♠♥♦♣♠♥♦♣♠♥♦♣♠♥♦♣♠♥♦♣♠♥♦♣♠♥♦♣♠♥♦♣♠♥♦♣

MIDDLE LIMIT HOLDEM POKER

Bob Ciaffone and Jim Brier

♠♥♦♣♠♥♦♣♠♥♦♣♠♥♦♣♠♥♦♣♠♥♦♣♠♥♦♣♠♥♦♣♠♥♦♣

COPYRIGHT

DEDICATION

Bob Ciaffone: I dedicate my effort in this book to the person on our planet who has influenced me the most. This is my father, Alfred J. Ciaffone, who passed away on July 21, 2003. He taught me nothing about poker or any of the other games I play, but he taught me what matters above all: how to treat my fellow man.

Jim Brier: I dedicate my effort in this book to my loving daughter Ann, whose love and encouragement have been such a source of joy in my life.

WE THANK

Dr. Alan Schoonmaker for his editorial assistance.
Barry Tanenbaum for his advice with various poker problems.
Mike Giordano for his cover photography.

THE COVER

Our cover photography is by Bob's friend Mike Giordano.

The cover of our book illustrates a holdem match-up between two hands, J♦–T♦ and A♥–K♠. As the hand developed, the J-T suited flopped a nice draw, and the A-K flopped top two pair. Both sides improved, so the A-K won the pot with a full house.

We decided to use this not-so-extraordinary hand for the cover of our book because it illustrates some useful poker ideas. First, the J-T suited is better fitted for a multihanded pot than a heads-up confrontation. Here are the odds against the J-T suited against the typical raising hand, assuming the pot is played out all the way. If the J-T suited runs into an overpair, it is about a 3.5-to-1 underdog; if it runs into two overcards like A-K, it is about a 3-to-2 underdog. Practically speaking, the odds are actually a bit higher than this against the J-T suited in an actual game, especially facing an overpair (which will hardly ever fold). If help is not bought on the flop in the form of a pair or draw, the J-T must fold. Therefore, we think the player with this type hand should prefer to get information about how the pot will develop before committing his money.

Second, it is easily possible when on a draw to make your hand and still lose the pot. Most poker players seem to be optimists. They look at the pot odds, then figure they can play despite lacking the full odds needed, under the assumption that the implied odds make it okay to stay. However, even though they will likely make some extra money if they make their hand, the other side of the coin is they can hit and lose. Each particular situation must be examined to see what the chance is of hitting and losing (always expensive).

Third, people play drawing hands strongly these days—sometimes too strongly. We often play a draw strongly ourselves, but not in as many situations as some of the more rabid players. Most players are optimists in calculating the chances of a drawing hand, figuring they are in good shape if the opponent only has a pair. But if he has two pair, as here, the odds change quite a bit. A redraw and a lockout enter the picture. This would be even more pronounced if we had given the made hand as a big pocket pair that had flopped a set—a not-so-unlikely scenario.

TABLE OF CONTENTS

MEET THE AUTHORS

BOB CIAFFONE

Bob Ciaffone has played poker since his childhood, and has been a professional player and familiar Las Vegas face since 1980. Ciaffone has an excellent reputation as a poker player, writer, teacher. He has competed in the $10,000 buy-in World Championship (no-limit holdem) seven times, with a 3rd place finish in 1987. His books *Omaha Holdem Poker, Pot-limit And No-limit Poker*, and *Improve Your Poker*, have all been well-received by the poker community. His book *The Official Rules of Poker* is the first comprehensive poker rulebook ever written. His latest rulebook, *Roberts Rules Of Poker*, which he believes to be the best set of poker rules in the world, can be downloaded for free from his website. Ciaffone has had a popular regular poker column in *Card Player* magazine for over a decade. Since moving back to his home state of Michigan in 1996, he has been giving poker lessons over the phone and by email. He charges reasonable rates, and is experienced at all the major poker forms. Ciaffone is a highly skilled all-around games player, being a life master at both bridge and chess, and an excellent backgammon player.

JIM BRIER

Jim Brier is a professional poker player who is presently based in Las Vegas. His favorite poker form is limit holdem, and he spends his time playing poker in exactly the kind of games written about in this book. He is a frequent contributor to *Card Player* magazine, where his articles featuring commentary on typical middle limit poker situations have proved popular with the readers. He has a lot of experience discussing poker hands on Internet forum sites, where the regulars know him well and respect his opinion. Brier was Ciaffone's student before becoming a professional player, so he has a keen sense of what a person who aspires to do well at holdem needs to know to go from a low-stakes player to the much tougher games at the middle limits.

ABOUT THIS BOOK

Here is how this book came about. In 1996, I (BC) moved from California back to my home state of Michigan, because of a family situation. There was not enough poker to accommodate me in the manner which I had been accustomed (I had been working as a fulltime proposition player at Hollywood Park Casino in Inglewood, California), so I started teaching poker. Most people who came to me for help were interested in playing holdem, particularly $10-$20, $15-$30, and $20-$40 limits. I began putting together instructional material aimed at those players.

Jim Brier, my co-author for this book, was one of those early students. He was a promising player, and worked very hard to improve his game. At my request, he kept a record of all the hands that involved a decision on which he wanted feedback. Every month or two, he would mail me a set of a hundred or so hands, and I would send him back written answers and explanations. He grew steadily in proficiency, and within a couple of years, retired from his job to become a professional player.

In 2001, Jim began writing articles for *Card Player* magazine (the poker publication I write a regular column for called *All About Poker*.) He told me he was putting together material for a poker book on limit holdem. I had been planning to write a book on the game myself, but had not really buckled down properly to work on it. I realized that the problems I had been answering for Jim and some other students were the excellent nucleus of a book. I felt that my writing and playing experience was a perfect blend with Jim's organized material and diligent work habits, so I offered to join our skills. Here is the result of our alliance.

What is the best way to teach poker—or any other game? One must both impart the general principles of play and use concrete examples to illustrate those principles being put to work. The authors feel that a general discussion of ideas followed by specific hand analysis is the best way for players to improve their game. For most players, it is through a discussion of specific hands that the various factors present in all holdem decisions are brought out. Factors such the number of opponents, your position, and the previous betting action are all important in deciding how to play a

1

hand. Most poker decisions are based on several factors, so one must see how general ideas are applied to a specific situation. We will observe when a principle applies and when it doesn't. Often, multiple principles pertain to a situation. If so, they will be discussed and the most pertinent one will be pointed out.

It is because specific hand analyses are so important that we began writing down many poker hands. Some are hands we played ourselves. A lot came from poker students. We also wrote down hands that friends of ours had given us, as well as hands that were posted on the Internet forums. We have a library of several thousand hands with annotated comments on each that we have accumulated over the past several years.

The vast majority of the hands and situations in this book actually took place in a real poker game. Only a few problems were constructed by us to illustrate a point.

We have avoided using any problems where a silly play was made that would be unlikely to occur in a real game. **This does not mean we endorse all the previous actions taken.** Sometimes a questionable play was made by a player or his opponents.

The limits in those games ranged from $10-$20 to $40-$80. These are the middle limits, so it seemed natural to call our book *Middle Limit Holdem Poker.*

The spelling we use, "holdem," rather than with the usual apostrophe between the "d" and "e," is because we believe the word will eventually evolve to this spelling, and we want to push progress along. Yes, we know that the apostrophe is there because the game is named from the expression, "hold them." That is how words get started—but usually, not how they wind up.

By reviewing the problems that are present in this book and then comparing your answer with our solution, we believe you can greatly increase proficiency in your play. The problems are laid out on the page so that you can cover the recommended solution and try to answer it yourself before seeing our answer.

Unless otherwise stated, it is assumed that we are dealing with a full table of ten players and a betting structure that doubles on the turn betting round. We call this the standard betting structure. In the chapter "Non-standard games," we discuss other structures such as that used in $15-$30 limit ($10 and $15 blinds).

ABOUT THIS BOOK

The opponents are not novices, but they are not world-class either. Assume that you are up against the typical decent players who have the bankroll and the experience to be playing in middle limit holdem games. Unless otherwise mentioned, the game has a normal tempo; it is not extremely aggressive or overly passive.

Player tells, mannerisms, and psychology are normally not part of the problem. Most of the decisions would be the same with a slightly different cast of players, or a different cardroom. (Every once in a while, we do mention a particular type of player, such as a wild man or a calling station, but this is rare.)

The problems are not designed to be tricky or especially difficult. They represent some common situations you are likely to encounter in a typical playing session. Try to answer each question in the same amount of time you would use if you were at the table. Spend some time going over the recommended solution, making sure that you understand the rationale behind the decision.

We had so much good material to work with that there was no reason to include those few problems where we diverged on the best course of action, or the reasoning. Our general philosophy of the game is very similar, so the prose accompanying the problems is also a combined effort. As a result, everything in this book is fully endorsed by both of the authors.

This book is not intended for novices. Rather, it assumes that the reader is an experienced player who is familiar with the mechanics of the game and common holdem terminology.

To make sure we are all on the same wavelength, here are a few of the terms used. The betting round before the flop, made on starting hands, is called preflop. The flop, of course, is the three board-cards that are put out by the dealer for the second betting round. The fourth card on the board is called the turn, as is the associated betting round. The fifth (last) card and betting round is referred to as the river. The names for certain of the various positions around the table are the small blind, big blind, under-the-gun (first player left of the big blind), cutoff seat (player on immediate right of the button), and the button (person acting last).

This book is designed to be read more than once. Because of the way it is organized, it can act as a reference book for problem hands and situations. The reader will encounter poker situations

3

such as: (1) He raised preflop and then flopped overcards with several opponents. (2) He had a good hand, but got raised or check-raised on the turn. (3) He had a fair hand that he has been betting all the way, and wants to know if he should bet the river. If the reader becomes familiar with this book, he can probably locate a problem which is very similar to the one he encountered at the table. There are over 400 problems in this book, which are logically grouped so that they can be readily accessed. So to get the most out of the book, and "be all you can be," write down a few hands each session that you found interesting or unclear. Then check out the problems from the related section of our book.

Higher-limit games are characterized by highly aggressive play. The fact that the number of players is much fewer means you gamble with the same people repeatedly, so deception is essential. The dividing line between middle limit games and each of the other two is not rigid. You may have to slightly adjust your play from our suggestions because of this. For example, in some of the situations where we say you should fold, the advice should not be followed when against a tricky, aggressive, and skillful opponent. Our recommended plays are for the center, not the poles.

Even though our book is aimed at the middle limits, we are aware that some low-limit players will be reading this book, and that a middle-limit player may sometimes be playing in a smaller game. So we added an additional chapter in our 2004 reprint titled, "Low Limit Poker." There are some adjustments that you should make to our strategies when playing in a cheaper game, where there is usually more calling and less raising.

We believe that this book will be instrumental in improving the play of many players who wish to have better success in middle limit holdem games. The style of poker we recommend is not the only way to beat a middle limit holdem game, but it is the easiest one to teach and play. Those players who seem to be able to play a lot of starting hands and come out on their feet actually have a lot of fluctuation in their results—and have few followers to whom they can successfully impart their style of playing. We are sure you will receive a poker education from us that will make middle limit holdem games a nice source of profit for you.

1 - HOLDEM POKER

The game of holdem was invented in the early part of the twentieth century. Nobody knows who conjured up this wonderful poker form. As for where it was invented, most of the old-time Texas poker players are of the opinion that it was first played in Robstown, Texas, near Corpus Christi. Johnny Moss said it came to Dallas in 1925, but did not originate there. We all owe a great deal to whoever was the game's inventor.

Some things that make holdem attractive are that many people can play it at one table, the best possible hand anyone can have (the nuts) is known to all the players, and there is a lot of bluffing because it is not easy to help the starting hand. Two unpaired cards are about 2-to-1 against improving on the flop; a pocket pair is over 7-to-1 against improving on the flop by hitting a set of trips.

Holdem has four betting rounds. The first is before the three-card flop, one after, one on the fourth board-card, and one after all the cards are out. Our book is organized according to the betting round. Even though a book of necessity must be grouped into sections, you should be aware of the inter-relation of the betting on earlier rounds to the betting on later rounds. For example, whenever you show power on one round, the opponents have a tendency to check to you on the following round, giving you more options. Another example is getting a better understanding of the reason a holdem player is very tight on play of starting hands in early position, as you watch how good position can be made to work for you later on, especially with a drawing hand. So notice how the ideas in an earlier section affect the strategy in a later one.

This book is aimed for the player who is already familiar with holdem, and has had at least some low-stakes playing experience. The differences between low-stakes holdem and the middle limits ($10-$20 up to $40-$80) are considerable, and require both an adjustment in strategy and the acquisition of new skills. Let us compare the two, keeping in mind that the actual dividing line is a little blurry, since you could have a $6-$12 game with a lot of the characteristics of a higher-limit game and a $15-$30 game with a lot of the characteristics of a lower-limit game.

5

Generally speaking, the skill level of the players increases as the stakes are raised. As we know, the number one deficiency of weak players is they are in the pot too much when they should fold. They play too many starting hands and they call on too many hands later on. This means there are usually a crowd of players contesting each pot. Bluffs have little chance of success, and tricky moves are mostly wasted. So the way you beat a low-limit game is to play only good hands and let nature take its course.

You can probably beat a middle limit holdem game using this same basic tool of sticking to good hands. But you will not beat it for much, and your results will deteriorate after a while as the opponents see what kind of player you are and make adjustments. To beat a middle-limit game for decent money, you will need to take a different approach in your play, and learn some new tricks. We will help you accomplish this goal.

You will find that the number one thing we stress throughout this book is to gear your play to the number of opponents you have. Against a crowd of four or more people, you play the same stodgy and solid poker that made you successful at low-limit holdem. But against only one or two opponents, you must play a far more aggressive brand of poker than worked at low-limit play. (The three-handed pot is the dividing line between aggressive and solid play.) A lot of pots in bigger games are heads-up or three-handed, so your results will be greatly affected by how you handle these short-handed situations. Your game must transform, because you have so few opponents between you and the money—and many of them are capable of throwing a hand away when they think they're beat.

In a short-handed pot, you do not want to be a caller. You are seldom getting big pot odds, and your chance of winning with a bet is reasonable. Certain texture flops scream for a bet, so you can fling some chips on some very light hands—sometimes nothing. If an opponent acting before you bets, a call is seldom the best play. If your hand is worth playing, try to win the pot with it by raising. If the bettor calls, then checks the turn, you can either follow through with a bet or take a free card.

With exactly three opponents, sometimes you hunker down, and sometimes you blast away. Three opponents is the dividing line between straight-forward and tricky play. The texture of the board has a lot to do with your strategy in this type of pot. We refer to the cards belonging to the top part of the deck (aces down through nines) as being in the "playing zone." These bigger cards win most of the pots, so of course they get played more often. With two or three flop-cards in the playing zone, it is hard to steal, because one or more opponents figure to have made a pot contender. With none or one flop-card in the playing zone, you are less likely to run into a contender, so some larceny is in order.

Observe the typical middle-limit game, and your first reaction is likely to be, "They do an awful lot of betting on some pretty crummy hands." This is true. But on closer inspection, you will see—or should see—that the betting does not go this way all the time. It goes this way when only a few people are contesting the pot, and when the player being aggressive has good position. Acting after the other guy enables you to a lot of betting and raising. A lot of this aggression is displayed on the flop betting round. The player is trying to position himself well for when the limit doubles. If a bet or raise has reduced opponents to passivity and they check to the pumper, that person can either continue to bet or take a free card. Frequently, the effect of putting in extra money on the flop when in position is to actually reduce the cost of playing the hand out, instead of increasing it. An extra half-bet is spent on the flop, but a full bet is saved on the turn. You raise on the flop, they check the next round. Of course, if the pumper has a high-quality hand, or has hit on the turn, he can continue to carry the betting.

This same idea of aggression in position can be used on the turn, with the idea of either getting a free showdown on the end, or getting extra bets into the pot in case the river card helps the hand. For example, if you have a pair and a flush-draw, you pop the bettor on the fourth card, with the idea of answering his last-round check by turning your hand up if you do not improve, and betting again if you do.

Since fewer people are entering the pot in a middle-limit game, a player in late position will get more chances to raise the pot and pocket the blind money. (Once a player has called, this opportunity evaporates, since a player in for one bet virtually always calls a raise.) Play against the blinds and defending against a raise when in the blind both become very important when you move up in class. It is standard practice at the middle limits for a player who opens in steal position to do so by raising. A raise gives the chance for immediate victory, whereas a call does not. When the blinds are faced with a raise from an aggressive player in steal position, they do not give the player the same degree of credit for a good hand that they would if a player were in early or middle position. We consider "steal position" to be the button and the first seat right of the button, referred to in this text as the "cutoff seat." Of course, you must watch to see how far around the bend a particular opponent is opening on light hands to steal the blind money, since some people treat middle position as we treat late position. No one likes to have an opponent run over him with heavy betting on mediocre holdings. A lot of the hands you play in a holdem game will be in these shorthanded pots where there is a fight over the blind money, so we cover this in great depth.

The fast-paced play, heavy betting, and tangling with the same aggressive player over and over has a much greater tendency to put one on tilt than happens in lowstakes poker. A player on tilt wants to get even, and the method is to increase the money swings by pumping up pots preflop, then trying to steal the money or get lucky on a longshot after the flop arrives. The three most common words in the steamer's vocabulary are "bet," "raise," and "wins." A steamer on tilt is playing much less effective poker than normal, but still can get lucky, hold very good cards, and injure your bankroll. So you cannot assume that they always have zero.

Of course, going on tilt is something you yourself must avoid. Once you start flying around on next to nothing, having read this book is not likely to save you from putting on a party for your opponents. Knowing how to play winning holdem poker is only half the battle; you must have the self-discipline to stick to the game plan. We will supply the knowledge half that you need; we hope you will have the discipline to properly put into practice what you are taught.

2 - COMMON CARDS

The basic nature of holdem is to use cards common to the hands of all players, which means the better hand is more likely to preserve its position on the leader-board than in poker forms that use only individual cards. (Even so, a holdem player will still take many bad beats.) The tendency of the best hand to stay on top is most apparent in match-ups of a similar nature, such as a made hand against another made hand, or a draw against another draw.

In made hand against made hand, the inferior hand is really hurting at holdem. An example is the common matchup of aces with one player having a bigger kicker, such as A-K against A-Q with a layout of A-x-x on the flop. Here, only the remaining three queens help the underdog. In holdem parlance, the A-Q is playing a three-out hand. (An out is a card that improves your hand.) With only three outs, the A-Q is more than a 7-to-1 underdog to win the whole pot. Some data on this matchup for you math buffs; in 1980 deals, the A-K wins 1710, the A-Q 240, and there are 30 ties.

For drawing hands that are trying to make the same rank of poker hand, the huge advantage of the higher-ranking draw is easily apparent. For example, if there are two hearts on the board, the A♥-9♥ has the K♥-8♥ in a terrible bind. The A♥-9♥ wins whenever a heart comes, and all the situations where it does not except when the K♥-8♥ pairs and the A♥-9♥ fails to achieve a bigger pair. Overall, the A♥-9♥ is a 4.5-to-1 favorite on the flop.

If the two hands involved are of a different nature, such as a made hand against a draw, than the cards to come being common cards does not protect the presently superior hand. However, the players can see when there is a potential flush or straight on the board, so the payoff for making a draw will normally not be quite as great as in a game when the coming cards are concealed.

An important part of holdem strategy is avoiding as best you can these traps of being pinned beneath a superior hand. The way to do this is to fold hands preflop that are most susceptible to becoming traps. For potential drawing hands, this means folding a king-high or queen-high suited combination when the sidecard is lower than a nine. For hands with high-card strength, avoiding traps means folding when a raise by an opponent has served notice that there may well be a hand of superior strength held by the opposition. Hands like an A-J or K-Q are good holdings in unraised pots, because you are not likely to be up against a hand that dominates you by tying up one of your cards or forcing you to hit the hand twice to win. You are dominated if up against a pair the same rank as one of your cards, or a card of the same rank coupled with a bigger sidecard. A higher-ranking pocket pair against a lower pocket pair is similar to domination, since the underpair is over a 4-to-1 underdog before the flop. These are all hands of such a high quality the opponent is likely to raise with them preflop, alerting you of the potential problem. The raise serves notice there is a strong possibility you hold a trouble hand dominated by the opponent's holding. Poker is the art of avoiding the opponent's high-quality hands, as judged by the betting, but collecting on your own high-quality hands.

Unfortunately, you cannot wait to have no vehicles visible anywhere on the highway before you cross it. Poker involves some risk-taking. There are certain situations where you should play a possibly dominated holding despite an opponent's preflop raise.

First, if you enter a pot and then get raised, you are obliged to call. There is no preflop situation in holdem where you call the blind and then fold for a single raise that charges the same admission price you just paid. (If you face a double raise, or are in a non-standard structure where the raiser can do more than double the bet, then a fold is likely in order.)

Second, if the raiser is in steal position and a player who is reasonably aggressive in trying to win the blind money, you can go ahead and call. An open-raise when in the cutoff or button position is what we consider a steal-raise. (However, no one can guarantee you that a player who opens in an earlier position is pure of heart.) Some poor players do not adjust their game for their position relative to the button. You should notice any player who always has a strong hand for a late position raise, instead of sometimes trying to steal the blind money, and adjust your game.

Third, if the raise is made by a player who appears far more interested in building a big pot than having a hand suitable to do so, you may of course take this into consideration. This happens most often when a player is stuck in the game, and wants to pick up the pace to increase the size of the pots. This steaming usually backfires, but there is no reason to let such a person drag you down the tubes with him. Guesswork is involved, and even great players make some bad guesses on occasion.

When playing a common-card type of poker, you have to be aware of what a card that helps you can do for someone else. One of the poker terms used regularly in our book's problems is "tainted." Webster's Unabridged Dictionary defines taint as, "To touch or affect slightly with something bad or undesirable." How does a word meaning affected by contact with something bad describe an element of poker strategy?

A key holdem concept is to be aware of how a board-card that helps your hand affects the possible hands of your opponents. When two or more players are helped by a card, they often put a lot of money into the pot, but only one of them will be smiling at the end (assuming it is not a tie). You want to be the person flashing those pearly teeth and stacking the chips.

When you draw at a hand, if there are helping cards that do not make you the nuts, you need to be aware of exactly what they do for the opponent, as well as the likelihood of an opponent having such a holding, and make the appropriate mental adjustments. Here is an example. You hold A♥-6♥ and the flop comes Q♥-8♥-2♣, giving you the nut flush-draw. How many outs do you have? The answer is that it depends on what the opponents hold. True, there are nine cards that make a flush for you, but only five of them make the nuts. Three of them (the J♥, 10♥, and 9♥) could give someone a straight flush. The 2♥ pairs the board, creating the possibility of quads or a full house.

Should you worry about a straight-flush possibility? For the limit holdem player, both the likelihood of a straight flush and the penalty for running into one are sufficiently low as to be almost discounted. Worst case scenario has you losing a pot, not all your chips. Of course, we are talking about your attitude while drawing. For example, if the 9♥ comes at the river and someone bets, you raise, and the opponent now reraises, anyone holding the nut flush who still discounts the straight-flush possibility is a complete fool.

As for the flush card that creates the possibility of a boat or better, the betting on the flop will give you a clue as to the likelihood of a boat. If the flop was bombarded, beware! If not, there is still the possibility of an opponent slowplaying two pair or a set until the limit goes up.

A straight-draw has the virtue (as opposed to the flush-draw) of having no cards that make your hand filling the opponent. Still, you can sometimes lose to a flush or bigger straight. If there is a two-flush on the board, there are two of your eight straight-making cards that create the possibility of a flush. The number of opponents in the pot will give an indication of how dangerous this is. If you are heads-up, a flush-draw is only one of many hands the opponent might hold, and chances are the flush card that makes your straight is a winner for you. So you probably have eight outs. If it is a bet and three calls to you, treat the hand as a six-outer. In evaluating your hand, keep in mind that not only are two of your outs tainted, but also that the opponents probably have a lot more redraws than if the board were rainbow.

The straight-draw should also give concern when some of your outs could make a bigger straight. If you have a card combination with both cards ten or higher, all your draws will be at the nut straight. Otherwise, you will have some of your straight-cards tainted. If the cards on the board that form part of your straight-draw are higher in rank than your cards, as a board of J-10 when you hold 9-8, you are said to be drawing at the "ignorant end" of the straight, and should downgrade your holding accordingly. Particularly bad are one card straight-draws, like a board of 10-9-7 when you have an eight. You may have no winners at all, or just a few cards for a tie.

The character of the straight-draw is also affected by how close in rank the board-cards are. A board of 9-8-7 (cards in sequential rank) means more straight-making combinations for the opponents, plus a greater chance of the nut combination being played. Calling a lone six with those board-cards a "straight-draw," though true, is a bit misleading. It sounds like a hand worthy of contesting the pot, but much of the time it isn't.

An area where a lot of players are weaker than they should be is evaluating overcards, with respect to cards that could make someone a bigger hand. Having a two-flush on the board in a suit that you have none of is a serious detractor of overcard value. A card that pairs you but puts a three-flush on the board is a dubious catch. Two overcards are (hopefully) a six-out hand. A two-flush changes this to a likely four-out hand. And even if you hit one of the two suspect outs and no one has a flush, there is the danger of a fourth card on suit appearing, making your chances dismal.

The last possibility of a tainted board-card we will discuss is with overcards. Be aware of situations when pairing an overcard makes a possible straight. Here is an example. You raise on the button with A♥-K♦ after several opponents have limped, and wind up with four callers. The flop comes 10♥-9♣-3♠. A player in middle position bets and there are two callers. What do you do? We believe you should fold. The deciding factor is that king you are trying to pair may give someone with Q-J a very big smile, since they would now hold the nut straight. If you change the board by making the 9♣ the 8♣, a call is now reasonable, since none of your outs are tainted by a straight-making possibility for the opponents.

The overcards of largest value are the biggest ones. When you have A-K, if you pair, at least you will beat someone else who makes one pair with that card. Unfortunately, there is a greater possibility here than with other hands of running into two pair, either by the opponent already having two pair, or having the person improve with your helping card. This is of particular danger when you hit an ace, since an ace-something is so common a playing hand. Making a pair of aces with A-K or A-Q and running into aces up is one of the most common beats in holdem. We are not telling you to always fold overcards, but they are a lesser hand than a lot of players seem to think. If you normally go to the river with A-K, trying to make a pair, this is a big leak.

Holdem is a common-card game, and realizing what a helping card for you can do for opponents is essential for success in it. An out is supposed to make you a winner, not just improve your hand. Otherwise, it is worse than worthless, since you not only fail to win the pot, but spend extra money in the act of trying. Whenever possible, try to draw at winners, not just helpers. Notice how your needed cards may help others; avoid tainted draws.

3 - BETTING STRUCTURE

The standard structure for holdem betting is to have the bet size on the turn and river twice the bet size used preflop and on the flop. All our discussions assume the standard structure is used unless otherwise stated (even though there are some other structures in use, such as spread limit giving the bettor a range of options, or allowing a river bet twice the size of the turn bet).

The turn bet increasing to double the flop bet has immense impact in the betting strategy. The naturalness of the betting on the flop is distorted, so betting or raising often does not mean, "I am strong," and checking or calling often does not mean, "I am weak." Deception on the flop is rampant. A raise on the flop by a player in late position is often used as a tactical tool, rather than being based on a hand that figures to have the best chance to win the pot. A player with a marginal hand or a draw raises to induce his opponent to check on the turn, thus reducing the total price of playing the hand to the end. He may elect to bet again if he thinks there is a chance to induce a fold. Should he hit on the turn, extra money is already in the pot.

There is also a lot of slowplaying of a hand which is the likely favorite, in anticipation of the bet doubling before one's true colors are revealed. A player with a good hand delays pulling the trigger until he can milk the maximum price.

Let us first talk about using the raise on the flop to possibly purchase a free card on the turn. For such a raise to succeed, it should be necessary for the raiser to have position. Otherwise, you can simply see him check on fourth street, play him for failing to have the needed requirements for a raising hand, and bet your hand accordingly. This check by the opponent can be used as a move to get in a check-raise, but much more often it simply shows weakness. We should assume a check to be weak until we get evidence to the contrary, as there are a lot more weak hands than strong hands dealt in a poker game.

We seldom throw in a raise on the flop trying merely to get in for half price on the turn. This strikes us as a pretty picayune goal. If we have raised on the flop with a draw, it is because we felt there was an opportunity to win the pot. So if the player calls our raise on the flop and then checks to us on the next round, there is a good chance we will bet our draw again, because a lot of players fold a marginal hand when the amount of the bet doubles. If instead we take a free card, this would let the cat out of the bag, letting our opponent know that we are almost surely drawing.

To counter the "phony flop raise," there are a couple of things we can do. First, if we have a really good hand, we should keep our foot on the gas pedal for quite a while if there is a two-flush on the board. It is unusual at holdem to have more than eight outs against a concealed two pair or set without having a flush-draw as part of your hand. If we flop two pair or a set, we simply keep reraising until the point comes when we are suspicious that the raiser actually has a made hand better than our own. A raiser's first raise is suspect, and to a lesser degree so is his second. (However, his third is likely to be on what he thinks is the nuts.)

The second thing we can do is simply call the raise, but lead out on the turn if a non-threatening card comes. This is a technique we use frequently. The fact that you choose to not reraise on the flop does not mean that you should automatically check on the next round unless you help. The opponent's raise certainly did not commit him to betting again. When you check, he often checks it back if he misses his draw.

Our thinking out-of-position when raised goes something like this. "My opponent might have a good hand, though he's probably drawing. Even so, he may well have a big draw (bigger than just a straight-draw or a flush-draw). This would put him close to even money against me with two cards to come. If I have misjudged and he has raised on a made hand, I might be in a lot of trouble. But if I can take off a safe card, the math has changed considerably, and I have become a solid favorite over a draw." In this manner, you can avoid putting in an extra raise on the flop and then catching a card on the turn that makes you ill (such as a flush card that is close in rank to the other boardcards), yet still retain the initiative in future betting on the hand.

The opposite situation from the one described is encountering weak betting on the flop, but running into a power sequence on the turn. We do not use this tactic much, because it gives the opponent an opportunity to make a good laydown, whereas if we simply bet our strong hand straight through, he is apt to scratch his head at the end wondering just where he was supposed to get away from his hand. However, at poker we often run into thinking contrary to our own, especially from weaker players, but sometimes from strong ones as well. A lot of people like to put on a broken wing act for the flop betting round and then spring to life on the turn.

There is a simple poker rule that applies most of the time. *The truth is more apt to be in the later action than the earlier one.* This rule is particularly applicable to split-limit poker. Do not ever say to yourself after running into a raise on the turn, "I do not think he actually has a strong hand, or he would not have let me and the other players in on the flop so cheaply and have a chance to beat his hand. He's not that dumb." The truth of the matter is he really is that dumb – but you would be even dumber to assume that he wouldn't do such a thing! Don't reward people for playing poorly.

Do we ever make use of "the phony betting round?" Yes, we do, but not to the degree displayed by many others. For example, if we think a hand is worth a raise, such as when having flopped two pair or a set, we sometimes just call a bet and wait a round to pounce. But we are selective when using this maneuver. There are a couple of rules that we follow. First, we do not do this in a multihanded pot. The opponents have shown they think their hand is worth something now by putting money into the pot. After the next card, you may have lost your market. It is better to get your licks in while you can. Second, we do not do this when out of position. That way we don't allow a free card on the turn.

One of the biggest differences between the average holdem player and the expert is the latter's ability to make use of the fact that the betting doubles after the flop. He knows some tricks to use himself, and he is aware of the tricks that might be employed by the opposition. The flop is a phony betting round because it is half price, so do not give full credence to an action taken by opponents, and blow a little smoke yourself to cloud things a little.

Some weight in a decision may be given to a cardroom's rule on limiting raises. A bet and three raises is standard, but some places allow four raises. Particularly in preflop betting, a third raise that caps the betting is sometimes less threatening than a third raise that exposes the player to a possible reraise.

4 - POSITION

Position at holdem is a key factor, since it stays the same for you over an entire deal. As any poker player already knows, acting later in a hand is an advantage. You can get a sense of how a pot will develop, finding out how many players and how much it costs to play. You can see how others react to a card before making your own decision. A holdem hand's true worth is based not only on what it contains, but also where it is located.

The value of good position depends on how many players are contending the pot. With one opponent, position is of some importance, but less than in a lot of other situations. For example, a check conveys less information, since a player does not worry as much about giving a free card to only one opponent, as opposed to a group of people. There is also the bluff factor. Bluffing is stronger against only one opponent, because if you get him out, you win. Furthermore, you are less likely to run into a hand that can take the heat. So heads-up, the person acting first bets a lot of the time (assuming he understands the game). If he has a good hand, he charges you a price to stay in and beat it. If he has a bad hand, he tries to get you out. A bet is the tool of choice for both of these aims. In fact, when a good player checks heads-up and his opponent has not done anything to indicate a good hand, the check is a bit suspicious!

Position is of greatest value in three-handed and four-handed pots. Here, a player with a good hand tends to bet it, reluctant to give a free card. Yet there are not so many players in that one is afraid to bet a marginal holding if the others have checked. This gives you the opportunity to exploit your position by winning the whole pot with a bet. If someone else bets and you have only a fairish hand, you can fold, and hold your losses to zero on that betting round.

One might think that as the number of opponents continues to rise, so does the value of position. Not so. When you get a big crowd, the best hand wins. You are not going to be able to use your position to scamper off with the pot. True, you might be able to gain or save a bet, which is helpful, but the big swing of altering the winner is not likely to happen.

POSITION

So far, we have been talking about position with respect to all the other players. At holdem, there is another kind of position to be considered. That is your position relative to the preflop raiser. At no-limit play, this is extremely important, but it also plays a role at limit play. The preflop raiser is far more likely than any other player to bet on later betting rounds, especially on the flop. Naturally, you do not want to be on the bettor's immediate left, with the whole field behind you free to act on the bet.

There is also another aspect of position relative to the raiser. Because the raiser bets the flop so often, people tend to check to that person. When you are on the raiser's left, if some players check and the raiser checks, you cannot assume that the opponents are weak. Someone may have checked a good hand to the raiser—and bag you when you try to pick up the pot. It is far safer to bet a marginal hand if the raiser is in early position, checks his hand, and then the rest of the field also checks.

How should one make this decision on whether to bet when the field has checked? A concept that must be factored into a decision whether to take aggressive action is the effect of reopening the betting. Naturally, if you are looking at the nuts, it is almost always correct to view reopening the betting as a virtue. With a lesser hand, you must weigh the pros and cons. Here is an example showing the difference of whether the betting is reopened or not makes on a typical limit holdem decision of whether to bet.

You have pocket queens on the button. You open with a raise and get called by just the blinds. The flop comes K♥-J♦-4♣. The blinds check, you bet, and they call. On the turn comes the 3♠, a total blank. The opponents check and you must decide whether to bet again. What to do?

Who is a good enough poker player to always bet when having the best hand here and check when not? Most opponents don't do something to give the show away that easily, and you face two of them to boot. Most of the time we would do the same thing here; bet. Here is our thinking. We do not know if our opponents will fold, call, or raise. If they fold, wonderful. If they call, it is likely that we break even with the plan of checking on the turn and calling on the river; we invest one more bet. Checking the turn and folding the river would be too wimpy an option. In limit poker, if you show weakness that might induce a bet, and you have a passable hand, you have to pay off at the river.

The advantage of betting the turn in this setting is obvious, as the opponents are given an opportunity to fold, instead of an opportunity to draw out. But what if you get raised? Bad news, right? Of course, but not as bad as it seems on the surface. Against any normal human being, you can fold with a clear conscience. The only way your one pair is the best hand is if the opponent is bluffing, and for someone to run a bluff by check-raising out of position on the turn in a threeway pot is really rare. Of course, the chance your opponent thinks he has the best hand but is wrong about this is close to zero. So it looks like you need a queen—but there are only two of them to be caught. The point to this discussion is a bet is most unlikely to cost a pot that you could have won by checking, so you bet.

Here is a slightly different situation. Everything is the same as in the previous problem except your hand. In the new problem, with the same flop of K♥-J♦-4♣, you have A-J instead of two queens. The only discernable difference in hand quality is in the second problem you get half the pot against an opponent who has A-J, whereas in the first problem your queens won the whole pot. But here is an important difference between the two hands that arises if you bet the turn. In the second problem, if you get check-raised on the turn and fold, you have mucked a hand two and a half times more likely to improve as in the first problem. If we equate improving with winning (likely but not necessarily true), here you have folded a five-outer, whereas in the first problem, you folded a two-outer. Perhaps we should mention that we think a fold in the second problem feels right, since the pot odds are not there for a call. We are a lot more annoyed getting knocked out of the pot holding a five-outer as a two-outer. Actually, we are 2.5 times as annoyed!

As you go through our book, be sure to note the strong role your position plays in the answer to the problems. The better the player, the more effectively he uses his position for making extra money: to get away from losers, to save a half-bet, to pick up the pot with a bet. A master of holdem is a master of positional play.

5 - DECEPTION

Deception is an integral part of the game of poker. If the opponents always know what you have, they are going to play pretty well against you. It is essential that they be kept off balance to some degree. Furthermore, fooling the opposition is part of the fun that goes with playing the game. There is no question that deceptive play is a valuable—indispensable—poker tool.

What is deception at poker? Basically, there are only two kinds of deception in any betting structure where the amount of the bet is fixed. You can act weaker than you really are by checking, failing to raise, or failing to reraise; you can act stronger than you really are by betting, raising, or reraising without the normal requisite values for that action.

We are not going to be talking about mannerisms designed to throw the opponents off the scent. Much of the time, these simply give the opponent more information to aid him in making the correct decision. Bet with an even tempo and a consistent motion.

In writing this book, we have a task to achieve in giving you our recommended plays. The play we give as best is how we feel you should play against a stranger or nondescript opponent. You are not supposed to be making the same play every time you get into a certain type of situation. You will need to vary your game by using deception. We do not point this out whenever we give each problem. Why waste all that space? Instead, we will give you information about using deception, and let you decide how much of it to use, based on the circumstances concerning the game where you are playing and who is your opponent.

An important question we need to ask is, "How much do I need to deceive in the game I am playing?" After a player gets used to your style of play, he can alter his own game to take maximum advantage of this knowledge.

If you are basically playing against the same lineup, deception is very important. When playing in a home game, you can expect to be facing the same people over and over again, and it is a necessity to vary your play to keep them off-balance. If you are playing the middle limits in a big casino like the Commerce Club in Los Angeles, there is a large base of players, and varying your

20

game is of lesser importance. Between these extremes is the public cardroom that spreads only one or two games big enough for your liking, and a middle-of-the-road attitude to deception is appropriate in that type of setting.

We must remember that deception by definition means playing a hand contrary to the nature of our holding, departing from the usual play. To fool the opponent, we have to bet abnormally, and so each departure from straight-forward play involves a decision weighing gain against loss. Involved are both the immediate situation where we want the best result possible on a deal, and the long-run situation that determines how opponents might behave against us in the future.

There is no such thing as a free lunch, as the saying goes. There are some drawbacks to deceptive play, and looking at those drawbacks is needed before deciding how often to use it.

If we are going to give something up, let's not do it when a lot is at stake. An important rule of thumb is the more money in the pot already in proportion to what you can bet, the less important it is to deceive opponents. Your goal in such a situation should be to get the pot into your stack, and not to try and milk an extra bet along the way. If you check what looks like the best hand in a big pot, it should be with the idea of hoping to get someone to bet so you can confront the field with a double bet, and thus have a better chance to get opponents to fold. This can be a viable strategy on occasion, but you need to have a strong reason to expect a bet in order to employ this tactic. Even though a large field improves the chance of someone having enough hand to bet, it also freezes up people from betting anything marginal, so there is a real danger of the flop being checked by all.

There is a problem brought on by deceptive play that many players do not enter into the equation when deciding whether to employ deception. If the opponent knows what you have, his actions are likely to tell you whether your hand is good, enabling you to do the right thing. If he has been deceived, his actions are a lot less reliable in indicating the correct course of action for you. For example, if the opponent does not know we have a decent hand, any action he subsequently takes is suspect, because it may have been taken on the misinformation we put out. By using deception, not only are you giving up the normal play, but you also are making it harder for yourself to make accurate decisions later on in the hand.

Poker can be an easier game to play when you bet in a straightforward manner. Bill Seale, a strong player from Houston, calls betting a good holdem hand on the flop "purifying the flop." He likes the idea that subsequent poker decisions are a lot easier because knowing the fact that the opponent had enough hand to call a bet on the flop considerably reduces the number of possible hands he might hold, enabling one to take the right course of action in situations arising later on in the play. This reasoning has a lot of merit. The turn-card makes a huge increase in possible card combinations a person might be playing to stay for the river.

Let's look at a common situation, and see how under-betting your hand leads to a difficult guess. You pick up a pair of jacks in the big blind. Three players limp in with calls, so you raise, and they of course call. The flop comes down 9♥-7♣-3♦. You bet and get two callers. The turn-card is the K♠, an unwelcome sight, as overcards are always unfriendly when all you have is one pair. What do you do? If you check and someone bets, did he bet because you showed weakness, or did he get helped by the king? The weak player checks because he no longer has a guarantee that his hand is good, and then pays off the hand because he thinks he may have induced the bet by his cautious check, which in fact "lied" about the strength of his hand. A strong player simply bets, not knowing whether his hand is good, but not wanting to lose the initiative. If the opponent raises after he bets, there is a good chance the player has him beat. If a preflop raiser "says" he likes a king, few opponents will try to take the pot away from him.

Here are five important principles of deception at poker:

(1) *Deception usually means giving something up.* By playing a hand unusually, you are playing a hand in a manner that is less than optimum. Many players act as if they are unaware their deception is a concession. They make a lot of plays that are so unsound that they cost big bucks, instead of looking for ways to deceive that are relatively inexpensive.

(2) *A little bit of deception goes a long way.* This may be considered a corollary of the first principle. Since we are doing something unsound, we don't want to do it too often. When you do something strange and it gets discovered, people will notice and remember. Last month—maybe last year—this guy reraised before the flop holding the 9♣–8♣. Most poker players make these cute plays too often, and as a result give up too much.

(3) *Deception is more effective against stronger players.* It can be completely wasted on the weakies. A novice may not be fooled no matter how clever you are. He hopes to improve his hand and wants to see what you have, so you may expect him to stay in there despite fierce betting. If you check a good hand to him, he will usually be pleased to check it back and gratefully take a free card. So be careful about whom you try to impress with fancy footwork. This book is aimed at people who wish to play $10-$20, $15-$30, $20-$40, $30-$60, and $40-$80 limits, so the degree of deception needed works its way up this stakes scale, with $40-$80 the level where it is needed the most, because those players tend to be the strongest. You will, of course, find that the opponents are using deception against you more often as you go up this scale. Some opponent plays such as bluff-raising you on the end when you are suspected of pushing a draw that never connected (when the raiser cannot even beat a busted draw) are hardly ever seen at the low end of this spectrum.

(4) *Don't make a deceptive play that is almost surely not going to work.* Even though we hope to make some extra money on our normal plays in the future as a result of our deceptive plays in the present, this is something that will take care of itself. When you make a cute play, have some reason to think it will help on the present hand. Don't deliberately throw away money by making a move that you know will be unsuccessful, hoping to recoup later.

(5) *Use less deception when stuck in the game.* The part of deception that involves betting or raising with a hand lacking the usual values for aggressive action is seldom applied in a random manner. A player is much more likely to overplay his hand when his luck has been bad and he is losing in the game. It is human nature to want to get even when stuck. The typical way to do this is to try building a big pot without having a big hand. The opponents of such a player are aware of this trait of human nature, and are less likely to be taken in by it and throwing their hands away than in a normal setting. This means the most effective time for aggressive play is when you are winning, not losing. Go contrary to the usual nature of man to fool somebody.

We see that deception is not to be indulged in frequently and randomly. We should be careful to apply it in an inexpensive manner. Let us look at some ideas on how to do this.

An important element in applying deception cheaply is position. When you have position, you can often throw in an extra bet or raise on modest values without an increase in the cost of playing a hand to conclusion. If the opponent checks and we bet, he tends to check to us again on the next betting round. If the opponent bets, we raise, and he calls, he again tends to check to us on the next betting round. We can take advantage of this tendency of the opponent to check whenever we have shown strength on the previous round. If we wish, we can take a free card and recoup the "loss" incurred by our previous bravado. Quite often, the total amount spent will turn out to be the same as if we had simply called. In fact, if the free card comes on a more expensive betting round, we actually save money, if the opponent would have bet into us on the next round had we not shown strength. And if we help, an extra bet is gained.

The typical positional raise is made on a drawing hand. Extra money is already in the pot if you hit. If you miss, you may well get the option of playing the deal out at a cheaper price than if you had not raised. We will see many examples of the positional raise in our chapter on drawing hands, and elsewhere in the book.

Contrast this raise in position with throwing in an extra bet or raise when out-of-position. There, you have to either bet again, or give the show away when the opponent can immediately capitalize on this. Your show of strength seldom accomplishes anything if followed up by a check when the opponent has yet to act.

Another idea you can use to reduce the cost of deception is that a raise doesn't cost nearly as much if you were going to play anyway. For example, suppose you are in the cutoff seat with a made-up blind. If you raise on a marginal hand, this in a sense only costs a fraction of a bet. If you don't have any money in the pot and raise on a hand not even worth a call, this is expensive. Prefer to spend small bucks when laying down a smokescreen.

DECEPTION

It is nice, when throwing in an extra bet, if the opponents have already limited their hands. An example is when you are in the big blind and no one has raised. If you pop it on a hand worth only a call, the absence of a powerhouse against you means that your expenditure is small, since the opponents probably have a hand around the same caliber as your own. So you are playing for twice as much money, but your equity in the hand is no less, as you are winning about the same percentage of the time in many situations.

Suppose you are playing in a $20-$40 limit holdem game. What are some situations where you can practice preflop deception without giving up too much?

Suppose you hold 7♣–6♣. If you open in early position with a raise, this gives up a lot. Your hand was not even good enough to call. Furthermore, you are thinning out the field with a drawing hand that begs for multihanded action. With all those players behind you yet to act, someone may reraise you. Yes, some deception is desirable, but putting in two or three bets heads-up before the flop on a piece of junk is a bit expensive, don't you think? But when we have our 7♣–6♣ in the big blind, and three or four players limp in with a call, a raise does not give up nearly as much. We already have a multihanded pot, and the betting has indicated that none of our opponents has a high-quality hand, as evidenced by their failure to raise on the initial round. Furthermore, you are raising in a situation where everyone is going to call (rather than in a possible steal situation), meaning you will surely be played for high cards or a big pair.

It is of course true that the first play, opening with a raise, is the more deceptive play. But it is by far the more expensive play. Either play would accomplish your goal of varying your game and keeping the opposition off balance. Who do you think you're playing against: Harrington, Reese, and Chan? Few opponents will observe your plays that precisely. In either situation, if the opponents discover your holding, a portion of them will hardly be paying attention. Most of the remainder are simply going to make a mental note, "This player sometimes raises on hands like the 7♣–6♣." Prefer to make the deceptive play that is less expensive.

A type of deceptive play that costs very little is reraising when you were going to call a raise anyway. Here is an example.

DECEPTION

Suppose you are in the big blind holding the Q♠–J♠. The player just to the right of the button opens the pot with a raise, and the remaining players fold. The raiser may have a good hand, but there is a reasonable chance he has a rather modest holding and is hoping to steal the blind money. Your hand is easily good enough to call the raise, although it is unlikely to be better than your opponent's holding. A reraise is not indicated on values, but this is a good spot for deception. Pop him back and see what happens. You may win some extra money, or you may even win a pot you would have otherwise lost. Showing aggression before the flop at holdem often puts a player in position to win the pot after the flop.

The best position is, of course, the button. This is a good place for a preflop raise on an ordinary hand. You pick up J♥–9♥ and several people limp in. Even though your hand is scarcely worth a call, a raise is not a costly proposition. Most of your opponents have already acted, denying a strong hand. A raise, besides being deceptive, may get you a free card on the flop betting round. Players often check to the preflop raiser, anticipating a bet. Here, with a substantial number of opponents, you do not intend to bet unless you hit, but the opponents do not know that.

Contrast the preceding play with a player who is on the button with the 9♠–7♠ facing a raise and a call, and elects to make it three bets. This kamikaze pilot has a hand that does not belong in the pot for one bet, let alone three bets. He is simply spending too much money in order to vary his game.

We have been looking at preflop examples of deception. Later on in the hand, deception can of course be used as well. In fact, this is the more important area for deceptive play.

When you raise the pot on two big cards like A-K and miss the flop, it is normal to make a play for the pot if there are not too many opponents. However, if someone shows strength before you have acted, it may be wise to give up. But there is an alternative. You can raise the bettor, and follow up with a bet on the turn. This tool is important in keeping the enemy off-balance. If one were going to pretend being dealt two aces, it is better to do it after the flop with A-K than before the flop on 7♣–6♣.

The companion tool to playing A-K like A-A is playing A-A like A-K. For slowplaying after the flop, aces are vastly superior to any other unimproved pocket pair, because there are no overcards. Just remember that one pair is a fragile holding in holdem; don't slowplay it too often or against multiple opponents.

Most deceptive shows of strength have good position as one of their components. Here is an example of a positional raise from a $20-$40 holdem game. You hold A♥-7♥ on the button. Someone limps in, you call, the big blind raps, and the three of you are in for flop of A♣-8♣-3♦. The big blind bets, the limper folds, and it is up to you. The opponent could have a flush-draw or a small piece of the board, but he probably has an ace. If so, your kicker is weak, though not hopeless, especially against a blind entrant. The hand is certainly worth a call, so consider throwing in a raise. If the opponent just calls, you can see what comes and how the opponent reacts to it before you decide how to play the turn. If a blank comes, the normal course of action would be to go ahead and bet the turn, then try to make a good guess on the end whether to just show the hand down or make a final bet.

Not all deception consists of betting. Here is an example. You open with a raise on A-K, get one player behind you, and everyone else folds. The flop comes down Q-8-3 rainbow. Suppose you check (a strange play for a preflop raiser when heads-up). Anyone familiar with your game knows that a bet here is virtually automatic—and you know it. He is liable to be so suspicious of your check that he checks it back to see what's going on. Of course, you'll likely bet the turn, and have a good chance to win the pot. Don't be surprised if your opponent asks you after folding whether you had flopped three queens! Smile and say nothing.

Poker players appreciate the value of deception, but they often give up too much to achieve it. By avoiding the four errors of making a tricky play with a hand that should be folded, making a tricky play too often, making a tricky play out-of-position, and overplaying a hand when stuck, you can vary your game without much cost. Most players will give you action if they have ever seen you out of line, so there is no reason to pay big bucks to fool them. Many players overwork deception. If you use the tool sparingly, you are going to find out something very pleasant. The less often you indulge in deception, the more likely your effort to deceive will be successful.

6 - HOLDEM MATH

It is possible to be a good limit holdem player without doing mathematical computations in your head. But just because we don't have to do math at the table does not mean we can dispense with acquiring a feel for the odds. Reading about the odds is helpful even if you do not actually memorize any particular prices. For those of you who enjoy the mathematical aspect of poker, this chapter should be helpful. For those that don't, better read this stuff anyway.

The way to calculate your odds on making a hand is by comparing the number of outs you have with the number of unknown cards. On the flop at holdem, that number of unknown cards is 47. This is derived by deducting the 5 known cards (three board-cards and two cards in your hand) from the total number of 52 cards in the deck.

An out is a card that helps your hand. If we are drawing to an open-end straight, we have eight outs. For example, if we have a Q-J-10-9 combination with our hand and the board, there are four kings and four eights that make the straight, a total of eight cards. That is 8 out of 47 cards that make our hand. Since 8 help us and 39 do not, the odds are 39-to-8 against us. That is 4 7/8 to 1 against.

How does a poker player obtain this type of odds information at the table? Certainly not by dividing 8 into 47 while playing a hand. That would make poker a tedious mathematical exercise, slow up the game, and provide more accuracy than needed to make an intelligent decision. In practice, a straight-draw is so common that the player simply memorizes the odds on hitting it. There is no necessity that the compound fraction 4 7/8 to 1 be committed to memory; just be aware that the odds are a little under 5-to-1.

The other common draw is a flush-draw, which is nine outs. The number nine is derived from the fact that there are 13 cards of a suit, so if you have a four-flush, nine cards of that suit are available for you to hit. So your chances are 9 out of 47, which is 9 that help you and 38 that do not, or just over 4-to-1 against.

This is how we know that on the flop, the odds on hitting an open-end straight on the next card are just under 5-to-1, and hitting a flush on the next card are just over 4-to-1. If you are drawing on the turn, there are only 46 unknown cards (instead of 47), since there are four board-cards instead of three. So your odds are a tiny bit better, but not much, and the odds of "Just over 4-to-1 for a flush-draw" and "Just under 5-to-1 for a straight-draw" still apply. Of course, this same principle of the odds of hitting on the next card being almost the same for the flop and the turn applies to all types of draws. We need to memorize only one set of numbers, because we are rounding off, and the difference between the flop and turn is so insignificant.

Another number that arises frequently and should be memorized is a four-out draw. You have four winning cards when drawing to a gutshot straight, or when holding two pair and needing to fill. The odds on hitting a four-outer on the turn are 4 out of 47, which is 10.75-to-1 against. We round this number off to 11-to-1, and should commit that figure to memory.

If we are calculating whether we have enough outs to justify calling a bet, all we look at are what happens on the next card. Obtaining two cards is a different price and requires a different calculation. With two cards to come, the odds on making a longshot draw will shorten about in half if we are looking at playing the hand to see both cards. For a thorough discussion on how to calculate the odds on completing a draw on the flop by staying until the end, see the odds tables in the back of the book.

To make an intelligent decision whether to draw at a hand, we need to know much more than the "pot odds," which is the ratio of the money it costs us to call compared to the amount presently in the pot. When someone bets and we are thinking about calling, there are several other questions besides the pot odds that we must ask ourselves.

First, "How much is it likely to cost me to see the next card?" If you have one opponent, the amount is just the one bet. But in multihanded pots, the answer is more complex (unless we are the last player to act on the wager). If there is one player behind us, and that player has checked, the threat of an additional charge is small. If there are several players behind us, and none have acted yet, the threat of an added fee is a strong consideration. Between these extremes, there are of course shades of gray.

Second, we must ask ourselves, "How much added money can I expect to gain if I hit?" Much of the time, since this is limit poker, a hand will make money after hitting, at least to the extent that the eventual pot won will be larger than the present one. Hitting a straight figures to get paid off in a greater quantity than hitting a flush, since a flush-draw getting there tends to make someone who has been carrying the betting pull in the reins and check. Of course, if you are hitting to the nut flush in a multihanded field, there is a chance you will have the pleasure of gaining several extra bets. Trapping a hand underneath you is another reason why it is much better to be on a nut draw, especially if a lot of players are in the pot.

Third, we must ask ourselves, "Is there the possibility of winning the pot by a bluff?" For example, if you are drawing to a straight and there is a flush-draw on the board, this reduces your chance of winning after you hit—but there is an upside. If the flush comes, you have the opportunity to represent it in the betting. The opponent, who did not know what you were drawing at, will fear the flush if he does not have one. Of course, there is no guarantee the opponent will respect your show of strength and fold. He may have a big card in the suit and be hoping to redraw, then call on the end because it is only one last bet. He could even have been betting on the come with a flush-draw, and now you are representing his hand, in which case you will both lose your money and feel a little foolish. Bluffs are by their nature risky, but this does not make us abstainers.

Fourth, we must ask ourselves, "How sure is it that I will win if I hit?" You may hit one of your outs, but fail to win the pot. This could happen if you are drawing to a hand the opponent has beat, if the card that helps you helps him even more, or if he redraws to make a bigger hand on the last card. This last factor must be discussed in greater detail.

Let's look at drawing to a gutshot straight on the flop. You hold K♠-Q♠ and get a flop of 10♣-9♦-2♥. The board is rainbow, so you think of your hand as "hitting to the nuts." Yes, hitting the straight on the next card would give you an unbeatable hand—if there were no more cards coming after the turn. But the rules of the game provide for a river card. How often will your hand be the nuts when all the cards are out? Let's analyze.

There are twelve cards that pair the board, creating the possibility of a full house. There are six cards that pair your hand, creating the possibility of a bigger straight. We must also remember that three of the four cards completing the straight also create a two-flush on the board, so three-quarters of the time that you hit, you must contend with a flush-draw going into the last card. The actual odds on your hand still being the nuts at the river is only about 53 percent. Naturally, someone has to have that better holding that beats you, but the whole point of this discussion is to show you the difference between hitting to the nuts after the flop and hitting to the nuts after the turn. With two cards to come, a lot can go wrong. The next time you try to figure the implied odds for your "nut" draw **on the flop**, consider the possibility of hitting and losing into your mental guesstimate of the situation.

One of the mathematical underpinnings of holdem is the difficulty of making a decent hand on the flop. It is rare to start with a pocket pair in holdem. Whatever your first card may be, there are only 3 cards out of 51 that match its rank. That is 1 out of 17, or 16-to-1 against making the pair. If you do not have a pair, you will make one on the flop only about a third of the time. These statistics show why holdem is played so aggressively in a short-handed pot. A player is anxious to put the burden of hitting the flop on the opponent, and scamper off with the cheese every time that opponent fails to connect. He often does this by raising preflop, as if he might have something good. Of course, if your opponent is the preflop raiser, there is no reason to let him succeed with this strategy.

The odds tables in the back of the book show three things:
(1) The price on making your hand on the next card, based on the number of outs you have.
(2) The odds on making your hand on either of the next two cards, and a number of common match-ups on the flop.
(3) The odds on various preflop match-ups.

7 – INTRODUCTION TO PREFLOP PLAY

"What you sow is what you reap." In a game using common cards, this old adage is particularly applicable. The person with the superior starting hand is the one who figures to be on the good side of whatever comes on the flop if two players connect. Be fussy about which hands you play. Use the information provided by the preflop betting to avoid being on the wrong side of a trap. The fold is an important weapon; don't be afraid to use it.

For our starting hand guidelines, we are assuming that the game is a typical middle limit game found in Las Vegas, Los Angeles, or any other major area where public poker is readily available. It has been our experience that in these games most pots are getting raised, and there are about three players on the average taking a flop. Of course, this will vary depending upon the particular lineup of players. Some passive games will hardly have any raising before the flop. Some loose games will have many players taking a flop. Correct preflop play is a strong function of how loose or tight the game is, as well as how passive or aggressive the game is. The looser and more passive the game, the more hands you can play, and rigidly adhering to our guidelines may not produce optimum results. The tighter and more aggressive the game, the fewer hands you can play, and blind adherence to guidelines may result in you playing too many hands.

Unlike low-limit poker (stakes up to $9-$18), good preflop play by itself in middle-limit games will not make you a winning player. However, poor play before the flop can easily make you a loser, regardless of how well you play once the flop arrives. It has been our experience that most of your income in a middle limit holdem game stems from showing down the best hand. Of course, stealing the blinds and bluffing account for a good share of your earn as well, but in limit poker it is very difficult to win a major pot without ending up with the best hand. What you can bet is small relative to what is already in the pot, and your opponents are almost always getting pot odds of 5-to-1 or better. This results in most bets getting called, and it usually takes the best hand to win.

There are two ways to end up with the best hand. You can start out with the best hand and have it hold up, or you can draw out on the best hand. This means that you have to enter pots with either a good made hand, or with a good drawing hand where you get favorable pot odds. In either case, proper starting hand selection is fundamental to ending up with the best hand.

One is often told that it is important to "vary your play" and not become too predictable. The contention is that if you don't vary your play often enough, your opponents will play very accurately against you, and this will work to your detriment. While we agree that some variation in your play is advantageous, we feel that it is over-emphasized by many players, because they are playing in a public cardroom or Internet site where there is a wide variety of different opponents.

For example, suppose you decide to limp in under-the-gun with a hand like seven-six suited in order to vary your play. The problem is that your hand is unlikely to survive all the way to a showdown. In the vast majority of cases, you will miss the flop, and be bet out of the hand with no one ever knowing that you varied your play. Couple this with the fact that the pot will frequently get raised behind you, forcing you to spend another bet to take a flop. You will typically have an up-front investment of one or two small bets. You may find yourself having to do this many times before you finally catch a hand that gets shown down.

Another problem is getting one of your astute (?) opponents to notice that you varied your play, and how you can take advantage of this on subsequent hands. If you play every day in a cardroom where there is likely to be only one table at the limit you want, so you are against much the same lineup of players every session, then this may not be a problem. You will find there are quite a few regular players who you will be facing for many hours.

If playing in a major cardroom, varying your play may not make much of a difference. Your unusual play will be good for a herring only in the game where it was used—and the opposing lineup changes rapidly.

Let us discuss some of the factors that might lead us into altering our preflop guidelines. The first would be if the game became short-handed. Later on in this book, short-handed play is discussed, so we will not dwell on this. For now, it is sufficient to say that if you are in a game with fewer than eight players, you should be playing looser than what we advocate in this section. Be attentive to players leaving the game. It is not how many seats there are at the table that affects your strategy; it is how many are actually dealt in.

We would loosen up our play some if the game were passive, meaning that there was very little raising before the flop. Let us further subdivide a passive game into one that is tight with a small number of players taking a flop and one that is loose with a larger number of players taking a flop. Knowing that you can enter a pot and probably not have to face a raise makes medium-low pocket pairs quite playable. Even in a tight game, you may be getting the right implied odds to try to flop a set. In a loose game you are definitely getting the right odds for this. Suited connectors become more playable, but you still cannot take them too far. The reason is because with suited connectors, you still have to make a hand after flopping a draw and have that hand hold up as the best hand. What you want for suited connectors is not only a passive game before the flop, but you want a game which is passive from the flop on, so that you are unlikely to have to pay a high price to pursue your draw. Such a game is much more likely to be found at low limits than middle limits.

Another problem is that if you are in a loose and passive game, it will be harder for your hand to hold up even when you hit your draw. In a loose game, it is common for one flush to lose to a higher flush, or for a straight to lose to a flush, or one straight to lose to a higher straight. When a lot of hands are getting played preflop, one of the common hand types the loose players seem to like is a suited facecard like Q-x or J-x. This means your 8-7 suited has less of a chance to be drawing live at a flush. The more opponents involved, the more important it is to be drawing to the nuts. For this reason, a hand like ace-little suited is playable in this type of game, while ace-little offsuit is not.

Unsuited big cards like A-T, K-J, and worse are still not playable up front. The risk of domination is still present, and if there are a lot of players, a pair, even top pair, does not rate to hold up as the best hand anyway. Being suited is of more importance in a game with a large field of players contesting the pots.

8 - EARLY POSITION

By early position, we are referring to the first three positions to act immediately after the big blind. It makes a big difference as to whether or not the pot has been raised ahead of you. There are also some special situations which develop that merit a separate discussion. Therefore, we have subdivided our early position guidelines into unraised pots, raised pots, and special situations.

Unraised Pots

You should prefer to open with a raise (or raise a limper) if you have A-A, K-K, Q-Q, J-J, T-T, A-K suited, A-Q suited, A-J suited, or A-K offsuit. With A-Q offsuit, we recommend raising about three-quarters of the time. Be more prone to raise with this hand when no one has opened or when you feel that the players are coming in with weak hands.

With 9-9 or 8-8, especially the former, you can raise if the game is so tight that you have a decent chance of grabbing the blind money. We prefer a call in a normal game.

An A-J offsuit is likely a fold against tough competition in a ten-handed game. We know some excellent high-limit players that normally fold the hand. In our experience, the hand is playable in the typical game where there are some weak players that you want to gamble with, especially if the game is nine-handed or less. Most games in the lower end of the middle limits are of a character for the hand to be played. In early position, you may treat a K-Q offsuit the same as you treat an A-J.

With A-T suited, we usually limp, but a raise is acceptable on occasion to vary your play if it is a loose game. You should open limp or limp behind others having 7-7, K-Q suited, or K-J suited. King-high hands are too weak to show down on the end, even against a possible busted draw, so don't start them out with a raise.

Raised Pots

When the pot is raised ahead of you, there are two things to keep in mind. First, it now costs you a double bet to play. Second, the raiser usually has a premium hand, since he is raising from early position. Against the typical player, you almost always reraise with A-A, K-K, and Q-Q. The holding of A-K (nicknamed "big slick"), whether suited or not, is a flexible hand. You can either reraise or just call, depending on a number of factors. You can normally cold-call with J-J, T-T, A-Q suited, A-J suited, and A-Q offsuit. Cold-calling a raise from a solid player with A-Q offsuit would be dangerous if the raiser adhered to the same high standards for his early position raises as we advocate. Since most players do not, we believe you can cold-call a raise with A-Q offsuit against typical players. Hands like K-Q suited, A-10 suited, and 9-9 are marginal, and a close decision whether to call or fold. With worse hands than these, a fold is advisable in a full game.

There is a school of poker thought that says if you hold a pocket pair and someone in front of you opens with a raise, you are in a reraise or fold situation. With a hand like J-J or T-T, you can't just call, but must take a committal stance. This isn't our practice, but we admit the idea has a lot of merit. A pocket pair like these is not looking for a volume pot. It does better heads-up.

Special Situations

Limping in early position with hands like Q-J suited and J-T suited is a marginal play. If the game is passive with not much preflop raising, then limping in is acceptable with these hands. In tough games where most players fold and there is usually one raiser, a fold is better, as these hands play quite poorly heads-up out-of-position. If you are in the second or third early-position seat and someone enters the pot ahead of you, then coming in with these hands is usually all right, because even if the pot is later raised, it figures to be a volume pot.

The next group of hands illustrate some important concepts in early-position play.

(1) You have J♣-T♣ under-the-gun. What do you do?

Answer: Depends on the character of the game. Jack-ten suited is grossly overvalued in certain older holdem literature. The hand plays well in unraised pots against a large field. It is not designed for heads-up play. The problem with coming in under-the-gun with this hand is that you have no idea as to what your ultimate cost will be to see the flop or how many opponents you will have. This hand is a speculative investment from early position and should be folded in a tough game.

(2) The under-the-gun player limps in and the next player folds. You have K♦-T♥. What do you do?

Answer: Fold. King-ten offsuit is not normally a playable hand. Fold unless you are: (1) in the blinds, (2) limping in from late position behind others, or (3) trying to steal the blinds from late position after everyone else has folded. This holding can frequently develop into an expensive second-best hand, and makes it especially dangerous to enter the pot from early position with the rest of the field yet to act. You definitely don't want to have to call a raise with this hand.

(3) The under-the-gun player raises. You have A♠-Q♣. What do you do?

Answer: Depends. This unsuited hand is just barely good enough to call against typical players. Against a solid player it is a fold. Had it been raised and reraised ahead of you, then a fold would clearly be in order. It is very easy for the raiser to have cards that dominate yours, meaning that if you hit the flop, he will have a better kicker or higher pair. An A-K is probably the commonest raising hand in the game, and you are in trouble against it.

(4) You limp in with the A♠-J♦ behind a call from the under-the-gun player. The next player raises and everyone folds to the small blind, who reraises. The big blind folds and the under-the-gun player calls. What do you do?

Answer: Fold. After limping in with this hand, you have to call a single raise back to you, but should not call a double raise. Between the raiser and the reraiser, it is too easy for someone to have pocket aces, kings, queens, jacks, or even a bigger ace. This would make it hard for you to improve to the winning hand, and easy to get into a trap against a stronger holding.

(5) An early player opens with a raise and you are next to act having 8♥-8♣. What do you do?

Answer: Fold, against normal people. An early position raiser normally has either a bigger pair than you or two big cards. With the former, you are a big underdog. With the latter, you are a small favorite. Overall, this makes you a long term money-loser in this situation. It is true that reraising could drive everyone else out and get the pot heads-up, but there are problems. First, it is costing you an extra bet to do this. Second, there are many players still to act, so you can run into a very good hand. Third, getting the pot heads-up is the last thing you want to do if you do not have the better starting hand. You do get the initiative by a reraise, and have position, but should venture this ploy only against a player who raises far too often in early position, making you feel that you are a favorite to have a clear advantage more often than running into an overpair. To have such an advantage, you need to have either a bigger pair or catch the person with only one overcard.

(6) You are playing in a Las Vegas game where the limit is a bet and four raises. The under-the-gun player opens with a raise. You are sitting right next to him with the A♥-A♦ and reraise. Everyone folds to the big blind, who calls. The under-the-gun player makes it four bets. What do you do?

Answer: Go ahead and cap the betting. The presence of a third player, the big blind, means that you should not slowplay here. It is important to force the big blind to pay the maximum price to take a flop. You know you have the best hand, and by capping it you will force the big blind to pay two more bets (or you will drive him out). If he calls, then you have collected an extra bet from both the big blind and the under-the-gun player by capping. Slowplaying by just smooth-calling would be acceptable if you were heads-up with position over your lone opponent. In that situation, you are willing to forsake collecting an extra small bet now in order to hide the strength of your hand. Don't slowplay a big pair against multiple opponents.

(7) The under-the-gun player opens with a raise and the player on his left calls. You are next with the K♥-Q♥. What do you do?

Answer: Call, against typical opponents. King-queen suited is a borderline hand. We do not advocate raising with it up front in a typical, full-table limit holdem game, but we are usually willing to call if someone else raises, provided we think that player is not a rock, and someone else has called in front of us. If the hand were unsuited, it would be a clear fold, since the threat of domination is quite real. However, being suited in a multihanded pot makes this nice hand worth playing against most opponents. We would fold a king-jack suited here, but that is a clearly weaker hand.

(8) A solid player raises under-the-gun. Another solid player sitting right next to him reraises. You are next to act holding the A♦-Q♦. What do you do?

Answer: Fold. The reraiser will normally have A-A, K-K, Q-Q, or maybe A-K. You are badly dominated, and may well have to make a flush or a straight to win. Having to pay three bets up front is too steep a price to try and do this. Furthermore, the other players will probably fold, making this a three-way pot with you having very much the worst of it. If you get lucky, and the reraiser is in there lighter than normal with J-J or 10-10 trying to isolate on the raiser, that doesn't mean you'll win the pot. The original raiser could have A-K or better, or you might not flop anything. If you do hit the flop, it is more likely that you will make a pair than the big draw you are hoping for.

9 – MIDDLE POSITION

By middle position, we are referring to the fourth, fifth, and sixth positions to act after the big blind in a ten-handed game. You can loosen up some from these positions because you now have a better feel for how the hand will develop. In addition, the prospects of picking up the blind money by raising are improved over the chance of this in early position. If you have a pocket pair and no one has opened, you should consider yourself in a raise-or-fold situation. Big cards like A-J and A-T are also raising hands.

Unraised Pots

All hands that were raising hands from early position are raising hands from middle position, whether or not players have limped in ahead of you. If no one has limped in, then you can open with a raise having 9-9, 8-8, 7-7, 6-6, A-J offsuit, A-T suited, and A-T offsuit as well. Given that up to half the field has folded, these additional hands have grown in strength. A raise will frequently fold the remaining players, while forcing the blinds to pay additional money if they choose to play. All other limping hands from early position are limping hands from middle position, whether or not anyone has called ahead of you. In addition, you can now limp in with hands like a suited ace, K-T suited, Q-J suited, Q-T suited, J-T suited, and K-J offsuit.

Sometimes you can be in middle position and still have three or four callers in front of you. A crowd gives you a much better price on flopping a set, so it is now more attractive to come in with small pairs. Pocket pairs like 5-5 and 4-4 look playable, and even the littlest twins can come under consideration.

Raised Pots

When a pot gets raised ahead of you, especially by an early-position player, then you should fall back on the early position guidelines outlined in the previous chapter covering raised pots. Having to cold-call a raise coupled with the threat of a reraise by any of the remaining players means that your implied odds are still

40

badly damaged even if multiple players have come into the pot. Every so often, there is someone in the game who raises very light in early position. You can three-bet such a player when you have J-J or 10-10. There is nothing wrong with isolating on a soft target.

The next set of hands bring some of these ideas into focus.

(1) You have A♠-3♠. Two early players limp, a middle player raises, and another middle player calls. What do you do?

Answer: Fold. Ace-little suited is a good hand against a large number of opponents in an unraised pot. But having to pay two or more bets upfront to see a flop makes this hand unprofitable in the long run.

(2) You have Q♠-Q♥. An early player limps, another early player raises, and the player to your right calls. What do you do?

Answer: Reraise. You are likely to have the best hand. Make your opponents pay dearly to see the flop. You never have a better opportunity to get more money in the pot when you have the best of it then before the flop. The raiser is far more likely to have a lower pocket pair or two big cards than he is to have pocket aces or pocket kings.

(3) You have A♠-J♥. An early player and a middle player limp. What do you do?

Answer: Call. This unsuited hand is not good enough to raise with, and it is too good to fold. Occasionally, you may want to raise with this hand if you have noticed that players have been coming in early with weak cards. But you would do this only to vary your play; it should not be something you do routinely.

(4) All four players ahead of you fold. You have the A♥-T♠. What do you do?

Answer: Raise. This is a decent hand to open with a raise when in middle position. You want to eliminate the remaining players if possible, and use your position over the blinds if they choose to play. If everyone folds, you are happy to take the blind money.

(5) The under-the-gun player opens with a raise. You are in middle position with the J♥-J♠. What do you do?

Answer: Depends on who raised, and your style. Our normal play is to just call unless the raiser is someone who is flying around on light hands. If you know the player is prone to raising on weaker hands than yours, you should three-bet, trying to get the pot heads-up having the better hand. Some strong players treat having a pocket pair on the immediate left of the opener as a raise-or-fold situation, because their hand is so hard to improve.

A solid opponent is likely to have a bigger pocket pair or two overcards. Three-betting someone who has a normal raising hand up front may get the pot down to two players, but getting heads-up is a laudable goal only if you are ahead. So who raised?

(6) An early player and a middle player limp in. You have 6♥-6♣. What do you do?

Answer: Call. This medium pocket pair is good enough to enter with when others have come in. You are hoping to see a flop cheaply and flop a set. Had the pot been raised, you should fold.

(7) Two early players and two middle players limp in. You have the 4♠-4♣. What do you do?

Answer: Call. The problem with little pocket pairs is that they can almost never be an overpair to the board, so your only "out" so to speak is to flop a set. However, given that four players have come in, the implied odds will be there for you to have a decent play. These small pairs need an unusually large field to be playable.

(8) An early player and a middle player limp. You have K♦-J♠. What do you do?

Answer: Call. This hand is marginal, but it is all right to limp in from middle position when others have come in ahead of you without raising. Someone who might have your holding dominated by having pocket kings, pocket jacks, ace-king, ace-jack suited, or even king-queen suited might have raised. You're also in trouble if someone limped in with either king-queen or ace-jack offsuit.

(9) You have the J♦-T♣. The player on your immediate right, in early position, limps in. What do you do?

Answer: Fold. Don't limp in with jack-ten offsuit from middle position when only one player has limped in ahead of you and there is still more than half the table yet to act. The likelihood of the pot getting raised with this many players behind you is too high to play a weak, speculative drawing hand like this. If you call and it gets raised, you will be obliged to call the raise, resulting in you having to pay two bets to take a flop. If your hand were suited, then you could play. If you were in a later position with more players limping in, then you might have a play.

(10) An early player and a middle player limp in. You limp with the K♣-T♣. The cutoff raises, the button reraises, and both blinds fold. Both limpers call. What do you do?

Answer: Fold. You limped in with his hand behind a couple of other players hoping to see a flop cheaply with a large field. But now it has been raised and reraised behind you, so it costs you two more bets to play. Furthermore, it may get raised again. Having to pay multiple bets to take flop with this hand seriously damages its implied odds. If you flop something like top pair, it figures to simply cost you money, since someone will likely either have an overpair or have you outkicked. You need to flop two pair or better, or flop a draw and get there, in order to end up with the best hand. This is too remote to pay another two bets.

10 – LATE POSITION

By late position, we are referring to the button, and the seat just to the right of the button, called the cutoff seat. If no one has come into the pot yet, attempting to win the blind money is very much on your mind (and minds of the remaining players). For this reason, the normal play from these two seats when opening is to bring it in with a raise. This not only gives you a chance to win the blind money without a fight, but also gives you the initiative in a shorthanded, perhaps heads-up, pot. As we know, it is not so easy to have a playable hand and then hit the flop, so a lot of shorthanded pots are bought by the first purchase order.

With one or more players calling ahead of you, a raise will not win the blind money. For someone to call and then fold for a single raise is extremely rare, as well as incorrect. So you do not want to raise without a hand of superior value if winning the pot immediately is not a possible result.

Some people seem to think that being in late position, especially the button, gives you an extraordinary advantage. They raise on marginal hands in the cutoff seat "to get the button." They raise on the button with junk. Many players over-estimate the amount of this advantage in limit poker. To reiterate, in a limit holdem game it will usually take the best hand to win most major pots. Being in late position may allow you to collect an extra bet or two when you have the best hand in large pots, but it does not necessarily make a weak hand magically playable. And if there are many players competing for a pot, having the button is of less value than when there are only two or three players competing.

Suppose you limp in from the button with a hand like 8-7 offsuit because there are a lot of players limping in. If you miss flopping a straight-draw but accidentally catch top pair instead, you will find that it is far less likely to hold up than when you have just a few opponents. Furthermore, you will frequently get "pot stuck," meaning that you are thrown into marginal situations where your outs are few, the opponents are many, and the pot is large. When you look back to see where the errors for a large loss on that hand occurred, you may find that the odds were always

10 - LATE POSITION

sufficient to pursue your longshot. The mistake was getting involved initially; you had no business calling preflop.

All that being said, you can of course enter the pot with more hands from late position than from the other positions, since you have a better understanding of how the pot has developed and what your cost will be to take a flop. That late position is advantageous is not disputed by us, only the degree of advantage this confers, and its impact on which hands are playable.

Unraised Pots

This discussion assumes that at least one player has limped in from early or middle position. All limping hands discussed in previous chapters are of course playable in late position as well. With three or more limpers, you can limp in with 5-5, 4-4, 3-3, and 2-2. With one or two limpers, you should normally fold these small pairs.

With suited connectors, you can now limp in with a T-9 suited. The one-gap hands of J-9 suited and T-8 suited are also playable. The two-gap hand of Q-9 suited may be played, but nothing with two gaps that is worse than this. Keep in mind that these hands are very marginal, and whether you call or fold is not a big deal either way. If there is one caller who is a tough player, or someone behind you on the button usually raises, a fold is fine.

You can limp with ace-little suited and king-nine suited. We do not recommend limping in with king-little suited or worse. The problem with limping in with just any suited king, queen, or jack is that against a lot of opponents, drawing to the nut flush becomes increasingly important. Contrary to what many players seem to believe, when many players take a flop, it is common for one flush to lose to another flush.

Unsuited big cards like K-T offsuit are playable in late position, as well as Q-T and J-T offsuit from the button. In the absence of a preflop raise, if you flop top pair, it has a better chance of being good. However, we do not recommend limping in with ace-little offsuit. A lot of aces with a kicker bigger than yours get played, so you may well be building a dominated hand. You can limp in with unsuited connectors no worse than J-T offsuit.

10 - LATE POSITION

Limping in from late position with a weaker suited connectors like 9-8 suited, 8-7 suited, 7-6 suited, or 6-5 suited is a very marginal play. We feel you need to be on the button to even think about doing this. In the cutoff seat, you have to consider the likelihood that you will not get last position on the deal, because the button standards for most players is far looser than ours. There is also the possibility of the button raising behind you, which would be most unwelcome on this type of hand.

Raised Pots

When the pot is raised ahead of you, follow the same standards as you would if you were in middle position, unless you are up against a steal-position raise, as on the button when the cutoff opens with a raise. In this case, you should consider reraising with any medium pocket pair or two big cards headed by an ace like A-K, A-Q, or A-J. You want the blinds to face a double bet, and you want the initiative if the pot becomes heads-up. Many players try to steal from the cutoff seat by opening with a raise on a hand like 4-4, 9-8 suited, J-T offsuit, or even worse. Punish these players by playing back at them when you hold a decent hand. Their game plan with such a hand is to use their raise to put the burden of hitting a flop on you. They intend to bet the flop whether buying help or not. Your reraise puts the task of helping back on them—as it should be if your hand is better than theirs.

Of course, you will get better results with this play of reraising if you use it only against a player who has a bit of gamble to him, and may well be on a steal. Beware of reraising a rock who in any position always has a big hand for a raise.

Stealing The Blinds

If you are in late position and everyone so far has folded, then you should be raising on a lot of hands that you would have just limped in with from earlier positions, or even folded. You could now have the best hand, and you have position if you get played with. The blinds may fold a lot of the time anyway.

10 - LATE POSITION

When you get called by someone, being the preflop aggressor is helpful, because it tends to put the burden of hitting the flop on the opponent—and he is a big underdog to be helped by the flop. Since you are always going to bet the flop into one calling opponent, he does not even figure to fight the majority of the time, so when you both miss the flop, you win the pot.

The big blind is the hardest person to get through with your preflop raise, because he has a sizable investment that he wants to protect. The style of play by the big blind can vary from never folding to giving up unless he has a solid hand, so you must observe this person closely in judging how often to attempt a steal. The type of opponent you want is the kind that seldom calls your raise, and does not make a play for the pot unless he hits the flop.

In general, when open-raising from late position, you want high-card strength. Being suited is not worth that much. In a shorthanded pot, any pair can be good, or even an ace-high hand. You should open with a raise on any pair higher than fives, any ace, or any two big cards higher than an eight. From the button, you may want to open raise with 5-5, 4-4, 3-3, or 2-2, depending upon how the blinds play and how they perceive you. It is obviously better with such a hand to win without a fight.

One other point. Do not just limp in with your premium hands like A-A, K-K, and so forth. Since the blinds expect you to try and steal, you might as well raise with your good hands. You collect extra money when they choose to take a flop with you, and it camouflages the times when you don't have a premium hand. Another reason to raise is to get enough money into the pot so the opponent will be more likely to play a marginal holding on the expensive betting rounds, where the strength of your hand stops him from getting the proper pot odds to make calling correct.

The next set of hands discuss preflop play from late position.

(1) You are in the cutoff seat with the A♥-T♦. An early player limps and a middle player raises. What do you do?

Answer: Fold. This is a trouble hand, because you frequently end up with kicker problems when an ace flops against a preflop raiser.

In addition, the raiser could have cards that cripple your hand, making it harder for you to improve.

(2) You are on the button with the J♥-J♣. Everyone limps except the cutoff, who folds. What do you do?

Answer: Raise. With no one raising, you almost certainly have the best hand. An extra bet here pulls into the pot probably eight additional bets with you holding the best hand. It is true that you are an underdog against a collective of eight players, but when you win, you will win a bigger pot as a result, and win far more than when you lose. You have the most to gain by raising. The idea of not raising too large a field when you have an intermediate pair is correct, but jacks are a big enough hand to pop it with. There is a much better chance of flopping an overpair with jacks than a smaller pair. Even though an overpair is in jeopardy with this big a field, it is still a desirable flop. A pair of tens are marginal for raising, and nines should likely just call. Even though you are getting excellent pot odds, sets don't always win, especially against a huge field—and losing with them is expensive.

(3) You are on the button with the 7♣-6♣. Everyone folds to you. What do you do?

Answer: Fold. There are several things to consider when attempting to steal the blinds. First, compared to stud, stealing the blinds is not as alluring mathematically, since you are risking two bets to win one and a half bets, so these are smaller pot odds than playing a poker form that uses an ante. Second, be prepared to get called more often than otherwise, since your opponents expect you to try to steal, and they are partway in already. Third, astute opponents who are in the blinds with a half-decent holding like a medium pair may well play back at you with a reraise. Finally, you are playing against only one or two opponents, which means that making a straight or flush is less necessary to win the pot, and does not provide as big a pot to win. A decent-size pair is usually enough to win in a short-handed pot, so a hand with high-card strength will play better here than a small suited connector.

10 - LATE POSITION

Every once in a while, you will run into a player in the big blind who makes no attempt to fight against steal-raises, and just keeps throwing his hand away. You can raise such a player on small suited connectors—and a lot of other trashy hands as well.

(4) You are in the cutoff seat with the K♣-J♣. Three players limp in. What do you do?

Answer: Call. King-jack suited is normally not a raising hand. You want to see a flop, but not pay a high price to do so.

(5) You are on the button with the 10♦-9♦. Three players limp and the cutoff raises. What do you do?

Answer: Fold. You would have limped in with this hand and seen a flop with a lot of players. Unfortunately, having to call a raise now makes the price too high. In addition, the pot could get raised again, costing you even more money to take a flop.

(6) You are in the cutoff seat with the A♦-A♣. Everyone folds to you. What do you do?

Answer: Raise. Since the button and the blinds expect you to try to steal, you should raise with your good hands. To just limp and give the blinds a free flop is a mistake. If they flop a hand that beats yours, you will lose a lot of chips to a hand they might not have played otherwise. The extra money in the pot may tempt someone in after the flop that would have folded in a smaller pot.

(7) You are on the button holding 6♦-6♥ and the player on your right, who has been in the game a half-hour without raising any pots, open-raises this one. What do you do?

Answer: Fold. You should reraise the typical player who pops it in steal position. However, if the pot is raised by a total rock, you must fold. Being on the button with a pocket pair and encountering an open-raise by a player in the cutoff seat puts you in a reraise or fold situation, so abandon ship against this type of player.

11 – INTRODUCTION TO BLIND PLAY

Play in the blinds is radically different from play in any of the other positions, because the ratio of what you must put up to see the flop compared to what you can win is much different. To view your blind money as "a loss" is to be making a big mistake. Since you are already partially in, the pot odds you are getting to take a flop are much better than anyone else's. This usually more than compensates for the inferior position you have on the remaining three betting rounds.

On the other hand, you build a lot of hands that are a bit shaky, such as top pair with a weak kicker, and are out-of-position to boot. To take advantage of the discounted entry fee and show a profit, you have to play circumspectly after the flop. When you run into resistance, be willing to fold instead of being a bulldog.

You should raise with your premium hands from either blind against limpers. Raise with A-A, K-K, Q-Q, and A-K regardless of how many people come into the pot. Against one to three limpers, you should raise with J-J and A-Q as well.

An important aspect of being in the blind is how you defend against a late position steal-raise. A player in the cutoff or button seat will normally raise with any hand he comes in with, if no one is in the pot yet. You cannot treat such a raiser as you would treat someone who had raised in earlier position, even though any seat can pick up a big pair. From the small blind, be more inclined to reraise than just call if you are going to play, since driving out the big blind and seizing the initiative is important in these situations. From the big blind, it is somewhat less necessary to reraise, since you will not be eliminating anyone. Even so, the initiative conferred by getting in the last word preflop is worth something.

One important point is that small and medium suited connectors are not worth much in raised, shorthanded pots, especially when you are out-of-position. You are not trying to make a straight or a flush; you are trying to build a pair or better. Frequently, a good ace will win in these situations. Pairs and high card strength are what is important here.

12 – SMALL BLIND

From the small blind, being halfway in when there is an unraised pot lets you call with a vast array of ugly hands. Any pair is playable. For suited cards, you can play hands such as six-five suited, eight-six suited, and even ten-seven suited. Offsuit hands as bad as nine-eight, jack-nine, and queen-eight become playable. But having the worst position at the table means you are forced to play conservatively after the flop. Get out quickly with these hands unless others seem very weak or you catch a big flop.

One common mistake is to think a bad hand should be played if there are enough opponents. Wrong. Look at all the people you have to beat. In shorthanded pots, the value of just being in is a lot. You can launch a bluff that might succeed, instead of having to show down the best hand—which is hard to do with junk.

For raised pots, it makes an enormous difference where the raise came from. An early raise or raise of someone who limped in early position must be respected. An open-raise from the cutoff or button is suspect, requiring much more aggressive treatment. An open-raise from middle position or raise of a middle-position limper is closer to being considered a solid raise.

When dealing with a legitimate raise from an early or middle player or from a late player who raises after others have limped in, we like the "Ciaffone Rule." *If you would not call the raise on the button, then you should not call the raise when in the small blind.* In a raised pot, the button ought to be worth about half a small bet.

Against a steal-position raise, you should reraise with any pair that you decide to play. All pairs present a raise-or-fold situation because your chance of winning increases greatly if you can get out the big blind.

You should reraise with an ace if you feel that the raiser is the type of player who will try to steal the blinds on a wide range of hands. A-K and A-Q are good enough hands to play back at nearly anyone. How much lower you go than this in kicker quality depends on how you view the player who is coming in with a raise. Whether you are suited is not of such great importance in this type of situation, since the pot will probably be heads-up if you reraise, and at most threeway.

12 – SMALL BLIND

For the following hands, you are in the small blind:

(1) You have the Q♥-6♥. Three players limp, a middle player raises, and the button calls. What do you do?

Answer: Fold. Queen-little suited is not normally a playable hand, and calling raises with it even from the small blind is a bad play. The odds are likely over 20-to-1 against making a flush and having it hold up as the best hand.

(2) You have the Q♦-10♦. An early player limps, a middle player limps, and the cutoff raises. The button folds. What do you do?

Answer: Fold. Though this suited connector is better than most, it is still not good enough to call a raise out of your small blind.

(3) You have the A♠-Q♥. Two early players limp and the button raises. What do you do?

Answer: Call. The button's raise is not a steal-raise here, since two other players have voluntarily entered the pot. This means that the button likely has a legitimate raising hand. Your hand is not good enough to reraise. Since you are partially in, you can call.

(4) You have the 5♠-5♥. The cutoff seat, a stranger, opens with a raise. What should you do?

Answer: Fold. The weaker the opponent, the bigger hand they are likely to hold when raising in steal position—and the more likely they are to call you down throughout the hand. A stranger often turns out to be a weak player (or else he would be playing often enough for you to get to know him). You are in a reraise-or-fold situation. A lot of players who know this is the character of their situation use it as an excuse to take a more aggressive action than their hand warrants. Against a caller type of player, and one who may not be raising because he is in a steal situation, you can't be as aggressive as you might be facing someone else.

13 – BIG BLIND

Being halfway in is a strong incentive to call a single raise. Despite the big blind having bad position, many more hands are playable there than if you were in late position and had to cold-call the full amount of the raise. A major consideration is what position the raise came from (and the raising habits in that spot of the player who did it).

An opening raise from the cutoff or button positions is considered to be a steal-raise. Many players who open-raise in steal position have shabby holdings for this action, and you must fight fire with fire. However, if there is already a caller, especially one in early position, the raiser is expected to have a decent hand regardless of his position.

Against a steal-position raise, you should reraise most players if you have 9-9 or better, A-K, or A-Q. How you handle hands like 8-8, 7-7, 6-6, A-J, or A-T is of course dependent on the raising habits of that particular opponent. Most opponents try to steal the blind money on a wide range of hands, but there are a few rocks who do not loosen up their raising requirements in late position.

Here is how to play heads-up against a raise that is not a steal-raise. Call with any pair or a suited ace. Against typical players, usually call with any two cards of ten and above. But be aware that a call is based on your playing the hand properly after the flop, which means not marrying it when the raiser says by strong betting that you are beat. Avoid confrontations with solid players on this type of holding. These hands play poorly against a big pair.

For a three-handed pot, don't play the small connectors when gapped, but you can play something like a 9-8 suited. If you are getting at least four-way action, then you can call with suited connectors down to 5-4 suited, and one-gaps like 9-7 suited.

Reraise a raise from any position if you hold aces, kings, or queens. Vary your play when holding A-K, sometimes calling, other times reraising. "Big Slick" is a flexible hand.

In considering how to vary your game, it is reasonable to sometimes reraise on hands not really worth such an action. We saw that when fighting against the steal-raise. The value of the preflop initiative is important in heads-up play.

13 - BIG BLIND

Here are some problems where you are in the big blind.

(1) You hold the T♥-T♦. Everyone folds to the button, who raises. The small blind folds. What do you do?

Answer: Reraise. You have a raising hand yourself, and since the button could be on a steal, you should reraise and charge him extra for taking a flop. Failing to be aggressive in this situation is bad poker. This is especially true if the button is the type of player who likes to steal on little connectors.

(2) You hold A♠-K♦. Two early players, two middle players, and the button limp. The small blind folds. What do you do?

Answer: Raise. You almost surely have the best playing hand when no one raises. You will flop top pair, top kicker or better about one third of the time. Another five percent of the time you will flop some kind of draw like a gutshot straight draw or a flush draw. For one extra bet, you pull into the pot another five bets, and you have a better chance than anyone else of ending up with the best hand. If the flop misses you completely, you can check and fold in many cases, since there are too many opponents to try a bluff. One raises to build a bigger pot holding the best hand; the fact that you can't eliminate anyone should not deter you from sweetening the pot.

(3) You have the A♠-5♦. Four players limp in, the button raises, and the little blind folds. What do you do?

Answer: Fold. Yes, we see the big odds you are getting with this many players. We also see a lot of people you have to beat in order to win the pot. Don't be an optimist and fall for the big pot odds. This hand is worse with a lot of players, because here it is quite likely someone has an ace with a bigger kicker. To win, you have to hit the hand bigtime, like two pair or better. The pot odds are not big enough to justify this. On top of everything else, your position is the worst it could possibly be: acting first, with the preflop raiser on your immediate right.

14 – INTRODUCTION TO FLOP PLAY

The flop gives each player three more cards to go with his pocket two. Because there is such a large change in prospects as a result, it is this round of new cards that has the most to do with who eventually wins the pot. Two aces are a far superior hand to a 10-9, but a flop of 8-7-6 completely changes things in terms of the relative prospects. One of the biggest mistakes you can make in holdem is to not adjust to the new situation after getting three more cards. The preflop pecking order may well be history.

What constitutes a good hand on the flop? You can either have a good made hand or a good draw. The typical normal requirements for a made hand are top pair or better. For a drawing hand, an open-end straight-draw or a flush-draw are considered decent. Sometimes you can flop a super-draw, such as a flush-draw with two overcards or a straight-draw combined with a flush-draw. In that case, you have a premium hand, and it should be bet accordingly.

It is nice to flop an overpair after raising the pot. With typical raising hands like kings, queens, and jacks, there was always the threat of that ace or other bigger card than your pair to mess things up. But flopping an overpair is not the same as winning the pot. Quite often, someone who just called preflop decides to raise you after the flop. Does he think he has you beat, or is he just putting in a raise for tactical reasons? Hard to tell, since the typical holdem structure has the bet on the flop only half the size of the bet on the turn, delaying for a betting round the real truth of his opinion. So what should you do with your overpair if you get raised on the flop?

Although each situation must be examined on its own merits, a lot of your decision on whether to reraise or call is based on your position. If you are acting first, prefer to reraise (unless the board is really scary), because a lot of the time the raiser is simply trying to get a free card or test you. However, if you have position, just calling is probably right, because to raise you there, a check-raise is needed, which is a much stronger play than just a raise. With position, you can see how the player acts after the turn-card comes. He will not be able to take a free card. If he checks, you bet. If he bets, you can make a decision at that point how to handle things. The important thing is not to let a player who has position on you raise on the cheap street and get a free ride as a result of his small investment.

When should you play aggressively on the flop by taking the lead in the betting? Our approach places great emphasis on the number of opponents you are facing as a critical factor in deciding whether to play aggressively by betting or raising. In general, we like leading on the flop when we have any piece of the board, the pot is unraised, and we are facing a small number of opponents (usually less than three). The reason is you have a decent chance of winning the pot when betting into a small field.

How likely are you to get called when taking a shot at the pot by betting a marginal hand or bluffing? One factor to consider is the rank of the highest card on the board. The higher the top flop-card, the more likely someone is to have top pair. This is most obvious in a raised pot, as a raise says, "I have high cards." An ace is particularly dangerous, since so many hands one raises with contain an ace. An ace is often in hands of the callers as well. Even for unraised pots, the higher cards get played more often. Weak players like to play any ace, and the suited king is also alluring to them. If the top card is not in the playing zone, it is much less likely someone has paired with it. So betting something like middle pair with a big card on the board, especially an ace or king, is more dangerous from the standpoint of running into top pair than when the flop is headed by a lower card.

On the other hand, an ace or king on board is also of a certain benefit when you are trying to pick up the pot on a draw or marginal holding. The hand one puts a bettor on first is top pair. The opponent may be more likely to believe you have the hand you are representing, because these hands are played so often. And fewer hands he may hold are playable if you actually do have that hand. The higher the top card on the board, the less likelihood of running into two overcards, or some hand where having one overcard would probably make it a playing hand, like a gutshot straight. So we are not saying that it is unattractive to bet when there is an ace or king on the board and you have less than top pair, because those other factors are at work. We just want you to be aware of all the various elements in deciding whether to bet.

Betting something of shaky quality is only for pots with few opponents. When the number of opponents is increased to a large field of four or more, we tend to shy away from leading with anything less than top pair, good kicker or a super draw like a flush-draw with overcards. The reason is simple. As you increase the number of opponents, the likelihood of you picking up the pot with a bet goes down dramatically. Furthermore, the likelihood of your getting raised, especially when having less than top pair, goes up even more dramatically as you increase the size of the field. If we don't have the best hand, then we are drawing, and we do not want to spend any more money than necessary to draw at a flush, straight, or lesser hand. We believe that leading into a crowd of players on tenuous holdings will cost you a lot of money.

Should you get aggressive against a crowd and do everything possible to win a pot that has gotten quite large? This might include betting, raising, or check-raising on a second-best hand in an attempt to drive out worse hands which might overtake your hand. But in order for this idea to work, a longshot parlay is required. Specifically: (1) You improve. (2) Your improvement results in a better hand than the currently best hand. (3) One of the opponent's hands would have improved to a better hand than your improved hand. (4) That opponent's hand will be folded because you bet or raised (much less likely in gigantic pots). (5) No one else improves to beat you. So what we are dealing with is the combined probability of all of these events occurring on a deal.

Combined probabilities of independent events are computed by multiplying the individual probabilities of each event. (This is a fraction, and multiplying fractions of course makes the resulting fraction smaller.) The likelihood of this parlay occurring is frequently on the order of one or two percent. So unless the pot has something like fifty bets in it, or the hands you may drive out greatly increase your chance to win, spending an extra bet doesn't increase your prospects enough to be worth the cost.

Let's put what we are talking about here into concrete terms. Our gunner opens with a raise on A-K and gets four callers. Now the big blind three-bets and everyone calls. Six players take the flop, which comes down with all small cards. The big blind bets—and our gunner raises. If you ask him why he is raising with what is obviously not the best hand, the explanation is something like this. "I know that I am not going to win the pot with this raise, but the pot is large. If I make my hand, the raise gives me a better chance of it being good. For example, I might get someone out that already has a pair, and an ace or king kicker with it." In addition to our previous arguments on the very small likelihood of the raise achieving everything that needs to take place for the raiser to win a pot he otherwise wouldn't have won, we must mention that the raise is likely to knock out people who would **not** have deprived our gunner of the pot. So the raise lessens the amount he wins when hitting. It also exposes him to a reraise. Our conclusion is that such a raise is just bad poker.

Let's be clear that throwing in an extra bet to try to win a pot is a normal tool used by good players. We are only knocking its use when it is obvious that you do not have the best hand, and the raise may well be more detrimental than helpful.

Let's now take a look at flop play from the perspective of someone who was not the preflop aggressor. The poker expression "Check to the raiser" is in common usage. The raiser has indicated strength on the prior betting round, and often bets if checked to on the next round. The player who checks is saying, "You have indicated that you think your hand is the best, so a bet is expected from you. By checking, I will defer my decision until you act, and then I'll let you know if I think your hand is still the boss." Usually, the raiser bets—but not always.

Despite its common occurrence, habitually checking to the preflop raiser is one of the damaging mistakes made by holdem players. Of course, checking is often the correct play, but it should be far from an automatic action. Here we will talk about when you should **not** check to the raiser.

Why does the raiser usually bet the flop in holdem, even if he has no pair and fails to buy help on the board? Simply because the mathematics of the situation dictates that he do so even if he winds up with a poor hand. It is about 2-to-1 against improving a pairless hand on the flop. In a heads-up situation, if the raiser actually had the better preflop hand, he is the favorite to still be in the driver's seat. Against two opponents, one of them will help more often then not, but it is still worthwhile investing a bet to see if this has happened. There is a reasonable chance of winning an uncontested battle. As the number of adversaries increases, so does the chance that one or more of them will improve. To bet into a crowd requires a real hand—for circumspect people—and the raiser does not always have such a hand, even if he is a solid player. A fine holding like an A-K suited is still likely to be only a pair-draw after the flop (it is about 2-to-1 against pairing). So the more people who see the flop, the less chance of getting the raiser to bet your hand.

Naturally, if you start with A-Q and the flop comes with two aces and a queen, there is no reason to bet and protect your full house. As any terrorist knows, it is the soft targets that need protection. The most vulnerable hands among the decent ones are one-pair hands where an overcard can make someone a bigger pair. If you start with A-Q and make a pair of aces on the flop, it is not so easy for someone to outdraw you on the next card. However, on a flop of 8-5-3, a hand such as an overpair like 9-9 or top pair like A-8 may well be the boss for the moment, but is in dire need of a bet to give it protection against being outdrawn. An overcard can make someone a bigger pair, a lower-ranking card makes a bunch of possible straights, and even pairing the board may enable someone to make trips and beat you.

There are many hands that the opponent might throw away if you bet. Overcards, gutshot straight-draws, and small pairs may wish to drop out of contention if there is a bet on the flop—and of course should be charged a price to draw if they choose to stay in. The situation screams for you to bet.

In poker, as in life, it is unwise to rely on someone else to protect your vital interests if you can do so yourself. If you are fortunate enough to flop top pair with intermediate-ranking cards, it is your job to bet the flop. Do not rely on the raiser to bet and protect your hand for you. Poker isn't supposed to be a game played by rote. But in this situation, where you flop a hand that figures to be the best but can easily be overtaken, it seems automatic to bet.

Your goal should be commensurate with your hand. The goal of a decent but not extraordinary hand should be the modest one of winning a small pot. You simply want to get the goods home without a big fight. But the way many players behave in the situation we are discussing is to provoke a conflict. They check the flop, call when the raiser bets, and then check again on the next round "to see if the raiser is serious."

Let us now look at the situation from the raiser's perspective. If he isn't an aggressive person, he will most likely check it back on the turn, hoping to draw out, and willing to give up the pot when he does not (which is the vast majority of the time). However, an aggressive player may well decide to keep betting, since his opponent has not indicated a lot of strength with the sequence check-call-check. He may keep coming with the hand, betting the turn, and possibly even again on the end. Of course, the raiser cannot be certain that his opponent isn't slowplaying a big hand, but the odds are always way against a behemoth. Such a hand is not easy to get, and might not have been slowplayed had the person gotten one. Just how far are you willing to go with a modest-sized hand against strong betting? A lot of pots are lost by someone with a hand that would have won a showdown, but the person was pressured into folding.

Adopting a weak betting sequence is "cornering the raiser." It may be okay to corner a pussycat, but beware of cornering dangerous animals. An aggressive player is a dangerous animal. The way to give yourself the best chance to win the pot is to make a probing bet on the flop and let him know you have something. If you also lead a lot with your very good hands—as you should—the opponent may well decide to concede a small loss rather than try to represent a big pair, which may not be the best hand even if he has it. Bet right into the raiser and give him a chance to get out cheaply, rather than provoking a big fight by acting weak and staying in, and you will win most of those small pots, instead of turning them into big pots when your hand doesn't warrant it. So if you stay for a raised pot on A-J suited or A-10 suited, bet when that ace comes. When you have an intermediate pair such as J-J, 10-10, or 9-9 and flop an overpair, go ahead and lead with it.

If you encounter strong resistance after betting the flop, it is a lot easier to turn a hand loose after having shown some strength than if you have shown nothing but weakness. A shrimp does not know if someone kicking sand in his face is simply acting that way because of his small stature. A guy built like Atlas knows that someone getting aggressive with him is likely to be real bad news. Let the opponent know you do not have a shrimp hand by betting the flop, and he is not likely to try bullying you into folding.

So far we have been looking at modest-sized hands. When you are fortunate enough to flop a really big hand like a set, it still may well be right to lead with it. This applies even if you feel sure the raiser will bet the flop. One reason to lead, at both limit and pot-limit play, is to avoid a power sequence that enables the opponent to get away from his hand. Check-raising the raiser shows a lot of strength, and may enable the opponent to make an astute laydown. If you bet the flop and keep betting on later streets, the raiser often hangs in there until the bitter end, scratching his head after taking a sizable loss, and wondering just when he was supposed to have folded. It is also quite possible he may raise you at some point, as a lot of players are so used to an opponent with a big hand using a check-raise strategy that they fail to show the bettor respect.

There are certain classes of flop play that can be logically grouped and studied. Hands such as overcards, overpairs, top pair, and various draws are extremely common and often misplayed. Most of the problems players have in these situations are over-valuing their holding. Fairly often, you will find a player whose preflop play is reasonably solid, but whose flop play is so loose as to constitute a major leak in his game.

Why do so many players stay in too long on inferior hands? Part of the problem is that they misunderstand the concept of outs. An out is a card that (hopefully) will improve you to a winner. The idea of having an out is that if one of your outs arrives, you end up with the best hand and win the pot. There is no prize for simply improving. But sometimes your "out" does not give you the best hand, either because an opponent already has a better hand, or your "out" improves your opponent's holding as well. This is commonplace when all you have is overcards, and are trying to make a pair, or you are drawing at the nut flush and make a pair of aces instead of the hoped-for nuts. One pair is a fragile holding. Another way to hit and still lose is to improve to the best hand on the turn, only to have your opponent make an even better hand at the river (the redraw).

A related problem is the failure to consider pot odds, both current and implied. When pots start getting raised and reraised on the flop, your implied odds get damaged, because you may be drawing dead, or have someone redraw after you hit. A lot of hands have to be thrown away when the pot gets bombarded. Many players ignore current pot odds and figure that they can play on for profit because of all the extra money they will collect on the expensive streets when they hit their hand. But this often assumes faultily that they will win every time they hit, which for the reasons stated previously, is not the case.

In poker, we do not necessarily give up just because we know the opponent has a better hand. Instead, we try to overtake him. At limit holdem, if we fail to help significantly on the flop, the fact that it is the cheap street means we may well opt to take a card off and hope to buy help. Let's talk about what induces us to call a flop bet holding a sub-par hand, and when to abandon ship.

The type of hand we will be talking about here is one lacking in the normal requirements for staying on the flop in multihanded pots. The type of hand we might stay on if the circumstances are right would be hands such as second or bottom pair, a couple of overcards, or a gutshot straight-draw.

The first question that needs to be answered is, "How much money is in the pot?" Since we are trying to help a longshot, we need to be getting good odds. None of the marginal hands we are talking about are worth playing if the pot has not been raised preflop. The odds simply do not justify playing a longshot unless there is added money in the pot from a raise. In an unraised pot, even if a lot of players saw the flop, seeming to create good odds, the fact that you have to defeat so many opponents will usually make playing marginal hands unattractive.

Naturally, a pot that has been reraised or capped before the flop contains a lot of money in proportion to the half-size bet allowed on the flop, so the inclination there would be to play most sub-par hands that had an outside chance. This means the usual situation where considerations other than the pot size come into play and become important factors will be when there has been precisely one preflop raise, so assume this is the case in the examples we will discuss.

The second question needing to be answered is, "How much is this going to cost me?" We are assuming that there is only one bet to you on the flop round of betting. But unless you are last to act, there is the possibility you will be snared by an installment plan into paying additional expenses by one or more raises behind you. The more players acting after you do, the greater the threat of getting charged additional fees to continue playing. Particularly dangerous is a bet that the preflop raiser hasn't had an opportunity to act on yet, as he is likely to raise if holding top pair or an overpair—and may pop it even if he does not. So anytime you consider continuing on marginal values, evaluate the threat of getting charged more than just the amount of a single bet. This jeopardy of added expenses changes many hands from being a marginal call into a clear fold.

There are other factors to consider when contemplating a call on a marginal hand other than how much you can win and how much you might be charged. The most important of these is the possibility of helping your hand and still not winning the pot. We can assure you, after working with a lot of people on improving their poker game, that the typical player has a lot of trouble in this area. People hardly ever seem to fold a hand that is worth a call. Virtually all the errors are on the side of the ledger where we keep track of hands being played that should be folded. Of course, this should surprise nobody.

Here are some hands and situations that are easy to improperly evaluate. We will give the general category, the hand, the board, and the type of explanation that you often hear used to justify playing, then comment on the situation.

A gutshot straight-draw. You hold K♠-Q♠ and the board is A♥-J♥-3♠. "I have an inside straight-draw and a backdoor flush-draw." One of the most common mistakes on a marginal hand is drawing to a gutshot straight when there is a flush-draw on the board. On this hand the 10♥, one of your cards to make a straight, would put a third heart on the board, creating the possibility of a flush. You should not be so concerned about this if heads-up against the preflop raiser, as he is much more likely to have a made hand than a flush-draw. But any other players in the pot may well be in there trying to make a flush. The more people that saw the flop, the more likely that the card which makes both your straight and a possible flush will be a curse rather than a blessing. And even if you make your hand with a ten not of the flush suit, that two-flush on the board means your straight will get cracked by the river card much more often than if a flush were impossible. Nearly all gutshot straight-draws should be folded if there is a two-flush on the board. As for the backdoor flush-draw, that is not enough to make a silk purse out of a sow's ear.

Two overcards. You hold the A♠-K♠ and the board-cards are 10♠-7♥-4♣. "I have two overcards and a backdoor flush-draw." Fine; take a card off and see what develops. But here are some other hands where you have a couple of overcards and you have no business in the pot.

You hold K♠-J♠ and the board comes that same 10♠-7♥-4♣. Remember, we are assuming the pot has been raised preflop and you were not the one who did it. Calling a raise cold on a king-jack suited is not recommended, but we can suppose you were in for one bet and then called a raise. When you did so, you were a bit leery that if you made top pair, the raiser or someone else would have either an overpair or a bigger kicker. These conditions still exist; pairing may well not win the pot for you. When your overcards are shaky in value, they are not enough reason by themselves to continue in the pot. Overcards of this nature do somewhat increase the value of a straight-draw or flush-draw, but if you had this type of hand, you would be continuing to fight for the pot anyway. (Also note that hitting a jack could make someone a straight; another drawback to this particular hand.)

You hold A♠-K♠ and the flop comes Q♠-8♣-8♥. Yes, you have two overcards, but are you drawing live? When there is a pair on the board, someone may already have trips. Once again, you should not be so afraid of the raiser; he is much less likely to have an eight than one of the callers.

Lastly, you hold A♠-K♠ and the flop is 9♥-8♠-6♦. "I have two overcards and a backdoor flush-draw." Once again, you could easily be drawing dead, since there is a possible straight on the board. With middle-sized cards, there is also a greater chance of a set being out against you than normal. Furthermore, when the boardcards hook up in rank like this, it hurts you. An enemy two pair is more likely. And even if you pair on the turn and it turns out to be good at that point, the last card is going to be more toxic than usual. Any ten, seven, or five likely spells doom. Even if someone does not actually make a straight with it, chances are good you will be facing two pair or trips. Lastly, your backdoor flush-draw is about a 23-to-1 shot against coming home, so it does not turn a fold into a call. Playing a hand like this is a big mistake.

As you can see, to take off a card on the flop to a marginal hand is sometimes the correct play, but far more often it is an error. Conditions have to be just right to stay. If there is anything about the situation that makes you uncomfortable, throw the hand in the muck. People make far fewer bad folds than bad calls.

One of the ways we can separate the various flop types into categories is by how many cards of a suit are on the board. One card, two cards, and three cards of the same suit are the possibilities, and each group has its own character.

The expression "rainbow" has come into poker parlance in perhaps the last decade or so as an adjective meaning, "Of all different suits." Whoever originally introduced the term did poker players, and especially us poker writers, a big favor. Thanks.

At holdem, the flop comes rainbow about a third of the time. Although there is no flush-draw on the board, someone can still make a runner-runner flush. There are 49 unknown cards, of which 36 will put a two-flush on board. There are only 13 cards of the missing suit that stop the possibility of a flush on that deal. A three-flush will show on the board by the river about one time out of six. So a rainbow flop is not insurance against flushes.

If you are trying to backdoor a flush yourself, the odds are much against you, as only 10 cards out of 47 even keep you in the running, and there are but 9 to catch at the river if you are still an eligible receiver. This means the parlay odds of your backdooring a flush are about 23-to-1 against.

How do we use this math? First of all, when we have a backdoor flush possible, it is rarely a sufficient factor to turn a fold into a call. If our backdoor flush is not to the nuts, there is even a chance that our longshot will come in, but we will still lose. The only time a backdoor flush possibility might turn a fold to a call is in one of those many-handed jammed pots that has been capped before the flop. In those pots, you more or less divide hands into those that can win once in a blue moon or oftener, and those that cannot win, and stick it out with the former. For other pots, you are better off playing as if your backdoor draw does not exist.

Second, beware of overrating your chance on a straight-draw. Hitting to the nuts on the flop does not necessarily mean winning the pot if you connect. On the flop, there are two cards to come, and after you make the nuts you still have to survive the river card. Full houses and flushes beat straights, and so do bigger straights.

Let's look at a situation where you are hitting to a gutshot straight on the flop. Suppose you hold the 10♦-9♦ and the board is J♥-7♣-3♠. Someone in early position bets, there are a couple of callers, and it is up to you, with nobody behind you that might pop it. Do you call or fold?

Here is the way the typical good poker player thinks. He knows the pot odds, adds into the equation the fact that he rates to make some extra money besides what is in the pot, and makes his decision. (He is described as a good player to separate him from those players who make their decision by criteria like whether they think the stars favor success or whether the pot will grow to be big enough to get even for the session. Naturally, the people who use this type of less effective analysis tools are not likely to be reading this book, favoring publications such as "Popular Astrology" for obtaining their poker advice.) At any rate, even a pretty good player may fail to take into his decision the possibility of hitting and losing. Yet if he makes his hand on the next card with any eight other than the 8♦, there will be 21 cards that leave him without the nuts anymore. There are 10 cards that pair the board (we assume that the opponent is holding two of the cards that contribute toward filling up), 7 more cards that make a possible flush, and 4 more cards that make a possible bigger straight. Even though it is probably less than even money someone will actually have a hand that exploits a possibility offered by the board, it is obvious that the chance of hitting and losing is serious enough to affect the decision on the flop whether to stay or fold.

Here is our advice. Unless you relish doing math problems in your head while trying to play a poker hand, do not try to run all the information about the added bets you figure to make minus the times you might hit and lose into that computer between your ears in order to calculate an accurate answer for situations with two cards to come. Make life easy on yourself. Simply ignore the implied odds and go by the pot odds. If you hit your hand, you will make some extra money, but run the risk of losing the pot. Pretend those two factors cancel each other out, and do a simple decision based on the amount in the pot. Implied odds at limit poker are more practical to use when there is only one card to come, when they favor the person drawing because redraws no longer exist.

These days, when there is a two-flush on board and someone raises, the tendency is to put him on a flush-draw and pay him off. Whether this is a wise policy based on the way people play or wishful thinking when you are stuck is a matter of debate, and the answer varies with the circumstances. But when the board is rainbow, the opponent cannot fall back on this excuse that the player may be flushing, and he may actually consider a fold. The bluff is a far more effective weapon with no flush-draw showing on the board.

The opponents are much more willing to put you on a flush-draw than a straight-draw. So when you get a rainbow flop, it is often a good idea to bet a straight-draw strongly. A straight-draw has almost as many ways to hit as a flush-draw, but has the benefit of being much better concealed. This gives you a better chance to win if you miss and get paid off if you hit, compared to pushy betting with a flush-draw.

Here is a poker problem. The board is K♥-7♣-5♠. You were in the big blind, and after the flop are first to act in a threeway pot with an early position caller and a middle-position caller. What is your action on each of the given hands: A♦-7♦, 8♦-7♦, Q♥-5♦, 6♣-5♦, 8♣-4♦, and 9♥-2♣. To save you some mental effort, there are two hands with middle pair, two hands with bottom pair, one gutshot straight-draw, and one complete abomination.

The answer is you bet. If you have second pair with a good kicker, you might have the best hand. If you have a pair or some kind of draw, you might improve. If you have nothing, betting is the only way you can win. Basically, with this texture flop of one big card and two little ones combined with a rainbow board, you bet because it is a good steal-flop.

A steal-flop is one that gives the bettor a good chance of not getting called. You should bet steal-flops a good bit of the time regardless of your hand, if there are not too many people in the pot. Here, all you have to do is win one out of three to break even, and a bet will probably win over half the time against sane opponents. In poker it is a good idea to vary what you do instead of being mechanical, so do not bet this kind of flop into a small field every single time—just whenever you're not busy eating or gawking at a sporting event on the tube.

As you can see, the number one thing to remember with the rainbow flop is the opportunity it presents to be aggressive. The opponent is more likely to put you on a real hand and fold. For you players who are highly selective about starting hand selection, here is a good chance to put that tight image to work pulling in extra chips. Bet those rainbow flops and get the pot of gold.

Next, we will talk about the implications of a two-flush on the flop, and compare it to betting with a rainbow flop.

The typical holdem player fails to make enough adjustments in his strategy and hand evaluation to allow for a two-flush on the board. Nearly everybody has the sense to do some adjustment when the third card on suit arrives, but that is like heading for higher ground only when the storm surge of a hurricane actually hits the shore. Once the flop comes, nobody can make a flush without the hurricane warning of a two-flush on the board first, so a wise poker player makes strategy changes ahead of time.

The number one adjustment you should make in hand evaluation when a two-flush arrives on either the flop or on the turn is unless that two-flush makes you a four-flush, your made hand has been somewhat devalued. This applies to excellent hands like a set, decent hands like top pair or an overpair, or poor hands like middle or bottom pair. When you have a made hand, the two-flush increases the chance of it being cracked, and usually injures your chance to improve to a winner as well.

Drawing hands like an open-end straight-draw, a gutshot, or two overcards are also devalued by a two-flush. When you have a drawing hand, you are doubly hurt. Some of your "outs" may be making one of your opponents a flush, and if you make your hand, there is an increased chance that someone will outdraw you on the last card. Any way you look at it, all these holdings have been reduced in value from what they would be with a rainbow flop.

Let's look at some specific hands and see how the presence of a two-flush affects your play. Suppose you hold the Q♥-J♥ on the button and two people call preflop in front of you. You call, the big blind raises, and everyone dutifully calls. The flop comes down A♠-10♠-3♣, giving you a gutshot straight-draw. The original raiser bets, the other two players call, and it is up to you. What do you do?

If the flop had been the same texture but rainbow, you would have had four outs to a straight that was the nuts. The pot would be offering you 11.5-to-1 money odds on a 43-to-4 chance of making the straight, which is 10.75-to-1. Not only would the pot odds be there for a call, but the implied odds would even improve your prospects, as if you make your hand there would be the full expectation of making some more money afterward. Even though it would be possible to make your hand and lose to a full house by the board pairing and someone filling up, you would have a clear call with a rainbow flop. Nobody is behind you to raise after your call, and you have perfect position if you make your hand. Perhaps we should mention that despite the derision going for an inside straight has received in poker lore, there are a large number of occasions at limit holdem where it is a perfectly acceptable play.

On the actual flop given, there is a two-flush on board, so going for that gutshot is simply bad poker. You need not be initially too concerned about the preflop raiser possessing a flush-draw, but there sure is a good chance that at least one of the callers is trying for spades. The K♠ is likely to fulfill the old adage that getting what you want may be the worst thing that can happen. You have probably only three outs instead of four, which changes the math to 44-to-3 against, making you over a 14-to-1 dog. Not only are the pot odds insufficient, but the implied odds are in all likelihood against you, because a flush-card on the end could easily turn your momentarily proud holding into garbage. A fold is clear with that two-flush on the board.

Let's look how a made hand would be affected by a two-flush on the board. Suppose with the same flop your hand had been the A♥-K♥. Since the flop was A♠-10♠-3♣, you have top pair with the best possible kicker. We will assume you had been in late position, some people limped in, you raised, and wound up with three callers in front of you. They all checked the flop, you bet, the initial checker raised, and there was a caller. Should you reraise? There may well be a difference of opinion on how this hand should be played, but you should be quite uncomfortable with your hand in this situation. You can lean toward aggressiveness if a reraise had a decent prospect of knocking someone out of the pot, but here the opponents are obviously in for the ride. Few things are as annoying as three-betting the flop and then having a card come off on the turn that destroys the value of your hand. Just call for now, trying to get a safe card on the turn, and reserving the possibility of aggressive action if a non-threatening card comes.

You should be more inclined to push your luck by three-betting in the situation described if your kicker were the king of the two-flush suit (K♠) instead of the K♥. That way, you have one of the cards in your hand that someone is likely trying to catch. If another spade comes on the turn, you are still in contention, since you would now have the nut flush-draw. With a two-flush on board, having the boss trump in your hand measurably improves it.

A second way a two-flush on board affects the play is by reducing your chance of a successful bluff. It is human nature for a poker player to put the opponent on a hand that he can beat. We would all prefer to play rather than be a non-participant. A two-flush on board gives the opponent the opportunity to say to himself, "There is a good chance that guy is pushing a flush-draw, so I am going to call." In a situation that is borderline where you are considering a steal try with cards to come, tend to the conservative course of action with a two-flush on the board.

Besides the problem you have of the opponent putting you on a draw and calling, there is also the problem caused by the two-flush of creating uncertainty in your mind; is the opponent calling on a draw or not? For example, suppose the flop is A-7-3 and you are thinking of running a bluff on nothing, because there are only a small number of contenders. If it is a rainbow flop and you get called by a sane human being, you know to back off, as there is little for him to have besides an ace. You can be happy to run a bluff in this spot because it will be a small and limited expense. With that same flop and a two-flush, it is more of a guess what to do later on, and a greater temptation to keep firing.

We will now look at flops that come all of one suit. It is rare for a three-flush to come on the board, but if you play a lot of poker, it will happen enough to make it worthwhile for you to study how to play in that situation. In our discussion of two-flush flops, we saw that if you do not have a possible flush, you should devalue your hand. Of course, this type of devaluation applies even more with a three-flush on the board.

Some people think if it is a weak game with lots of players seeing the flop, there is a less likely chance of people holding suited starting hands (and thus less likely of holding a flush). We do not think this is true. Weak players love suited cards. They never fold a suited ace in any position. King-rag suited is considered a reasonable playing hand. A suited queen-rag or even jack-rag is okay in late position—or earlier position for reasons such as the game is good, the player is stuck, the stars are right, there was a near-miss at winning the previous pot on such garbage, or sundry similar excuses. If another player is seeing twice as many flops as you are, the vast majority of those extra hands he plays are suited, and being played precisely for that reason. So if a three-flush hits on the flop and some loose goose starts acting as if he has a flush, do not ever think he does not really have it because he plays so many hands that he is not a favorite to be suited. The reason that he was in at the start was probably because his trash cards were on suit.

It does not matter whether the players seeing the flop are weak ones or strong ones. The number of players seeing the flop is a good indicator of the likelihood for someone flopping a flush regardless of who they are. With one or two opponents, you are obligated to find out if they have anything if you have top pair or

71

an overpair. There is a reasonable chance your hand is good. With a crowd in for the flop, one pair is an underdog to be the boss. You can probe by betting the flop against a group in the hope that everyone missed, but if you get raised, recognize that the raiser is very likely to have a flush. Even someone who raises a lot on the flop betting round usually respects a three-flush on the board, and is not pumping something like a smaller pair. On your really good days, the raiser may show up with the lone ace—and miss his flush—but most of the time you need to fill (good luck, pal).

Frequently, the right mental attitude with only one or two opponents and a three-flush comes on the flop is to say to yourself, "With so few opponents, there is a good chance the flop missed everyone. A player without a flush or the prospect of one is likely to be afraid of that board and fold if someone bets. Let's see if anyone has a decent hand." So you put out a bet and see what happens. If you get played with, it is probably best to switch off and give up on the pot. But your bet was getting money odds, so it does not have to work the majority of the time to turn a profit. And there is the chance when you do get lucky and flop a flush on some other occasion, someone will remember your brashness and pay you off on a marginal hand. The scarier the flop, the better the bluff. If you are in the big blind with the 3♣-2♠ against an early limper and the small blind, and the flop comes down K♥-Q♥-J♥, pretend you have just hit the Ponderosa and bet, if no one else has yet. It is perfectly all right to bluff with no outs into one or two other people, even if your only outs after being called are an earthquake or a lightning bolt, because outs don't matter if the opposition folds. You are taking only a single stab at the pot.

Of course, it is always nicer if you do have outs. With a three-flush on the board, even the deuce of the flush suit can win you a pot, but trying to pursue a non-nut flush-draw is far more dangerous here than with a two-flush on board and two cards of that suit in your hand. To fully appreciate the difference of the two situations, let's examine them mathematically, looking at the possibility of the nut flush-draw lurking in an opponent's hand. In a ten-handed game, twenty cards are initially dealt to the players. That means if a specific ace such as the ace of hearts is what we are looking for, the odds of someone receiving it are 20 out of 52, or just under forty percent. However, the chance of that ace being suited are only 12 out of 51, or just under twenty-five percent. The conclusion is if you have the second nut flush, it is about four times as likely you will run into the nuts with four-of-a-suit on board as you will with three-of-a-suit. The math given you is not perfect, as it is more likely that a suited ace will get played than an unsuited one. But if you are playing in a game where an ace gets played even when it is accompanied by an offsuit rag, these are roughly the odds.

If someone is really doing a lot of heavy betting, and there is a four-flush on board, you can forget everything that was said about the initial odds and simply put them on the nuts. It is hard for someone to get very far out of line in this situation without the boss card, because they would be afraid of running into it in someone else's hand.

One of the most frequent mistakes with a three-flush on board and a large field of contenders is for someone with a set or two pair to overplay his hand. Yes, it's okay to bet the flop. But if you get raised, proceed cautiously. First, you are probably up against a flush. Second, the opponent is not laying it down. At limit poker, even small flushes hardly ever get folded. The owner makes crying calls to see if the raiser or reraiser has what he is supposed to have. So the rule for flops with a three-flush is once you find out the opponent has something he likes, don't try to make him throw it away.

Players that like to bet the lone ace strongly should also heed this advice. If you are playing pot-limit, it is okay to put down the heat. At limit poker, that heat may get you a free card, but someone with a flush is not going to let you run him out of the pot.

So far, all we have talked about is the situations where you do not have a flush. Hey, every once in a while we flop a flush ourselves. The first thing to do is conceal your amazement. The second thing to do is realize any non-nut flush is in serious danger, as another card of that suit on the board may well cost you the pot. Bet, bet, and raise. Not only do you charge the opponents a price to draw out, but you also might run someone out of the pot that could have beat you. If your hand is the 10♥-9♥ and you flop a flush, that person with the lone jack or queen might fold, because he is not even sure that he is drawing live.

The last holding we will talk about is the nuts. You have a suited ace and three of your suit are flopped. You can smugly contemplate how to extract the most money from the opponents. The nuts is a flexible hand, and a good poker player varies what he does with it, sometimes betting in a forthright manner and other times slowplaying. We prefer to play the hand strongly more often than not. There are a couple of reasons for this. First, if someone else has a flush, he will give plenty of action. As mentioned before, he is not going to throw his flush away no matter how you play your hand. Second, if another card on suit comes, even though you still have the nuts (unless someone makes a straight flush) you may have lost your market. When we said that the opponent is not folding a flush, we weren't referring to the situation where four cards of a suit are on board, only three.

So play your flushes full speed ahead most of the time, and for all other hands, show caution if you get raised when there is a possible flush on the board.

An important factor of flop play is the fact that the limit will double on the next round. A lot of aggression can be shown if you have position on the opponent. It is a common tactic to raise with drawing hands or marginal holdings. If the opponent calls the raise, then checks to you on the turn, you have the option of taking a free card. Of course, if you help your hand, it is in your favor that there is extra money already in the pot.

Since the flop is a "cheap" betting round, it is often necessary to throw in a raise if you are even suspicious that you hold the best hand. The opponents who have not yet acted must be confronted with a double bet to protect your hand. And once again, it is nice to have position, so you can see how the opponents have reacted to your raise, and then you can adopt the appropriate turn strategy.

As you can see by our discussions, the flop betting round has a special character. It is strongly affected by the fact that in the standard betting structure, three new cards are on the board, often radically rearranging everyone's chances, but the betting limit stays the same as the preceding round. We often think of the flop as the phony betting round, because so much deception is used.

15 – OVERCARDS

The play of overcards presents some of the most difficult decisions in holdem. It is common to raise preflop on a hand like ace-king, only to have the flop miss you completely. You are now left wondering what to do. There is no pat answer. The more opponents you have, the less likely you are to win the pot by betting, and the harder it will be for your hand to hold up even when you improve. The worse your position, the harder it is to get a free card, and the more likely you are to get raised if you bet. Flops containing two-flushes, cards in the playing zone (jacks, tens, and nines), touching cards like queen-jack, and even paired boards make it more likely that players will either have a better hand than you or be justified in staying and trying to draw out.

In many cases, the right answer simply is to not bet. It may sound like wimpy poker to raise preflop with a hand like ace-king and then check, planning to fold when the flop gets bet, but that is exactly what has to be done in many situations. To sit there stubbornly and call bets and raises trying to take off cards to build one pair will prove costly. In holdem, when you are behind on the flop, you are often way behind, without much chance of winning.

There are times when you can play overcards aggressively, even when they are your only outs. Nearly all of these situations occur when you have a small number of opponents. With one or two opponents, a bet might be all it takes to win the pot. A hand without a pair helps only on about a third of the flops. In addition, the fewer the opponents, the less likely you are to encounter an enemy hand strong enough to raise.

You can, of course, play overcards aggressively when you have also flopped a draw to a straight or flush with them. The nice thing about any straight-draws or flush-draws you flop is that they will usually be to the nuts, making your outs "clean."

These hands illustrate some important considerations in the play of overcards.

(1) A $20-$40 game. You are in the cutoff seat and hold A♥-T♥. An early player limps in. You limp. The small blind limps. There is $80 in the pot and four players. The flop is: 8♦-3♣-2♠. The small blind checks. The big blind bets and the early player calls. What do you do?

Answer: Fold. With three opponents in an unraised pot, you should fold. You are getting 6-to-1 pot odds. You have a six-outer, which is about a 7-to-1 shot. You have no nut draws and little dough to chase. Overcard outs are risky. If the big blind happens to be betting top pair, top kicker, or the early player is calling with an ace in his hand, then hitting your ace will cost you money.

Many players routinely call with overcards in these situations. They think that they have six outs and will win a large enough pot to justify taking a card off for one small bet. What they overlook is the fact that their outs will not win all the time. This can happen in several ways. First, one of the other players may already have the hand they are hoping to make already beat, like by holding two pair or a set. Second, one of their outs may give someone else an even better hand, as if the big blind were betting top pair, top kicker in this problem. Third, they may hit one of their outs on the turn only to have one of their opponents make a better hand at the river (a redraw). An example of a redraw would be if someone had ace-trey, and a ten came on the turn, followed by a trey at the river. Any one of these scenarios would seem unlikely, but when taken collectively, they are all within the spectrum of possibilities, and they all weaken the argument for hanging around trying to hit.

(2) A $15-$30 game. You are in the big blind holding the A♥-K♠. Two early players, two middle players, the cutoff, the button, and small blind all limp. You raise and everyone calls. There is $240 in the pot and eight players. The flop is: 7♦-4♦-2♣. Everyone checks to the button, who bets. The small blind folds. What do you do?

Answer: Call. There is $255 in the pot and it costs you $15 to call. You are getting 17-to-1 on your call to play for six outs, which is a 7-to-1 shot. Even discounting the A♦ and the K♦ because of the two-flush means you have four outs, which is an 11-to-1 shot. You have such a large overlay that calling is right, despite the fact that you will not necessarily win if you hit. The alternative to calling is raising, a reasonable play. The idea is to drive out the other players by confronting them with a double bet. If the button is pairless, betting a draw, this is the best play. If anyone is slowplaying a set, it is not. Neither of these possibilities is the most likely scenario.

On the actual hand, two other players called. The turn and river were checked around and the player won with his ace-king. No one had a pair among all those players! This was highly unlikely, of course, but another small possibility in deciding whether to call.

(3) A $30-$60 game. You are in the cutoff seat with A♦-K♠. Everyone folds to the player on your right, who opens with a raise. You reraise, since he could be raising light, and you want to isolate him with position and a good playing hand. The button calls the three bets cold. Everyone folds to the preflop raiser, who calls. There is $320 in the pot and three players. The flop comes: J♦-9♣-7♦, giving you a backdoor nut flush-draw in addition to your two overcards. The original raiser checks and you check. The button bets. The preflop raiser calls. What do you do?

Answer: Fold. There is $380 in the pot and it costs you $30 to take off a card. A player who calls three bets cold and then bets a flop like this one will usually have K-K, Q-Q, J-J, or maybe an ace-king suited. Against K-K you have three outs, a 15-to-1 shot. Against Q-Q, you have six outs, a 7-to-1 shot. Against J-J, you have no outs other than backdoor diamonds with the board not pairing. Against ace-king suited, you are playing for a tie unless you make a backdoor flush. There is also a third player in the hand, who may have something that cripples your chances of improving. Finally, you may catch a card that gives you the best hand, but then get redrawn at the river. There are too many situations where you are playing with hardly any outs. In the other scenarios, where you do have a sufficient number of outs to play on, they are only to a pair, which may not hold up as the best hand anyway once all the board-cards are out.

(4) A $20-$40 game. You hold the A♦-K♦ and raise from middle position after an early player limps. The button and limper call.

There is $150 in the pot and three players. The flop is: 4♦-3♣-2♥, giving you a gutshot straight-draw and a backdoor nut flush-draw as well as overcards. The early limper checks. What do you do?

Answer: Bet. In addition to your overcards, you have some other outs, and only two opponents. You could win the pot outright, since you were the preflop raiser marked with a good hand. Even though your two opponents may suspect that this flop didn't help you, it may not have helped them either.

(5) A $30-$60 problem. You are in the big blind with the A♥-K♠. A middle player opens with a raise and everyone else folds. You call. There is $140 in the pot and two players. The flop comes: 7♥-5♠-4♣. You check. Your opponent bets. What do you do?

Answer: Call. There is $170 in the pot and it costs you $30 to chase your "six-outer," which is a 7-to-1 shot. However, there are some factors in your favor. First, you may actually have the best hand. Second, since you are a caller, you are well-placed to represent a straight if an eight, six, or three comes on the turn. Third, you may improve your hand to a winner.

(6) A $10-$20 game. You are in middle position with the A♣-K♥. You raise behind two early limpers. The cutoff, the big blind, and the limpers call. There is $105 in the pot and five players in the hand. The flop is: T♣-7♣-3♦, giving you a backdoor nut flush-draw in addition to your overcards. The big blind and the limpers check. What do you do?

Answer: Check. You have nothing but overcards and some remote backdoor possibilities. Raising preflop does not obligate you to continue betting against a large field after missing the flop. With four opponents and a two-flush on the table, your proper play is to check and hope to get a free card. Bet this kind of flop in heads-up and three-way pots when you are the preflop raiser, and make a good guess whether to bet or check in a four-way pot. Against a crowd, don't try to run over the whole crew.

(7) A \$10-\$20 game. You are in middle position with the K♥-Q♠. All five players in front of you limp. You limp. The small blind also plays, so there is \$80 in the pot and eight players. The flop is: T♦-7♣-3♠. Both blinds and two early players check. The third early player bets. Both middle players fold. What do you do?

Answer: Fold. There is \$90 in the pot and it costs you \$10 to take off a card. You have a six-outer, which is a 7-to-1 shot, so you have an overlay—if hitting will win and the pot does not get raised behind you. Those are two big drawbacks. When contemplating a call with overcards, the presence of a large number of active players behind you is a strong deterrent, even if some of them have checked. Your overcards do not complement the board, but there are a lot of people to beat with your hoped-for one pair.

(8) A \$15-\$30 game. You have A♣-K♣ and raise from middle position after an early player limps. The button, the blinds, and the limper call. There is \$150 in the pot and five players. The flop is: T♥-4♥-3♦. Both blinds and the limper check. What do you do?

Answer: Check. You have four opponents and there is a two-flush on the board. This means that you are very unlikely to win the pot outright by betting. Remove the two-flush and with three of your four opponents checking, one could argue that betting might be right here. But the two-flush makes people more likely to call or even raise than otherwise, plus it devalues your overcards. The A♥ or the K♥ may give someone a flush, or at least a draw to a flush, so not all your outs are clean, and there are probably more redraws than normal.

(9) A \$30-\$60 game. You are in early position with A♥-Q♣ and open with a raise. Only the small blind calls. There is \$150 in the pot and two players. The flop is: T♠-8♠-6♣. The small blind bets. What do you do?

Answer: Fold. With only six small bets in the pot, it is too small to merit an overcard call. There is also the serious problem of a compact board with three cards to a straight, plus a two-flush.

15 - OVERCARDS

There are innumerable scenarios where you could hit one of your outs, only to be redrawn at the river. For example, a spade, a nine, or a seven confronts you with a hideous board. On the surface, it may look like wimpy poker for the preflop raiser to fold when heads-up, but continuing to call bets trying to take off cards is a loser in the long run. Bail out of this deal cheaply right now.

(10) A $20-$40 game. You open with a raise from middle position with the A♠-Q♠. Only the button and the big blind call. There is $130 in the pot and three players. The flop is: J♦-9♥-8♣, giving you a gutshot straight-draw in addition to your overcards. The big blind checks. What do you do?

Answer: Check. Normally, the flop gets automatically bet when it is checked to a preflop raiser, unless there are a large number of opponents, or something else unusual is present. Typically, the preflop raiser bets, because he frequently wins the pot outright. If this were heads-up, you should bet. But the board is too coordinated, and flops that have combinations containing jacks, tens, nines, and even eights help limpers and callers more than preflop raisers. One of your overcards complements the board, making a straight possible if you pair it. Even if a ten comes, you could be splitting the pot with someone else who has a queen—or losing to K-Q. You have another player yet to act who cold-called your preflop raise. It is highly unlikely that you will win the pot outright by betting. That board rates to have given at least one of your two opponents a better hand and some kind of big draw. There are a large number of cards that could come off on the turn that could easily kill your hand. A king, queen, a jack, a nine, an eight, or a seven could all be very bad for you. Avoid getting involved with overcards when the flop probably helped the enemy.

(11) A $10-$20 game. You are in the small blind with the A♥-K♠. An early player limps and the button raises. You call. The big blind plays, as well as the early limper. There is $80 in the pot and four players. The flop is: Q♦-J♥-J♠, giving you a gutshot straight-draw in addition to your overcards. Everyone checks to the button, who bets. What do you do?

Answer: Fold. With two facecards on the flop, there is too great of a chance someone is already full, or has at least trip jacks. Furthermore, the ten you need for your gutshot straight would give someone having a jack-ten a full house. Jack-ten is a common limping hand. You are getting 9-to-1 pot odds, but an ace or a king is not a clean out at all. If someone has trip jacks, your only out is a ten, and when they don't, an ace or a king could still give someone a straight. Compact boards with touching cards all in the playing zone are dangerous because they can so easily connect with typical playing hands of your opponents.

(12) A $30-$60 game. You are in middle position with A♦-K♦ and raise after an early player and a middle player limp. The button, the big blind, and everyone else calls. There is $320 in the pot and five players. The flop comes: T♦-7♥-3♥, giving you a backdoor nut flush-draw in addition to your overcards. The big blind and the two limpers check. What do you do?

Answer: Check. You have four opponents, which is too many for you to win the pot outright with a bet. Furthermore, a check to the raiser is not like getting checked to in an unraised pot. Players in a raised pot often check, expecting you to bet. They may be afraid to bet into you, or they may have a good hand and be looking to raise. It is possible someone erred by checking, giving you the chance to get a free card and stay in contention. Also, there is the button cold-caller yet to act, who may well have a better hand than you, given this flop. The two-flush on board hurts your chances of winning the pot outright by betting. You should check. If the button bets and no one raises, you can call and take off a card.

(13) A $20-$40 game. You are in middle position with the Q♥-J♥. Two early players and two middle players limp. You limp. The cutoff raises, and everyone calls except the button and small blind, who fold. There is $290 in the pot and seven players. The flop is: T♦-7♣-3♠. Everyone checks to the cutoff, who bets. One middle limper calls. What do you do?

Answer: Fold. There is $330 in the pot and it costs you $20 to call. But despite the great pot odds, all you have are six outs to a pair of jacks or queens, which may not win against a preflop raiser, who could have A-A, K-K, Q-Q, J-J, T-T or A-Q. The only legitimate raising hand you have six outs against is A-K. You have some remote backdoor possibilities, but that does not turn a fold into a call. Even if the cutoff raised on garbage like queen-ten suited, jack-ten suited, or king-ten suited, you are still drawing very slim. Beware of overcards that could easily be no good even if they pair, given the preflop betting. In addition, with mid-sized cards like these, even if you were lucky enough to be drawing to a better hand than the current top one, the card that hits you could easily make someone else the same hand with a better kicker.

(14) A $10-$20 game. You open with a raise from middle position with the A♥-T♣, and the button and blinds call. There is $80 in the pot and four players. The flop comes: 9♦-8♣-3♥. Both blinds check. Do you bet or check?

Answer: Check. You shouldn't bet your overcards here. The flop has two touching cards (nine-eight) and if a ten turns up, that would complement the board, making a straight possible. So a ten is not a clean out for your hand. Furthermore, there is a player behind you, and you have three opponents. (Reduce the number of opponents to two and betting would be much more reasonable; against one it would be practically mandatory.) You could easily get a free card here by checking, since the button may well check with this many players in the pot if he doesn't have much.

(15) A $15-$30 game. You are in middle position with the A♦-J♣ and open with a raise. Only the button calls. There is $85 in the pot and two players. The flop is: 7♠-5♥-3♦. You bet and the button raises. What do you do?

Answer: Fold. You have six outs, assuming your opponent has a pair. There is $130 in the pot and it costs you $15 to take a card off, so your pot odds are almost 9-to-1, and a six outer is a 7-to-1 shot. Consider the following reasons to fold:

1. You are only building one pair, which can be easily beaten, given your opponent's play here.

2. If your opponent has a pair with an ace sidecard, then you have three outs, not six, and if an ace comes it could get very expensive for you.

3. If your opponent smooth-called your raise with a big overpair like K-K or Q-Q, you have only three outs.

4. Your opponent could have more than just a pair. He might have flopped a set, which means you are drawing dead.

5. You're out of position, so you can't get any free cards.

6. If the next card is a blank, you will be folding if your opponent bets after you check, since the pot odds are no longer there for staying only on overcards.

7. The opponent may have A-K or A-Q for his preflop call. He thinks he is putting a play on you—but actually has you beat.

All that being said, if you think for some reason that you have an image problem at the table because you have been losing or have been folding a lot, and your opponent is a super-aggressive player who may well be moving around on nothing, you may want to stay in the pot. If so, it is better to play back with a reraise and keep firing than to just call. Under normal conditions, folding is surely right.

(16) A $30-$60 game. You open with a raise in the cutoff with the A♥-Q♣. The button and small blind fold. The big blind reraises and you call. There is $200 in the pot and two players. The flop is: J♥-8♥-3♦, giving you a backdoor nut-flush draw in addition to your overcards. The big blind bets. What do you do?

Answer: Fold. There is $230 in the pot and it costs you $30 to call. But what are your outs? You have six outs plus a backdoor possibility. Your six outer is a 7-to-1 shot, and this is about what the pot is offering, but you will not win all the time when your outs arrive. The big blind three-betting frequently means a big pair or ace-king. Against ace-king you are dead to a queen, and an ace showing up will cost you some money. Against a big pair you need an ace—or a doctor.

(17) A $30-$60 game. An early player opens with a raise and you call from middle position with the A♣-K♦. The next player reraises and only you and the early raiser call. There is $320 in the pot and three players. The flop is: 9♦-7♥-3♣. The early raiser bets. What do you do?

Answer: Fold. With the early raiser leading into you and a three-bettor yet to act, you have a clear fold. You have no pair, no draw, and no hand. You could even be drawing dead, and the pot may well get raised. When unimproved, slick is a poor hand in most three-bet pots, because you are up against aces or kings too often.

(18) A $20-$40 game. You are on the button and have A♥-K♥. Two early players limp, one middle player limps, and the cutoff limps. You raise and everyone calls. There is $280 in the pot and seven players in the hand. The flop is: J♥-T♥-3♦, giving you the nut flush-draw and a gutshot straight-draw, as well as your two overcards. Everyone checks to you. What do you do?

Answer: Bet. It would be wimpy poker not to find a bet here. You have nine outs to the nut flush, three more outs to the nut straight, and six outs to top pair, top kicker with two cards to come. You are mathematical favorite to make the nut flush, the nut straight, or top pair, top kicker by the river. You should bet and not be intimidated by all those limpers. You have a hand that can take a lot of heat, and you will be going to the river anyway in almost all cases. You should want to build a bigger pot, since you are the individual favorite to win the hand. Don't let some yo-yo with pocket deuces get a free card to hit a set on you. We have been downgrading the value of overcards, but when combined with a flush-draw or straight-draw, their value dramatically increases.

(19) A $15-$30 game. You are in middle position with A♠-Q♠ and raise after an early player limps in. Only the big blind and the early limper call. There is $100 in the pot and three players. The flop is: T♥-9♣-8♦, giving you a gutshot straight-draw in addition to your two overcards. Both opponents check. What do you do?

Answer: Check. Take a free card. This is not a flop you should be betting, given your holding. You have no flush-draw and your overcards are weak with this board. A queen gives you top pair, top kicker, but anyone with a jack would have a straight. A jack gives you a straight, but anyone with a queen has the same straight. Someone could easily have top pair or two pair and decided not to bet because you raised preflop. There will also be times when you are up against a straight, leaving you with maybe three outs to a tie. It is unlikely that you can win the pot outright by betting, given the coordinated nature of the board, and you may well get raised.

(20) A $20-$40 game. It is a shorthanded, seven-player game, and the under-the-gun player opens with a raise. You reraise with the A♦-K♠. Two players behind you cold-call, with everyone folding back to the raiser, who makes it four bets. All call. There is $350 in the pot and four players. The flop comes: J♥-T♥-T♠, giving you a gutshot straight-draw as well as your two overcards. The preflop raiser bets. What do you do?

Answer: Fold. An opposing full house is a big threat. The queen that gives you a straight could easily give one of your opponents a full house in a four-bet pot like this with three opponents. There may be a full out already. You have two players behind you who called three bets cold preflop. An ace or a king coming off on the turn would probably not give you the best hand, but instead could give one of your opponents a monster.

(21) A $10-$20 game. You are in middle position and raise with the A♠-Q♦ after two early players limp. The cutoff, the button, the big blind, and the other players call. There is $125 in the pot and six players. The flop is: 9♣-3♠-2♠, giving you a backdoor nut-flush draw in addition to your overcards. The big blind checks. The first limper bets and the next one calls. What do you do?

Answer: Call. This is a decent situation for an overcard call. It is a raised pot, and neither of your overcards complement the board. The board is ragged, although the two-flush is a concern.

However, you have the ace of the flush suit, which somewhat mitigates this. If the flush comes on the turn, you will at least have a playing hand. Raising the flop bet is a reasonable alternative.

(22) A $20-$40 game. A shorthanded game with only six players. The first two players fold and you open with a raise having the K♠-Q♣. Only the big blind calls. There is $90 in the pot and two players. The flop is: J♣-7♦-3♥. Your opponent checks. What do you do?

Answer: Bet. You are the preflop raiser marked with the good hand, and your lone opponent has checked to you on a ragged, rainbow board. You will win the pot outright a significant percentage of the time, and you have six overcard outs if you get called by a better hand. As the preflop raiser in a heads-up situation, you must fulfill your obligation to find out if the opponent has anything.

(23) A $10-$20 game. You have the A♣-K♥ in middle position and raise after an early player limps in. The cutoff, the small blind, the big blind, and the early player all call. There is $100 in the pot and five players. The flop comes: J♦-5♦-2♣. The small blind checks. The big blind bets. The early player folds. What do you do?

Answer: Fold. A player who leads into a crowd of four opponents, including a preflop raiser, should be given credit for a better hand than yours. Furthermore, the two-flush kills two of your outs (the A♦ and the K♦), since it could give someone a diamond flush or a diamond flush-draw. Your current pot odds are 11-to-1, but your four clean outs are only to a pair. Even hitting top pair, top kicker on the turn will not win the pot for you all the time.

16 – OVERPAIR AND TOP PAIR

When you flop an overpair, or top pair with a good kicker, this is normally a strong holding and a profitable situation. In general, you need to play aggressively in these situations, betting or raising to knock players out and protect your hand. This applies even more so when the pot has been raised preflop. The reason is your hand can be easily overtaken, especially when you have a lot of opponents, and it is important to force the other players to pay heavily to stay with you.

You should seldom be bothered by eliminating the field and winning only chips already out there, especially in a raised pot. If someone bets, and you have top pair or an overpair, it is nearly always right to raise when you can confront other players in the pot with a double bet. There will be many times when you consider a raise, but do not have full confidence in your kicker being the best. Normally, you raise anyway. (The rank of the top card and texture of the board are important, because they determine how desperate you are to get the remaining players out.) If there is a reasonable chance that your hand is good, you must try to protect it. A lot of the time, you will not lose any extra money by raising with a hand that turns out not to be good, because you have position, and can get the bet back later on. In fact, you figure to save a half-bet, because if you get the bet back, it will be on one of the two rounds where the limit is doubled.

There are many cases where due to some combination of the texture of the board, the number of opponents, and the heavy betting action, you will have to fold. Poker is highly situational. You may think you have a strong holding, but you must realize that a pair, even an overpair or top pair, is still just one pair, so it can be easily beaten. If the betting action combined with the texture of the board leads you to conclude that you are behind, you need to think about folding, since your outs may be too few to continue. If someone has a made hand like a straight or a flush, you need to catch two perfect cards to end up with the best hand at the river. When this situation occurs, you are almost never justified in continuing. Similarly, if you flop top pair, but someone else has flopped a set, you need two perfect cards. If you flop top pair along with another player who has you outkicked, you are playing three outs, which is a 15-to-1 shot, and the pot odds will normally not be there to try to take off a card.

The next set of problems demonstrate some important factors in decisions regarding an overpair or top pair.

(1) The game is $10-$20. You are in the small blind with A♠-K♣. An early player, a middle player, and the cutoff limp. The early player is an elderly lady who rarely raises or plays strongly unless she has excellent cards. On the other hand, she will faithfully check and call if she has any chance of winning. You raise. The big blind folds and the other three players call. There is $90 in the pot and four players. The flop is: K♦-7♥-7♣, giving you kings over sevens with an ace kicker. You bet. The lady raises and the other players fold. What do you do?

Answer: Call. There is $120 in the pot and it costs you another $10 to call. If the lady has a seven, you are playing two outs, which is a 23-to-1 shot, and you are getting only 12-to-1 on your money. However, you would rate to pick up another $40 or so on the turn and river if you hit a king. The lady might have a king, which means you are in good shape. In looking at the board, there is no flush-draw or straight-draw for her to be raising on (and she would likely not raise on a come hand anyway). The decision is between calling and reraising. Calling is the best play, since you can check the turn if a blank comes, and she will continue betting a worse king, if that is her hand. In that case, she only has three outs, so you prefer to leave her in. On the actual hand, she had king-queen. The turn and river were blanks, and when checked to she continued to bet.

(2) The game is $10-$20. You are in middle position with Q♣-J♠. An early player and a middle player limp. You limp. The button and small blind limp. There is $60 in the pot and six players. The flop is: J♥-9♣-8♣, giving you top pair, decent kicker plus a gutshot straight-draw and a backdoor flush-draw. The small blind bets. The big blind folds. The early and middle limpers both call. What do you do?

Answer: Call. The field is already committed by the flop call, so raising will likely not drive out anyone other than the button, who might be folding anyway. The small blind leading into a field of five opponents will usually mean that person has at least top pair, and frequently something more. The board is highly coordinated, plus there is a two-flush. A ten turning up does not give you the nuts. Even if your hand is good, anyone with another queen splits the pot with you, thereby cutting your win in half. In fact, you have no nut cards at all. Even backdoor clubs gives you only the third-best flush. The other problem with the raising is that you open yourself up to a reraise, thereby increasing your cost to see the hand through.

On the actual hand, the player raised to $20. The button folded. The small blind reraised to $30 and everyone called. The turn was the 5♠. The small blind bet $20 and everyone called. The river was the A♣ and everyone checked. The small blind won with Q♦-T♦ for a flopped straight. The Q-J was playing with three outs to tie.

(3) The game is $15-$30. You are in the small blind with K♦-J♣. A middle player and the button limp. You limp. There is $60 in the pot and four players. The flop comes: K♥-9♠-3♦, giving you top pair, decent kicker. You bet. The big blind folds. The middle limper raises. The button reraises. What do you do?

Answer: Fold. There is no flush-draw or open-ended straight draw for your two opponents to be betting or raising with here. You probably need a jack, and could even be dead if someone happens to have a set (unless you catch perfect-perfect, which is too remote to consider). While it is possible the first raiser could have top pair with a weaker kicker, when you add in the presence of a second player who reraises, this means that you are badly beaten at this point in at least one spot, and possibly both spots. It is costing you $30 right now, and could even get capped back to you.

On the actual hand, the player called, as well as the first limper. The turn was the Q♥. He checked. The first limper bet and got raised. The player finally folded. The other player called. The river was the 2♠. It was checked to the button, who bet, and he got called by his lone opponent. The pot was split, since they both had king-queen offsuit. On the flop, the player had three outs, and from the flop betting could have had no outs. But even a three-outer is about a 15-to-1 shot, and would require about a $400+ pot to merit continuing.

(4) The game is $20-$40. You are in middle position with A♣-T♦. Three players limp in ahead of you. You limp. The small blind calls. There is $120 in the pot and six players. The flop comes: T♥-9♣-8♠, giving you top pair, top kicker. Both blinds check. An early player bets and the next player folds. The player on your right now raises. What do you do?

Answer: Fold. Though you have top pair, top kicker, this board is highly coordinated, and it has been bet and raised to you. If someone has a straight, you are practically drawing dead, with only perfect-perfect saving you. Between the bettor and the raiser, someone could easily have two pair, or even a set. If you are up against two pair, you could have as little as three outs. It is costing you $40 now with $180 in the pot. A three-outer is a 15-to-1 shot. Against a set you are practically drawing dead. The blinds checking does not mean for sure they are broke. The pot could even get raised again, costing you $60 or even $80 to take off a card. Even if you have "erred" by folding the best hand at the moment, your hand is exceptionally vulnerable to being overtaken, so the fold may work out anyway. When you see dark clouds on the horizon like this, don't wait until the storm hits before paddling to safety.

On the actual hand, the player called two bets cold. The blinds folded and the early player reraised to $60. The next player capped the betting at $80 and the player also called that, along with the early player. The turn was the Q♦. It was bet and raised to the player, who finally found the good sense to fold. The bettor called, the river was a blank, and the other two players split the pot. One player had Q♥-J♠, having flopped the nuts; the other had J♣-T♠.

(5) A $10-$20 game. You are in middle position with the A♠-7♠. An early player limps and everyone folds to you. You limp. Only the cutoff limps. There is $45 in the pot and four players. The flop is: 7♥-5♥-2♣, giving you top pair, top kicker. The big blind checks. The early limper bets. What do you do?

Answer: Raise. You should try to drive out the other players and make the flush-draws and straight-draws pay double. You want to drive out anyone like the cutoff who might have limped in on overcards and is hoping to take off a card cheaply. You could easily have the best hand. It is possible the bettor limped in with pocket eights or nines, and has you beat, but more likely he is betting top pair with a worse kicker than yours, or betting a draw.

(6) A $10-$20 game. You limp in under-the-gun holding 8♠-8♥. An early player limps, a middle player raises, the big blind calls, you call, and the early player calls. There is $85 in the pot and four players. The flop is: 6♠-3♥-3♦, giving you an overpair. The big blind bets. What do you do?

Answer: Raise. The other two players could be playing just big cards. Your raise may drive them out. Someone with a bigger overpair might fold anyway, fearing that either you or the big blind has a trey, reducing them to two outs. Your raise could also get you a free card later, as you have position over the bettor. For an extra small bet, you significantly increase your likelihood of winning the hand. The big blind may well not be leading with trips. A player who flops a small open set of trips with another small board-card will often prefer to try for a check-raise, or even slowplay by waiting until the expensive street to pull the trigger.

(7) A $15-$30 game. You are in the big blind holding the K♠-3♥. An early player, two middle players, and the small blind limp. You get a free play. There is $75 in the pot and five players. The flop is: K♣-J♦-8♥, giving you top pair, no kicker. The small blind checks. What do you do?

Answer: Check. You have four opponents with two flop-cards in the playing zone and the eight just outside. The problem with betting is that you have very little chance to win the pot by a bet, and you may well get raised. Even if you have the best hand, you can't take heat with it. Top pair is not an automatic betting hand; there are exceptions. When your kicker is weak, the opponents are many, and the board-cards are high and close in rank, discretion is the better part of valor.

(8) A $20-$40 game. You are in the small blind with the A♠-5♠. An early player limps and an elderly lady in middle position limps. She is a tight-passive player that only bets or raises when she thinks she has the best hand. But she will faithfully call to the river with any chance of winning just to see who wins. You limp. There is $80 in the pot and four players. The flop is: A♥-8♦-6♠, giving you top pair, no kicker and a backdoor nut flush-draw. You bet. The big blind folds and the early player calls. The lady raises. What do you do?

Answer: Fold. With her raising, you are almost certainly looking at a better ace at least. You have three outs at best, a 15-to-1 shot. Right now there is $160 in the pot and it costs you $20 more to call. These are pot odds of only 8-to-1. Your backdoor flush-draw and backdoor straight-draw do not add enough value for you to be calling. With such a small kicker, you may not win even if you help; she may have two pair or a set.

(9) A $10-$20 game. You are on the button with the K♠-T♥. An early player, two middle players, and the cutoff limp. You limp as well as the small blind. There is $70 in the pot and seven players. The flop is: K♦-Q♣-3♦, giving you top pair, fair kicker. Everyone checks to the second middle limper, who bets. The cutoff raises. What do you do?

Answer: Fold. It is costly to be cold-calling a bet and a raise on the flop with top pair, weak kicker. A common scenario is one player is betting top pair and the raiser has two pair or better. A more favorable scenario for you would be if one player is betting just top pair and the other player is betting or raising with a flush-draw or a straight-draw. But in most cases, you are playing with three outs at best, and the T♦ could give one of your many opponents a flush (or a draw to a flush, which they end up making at the river). If you happen to have the best hand, you will find that you can be easily overtaken, since anyone on a flush-draw or straight-draw will be hanging around. The bottom line is when you are behind, you are really buried, and when you are ahead, you are only a marginal favorite. There are also several other players yet to act, and it could get raised again.

(10) A $20-$40 game. You are in the big blind holding K♦-9♠. Two early players, all three middle players, and the small blind limp, so you get a free play. There is $140 in the pot and seven players. The flop is: K♣-T♣-T♥, giving you kings over tens with a weak kicker. The small blind checks. What do you do?

Answer: Check. Leading into a field of six other players with an open pair on the table, a two-flush, and two cards in the playing zone is a bad idea with your hand. In fact, you should plan on folding if it gets bet and raised back to you after you check. In many cases, you should fold if it gets bet with several callers. When someone bets into a large crowd like this with a high pair on the board, you should hit the door. With all these players, it is too easy for someone to have a ten or a bigger king. Furthermore, even if you are in the lead, it may not be for long, because with this many players there will be all kinds of drawing hands against you. There are a multitude of cards that can come on the turn (or river) and destroy your hand. Any club, an ace, a queen, a jack, and a nine are all bad.

(11) A $10-$20 game. You raise under-the-gun holding K♦-K♠. An early player, three middle players, and the big blind call. There is $125 in the pot and six players. The flop is: 9♣-4♣-4♠, giving you an overpair. The big blind checks. You bet, the next player calls, a middle player raises, the next two players fold, and the big blind reraises. What do you do?

Answer: Fold. With this many players taking a flop and two players raising and reraising with the open pair on board, it is likely that someone has trip fours or better. You are reduced to playing a two-outer. The pot may even get raised again. Continuing on is normally a serious mistake. (We admit the type of player who reraised has to be taken into account. An imaginative player who knows you might throw away an overpair could put a move on you here.)

(12) A $10-$20 game. You open-raise in early position with the A♦-K♠. Only a middle player calls. There is $55 in the pot and two players. The flop is: K♥-J♦-7♣, giving you top pair, top kicker. You bet and your opponent raises. What do you do?

Answer: Reraise. You do not want to be put on the defensive with this hand. Your betting tells your opponent that you got at least a piece of this flop. His raise says he probably has a king. You reraise because you have the top kicker. In a heads-up situation like this, especially when you are out of position, it is important to be aggressive when you have a good hand. Many opponents like to throw in a raise on the cheap street if they decide to play a hand, figuring to either pressure you off a weak holding or get a free card on the more expensive round. There also can be a macho element in heads-up situations that causes an opponent to overplay many hands. When you have this good a hand, you should try to stay in the driver's seat. It is not so easy for a single opponent to flop a better hand than this, and even if he did, he might have waited until the limit doubled before raising. When there is no one else but you and the opponent in the pot, a raise on the flop is frequently a probe or ploy rather than an indicator of a big hand.

(13) A $30-$60 game. You are in the small blind with the K♣-K♦. An early player opens with a raise and everyone folds to you. You reraise and only the raiser calls. There is $210 in the pot and two players. The flop is: Q♦-8♥-6♥, giving you an overpair. You bet and your opponent raises. What do you do?

Answer: Reraise. Your opponent's most likely holding is A-Q (12 hands given the queen on the board) versus Q-Q (3 hands given the queen on the board) or A-A (6 hands). He could even have A♥-K♥ or A♥-J♥ or K♥-Q♥ (3 hands), which you can also beat and which he would have raised with preflop. This assumes he actually has some kind of hand; he may not be even that good.

(14) A $30-$60 game. An early player limps and you limp in early position holding the 9♥-9♣. Two middle players, the button, and the small blind (a top pro) all limp. There is $210 in the pot and seven players. The flop is: 6♠-6♥-2♣, giving you an overpair. The small blind bets. The big blind and the early limper fold. What do you do?

Answer: Call. Raising would be a risky play in this situation. Normally, when you flop an overpair in an unraised pot, you should raise when someone bets. But this is an exception. A top pro will probably not lead into a field of six other players from the little blind position without trips when the board pairs small like this and the odd card is lower-ranking than the pair. The only legitimate betting hand you can beat is a pocket pair of sevens or eights. But the small blind is far less likely than anyone else to have started with a pocket pair, especially in a structure where he is two-thirds of the way in already, as in $30-60. (He is also less likely to be suited than any of the other players.) Moreover, someone behind you may have a six even if the bettor does not.

(15) A $30-$60 game. You are in the cutoff seat with the A♦-J♦. A middle player limps in and you raise. The big blind and limper call. There is $200 in the pot and three players. The flop comes: J♠-9♠-7♠, giving you top pair, top kicker. Both opponents check. You bet and the big blind calls. The limper now raises. What do you do?

Answer: Fold. It is tough to dump top pair with an ace kicker, but when the board flops all of one suit, it is too easy to be drawing dead to a backdoor boat. If another spade shows up (other than the ace), your hand is instantly dead. You could also be looking at a straight or two pair. There is a chance the raiser could be check-raising with a pair and a spade, but even then you are not a huge favorite, and there is still a third player to worry about. You should fold, because you are quite likely beaten with hardly any outs, and even if you are folding the best hand, you could be easily overtaken. To call now does not accomplish much, because you will be probably folding on the turn. It often happens that calling with the best hand doesn't win, because it can't go the distance.

(16) A $20-$40 game. An early player opens with a raise and you reraise with the K♦-K♣. The big blind and the early player call. There is $190 in the pot and three players. The flop is: J♠-T♠-3♣, giving you an overpair. The big blind checks. The early player bets. You raise. The big blind makes it three bets. The early player caps the betting. What do you do?

Answer: Fold. You have to be badly beaten here. To call two more bets back to you would be a clear error. If someone has a set, you are playing two outs at best. Not having the K♠ also hurts, since this helping card makes a spade flush possible. If someone has two pair, you have five outs at best, and a set is a distinct possibility on the preflop betting, where J-J or 10-10 are more likely enemy hands than J-10.

On the actual hand, the big blind had flopped a set of jacks and the preflop raiser had the A♠-Q♠. A spade came at the river, giving the preflop raiser the winning hand with a spade flush. The player finally found the good sense to fold on the turn when his two opponents kept raising.

(17) A $30-$60 game. You are in the big blind holding T♣-6♣. Everyone limps except two players. You get a free play. There is $240 in the pot and eight players. The flop is: 6♦-4♠-2♥, giving you top pair, weak kicker. The small blind checks. What do you do?

Answer: Check. With seven opponents, it is not a good idea to bet top pair, weak kicker when there are three cards clustered together on the flop. Even when your hand is good, it cannot take any heat, and does not rate to hold up. You should check. If you are constantly leading into crowds on these kinds of hands, you will find yourself frequently getting raised.

(18) A $30-$60 game. There is an early limper and you raise from middle position with the K♥-K♦. The cutoff, the big blind, and the limper call. There is $260 in the pot and four players. The flop is: J♣-9♥-8♣, giving you an overpair. The big blind bets and the early limper calls. What do you do?

Answer: Call. Normally, you should raise a flop bet when having a big overpair, but in this situation it is a bad idea. It does not get much worse for you with a board of J-9-8 and a two-flush. You have the big blind leading right out and the next player calling. It is quite possible your hand is no longer good. Even if two kings are still the best, your hand can be easily overtaken. You should just call and await developments on the turn. If you raise it could get reraised, and you could find yourself playing with hardly any outs. There are many killer cards that could show up on the turn like a club, a jack, a ten, a queen, or even a seven. When this happens, you have to fold if the turn gets bet, since you will not have enough outs to merit continuing; maybe no outs at all.

(19) A $30-$60 game. You are in the big blind holding A♣-J♠. An early player, a middle player, the button, and the small blind limp. There is $150 in the pot and five players. The flop comes: A♦-9♣-8♣, giving you top pair, fair kicker and a backdoor nut flush-draw. The small blind checks. You bet. The early player folds. The middle player raises. The button reraises. The small blind folds. What do you do?

Answer: Fold. Your one pair must fold when raised and reraised. Someone almost certainly has two pair and maybe more. When you are beat, you are either dead to two perfect cards or playing three outs. If by some miracle you are ahead, you will frequently get overtaken on the turn or at the river. It could even get raised again. You do not have enough hand to be taking multi-bet rides on every street.

(20) A $10-$20 game. You open limp from middle position with the Q♣-T♣. The cutoff limps. There is $35 in the pot and three players. The flop is: T♥-8♥-3♠, giving you top pair, good kicker. The big blind checks. You bet, the cutoff raises, and the big blind reraises. What do you do?

Answer: Fold. While one opponent may be on a draw, between the raiser and the reraiser, you probably don't have the best hand. The pot is not large enough, and you do not have enough outs to call for another two bets with this hand. It could even get raised again, and you could get taken for a four or five bet ride here.

(21) A $20-$40 game. You open-raise under-the-gun having the A♥-Q♠. An early player, a middle player, and the big blind call. There is $170 in the pot and four players. The flop is: Q♥-9♦-5♠, giving you top pair, top kicker. The big blind checks. You bet and the early player raises. The middle player calls, as well as the big blind. What do you do?

Answer: Call. You need to show some respect for the strong betting. Your flop bet got raised with two cold-callers on a rainbow board. Everyone assumed you had a good hand when you raised preflop under-the-gun. While you are probably up against one draw with perhaps jack-ten, between the other two players you could be up against two pair or a set. Keep in mind that the raise was on your left with two cold-callers. This means that the other players have better hands than normal, and are unlikely to be driven out if you reraise.

(22) A $15-$30 game. You are in the big blind holding A♥-9♥. A middle player opens with a raise and four other players call. You call. There is $190 in the hand and six players. The flop comes: A♠-J♦-T♥. giving you top pair, weak kicker and a backdoor nut flush-draw. What do you do?

Answer: Check. This hand was hotly debated on an Internet forum. This is a horrifying flop for you to be leading into a crowd of five other players. This board is highly coordinated, and has probably helped the preflop raiser more than you, plus there are four other players in this hand. Someone could easily have a better ace. If you lead, you will probably get raised, costing you two bets to take a card off. You may even get bet out of the hand. Furthermore, in the small percentage of cases where you are ahead, you will find that you can be easily overtaken. There will even be cases where you are practically drawing dead because someone has a straight. You should check and await developments.

(23) A $10-$20 game. You are in the big blind holding the 8♠-3♥ and get a free play when an early player, two middle players, and the button limp. There is $55 in the pot and five players. The flop is: 8♣-2♠-2♦, giving you top pair, no kicker. What do you do?

Answer: Bet. Despite having four opponents, you should bet top pair, no kicker when the board pairs small and is rainbow. If you get heat, you can fold, but cross your bridges only when you come to them. This is an unraised pot with no one showing any strength. You must initially protect your hand by betting, because it would be disastrous for it to get checked around, as any card higher than eight could give one of your opponents a better hand.

(24) A $15-$30 game. You are in the cutoff seat with the 8♥-7♥. Two early players and a middle player limp. You limp, as well as the small blind. There is $90 in the pot and six players. The flop is: 7♦-5♠-3♠, giving you top pair. Both blinds and the first early player check. The next player bets and the middle player calls. What do you do?

Answer: Fold. Top pair, no kicker is a loser in a six-handed pot with a bettor and a caller, despite the 8-to-1 pot odds. You are usually playing three outs at best, and an eight complements the board, making a straight possible for one of your numerous opponents.

17 – DRAWING HANDS

A drawing hand can vary in quality from a straight-flush draw with overcards to a mere gutshot straight. The decision how to play a draw is not easy, as there frequently are competing concepts involved. Should you just call and try to take off cards cheaply? Should you bet, hoping to win the pot outright, and having outs when you get called? Should you raise to get a free card?

The strength of your draw is a critical consideration. Obviously, the stronger your draw, the more aggressive you should be. Some draws are so strong that you are a mathematical favorite to hit your hand by the river. If you flop an open-ended straight flush draw, you have nine outs to a flush plus another six outs to a straight. (The remaining two of your straight cards have already been counted as flush cards.) This is 15 outs with two cards to come. You will make a straight or a flush 54 percent of the time by the river. A key point is that at limit poker you will be going to the river almost all the time anyway, even if you had just a normal flush-draw or open-ended straight-draw. Therefore, with a big draw, you should be aggressive on the flop. It's common sense to want more money in the pot when you are the favorite to win it, even if you do not have anything made yet.

Toward the other end of the spectrum, if you flop a gutshot, you have only four outs, which is about an 11-to-1 shot on the next card. In most cases, the pot odds on a gutshot will not justify calling a bet on the turn. Even on the flop, the pot odds may not be there to call and try to take a card off.

There are other ways to evaluate the strength of a draw besides the number of outs you have. An important consideration is whether you are hitting to the nuts. Few things in poker are more frustrating and expensive than making your draw, then finding out that your hand is no good. The draw can fail to win if someone makes a different type of hand that is better than yours. An example would be making a flush with a card that pairs the board. But with flush-draws, the most common way to hit and lose is simply to be drawing at a non-nut flush. While there are times playing such a draw cannot be helped, you can take some measures to avoid this problem. First, don't play so many small

100

suited starting hands. Second, bail out when the pot gets bombarded on the flop, since the nut flush-draw is often a party to doing the pounding.

An important factor in gauging the strength of your drawing hand is whether you are using two cards from your hand or only one card. Even though draw poker is the usual setting for the use of the term, "one-card draw," there is also a "one-card draw" in holdem. This is the situation where there are three parts to a straight on the board and you have a card that fits in with them. This layout can give an open-end straight-draw just like the normal type (a "two-card draw," meaning both cards in your hand are used) that can complete a straight with a couple of different cards. Here is an example of this. You hold A-10, and the board is J-9-8 on the flop. Between you and the board, there is a layout of J-10-9-8, and either a queen or seven will make a straight. This means you have the standard number of outs for a straight-draw of eight—but will the "outs" really get you a winning hand?

This one-card holding is overrated by many holdem players, and we want to illustrate to you how poor it really is. So we call it a "one-card straight-draw," to distinguish it from the normal straight-draw such as J-10 in your hand and 9-8 on the board, which is a "two-card straight-draw" because both cards in your hand are used in the straight.

When a person learns something new, the typical error is to link dissimilar items as equivalent because they fall under the same general category. For the poker player, the broad category is "eight-way straight-draw," and the error is failing to distinguish at holdem between a one-card draw and a two-card draw. Lets look at some reasons why we downgrade the one-card straight-draw.

The first drawback to a one-card draw is most of the time you are not hitting to the nuts. In the given situation, where you hold A-10 with a board of J-9-8, someone could have a K-10. In this case, the queen that makes you a queen-high straight makes your opponent a king-high straight. It is possible to construct a one-card draw that is to the nuts if you have your other card working in the straight, as the K-10 does here. But note that the seven which makes your straight on the low end does not give you a nut holding. We can conclude that a one-card draw that also has a card that will become part of the straight if you hit, such as our K-10 here, is superior to the typical one-card draw, but still inferior to a two-card draw. You can also be hitting to the nuts if your straight is ace-high. For example, if the board is K-J-10 and you have a queen (having a Q-2 in the blind is an example hand) an ace will make you the nuts. Of course, a nine will not, so your draw is of a similar character in this respect to the K-10 we discussed earlier, being to the nuts only on the top end. This draw with the queen is inferior to the K-10 draw, though, because with the latter you have the chance to beat a one-card draw out of a big pot.

The second drawback to the one-card draw is you are in much more danger of tying when you make your hand. All an opponent needs is the same key card as you. With the board of K-J-10, and your hand of Q-2, it would not be at all surprising to have a split pot. A two-way split is common, and a four-way split is possible. You can have someone else drawing at the same hand, or someone may already have the hand you are hoping to make. With a two-card draw at a straight, a split is of course also possible, but a lot less likely, because an opponent needs match **both** of your cards.

The third drawback to the one-card draw is the implied odds are worse. The implied odds are the extra money you expect to get after making your hand (in addition to what is already in the pot). Suppose you take that A-10 with a flop of J-9-8. You need a queen or a seven, but either of them will put a four-straight on the board. Looking at a board of Q-J-9-8 is pretty terrifying if you do not have a straight. It would be unusual for someone to bet your hand for you. Even top set is likely to just check and call. You simply cannot make as much money after hitting if there are four parts to a straight on the board instead of only three.

Of course, there are times at holdem when you will want to play a one-card draw to a straight. But keep in mind that it is similar to drawing at a flush with the board paired. You make these plays when a lot of money is in the pot preflop and you are playing limit poker. If you are about a 5-to-1 dog to make your hand and getting 15-to-1 or 20-to-1 pot odds, it is normally okay to draw at non-nut hands. You can afford to hit and lose a few times, and will still be better off playing the hand. It is not our goal to get you to automatically fold such hands every time. But you do need to go into these situations aware of the defects of your one-card draw, and take these defects into consideration when weighing whether and how to play your hand. Frequently, a fold is the favorite to be the right play with a one-card draw at holdem.

In "poker 101" we are taught that a drawing hand craves multihanded action, whereas a made hand wants to eliminate opponents from the pot. Here is an example. You have a flush-draw on the flop. Someone bets. It is in your interest to see the next card cheaply, and avoid a raise, which might get the pot narrowed down to just you and the bettor. If you are heads-up, the fact that you are about a 2-to-1 underdog means that the bettor has way the best of the situation. But with one or two other players along for the ride, as long as they are not flushing along with you, the odds have become attractive. If you raise, it seems that you are doing the bettor a favor, since the field may well get narrowed.

Let's sit behind an expert poker player. Sometimes you will see him doing exactly as is taught in a beginning poker class: just calling along with a draw in the hopes of multihanded action. Then along comes a hand where the expert plays his draw very strongly, betting and raising every time it is his turn. He may be doing this on just an ordinary size draw. Why this departure from basic principles? Doesn't he know his ABC's?

The truth of the matter is that how to play a draw can be a complex decision. Making sure you are getting proper pot odds through multiple opponents is only one approach to playing a draw. Sometimes this element predominates, but in other spots there may be a more important consideration at work. Let's look at what else there is to think about besides tailoring a pot so we get attractive odds on our draw.

Some pots can be won by simple aggression. You keep betting and raising, and after a bit you are the only one left in contention. Although it is possible to adopt this tactic on nothing, you will normally prefer to have a chance to win the pot by making a hand. So having a draw acts as a way to get lucky. You do not have the strong made hand you are representing, but if they keep calling to the end, you still can win the pot. This is "having outs."

Playing a drawing hand by betting or raising as if it were a strong made hand is called a semi-bluff. It is an important weapon in the arsenal of a good player. When properly utilized, it allows him to win in many situations without having the best hand. But the key is that there has to be a reasonable chance that the pot can be won at some point as a result of your betting or raising. If the texture of the board, the number of opponents, or the previous betting action indicate that this is not the case, then semi-bluffing is usually wrong. How far wrong it is depends upon the strength of your draw and how many outs you have.

Some of the biggest swings in holdem that favor strong players over weak ones are engineered by a player being aggressive with a drawing hand. By betting or raising, you prevent the opponent from winning the pot on anything that cannot stand the heat. If both you and the opponent are on a draw, you win. When the opponent has a shaky holding, you run him out of the pot, instead of him charging you to draw at your hand and then getting your money if you miss. The large degree of aggression in the style of play by good players at middle-level stakes is directly attributable to these factors. (At lower stakes, there are more players in for the flop, and they hate to ever fold, so aggression there has less to gain. A key thing to learn when you move up in class is the much greater value of aggression with a draw at the middle levels.)

With either a super-draw or a longshot, your course of action is usually clear. But with a regular draw to a straight (eight outs) or a flush (nine outs), you need to decide whether to be passive with the hand and just call, or be aggressive and bet or raise.

How can we identify a situation where obtaining proper pot odds is not as important as giving yourself a chance to win on power betting? The number one consideration is whether you have a chance to win the pot by taking aggressive action. (Realize that a bet or raise on the flop may be helping you to win the pot by a turn or river bet, as well as giving a chance to win immediately.)

The biggest determinant of whether aggressive action will provide a decent chance to win the pot is the number of opponents. With only one or two opponents, there are fewer obstacles between you and the roses. Also, the fewer people who stay for the flop, the less likely someone will hit a big enough hand to stand the heat. Frankly, it would be hard to find a heads-up situation where you would have a straight or flush draw and not bet or raise until you could see the opponent was in for the duration.

With exactly three opponents, you have to make a judgment on that individual case, looking at who those people are and the texture of the board. Are they loose players? Are there a lot of card combinations people could have where they will stay in? The presence of these factors would steer you to conservatism, and an absence to aggression.

With more than three opponents, back off. The reason why you should not be aggressive with an ordinary draw against a large field is poker does not offer a place or show prize on a hand. If you do not eliminate everyone, knocking people out is normally detrimental to a drawing hand. The larger the field, the better the pot odds, and the greater chance of making money after hitting your hand. A bet figures to knock some people out of the pot. And a raise not only eliminates players, but allows the original bettor (or someone else) to reraise. A reraise happens quite often, as the original bettor may strain to reraise because the other players are now confronted with a double bet.

An important factor in whether to be aggressive with a draw is your position. The later you have to act, the better chance you have to see if anyone else likes their hand enough to bet. For example, with three opponents, if you have to act first, a bet has less chance of success than if some of them have already checked. Furthermore, when you have good position, you can decide on the turn whether to keep the pressure on with another bet or simply take a free card. So a bet in late position not only has a superior chance to win the pot, but also places you well in subsequent betting rounds. Lastly, it may be that if you do not bet your draw, you might have to pay to hit your hand anyway. If you check, someone else may well decide to push a modest hand like middle or bottom pair because you showed weakness by checking.

Good position is also important when contemplating a raise. If you check-raise in early position, the opponent gets to see how you react to the turn-card. If the flush fails to come and you check, he probably will put you on a draw, so your ruse worked only for the flop betting round. But if you raise in late position, he has to act before you do, so you may well get a choice if you miss your draw of carrying on your semi-bluff or taking a free card.

Take note of the much greater value of a drawing hand when your position is good, and recognize how this has been applied to our starting hand requirements in the various positions. When a book is written, the material must be organized into chapters. For a holdem book, it seems logical to divide it according to preflop, flop, turn, and river betting. So when you read our poker book, do not compartmentalize each chapter, but pay lots of attention to how they are all related. Notice how your preflop action is based partly on how a hand will play out. Hands like J-10, J-9, and 10-9 build a lot of draws. When we counsel conservatism in early position preflop with these and similar character hands, it is not just to protect you against committing too much money on a longshot in preflop betting. It is also because this hand type plays much better with good position. This chapter on drawing hands should be helpful in illustrating the point with concrete examples.

Look for aggression with a draw when the preflop betting has been insipid. The weaker the hands preflop, the less likely the opponents have of holding something good after the flop. When you see wimpy betting such as an unraised pot with a late-position limper, the button, and the blinds being the only ones in to see the flop, this is a good indicator to bulldoze with a drawing hand.

At the standard split-limit betting structure, where the betting limit doubles on the last two rounds, it is routine to see a drawing hand take aggressive action on the flop with the not-so-lofty goal of trying to get a free card on the next round. The raiser is hoping his show of strength will cause the opponent to check on the turn. Note the importance of having position on the opponent when using this tactic, as check-raising on the flop and then checking to him on the turn is not likely to impress him into believing his hand is weaker than yours.

Frankly, throwing in a raise to save half a bet is probably an overrated poker ploy. Some of the time the bettor is going to reraise you, so you actually lose a bet by raising. Of course, when the person three-bets you, it is possible to once again raise. "I'm going to get a free card no matter what it costs" seems to be an oxymoron, but is a possible line of play. But suppose the bettor behaves like a good little boy or girl, just calling your raise and then checking on the turn. Rather than taking a free card and beating your chest in a Tarzan triumph at this accomplishment, consider being a pig by betting again trying to win the pot. The opponent backed off, so maybe a bet by you will take the cheese immediately. This surely is your only chance to win without making your hand, as if you check the turn, you can buy the pot on the end only from someone who does not understand poker.

In betting a drawing hand, you are mimicking a made hand. Thus, aggressive action on a draw can win you the pot when facing another draw, even when the opponent has bigger cards than you. For example, if you fire throughout the deal on a jack-high flush-draw, and the opponent has a king-high flush-draw, you will have a fine chance to win by a bet on the end. Here we have the paradoxical situation that you will win only by missing your draw. Obviously, taking the initiative in the betting on this type of layout is vastly superior than trying to draw as cheaply as possible. Don't be afraid to invest an extra bet for deception when drawing.

In this discussion, we have talked about a number of situations where someone with a drawing hand bets strongly, trying to narrow the field, rather than following "Classical Poker Theory" by letting the field come in. But don't get the wrong idea from what's been said. Following Classical Theory is right much of the time. In this era where the merits of aggression are appreciated by many poker players, there are people who seem to always throw in an extra bet or raise with a draw. It appears to be the only kind of poker they know. These loose cannons can book some big wins on good nights, but the converse is also true. Throwing in extra bets all evening with the worst hand is not good poker. The decision whether to bet a draw strongly is neither automatic nor easy. The weakies do their thing—either always calling or always raising—simply by rote. Using good judgment in this kind of situation is the hallmark of the accomplished player, who manages to make a lot of good decisions about when to pound and when to grovel.

The next set of hands illustrate how all these factors come into play on the flop in a full table, middle limit holdem game.

(1) A $10-$20 game. You are in the big blind holding the T♠-9♥. Two early players and two middle players limp in. The cutoff raises. The button and small blind both fold. You call. The early limpers call, as well as the first middle limper. But now the second middle limper reraises. The cutoff just calls. You call. The first early limper now decides to cap the betting, and everyone calls. There is $245 in the pot and six players. The flop is: J♦-7♣-6♣, giving you a gutshot straight-draw. You check. The first early limper, who capped the betting, bets. The next early limper raises. Everyone folds to you. What do you do?

Answer: Fold. You have an inside straight draw with any eight. The odds against you are about 11-to-1. There is $275 in the pot right now and it costs you $20, so your pot odds are about 14-to-1. It would appear that you have a call. The problem is that there is a two-flush on board and six players took this flop. The two-flush not only taints one of your outs, but it sets up redraws, making your implied odds much worse. In other words, the 8♣ could give someone a club flush. You have only three clean outs, which is a 15-to-1 shot. Furthermore, even if nobody makes a flush with the 8♣, it could give someone a club flush-draw, which means that you will not win all the time even when you hit one of your outs. Another problem scenario would be if a non-club eight arrives on the turn, giving you the nuts, and then a club shows up at the river, possibly giving someone a club flush. Again, this damages your implied odds, since you will lose a lot of chips when this happens. Finally, it could get raised again, and even reraised, forcing you to call another $10 or $20 to take off a card.

On the actual hand, the worst of all things happened. The player called. It was raised and capped back to him and he called. The turn was the 8♥, giving him the nuts. The betting got capped again. The river was the J♠, pairing the top flop card. The player lost to someone who flopped a set of sevens and filled up at the river. He lost another $140 on this hand.

(2) The game is $10-$20. You are in the cutoff seat and had to post a late position blind. Two middle players limp in. You rap the table, having the 3♠-2♠. Everyone else folds. There is $45 in the pot and four players. The flop comes: A♠-K♥-5♠, giving you a gutshot straight-flush draw. The big blind checks. The first limper bets and the next limper calls. What do you do?

Answer: Raise. You have 12 outs to a flush or a straight with two cards to come. You are almost even money to make a straight or flush by the river. With only three opponents, you are not so likely to be up against another flush-draw. Other good things might happen by raising as well. If a blank comes on the turn, you may be positioned to make a good semi-bluff bet on the expensive street. In other words, you may win the pot outright, and you still have a lot of outs if you are called. If no one folds, no spade or four arrives on the turn, and no one bets, you may be able to take a free card here if you like.

On the actual hand, the player raised. The big blind folded, and the first limper decided to fold. The second limper called. An ace came on the turn and the remaining opponent checked. The player bet and his opponent folded while flashing K♠-Q♦.

(3) The game is $15-$30. An early player opens with a raise. You are next to act having the K♥-Q♥ and call. The small blind calls. There is $105 in the pot and three players. The flop is: J♥-7♦-4♥, giving you a flush-draw with two overcards. The small blind checks. The early player bets. What do you do?

Answer: Raise. You have both a flush-draw and two overcards, so you could have as many as 15 outs with two cards to come. You are a mathematical favorite to make a flush or top pair by the river. This is a raised pot, and it is important to put pressure on the small blind. He might hang around for only one bet with a better hand than yours like middle pair, bottom pair, or even an ace overcard, but will likely fold rather than call two bets cold.

On the actual hand, the player just called, as well as the small blind. The turn brought the T♦, so he picked up an open-end straight-draw. The small blind checked. The early player bet and both players called. The river was a blank and it was checked around. The small blind won the pot with the 5♦-4♦ for a pair of fours. The small blind called the turn bet because he picked up a diamond flush-draw. The early player had the K♣-Q♣.

(4) A $15-$30 game. You are in the cutoff seat holding K♣-T♣. Two early players limp in. You limp as well as the small blind. There is $75 in the pot and five players. The flop is: A♠-9♣-7♣, giving you a flush-draw. The small blind checks. The big blind bets. One early limper calls and the other folds. What do you do?

Answer: Call. In a three-way pot like this, you should not raise the flop with a flush-draw when the ace is not of the flush suit. Change the flop to A♣-9♠-7♣, so you are hitting to the nuts, and you can consider a raise. The problem with this flop is that you can get buried if one of your opponents has the A♣ with another club, giving him top pair with a better flush-draw. He will be pounding the pot having both the best hand and the best draw. Another reason to avoid raising is that it may not be in your best interest to drive out players when you have a drawing hand like this. They should be encouraged to hang around with their pairs and straight-draws so you get better pot odds, and have a chance to collect some additional money when you hit.

(5) A $15-$30 game. You are in the big blind holding the K♠-8♠. Two early players, two middle players, and the small blind limp. You take a free play. There is $90 in the pot and six players. The flop is: Q♥-J♦-T♣, giving you an open-end straight-draw. The small blind checks. You check. The first early limper bets and the next player folds. The first middle limper raises and everyone folds to you. What do you do?

Answer: Fold. You should not call $30 cold despite having an open-ended straight draw. You have a "one-card straight draw," meaning that you are only using one of your two cards to make a straight. Your hand can be easily counterfeited, so that even if one of your outs arrives, you could be splitting the pot with someone else, or even losing it altogether. The greatly increased chance of a split pot against another king, or even losing the pot if a king turns up, makes playing on a mistake. Furthermore, the board is highly coordinated, and it could be reraised and capped back to you, costing you an additional $30 to take off a card after calling.

On the actual hand, the player called. It got raised and capped back to him and he called all that as well. The turn brought a nine. The betting got capped again. The river paired the nine. It was bet and called on the river in two spots. A player with pocket tens won a huge pot, having flopped a set and filling up at the river. The other player had ace-king. The player was playing three outs to tie.

(6) A $10-$20 game. You are in the big blind holding the J♣-9♣. An early player limps, a middle player raises, the cutoff calls, and the small blind calls. You call and the early limper calls. There is $100 in the pot and five players. The flop is: 4♠-3♣-2♣, giving you a flush-draw with two overcards. The small blind checks. What do you do?

Answer: Bet. You should bet despite having four opponents. You have two overcards that don't complement the board, and a flush-draw. You are a mathematical favorite to make a flush or top pair by the river. That board does not rate to have helped an early limper or a preflop raiser. It probably doesn't help the cutoff, who called two bets cold. Being in the big blind, you could have called a preflop raise with a wide range of hands. For all your opponents know, you could easily have a straight, a set, or two pair. If you get called or raised, you have outs. If you get called in only one spot and the turn-card pairs the top flop card, you can frequently bet and win the pot outright, since some opponents will fold overcards (possibly even overpairs) in this situation. If you do decide to check, it should be with the intention of check-raising. This would be a way to vary your play, but it is not so appealing to play a draw in this manner because you are in front position.

(7) A $15-$30 game. You are in the small blind holding 7♦-6♦. An early and middle player limp and then a middle player raises. Everyone folds to you and you call. Everyone else calls. There is $150 in the pot and five players. The flop is: T♣-9♠-4♦, giving you a gutshot straight-draw. Everyone checks to the raiser, who bets. What do you do?

Answer: Fold. You have a gutshot straight-draw, an 11-to-1 shot, plus a backdoor diamond draw. There is $165 in the pot, so you are getting 11-to-1 pot odds. But your draw and your play have some serious difficulties. The gutshot you are drawing to is not to the nuts. If you catch an eight, then someone with queen-jack or even jack-seven has a bigger straight than you. With four opponents, this will happen more often than you think, costing you a ton of money in the process. The other problem is that you are being bet into with three other players yet to act, so one of them might raise. Don't be fooled by all the checking into thinking they must be weak, since they may have been "checking to the raiser."

(8) A $15-$30 game. You are on the button with the Q♠-T♠. You open with a raise and both blinds call. There is $90 in the pot and three players. The flop is: A♠-8♠-3♣, giving you a flush-draw. The small blind checks and the big blind bets. What do you do?

Answer: Raise. You are still the preflop raiser, although a steal-raiser, and you could easily have a top pair of aces with a good kicker. Your opponent's lead bet here might be done on a draw, middle pair, or even bottom pair in this three-handed pot with one player already checking. You may not win the pot outright on this round, but you set yourself up to take it down on the next round when you follow it up with a bet on the expensive street (assuming your opponent checks). You have your flush outs to fall back on if your opponent stays with you. The ace being of your suit helps. Even if blanks come on the turn and river, you should plan on betting both rounds unless your opponent raises you somewhere.

(9) A $15-$30 game. You are in the small blind holding 5♣-4♣. An early player and a middle player limp. Another middle player raises. The cutoff and button both call. You and the other players call. There is $210 in the pot and seven players. The flop comes: A♠-6♠-3♥, giving you an open-end straight-draw. Everyone checks to the middle limper, who bets. The preflop raiser pops it. The cutoff and button fold. What do you do?

Answer: Fold. You should dump a straight-draw with a two-flush on board and two players betting and raising with other players involved. Two of your outs could be killed, and if not, redraws get created. The pot could get raised again, and you could be going for a multi-bet ride on every street.

(10) A $10-$20 game. You are in the big blind holding the 6♣-5♣. An early player, a middle player, and the button limp. You get a free play. There is $45 in the pot and four players. The flop is: A♣-Q♦-T♣, giving you a flush-draw. What do you do?

Answer Check. Even though you have a flush-draw, this is a very bad flop for you to be betting into three opponents. Your bet will not allow you to win the pot outright, and you can easily get raised, since an all playing-zone flop having an ace, a queen, and a ten figures to have helped the opponents.

(11) A $10-$20 game. You are in the big blind holding Q♥-3♣. A semi-maniac limps in under the gun, as does an elderly lady sitting right next to him who is the tight-passive player discussed in previous problems. Everyone else folds, so you get a free play. There is $35 in the pot and three players. The flop is: K♣-J♣-T♦, giving you an open-end straight-draw. You check. The semi-maniac checks. The lady bets. You call. The semi-maniac raises. The lady reraises. What do you do?

Answer: Fold. At this point you should fold rather than calling a double bet back to you. There is a flush-draw on board, so the A♣ or the 9♣ may not be outs. Your one-card straight-draw is bad, because if an ace or a nine shows up, you may be splitting the pot if someone has a queen. A one-card draw also hurts your implied odds, because your opponents will fear a board containing four parts to a straight. You could even be up against a completed hand with someone having ace-queen. Another problem is that the semi-maniac may reraise.

On the actual hand, the player called. The semi-maniac made it four bets, the lady capped it, and he called. The turn-card was a club. The semi-maniac won a big pot with the 7♣-6♣; the lady had A♥-Q♦.

(12) A $10-$20 game. After two early players call, you limp in from middle position with the K♣-J♥. The button and small blind limp. There is $60 in the pot and six players. The flop comes down: Q♦-T♥-7♠, giving you an open-end straight-draw. Both blinds and the first early limper check. The second early limper bets. What do you do?

Answer: Call. The choice is obviously between raising and calling, since folding an open-ended straight draw on a rainbow flop would be insane. There are too many opponents to be raising with a standard draw like this, and you should not want to eliminate players. Otherwise, you run the risk of getting heads-up between yourself and the best hand. The king overcard is shaky because it complements the queen-ten on the flop, so it's not a clean out here. When you have a straight-draw and one or two overcards, at least one of your pair-draw helpers will be tainted.

(13) A $10-$20 game. You are in the small blind with the K♥-J♣. An early player limps and you limp. There is $30 in the pot and three players. The flop is: Q♦-9♣-7♦, giving you a gutshot straight-draw. What do you do?

Answer: Check. You have a gutshot straight draw with any ten, and a king overcard. You have only two opponents, one of whom has a random holding, since he got a free play. So you could argue that a bet might well pick up the pot here, and if it doesn't, you have outs. But there are factors which weigh in against betting. One problem is the two-flush, which taints one of your four straight-cards. In addition, the cards on the flop are somewhat coordinated with each other, increasing the chance of getting played with. If the seven were a five or a four, then that would be much better for the chance of a bet driving everyone out. Also, the pot has only three small bets in it. Check and hope to get a free card; fold if someone bets. The pot is too small and the board is too tough to bother getting involved.

(14) A $30-$60 game. You limp in under-the-gun with K♣-Q♣. An early player raises and a middle player, the big blind, and yourself call. There is $260 in the pot and four players. The flop is: A♣-T♣-3♥, giving you a gutshot to a royal flush. The small blind checks. What do you do?

Answer: Bet. You have a super draw, with nine outs to the nut flush and three more to the nut straight with two cards to come. You are almost even money to make a flush or a straight by the river. Your three opponents may fold if no one has an ace.

On the actual hand, the player checked and it got checked around. The turn was the A♦ and everyone checked (betting on the draw would have been preferable). The river was the 2♦. The preflop raiser bet and was called in one spot. The preflop raiser won the pot having the J♠-J♣. Who knows what would have happened had the player bet the flop, but it was ridiculous to let a pair of jacks take the money without a fight. The player actually had six additional outs, with any king or queen.

(15) A $30-$60 game. You are in early position with the A♣-K♦ and call an under-the-gun raiser. Two middle players and both blinds call. There is $360 in the pot and six players. The flop is: Q♥-J♥-J♠, giving you a gutshot straight-draw. Both blinds and the preflop raiser check. You check. The first middle player bets. The second middle player folds, as well as both blinds. The preflop raiser calls. What do you do?

Answer: Fold. You have three board-cards all in the playing zone. The queen and jack are touching in rank, increasing the chance of someone already having a full house. In addition, there is a two-flush on the table. The two overcards are probably useless, and even your gutshot draw may not win.

(16) A $30-$60 game. You are in the big blind holding K♣-3♦. Everyone folds to the small blind (who does not chop). The small blind raises and you call. There is $120 in the pot and two players.

The flop is: Q♣-J♠-T♥, giving you a one-card straight-draw with an overcard. Your opponent bets. What do you do?

Answer: Raise. In a heads-up situation like this, since you will go to the river, you must make a play for the pot at some point. Right now you have an open-ended straight draw with any ace or nine, with two cards to come. Your opponent may well fold a medium or small pocket pair or an ace with a low sidecard. If he calls, you have a lot of outs with two cards to come. If you hit, you got the money in before you could lose your market. The alternative to raising now would be making a strong play for the pot later.

(17) A $30-$60 game. You are in the big blind holding A♣-8♣. A middle player opens with a raise and the small blind calls, as well as yourself. There is $180 in the pot and three players. The flop is: J♣-9♣-5♠, giving you the nut flush-draw. The small blind checks. What do you do?

Answer: Bet. You have nine outs to the nut flush, plus an ace could be an out, giving you as many as 12 outs. You have only two opponents and there are two cards to come. You are almost even money to make a club flush or a top pair of aces by the river. You could win the pot outright, and you have lots of outs if you get called or raised.

(18) A $30-$60 hand. You open with a raise from middle position having the A♣-T♣. The player on your immediate left calls and everyone else folds. There is $170 in the pot and two players. The flop is: K♣-T♦-9♣, giving you the nut flush-draw and middle pair. You bet and your opponent raises. What do you do?

Answer: Reraise. In a heads-up situation, be aggressive whenever feasible. You have the nut flush-draw (nine outs), a middle pair of tens (two more outs), and an ace kicker (three more outs). This is 14 outs with two cards to come. You are about even money to make the nut flush, trips, or two pair. You raised preflop and you are now three-betting on the flop when it comes king-high. Your opponent might decide to fold a weak king, fearing that you have pocket aces, ace-king, or a set of kings. If he was raising on some kind of drawing hand like ace-queen, he may fold when you reraise. Most of the time he will call. If he continues to bet, you have plenty of outs. Plan on betting the turn if he calls and a blank comes. Some players will fold on the expensive street in the face of an opponent who keeps charging, unless they have two pair or better or a good draw. You have a big enough hand that you should retain the initiative.

(19) A $20-$40 game. You are in the big blind holding the 9♣-7♣. The under-the-gun player opens with a raise. An early player, a middle player, the button, and the small blind all call. You call. There is $240 in the pot and six players. The flop is: K♠-J♣-T♠, giving you a double belly-buster straight-draw with any queen or eight. It is checked to the early player, who bets, and only the middle player calls. What do you do?

Answer: Fold. There is $280 in the pot and it costs you $20 to call, so your pot odds are 14-to-1. In addition to your straight-draw you have a backdoor flush-draw. You have eight cards that make you a straight, but it would be a mistake to equate this with eight outs. The problem is that a queen means that anyone with an ace has a bigger straight. The 8♠ could give someone a spade flush or a draw to a spade flush. You have maybe three clean outs with any non-spade eight, and that is a 15-to-1 shot. But even then, there may be times when your jack-high straight won't hold up, because a spade comes at the river, giving someone a flush. An opponent could have A-Q for a straight made already. You have no nut outs and a two-flush is on the board. Fold and stay out of trouble.

(20) A $20-$40 game. You are in the small blind with the A♣-Q♣. An early player, a middle player, and the button limp. You raise, the big blind folds, and the rest call. There is $180 in the pot and four players. The flop is: K♠-T♦-7♦, giving you a gutshot straight-draw. What do you do?

Answer: Check. You have three opponents. Two of three cards out there are in the playing zone, plus the seven connects with the ten to yield straight-making possibilities. Your bet will not win the pot outright, and you may even get raised. A king-high flop rates to connect with limpers, since many playable hands contain a king. The two-flush hurts your hand. The flop may not get bet, and a free card would be nice.

(21) A $30-$60 game. You are in the big blind holding Q♣-8♣. The under-the-gun player opens with a raise and a middle player and the small blind call. You call. There is $240 in the pot and four players. The flop is: A♣-T♣-3♠, giving you a flush-draw. The small blind checks. What do you do?

Answer: Bet. Because the ace on the table is the ace of your suit, you will not get buried under top pair, nut flush-draw. By betting, you can represent an ace, and might win the pot here or on the turn. If you get called or raised, you have nine outs to the second nut flush with two cards to come.

On the actual hand, the player checked and it got checked around. The turn was the 8♠. The player bet the turn with his pair of eights and club flush-draw. He got called by the middle player and the small blind. The river was a blank and it was checked down. The middle player won the pot with a pair of nines, a ridiculous outcome. The player with pocket nines would be hard-pressed to call a flop bet with two overcards on the board and a two-flush. But when the turn came, the middle player figured that his pocket nines might be good, given the lack of flop betting.

(22) A $30-$60 game. The under-the-gun player opens with a raise and you call from middle position with the K♥-Q♥, with everyone else folding. There is $170 in the pot and two players. The flop is: A♥-T♣-T♠, giving you a gutshot straight-draw. Your opponent bets. What do you do?

Answer: Fold. An ace-high flop may well have helped an under-the-gun raiser. You are behind, chasing with a gutshot that may not win even if you hit one of your four outs. Both the pot odds and the implied odds are poor.

(23) A $30-$60 game. You are on the button holding the A♠-6♠. The under-the-gun player raises. An early player, a middle player, and the cutoff call. You call and both blinds call. There is $420 in the pot and seven players. The flop is: 7♦-4♥-3♣, giving you a gutshot straight-draw. Both blinds check. The preflop raiser bets. The early player and middle player both call. The cutoff raises. What do you do?

Answer: Fold. There is $570 in the pot and it costs you $60 right now to call. These are pot odds of about 9-to-1. You have four outs with any five, and that is an 11-to-1 shot. Furthermore, yours is a one-card straight-draw, which means if you hit, you will only be splitting the pot with anyone who happens to have a six. It costs you two bets to play. Adding to your woes is the possibility of it getting raised again. The implied odds are almost never there to play a one-card straight-draw that is a gutshot as well.

(24) A $20-$40 game. You open with a raise from middle position with K♥-Q♣ and only the big blind calls. There is $90 in the pot and two players. The flop is: T♥-9♦-3♥, giving you a gutshot straight-draw with two overcards. The big blind bets; what now?

Answer: Raise. You have 10 outs to a straight or top pair, plus you have a backdoor flush-draw. You are heads-up with position and you were the preflop raiser. You are most likely going to the river anyway, so you might as well begin the festivities with a raise. Give your opponent a chance to make a bad fold.

(25) A $30-$60 game. You are in the big blind holding K♠-J♠. The cutoff opens with a raise. The small blind and you call. There is $180 in the pot and three players. The flop is: Q♠-9♥-3♦, giving you a gutshot straight-draw. The small blind checks. What do you do?

Answer: Bet. This is a three-way pot with one opponent checking. The preflop raiser was in a steal-raise situation, so he does not need any kind of premium hand for his preflop action. You might win the pot outright, and you have outs if you are called or raised.

A ten is four outs. A king is three more outs. You also have a backdoor spade flush-draw. If you check, then you will have to fold on the turn unless a king, a ten, or a spade shows up, because at that point you will not be getting the right price to continue.

(26) A $10-$20 game. You are in the big blind holding the 9♠-6♥ and get a free play after three early players limp, a middle player limps, and the small blind limps. There is $60 in the pot and six players. The flop is: T♣-7♣-3♦, giving you a gutshot straight-draw. The small blind checks. You check. The first early player bets and everyone calls back to you. What do you do?

Answer: Fold. There is $110 in the pot, so you are getting 11-to-1 on your call. Your implied odds are even better if you hit your gutshot and it holds up. Nevertheless, folding is right here because of the two-flush. With all these opponents, the 8♣ could give someone a flush, so that kills one of your outs. Furthermore, if the 8♣ does not give someone a flush, any one with just one club has a redraw against you at the river. The point is that you will not win all the time even when you hit one of your four miracle cards. There are some lower-order concerns as well, which frequently occur when you have a lot of opponents. The straight you are trying to make is not to the nuts. Someone with jack-nine would have a higher straight. With the two-flush on board plus a lot of opponents, all kinds of draws and redraws are out there, so you will lose a lot of money if you hit but get beaten.

(27) A $20-$40 game. You are in the cutoff seat with the K♠-T♠ and call behind a middle limper. The button limps. There is $90 in the pot and four players. The flop comes: A♦-J♥-9♣, giving you a gutshot straight-draw. The big blind checks and the next player bets. What do you do?

Answer: Fold. There is $110 in the pot and it costs you $20 to call. You are getting about 5-to-1 to chase a gutshot straight with any queen, which is an 11-to-1 shot. The odds are not there to be chasing. A flop call would be bad for other reasons besides the poor pot odds. The board contains three cards in the playing zone, so it is quite likely that this flop has connected with one or more of your opponents. After your call, there will be two opponents behind you who have not acted, so you may get raised.

(28) A $10-$20 game. You limp in from middle position with the A♠-3♠ behind an early limper. Another middle player limps, the cutoff limps, and the small blind limps. The big blind raises and everyone calls. There is $120 in the pot and six players. The flop comes: J♠-5♠-3♦, giving you bottom pair and the nut flush-draw. The small blind checks. The big blind bets and the early limper folds. What do you do?

Answer: Raise. Between the nut flush-draw, your overcard, and your pair, you have 14 outs with two cards to come. You are a mathematical favorite to make a flush, trips, or two pair by the river, and most importantly, you will be going to the river regardless of what comes on the turn. Although a multi-handed pot is fine when you are drawing, if you have the best hand, it's not. If the preflop raiser has only two big cards, you do not want players.

(29) A $20-$40 game. You are in the big blind holding A♦-3♥. The cutoff limps as well as the small blind. There is $60 in the pot and three players. The flop is: J♦-5♣-2♥, giving you a gutshot with an overcard. The small blind bets. What do you do?

Answer: Fold. You are getting 4-to-1 pot odds and have four to seven outs, so your chance of improving is from 6-to-1 to 11-to-1 against. You also have a player behind you who might raise.

(30) The game is $10-$20. You are in middle position with the Q♣-J♦ and limp in behind an early player and another middle player. The small blind limps. There is $50 in the pot and five players. The flop is: K♥-T♠-3♦, giving you an open-ended straight draw. The small blind checks. The big blind bets and the limpers fold. What do you do?

Answer: Raise. The small blind, who is the third player in the pot, has checked, so it looks like facing a double bet will get him out.

Despite having an ordinary draw, you have position in a likely heads-up situation. The raise will give you some leverage on later streets if your remaining two opponents choose to play. Since the small blind has already checked, it is unlikely that he will cold-call a bet and a raise. It is even possible that the big blind may fold, if he was betting something other than top pair or a draw. Even when the big blind calls, you will have the option if a blank comes of either pursuing your semi-bluff play by betting the turn or taking a free card.

(31) A $30-$60 game. You limp in from middle position with the J♥-T♥ behind an early limper. The cutoff and the small blind limp. There is $150 in the pot and five players. The flop comes: K♥-Q♣-4♥, giving you an open-end straight-draw and a flush-draw. It is checked to you. You bet and the cutoff raises. Everyone folds to you. What do you do?

Answer: Reraise. With at least 15 outs (unless the opponent has the nut flush-draw) and two cards to come, you are a mathematical favorite to make a flush or a straight by the river. As well as reraising, you should plan on betting the turn in most cases. On the actual hand, the player called. The turn was the 6♦. He checked and the cutoff bet. He called. The river was the 8♦. It was checked down. The cutoff won a $390 pot with the Q♦-T♦ for a pair of queens. Had the player reraised on the flop, he might have won it right then. If not, a follow-through bet on the turn would have almost certainly picked up the pot. You should avoid letting a person on a modest holding that can't take heat charge you money to draw, and it is worth throwing in an extra raise to prevent this.

(32) A $10-$20 game. You are in the big blind holding K♦-5♥. A middle player and the small blind limp, so you get a free play. There is $30 in the pot and three players. The flop is: 6♣-4♣-3♦, giving you a one-card open-end straight-draw with an overcard. The small blind checks. What do you do?

Answer: Bet. With only two limping opponents, one of whom has checked, you have an excellent chance to pick up this little pot with a bet. You have outs to fall back on if you get played with.

(33) A $10-$20 game. You have J♠-9♥ in the small blind. Two middle players and the cutoff limp. You call. There is $50 in the pot and five players. The flop is: Q♠-T♦-3♣, giving you an open-end straight-draw. What do you do?

Answer: Check. Contrast this with the previous problem. In both cases you have a small unraised pot with an open-end straight draw, and you have the chance to lead at the flop. So why not bet? Because there are some significant differences that make a semi-bluff bet a poor one in this situation. Here you have four opponents, and no one has checked. In the previous problem you had only two opponents, with one of them checking. Furthermore, this board is coordinated, with two cards in the playing zone (the queen and the ten), making it more likely that one of your many opponents has a piece of it. In the previous problem, a board of all small cards does not rate to help anyone. When you semi-bluff, you want to have a reasonable chance of winning the pot outright by betting. By the way, you should note that with this type of straight-draw, with one of your cards lower in rank than both of the boardcards you are tied in with, you are not hitting to the nuts on the top end of the draw. In this case, a king would make someone with A-J a higher straight than yours.

(34) A $15-$30 game. After an early player limps, you call with J♥-10♥. The game has become very passive with hardly any preflop raising. Another early player, the cutoff, the button, and the small blind all limp. There is $105 in the pot and seven players. The flop is: A♥-10♠-3♥, giving you middle pair with a flush-draw. The small blind checks. The big blind bets. The next player folds. What do you do?

Answer: Raise. Even though you probably don't have the best hand on an ace-high board with six opponents, you can represent a good ace and perhaps drive players out who don't want to call two

123

bets cold. You have a "super" draw here with 9 flush outs, 3 outs to two pair, and 2 outs to trips, making you even money to end up with a hand that rates to win.

(35) A $10-$20 game. You open limp from early position with the J♠-T♠. Two middle players and the button limp, as well as the small blind. There is $60 in the pot and six players. The flop is: Q♥-9♦-5♣, giving you an open-end straight-draw. Both blinds check. What do you do?

Answer: Check. Despite having two of your five opponents check, you have too many other players taking a flop to merit betting out with a garden-variety draw like this. You are highly unlikely to win this one by leading, and you may even get raised, especially given two cards in the playing zone (a queen and a nine). When you get raised, two things happen, both of which are bad. First, a raise causes players to fold who you want in when you are drawing. Second, it now costs you more money to pursue your draw. Don't give the guy with the best hand a chance to thin the field by raising your bet. He profits at your expense.

(36) A $20-$40 game. You are in the big blind holding K♣-T♥. An early player limps and everyone folds so you take a free play. There is $50 in the pot and two players. The flop is: A♣-Q♣-9♥, giving you a gutshot straight-draw and backdoor flush-draw. What do you do?

Answer: Bet. You have but one opponent, who has only limped. With this board, he may fold a better hand like a small or medium pocket pair. You have few outs if you get called, but you will win enough pots to compensate for this.

(37) A $10-$20 game. You are in middle position with the A♠-5♠ and limp behind an early limper. Another middle player and the small blind limp. There is $50 in the pot and five players. The flop is: 8♠-6♥-4♠, giving you the nut flush-draw and a one-card gutshot. Both blinds and the early limper check. What do you do?

Answer: Bet. No one has shown any strength. The board is all small cards. Two of your four opponents have checked. You have an outside chance of winning the pot with a bet, but the real strength of the situation is your hand. You have 9 flush outs, 3 straight outs, and 3 overcard outs, for a total of 15 outs with two cards to come. You are about even money to end up with the winning hand anyway.

(38) A $20-$40 game. You are on the button with the 9♥-8♥. An early player and two middle players limp. You call, as well as the small blind. There is $120 in the pot and six players. The flop is: K♦-J♥-T♥, giving you an open-end, straight-flush draw. The small blind checks and the big blind bets. The early player calls. One middle player calls and the other folds. What do you do?

Answer: Call. Despite your having an open-end straight flush-draw, a semi-bluff raise is not a good idea. If the K♦ had been a little card, raising would be right. But right now your hand is a mirage. Given that board and four opponents, no one is folding if you raise. Furthermore, someone could have a straight and someone else a bigger flush-draw. Note that a non-heart queen that gives you a straight gives anyone with an ace a bigger straight and anyone with a nine the same straight. Your outs are too tenuous to be pounding the pot.

(39) A $20-$40 game. You are in middle position and limp in with the K♥-T♥ behind two early limpers. The big blind raises. All of you call. There is $170 in the pot and four players. The flop comes: J♠-8♥-3♥, giving you a flush-draw with an overcard. Everyone checks to you. What do you do?

Answer: Bet. You have three opponents who have checked. The board is only mildly coordinated, with a jack and an eight, and the two-flush is in your suit. A bet could win it. If you get called, you have 12 outs to a flush or top pair with two cards to come.

(40) A $20-$40 game. You are in the big blind holding A♥-9♥. The under-the-gun player raises and only the cutoff calls. You call.

There is $130 in the pot and three players. The flop comes down: Q♥-T♥-6♣, giving you the nut flush-draw. What do you do?

Answer: Bet. If the under-the-gun player was raising preflop with jacks or nines or ace-king he may well fold. Regardless, you have the nut flush-draw and an ace overcard with only two opponents, and two cards to come. You have too much hand not to bet.

(41) A $10-$20 game. You limp in from middle position with the K♣-T♣ after an early player limps. The cutoff calls. There is $45 in the pot and four players. The flop comes: A♣-7♣-3♦, giving you the nut flush-draw. The big blind bets and the early player calls. What do you do?

Answer: Call. Raising as a semi-bluff move would not be good. You have no chance of winning the pot outright, since two players are already committed for one bet. Furthermore, you have a common draw, and no desire to chase out the remaining player. A raise would give the big blind a chance to reraise and thin the field. When you are hitting to the nuts, you normally want to leave people in to make a worse hand than yours and give you a nice price on your draw. Note the difference with flopping the nut flushdraw with the king and the nut flushdraw with the ace. The king will never be both an overcard and the nut draw, because there has to be an ace on the board in this latter case. This is another reason we downgrade a suited king as a starting hand.

(42) A $20-$40 game. You are in the small blind with the J♦-T♦. A middle player limps, the button calls, you call, and the big blind raps. Four of you see a flop of 8♦-7♥-3♠. You have two overcards, a gutshot, and a backdoor flush-draw. What do you do?

Answer: Bet. You have only three opponents, none who have shown strength preflop. One of them is the blind. The flop is rainbow, good for your hand type. The flop cards are low enough that your bet has a decent chance of not getting called, and you have a reasonable hand to fall back on of someone plays.

18 – SINGLE-SUITED FLOPS

You are severely handicapped whenever the board flops all of one suit and you do not have a card in that suit. This applies whether you have a pair, two pair, trips, or a straight. You will find that if you play on, you are often fighting against a flush. If not, when another card of that suit appears, you usually have to throw in the towel unless you are a card away from a full house. Overcards are hurting when neither card is in the flush suit, since the chance of drawing dead is very high, especially against a lot of opponents. Top pair, even an overpair, without a card in the flopped suit go way down in value, and should often be mucked. Furthermore, playing on with just a pair can get very expensive if there are several players in the hand who are willing to bet and raise. Open-ended straight draws are typically not playable, even when you do not think anyone has a flush. Two of your outs are killed, and there will usually be a lot of redraws against you when one of your other outs arrive. Two pair is playable, and of course a set, because filling up means you can win a big pot.

Whether to play one of these holdings strongly depends on how the opponents react to aggression. Generally, you should not let the presence of a three-flush on board deter you from betting, but be prepared to pull in your horns if you get a lot of resistance.

Do not think that you can make an opponent throw away a small flush. The player with the lone "ace of trump" (ace of the flush suit) often plays his hand strongly, so the expected reaction of a player with a flush is to stay in the pot to the end and see what your heavy betting is based on.

With this type of flop, the size of the field is extra important. With a small number of opponents, you should try and protect a one-pair hand if you think it may be the boss. Bet and see what happens. You may well get someone to fold a one-card flush-draw at a small card of the "trump suit." But if you run into serious resistance, drop the hot potato before you get burned.

If a fourth suited card appears on the turn and you have a set, you still have ten outs to beat a flush, so the pot odds will almost always mandate seeing the river. With other hands, the normal reaction to a fourth card of the same suit on the board is to give up if someone bets. Of course, you are allowed to bluff. When you have a big card in the flopped suit, especially with something else like a high pair, you can play aggressively, especially against a small field, just as you would with a draw on a different type flop.

If a fourth suited card comes at the river, you may choose either to fold or pay it off. It is perfectly natural for an opponent to seize upon this situation as a bluffing opportunity. You should sometimes run this type of bluff yourself.

If you flop a flush, it should usually be played fast, unless it is the nut flush. You do not want someone with just one big card in the flush suit to draw cheaply. Even with the nut flush, you may choose to play full steam ahead, since the opponents may well think you are fooling around with the lone ace.

A word of warning. In a game where a lot of starting hands are being played, the reason the player chose to enter the pot on trash that you or any decent player would fold is because his two rags were of the same suit. Don't give a dolt too big a reward for flopping a flush with his J-4 suited.

The following hands illustrate some important considerations when the board flops all of one suit.

(1) The game is $20-$40. You are in the big blind with K♣-8♠. Only the cutoff and button limp in. You get a free play. There is $70 in the pot and three players. The flop is: J♣-6♣-2♣, giving you a flush-draw to the lone king. What do you do?

Answer: Bet. This is a small unraised pot, and you have only two opponents. You have the second nut flush-draw. A king may well be an out. This is a good flop to lead at. Frequently, you win the pot outright, especially if neither opponent has a club or a jack. If you get played with, you have many outs, as long as no one has the key ace. Most of the time, you will be going to the river with this hand. (But beware of playing the lone king strongly against a large field.)

(2) A $10-$20 game. You are on the button and are holding the A♠-K♦. An early player and a middle player limp. You raise and only the limpers call. There is $75 in the pot and three players.

The flop is: T♠-8♠-5♠, so you are drawing to the lone ace. The early limper bets and the next player folds. What do you do?

Answer: Raise. You have two big overcards and the nut flush-draw. You are heads-up against one opponent who bet into you. Your opponent might fold, fearful of a flush. He might call, and then check to you on the turn, giving you a free card (you may prefer to bet again rather than checking and giving the show away so early). He might reraise, in which case you would have to decide whether to just call or pop him again. He cannot get too frisky, since you have the ace of the flush suit; he's not holding the nuts. If he doesn't have a flush, but just a pair lower than kings, you have 14 outs with two cards to come, so you are a shade over even money to make a flush or top pair, top kicker by the river.

(3) A $15-$30 game. You are in the big blind and hold A♠-6♠. An early player opens with a raise. A middle player calls, along with the small blind. You call. There is $120 in the pot and four players. The flop is: A♣-7♣-5♣, giving you top pair. The small blind checks. You bet. The preflop raiser pops it. The middle player calls. The small blind folds. What do you do?

Answer: Fold. It would be horrible poker for you to do anything but fold. There is $195 in the pot and it costs you $15 to take off a card, so your pot odds are favorable at about 13-to-1. But you need to respect the betting action, and the fact that the possibility of a completed hand is very real with the board showing all of one suit. Against a made flush, you are drawing dead to two perfect cards. If another club arrives, your hand will be instantly dead unless it is the 6♣. If the raiser happens to have a better ace than yours, you have only three cards to improve (sixes), and one of them is the tainted 6♣. You really only have two viable outs, a 23-to-1 shot, and even this assumes no one already has a flush.

(4) A $10-$20 game. You are in the big blind and have A♥-T♦. Two early players, a middle player, the cutoff, and the small blind all limp, so you get a free play. There is $60 in the pot and six players. The flop is: A♣-7♣-3♣, giving you top pair, fair kicker. The small blind bets. What do you do?

Answer: Fold. With the board flopping all of one suit and you not having even a card in that suit, you could be in serious trouble here. You have top pair, decent kicker, which might be a raising hand under other circumstances. But, in this case, there are too many players and you do not have enough hand. Getting people out who are drawing with a club in their hand is a good play only if you have a strong reason to believe that you have the best hand. But the small blind could easily have an ace with a bigger kicker, two pair, or even something better, since he his leading into a field of five opponents.

(5) A $30-$60 game. You are in the big blind and have the 7♦-6♦. The cutoff opens with a raise, the button calls, the small blind folds, and you call. There is $200 in the pot and three players. The flop is: J♠-5♠-4♠, giving you an open-end straight-draw. You check. The cutoff bets and the button calls. What do you do?

Answer: Fold. There is $260 in the pot and it costs you $30 to pursue your straight-draw. These are pots odds of almost 9-to-1. If you discounted two of your eight outs because they are spades, then you could argue that you have six outs, which is a 7-to-1 shot. So you appear to have even a little bit of an overlay to call. But with two cards to come, any spade will arrive almost a third of the time, and you could be drawing dead. You will lose some serious money on the expensive streets if you hit and a spade arrives to make someone a flush, or in those cases where someone has flopped a flush.

On the actual hand, the turn brought the 8♣. The player bet and got raised. He called with his straight. The river was the A♦ and he check-called, only to be shown the 8♠-7♠ by the cutoff. His call on the flop cost him an extra $210, or seven small bets.

(6) A $20-$40 game. You are in the cutoff seat holding K♣-Q♠ and open with a raise. The button reraises and you call. There is

18 - SINGLE-SUITED FLOPS

$150 in the pot and two players. The flop is: A♣-8♣-3♣, giving you the nut flush-draw to your lone king. What do you do?

Answer: Bet. In these heads-up reraised situations, you need to make a play for the pot. His button reraise preflop could be done on a lot of hands, since he was responding to your possible steal-raise. He might well fold a hand like 7♥-7♦. If he calls or raises, you have the nut flush-draw to fall back on.

(7) A $10-$20 game. You are on the button and hold the A♥-K♠. An early player, a middle player, and the cutoff call. You raise, the small blind folds, and everyone calls. There is $105 in the pot and five players in the hand. The flop is: J♣-T♣-5♣, giving you a gutshot straight-draw with two overcards. The big blind bets and everyone folds to you. What do you do?

Answer: Fold. Your overcards and inside straight draw are a sick joke. With a player leading into a field of four opponents including the preflop raiser, you could be drawing dead, and another club means you have to hit the door anyway.

(8) A $10-$20 game. You are in the big blind and hold Q♠-3♣. Two early players, a middle player, the cutoff, the button, and the small blind limp. You take a free play. There is $70 in the pot and seven players. The flop is: J♠-9♠-2♠, giving you the third nut flush-draw and one overcard. It is checked to a middle player, who bets. Everyone folds to the small blind, who calls. What do you do?

Answer: Fold. Given that six players took the flop with you, what is the likelihood that at least one of them has the A♠ or the K♠, giving them a better flush-draw? If they just played random cards, we would have 47 unseen cards between our hand and the flop, of which 12 are in the opponents' hands. Without going through the math, the probability that neither of these two cards is one of the 12 cards that the opponents all hold is 55 percent. In other words, about half the time, if your opponents just played random cards, someone would rate to have a better flush-draw than you. Couple

131

this with the fact that players don't play random cards. Furthermore, a player that entered the pot in early position and then leads off betting into a big crowd when there is a three-flush on the board does not have a "random hand." This all makes it much more likely that someone has one of these two big cards than otherwise. So your flush-draw could be drawing dead, and you will lose additional money when a fourth spade hits and you lose to a bigger flush. Your queen overcard gives you some additional outs to top pair, but a queen also complements the board, making a straight or two pair more likely.

(9) A $20-$40 game. You are in the big blind and are holding the A♥-A♦. An early player, a middle player, and the small blind limp. You raise and everyone calls. There is $160 in the pot and four players. The flop is: J♥-7♥-3♥, giving you the nut flush-draw with your aces. The small blind checks. You bet. The early player raises. The middle player folds. The small blind calls. What do you do?

Answer: Call, don't reraise. When there is a three-flush with that texture board and you get raised, you should put your opponent on a flush, since it is unlikely he is holding two pair. It looks like you are drawing, and you do not want to eliminate the third player. A raise with a three-flush on board is often made on the lone ace of the flush suit—but you know he doesn't have that hand.

19 - OTHER FLOP PLAY

This chapter includes hands where you flop middle pair, bottom pair, or second pair (a pocket pair that ranks between top and middle pair). Typically, in these situations, you are chasing and playing a "money odds" game. You are balancing the pot odds, both current and implied, against your number of outs to determine whether or not you should play. On the other hand, especially against a small number of opponents in an unraised pot, these can be respectable holdings where you have the best hand. It is important for you to recognize when this is the case, and protect your fragile hand with a bet, not allowing a free card.

This chapter also includes good hands where you flop two pair, a set, or some kind of completed hand like a straight, a flush, or a full house. Many players routinely try for a check-raise or slowplay when they flop a good hand. They think they can get more money in the pot by playing this way, if not on the current round, then on future betting rounds. While this is occasionally the case, what can also happen is that they miss out on collecting an extra round of bets, since most players will call with more hands than they will bet. In addition, by their failure to bet, a free card is given to an opponent who would have folded, sometimes resulting in that opponent staying and going on to win the pot.

The following hands bring out some important considerations in playing these kinds of holdings.

(1) The game is \$20-\$40. You are in middle position with J♥-T♥. An early player limps in. You limp, and so does the cutoff seat and the small blind. There is \$100 in the pot and five players. The flop is: Q♦-T♠-3♣, giving you middle pair. The small blind checks. The big blind bets. The early limper calls. What do you do?

Answer: Fold. Between the bettor, who is leading into a field of four opponents, and the caller, someone probably has a top pair of queens, especially given the rainbow board. Your middle pair is no good. There is \$140 in the pot and it costs you \$20 to take off a card. You are getting 7-to-1 pot odds, but you have five outs at best (with any jack or ten). A five outer is over 8-to-1 against. If someone else has middle pair with a bigger sidecard, then you must hit your kicker, and have only three outs. Also keep in mind that your kicker puts three parts to a straight on the table, which further increases the possibility of the hand you hope to make not holding up, either because it makes a straight for someone, or it creates a straight-draw for a player, who then hits his hand at the river. One might argue that if you catch one of your outs, you can win enough money by collecting some double bets on the turn and river to make calling correct. But this mistakenly assumes that you win all of the time when you hit.

On the actual hand, the player called; the cutoff and small blind folded. A jack came on the turn, giving the player two pair. He was bet into on the turn and he raised. He got reraised to $120 and called. The river was a blank and he made a crying call at the river, only to be shown ace-king by the early limper, who apparently chose not to raise preflop with slick. His mistaken call on the flop eventually cost him $180.

(2) A $10-$20 game. You are in the big blind and are holding the 9♣-7♣. An early player, a middle player, and the small blind limp. You take a free play. There is $40 in the pot and four players. The flop is: A♠-7♦-6♠, giving you a middle pair of sevens. The small blind checks. You check, because with both an ace and a two-flush on board, you are unlikely to win the pot outright by betting into three opponents. The early player bets. The middle player and the small blind call. What do you do?

Answer: Fold. There is $70 in the pot and it costs you $10 to call. You are getting 7-to-1 pot odds to see the turn. From the betting, someone almost certainly has an ace, so you have five outs at best, which is an 8-to-1 shot. The problem is that the 7♠ or the 9♠ may well give someone a flush, so two of your five outs are not clean. A three-outer is a 15-to-1 shot. Furthermore, your kicker is bad, which means that if no one has an ace, then one of your three opponents could be hanging around with the same middle pair of sevens as you have, but with a better kicker.

On the actual hand, one of the players had K♥-7♥, turned two pair, and then lost at the river when a spade arrived. So the big blind was playing with two outs (9♥ or 9♦) on the flop, and would still have many redraws against him at the river even if a red nine came on the turn.

(3) A $30-$60 game. You are in the big blind and are holding the 7♠-5♠. An early player limps and everyone folds to the small blind, who raises. You call from your big blind and the early limper calls. There is $180 in the pot and three players. The flop is: K♠-J♦-7♥, giving you bottom pair and a backdoor flush-draw. The small blind bets. What do you do?

Answer: Fold. You have five outs at best, with any seven or five, which is an 8-to-1 shot. There is $210 in the pot and it costs you $30 to call, which are pot odds of 7-to-1. You have a backdoor spade flush-draw. Some players might rationalize calling. But you have a player behind you yet to act. The board contains both a king and jack, which are two cards in the playing zone. This flop probably helped the small blind unless that person was raising on specifically ace-queen. It may have helped the player behind you, which means the pot could get raised. It would be dreadful to have to pay $60 to take a card off. Furthermore, you will not win all the time even if you catch one of your outs on the turn.

On the actual hand, the player called and got raised. The turn was a spade, so the player called the turn bet as well, going for his spade flush. He folded at the river when the A♥ came.

(4) A $15-$30 game. You limp in under the gun with the A♥-J♠. Two middle players and the cutoff limp. The button folds and the small blind raises. Everyone calls. There is $180 in the pot and six players. The flop is: J♣-J♦-5♣, giving you trip jacks with an ace kicker. The small blind bets and the big blind folds. What do you do?

Answer: Raise. Don't slowplay your trips. With a two-flush on the table, five opponents, and a raised pot, you should play this fast and make your opponents pay through the nose to chase. Protect your money, and save slowplaying for situations when the opponents will lose if they hit, not be beating you out of a big pot.

(5) A $10-$20 game. You are in the big blind holding the 9♠-9♥. A middle player opens with a raise and only the button calls. You call. There is $65 in the pot and three players. The flop comes down: T♣-8♣-6♥, giving you second pair and a gutshot straight-draw. What do you do?

Answer: Bet. This is a good flop for your hand. You have but two opponents. The flop is only ten-high, so maybe the opponents missed. You should bet this flop despite the presence of a preflop raiser, who could have been raising on just two big cards. You do not want to see this flop checked around, thereby giving your opponents a free card. Middle-size pairs cry out for protection because there are so many overcards that could beat them.

(6) A $10-$20 game. You are on the button with the 6♠-6♣. Everyone limps except for three players. You limp as well as the small blind. There is $70 in the pot and seven players. The flop is: 7♠-6♦-3♣, giving you middle set. Four players check to a middle player who bets. The cutoff calls. What do you do?

Answer: Raise. Don't even think about slowplaying or sandbagging with your middle set. There are too many opponents. You cannot afford to have players drawing cheaply with an inside straight-draw or an overpair that might become a bigger set. Get people out, and build a pot with the remaining players.

(7) A $10-$20 game. You are in middle position with the A♣-6♣. An early player and two middle players limp. You limp. The small blind limps. There is $60 in the pot and six players. The flop is: J♥-6♦-3♠, giving you middle pair. Everyone checks to you. What do you do?

Answer: Bet. The board is not threatening. No one is betting, which likely means no one has top pair. You have middle pair with the top kicker, a decent hand under the circumstances. You should bet the flop while your hand is still good. A free card here rates to help one of your many opponents far more than you.

Anything higher than a six which comes off on the turn could easily give someone else a better hand.

(8) A $15-$30 game. You are on the button with the J♠-J♥. A middle player opens with a raise and everyone folds to you. The middle player, who plays aggressively, could be raising light to drive everyone else out and get position over the blinds, so you decide to reraise. You may well be three-betting with the best hand and the best position, and you want to get the blinds out. The blinds fold and your opponent calls. There is $115 in the pot and two players. The flop is: A♠-7♦-3♦, giving you second pair. Your opponent checks. You bet and he raises. What do you do?

Answer: Fold. An ace-high flop will touch many hands that a preflop raiser would raise with, especially one who open-raised from middle position (that is A-K, A-Q, A-J, A-T, and even ace-little suited). If this is the case, you are playing with only two outs, which is a 23-to-1 shot. You have no other draws. The check-raise is a strong move, usually signifying a good ace and maybe something more. A lower consideration is that there is a two-flush on the table, which means that the J♦ may not be a clean out, since it could give your opponent a diamond flush. You will be forced to fold on the turn anyway if your opponent bets, unless a jack comes.

(9) A $30-$60 game. You are on the button with the A♥-5♥. An early player limps and you limp. The small blind limps. There is $120 in the pot and four players. The flop comes: A♠-A♣-T♠, giving you trip aces. Everyone checks to you. What do you do?

Answer: Bet. Don't slowplay. There is both a two-flush and two cards in the playing zone (an ace and a ten) which means there can be gutshot draws out there from anyone who came in on K-Q, Q-J, or K-J. In an aggressive game, players are more likely to lead with a flush-draw even when the board has a high pair, since they can frequently win the pot outright. The lack of flop betting tends to deny the existence of a flush-draw if not too many opponents are in. With players limping in on big cards, gutshot draws are the more likely threat.

(10) A $15-$30 game. You are in the big blind holding K♥-6♥. An early player opens with a raise, a middle player calls, and the small blind calls. You call. There is $120 in the pot and four players. The flop is: T♥-8♣-6♣, giving you bottom pair and a backdoor flush-draw. The small blind checks. You check. The preflop raiser bets; the other two opponents call. What do you do?

Answer: Fold. There is $165 in the pot, so you are getting 11-to-1 to call with your five outer, which is an 8-to-1 shot. There is a two-flush, three cards to a straight, and three opponents. The K♣ could either give someone a club flush or create a flush-draw that beats you at the river. Any seven or nine on the turn could give someone a straight. Bottom line is that your outs are too weak to play on, given the coordinated nature of the board and the number of opponents you have. The implied odds are against you.

(11) A $10-$20 game. You call from early position with A♦-J♥. A middle player and the small blind call. There is $40 in the pot and four players. The flop is: Q♦-J♠-J♣, giving you trip jacks. Both blinds check. What do you do?

Answer: Bet. You should not slowplay your trips. There are two big cards to a straight on the table. You cannot afford to give out free cards to all kinds of open-ended and gutshot straight draws like A-K, A-T, K-T, K-9, or T-9. You might even be giving a free card to someone with a lower pocket pair who could hit their two-outer and fill. Since the third card on the board is large, you will probably get played with. On your good days, one of the blinds is slowplaying trip jacks with a worse kicker.

(12) A $10-$20 game. You are in the small blind with the Q♠-J♥. An early player and two middle players limp. You limp. There is $50 in the pot and five players. The flop is: K♠-Q♥-7♠, giving you middle pair and a backdoor flush-draw. What do you do?

Answer: Check. Betting middle pair into a crowd of four players with this texture flop is a good way to give back some of your hard-earned money. Your bet does not rate to win the pot outright. The flop contains a two-flush and two cards in the playing zone, so it rates to have helped some of your many opponents. Your bet could easily get raised by someone with top pair, since many of the hands that players limp in with contain a king. There figures to be some good draws out there as well. Someone could put down heat, so even if you do have the best hand, your frail holding will have to be mucked. Another problem is that your jack kicker complements the board. So you if you turn two pair, that also puts three parts to a straight on the table (king-queen-jack), making you a big dog to hands that hit like king-jack, ace-ten, or ten-nine.

(13) A \$10-\$20 game. You limp in with A♦-T♦ from early position behind another limper. Everyone folds. There is \$35 in the pot and three players. The flop is: J♠-T♥-2♠, giving you middle pair. The big blind bets; the limper calls. What do you do?

Answer: Fold. Middle pair, top kicker really isn't playable here. First, there is no serious money in the pot. It costs you \$10 to call with only \$55 in the pot. If the big blind is betting top pair or the limper is calling with top pair, you have five outs at best, which is an 8-to-1 shot, and you will not win all the time when you hit. Second, an ace would complete a possible straight if one of your opponents is playing with king-queen. Third, the two-flush on the table hurts you.

(14) A \$10-\$20 game. You are on the button holding the Q♥-T♥. Two early players and a middle player limp. You limp, as well as the small blind. There is \$60 in the pot and six players. The flop is: A♥-Q♣-7♠, giving you middle pair and a backdoor flush-draw. Everyone checks to the middle limper, who bets. What do you do?

Answer: Fold. Your pot odds are 7-to-1. A five outer is an 8-to-1 shot. You do have a backdoor heart flush working. Nevertheless, there is an ace on board, and with all those players, aces-up is a possibility. A ten coming would put three cards in a straight zone (A-Q-T). You need a real overlay on the pot odds to call here.

(15) A $15-$30 game. You are in the big blind holding the 6♥-5♥. An early player limps and a middle player raises. Another middle player calls. You call, as well as the early limper. There is $130 in the pot and four players. The flop is: K♥-5♠-2♣, giving you middle pair and a backdoor flush-draw. What do you do?

Answer: Bet. A flop of king-rag-rag is an excellent flop to bluff into, since you are representing a pair of kings. It is not so likely that someone without a king will hang around, as there is no draw on the board. You may win the pot outright by betting.

(16) A $15-$30 game. You are in the small blind with the Q♠-J♠. Only an early player and the button limp. You limp. There is $60 in the pot and four players. The flop comes: K♠-J♣-8♥, giving you middle pair and a backdoor flush-draw. What do you do?

Answer: Check. You should not lead with queen-jack into three opponents with a board of K-J-8. The board is too cluttered with cards close in rank, and you will seldom win the pot outright. Furthermore, your kicker is tainted; if you hit your second pair, this puts K-Q-J on the table, which can give someone a straight.

(17) A $20-$40 game. You limp in from middle position with the Q♥-J♦ behind an early limper. The cutoff also limps. There is $90 in the pot and four players. The flop comes: K♣-Q♣-7♠, so you have middle pair. The big blind and the early limper check. You bet. The cutoff calls. The big blind raises. The early limper calls. What do you do?

Answer: Fold. You are frequently up against kings-up, and you don't have enough outs to continue, especially with the two-flush on board. The J♣ could easily give someone a flush, given a cold-caller and a third opponent hanging around. If the big blind is check-raising with king-queen, you are drawing dead to two running cards like J-J, A-T, or T-9.

(18) A $20-$40 game. You open limp from middle position with the J♠-T♥. Only the button calls. There is $70 in the pot and three players. The flop is: K♣-T♦-7♠, giving you middle pair. The big blind bets. What do you do?

Answer: Fold. It is costing you $20 to call with only $90 in the pot. The pot odds are terrible for trying to improve, since a five outer is an 8-to-1 shot. The big blind probably has a king. A ten with a better kicker also beats you. There is another player yet to act. While it is possible you have the best hand, you should fold. If you called and did not improve, you would have to fold on the turn anyway if the player bets again. The pot is not large enough to get involved. On the actual hand, the big blind won the pot with ace-ten, so the player had only three outs, not five.

(19) A $10-$20 game. You are in the small blind with the Q♠-9♠. Everyone calls except three people who fold. You call. There is $70 in the pot and seven players. The flop is: Q♥-Q♦-9♥, giving you a full house. What do you do?

Answer: Bet. Although it is tempting to slowplay or sandbag, having flopped the nuts against a large field like this, it is better to come out betting with this particular board. There is both a flush-draw and a straight-draw on the flop. With this many players, there is a good chance several of them will at least call, which gets more money in the pot when you win it. They will put you on trips for betting a paired flop into a large field—but they can hit to beat that hand. There is no point in having it checked around and miss collecting all those extra bets. Some aggressive player might even raise your bet on a draw, not realizing that he is drawing dead.

(20) A $30-$60 game. You are in middle position with the 4♥-4♦ and limp behind three other players. The cutoff and small blind limp. There is $210 in the pot and seven players. The flop comes: 9♥-6♣-5♦, leaving you with an underpair. Everyone checks to you. What do you do?

141

Answer: Check. Five people checking to you with one opponent yet to act is far different than having only one opponent to start with. The player in question bet because he reasoned that no one had a nine and he could get someone with six or a five to fold, giving him the best hand and perhaps even winning the pot outright. But with many opponents and three cards to a straight on the board, his chances of winning the pot outright are poor.

(21) A $30-$60 game. Two early players limp, and you raise from middle position having the Q♠-Q♣. The big blind and the limpers call. There is $260 in the pot and four players. The flop comes: K♥-J♠-3♠, so you have second pair and a backdoor flush-draw. The big blind and the first limper check. The next limper bets. What do you do?

Answer: Fold. With three opponents, a player leading into you, and a king-high flop, you are probably playing two outs. You may be up against a draw, but unless a queen, a spade, or a ten arrives on the turn, you will be forced to fold anyway if the turn gets bet. Because you are getting almost 10-to-1 pot odds to call and there are 15 cards which allow you to keep playing, a case might be made that you should call. The problem is that 13 of these cards just give you a draw, and you have to pay more money to continue. Some might argue that raising would be good, since maybe you can drive out the other players and get it heads-up with the bettor. Now you may get a free card. But if you are only playing with two outs and some backdoor possibilities, a free card is not worth investing $60.

(22) A $30-$60 game. You are in the small blind with the K♣-Q♠. An early player and a middle player limp. The button raises. You call. The big blind folds. The other two players call. There is $270 in the pot and four players. The flop is: K♠-K♦-T♠, giving you trips and a backdoor flush-draw. What do you do?

Answer: Bet. With a two-flush, an open pair, two cards in a straight zone, and a preflop raiser, you will get played with. It would be silly for you to check in this raised pot with three other players and have it checked around. You are simply handing out free cards to all the possible flush and straight draws.

(23) A $30-$60 game. After a middle player calls, you call from the cutoff seat, having the 7♣-7♥. There is $110 in the pot and three players. The flop is: 9♥-7♠-3♥, giving you middle set and a backdoor flush-draw. Both opponents check. What do you do?

Answer: Bet. You should bet your hand, since there is both a two-flush on the table and three cards loosely connected, making various gutshots and other straight draws possible. If a heart, an eight, a four, and perhaps other cards show up on the turn and the turn gets bet, any raises you make will be made with no idea whether your opponent is chasing you with hardly any outs or whether you are chasing your opponent with ten outs. Suppose you check it down and a heart shows up on the turn. What do you do if one opponent bets and the other calls? Will you raise or just call? You would like to raise if you knew you had the best hand, but how can you tell? But suppose you bet the flop and get called in two spots. Now when a heart comes off on the turn and you are bet into, you can call, knowing that a raise would probably not be right, since you may well be up against a flush and get reraised.

(24) A $30-$60 game. You are in the small blind with the Q♥-Q♣. Two middle players and the button limp. You raise and everyone calls. There is $300 in the pot and five players. The flop comes: A♣-T♣-7♠, giving you second pair and a backdoor flush-draw. What do you do?

Answer: Check. This is a terrible flop for your hand, since it is with an overcard, and also highly coordinated. Among four other players, someone will normally have an ace. There is also a two-flush on board. You do not figure to win the pot outright by betting, and you will frequently get raised and have to fold anyway. You should check, and fold if the flop gets bet. Sometimes a guy with a weak ace might not bet, fearing a check-raise, and you might get a free card, but this is unlikely.

(25) A $20-$40 game. You get a free play in your big blind with the 6♠-4♥ after an early player, a middle player, and the small blind limp. There is $80 in the pot and four players. The flop is: 5♦-4♦-2♣, giving you middle pair and a gutshot straight-draw. The small blind checks. What do you do?

Answer: Bet. With all little cards on the board, there is a decent chance your hand is best, so you should bet. Big cards are in the playing zone for those who select hands to enter, so this board may be said to be in the blind's zone! It is a small, unraised pot with no one showing any strength. You may win the pot outright, may have the best hand, and have outs if you run into trouble.

(26) A $20-$40 game. The game is temporarily shorthanded with only six players. You open with a raise under-the-gun having the A♦-J♥. Only an early player and a middle player call. There is $150 in the pot and three players. The flop is: Q♦-9♣-7♠, leaving you with just an ace overcard. What do you do?

Answer: Check. Normally, you should bet in these shorthanded, raised pots when you were the preflop raiser. But this hand is an exception; the board has cards that are too high and close in rank for you to be betting. The likelihood of winning the pot outright even against only a couple of opponents is too small, and you have no hand to fall back on if you get called.

(27) A $10-$20 game. The cutoff opens with a raise and you are on the button with the A♦-Q♦. You reraise. Both blinds and the cutoff call. There is $120 in the pot and four players. The flop is: K♠-8♥-3♦, leaving you with an ace overcard and a backdoor nut flush-draw. Both blinds check; the cutoff bets. What do you do?

Answer: Fold. You have nothing. You are being bet into by the player on your right, which means one of the blinds could raise after you call, costing you even more money to stay. If someone in the blind flops a biggie, they often check, going for a check-raise of the preflop raiser.

(28) A $20-$40 game. You are in the cutoff with the J♥-J♦. A middle player opens with a raise and you call. The small blind reraises and the middle player and you both call. There is $200 in the pot and three players. The flop comes down: K♦-K♣-Q♠. Both opponents check. What do you do?

Answer: Check. Normally it is right to bet in shorthanded pots after your opponents check to you, since you can so often pick up the pot right then. But you should be very suspicious of a person who three-bet preflop and then checks a board like this. This flop should have helped a small blind who reraises out of position. More often than not, you are facing trip kings or a full house.

(29) A $20-$40 game. A loose player opens with a raise from early position, and you call from middle position with the 9♠-9♥. The big blind calls. There is $130 in the pot and three players. The flop is: K♥-T♣-7♦, leaving you with your pair of nines and two overcards on the table. Both opponents check. What do you do?

Answer: Check. Normally, it is good poker to bet the flop against a small number of opponents who check to you when you have a decent pair or some piece of the board. However, this hand is an exception. There are two overcards to your pair on the table. Furthermore, the cards are connected, meaning that it is less likely that you will win the pot outright by betting, since the likelihood of some straight-draws being out there are higher than normal. The other complicating factor is the preflop raiser who checked. Though he is a loose player, he may have decided to check A-A, AK, K-Q, K-J, or K-T, planning to check-raise.

(30) A $10-$20 game. You raise from middle position with the Q♠-Q♦ after two players limp in. The button, the big blind, and the two limpers call. There is $105 in the pot and five players. The flop is: K♣-9♣-5♠, giving you second pair. It is checked to you. What do you do?

Answer: Check. Betting after four players have checked would make more sense with your good second pair if you had not raised preflop. But the fact that you were the preflop raiser means that your opponents could be just "checking to the raiser," so a king is not denied. With four opponents, a two-flush, and a king-high flop with another card in hailing distance, you should check.

(31) A $20-$40 game. You limp behind two early limpers with the A♣-9♣. The small blind limps. There is $100 in the pot and five players. The flop is: K♦-9♦-3♥, giving you middle pair. It is checked to one of the early players, who bets. What do you do?

Answer: Fold. A player who bets into a crowd of four other players should be given credit for a better hand than yours. A king-high flop could easily touch many hands that players limp in with. The two-flush is also a problem. The A♦ may not be an out, or could set up redraws at the river.

(32) A $15-$30 game. You are in middle position with the 7♦-7♣. An early player limps and another middle player limps. The middle player is very loose and aggressive. You have noticed that he frequently bets with nothing and likes to bluff a lot. You limp. There is $70 in the pot and four players. The flop is: J♦-6♣-3♥, giving you second pair. The big blind and the early player check. The middle player bets. What do you do?

Answer: Raise. You should raise here because: 1) you may have the best hand, based on what you have observed about the bettor, 2) you could win the pot outright against three opponents, two of whom have checked, 3) there is no flush-draw on the flop and no real hand for you to be drawing at, which means your opponent is more likely to put you on a good hand and fold, 4) you can eliminate players by confronting them with a double bet, 5) you may get free cards to the river if you choose, since you have position over the bettor, and 6) you can get super-lucky and catch another seven. On the actual hand, the player raised and only the bettor called. The turn was the 4♦, giving the player a gutshot straight-draw to go with the sevens. His opponent checked. He bet and his opponent folded.

20 – INTRODUCTION TO TURN PLAY

Turn betting is a very complicated subject, and how you handle it has a lot to do with whether you are a winning or a losing holdem player. Honing your judgment in this area will improve your results dramatically.

We cannot discuss proper strategy on the turn without knowing the exact betting structure. Most limit holdem games use a two-tiered structure, with a lower limit before and on the flop and an upper limit that is twice the lower on the turn and river betting rounds. But other structures may be employed. For example, sometimes a single limit is used on all the betting rounds. We see that structure mainly when local or state government has restricted the stakes to a certain size, as any true poker player would prefer to have the amount you can bet increase as the pot grows. When the limit imposed by law is lower than the players would like, they may resort to this artificial structure because it allows the legal limit to be bet on every round, so they can gamble as high as the law allows.

In any structure, someone with a big hand tends to show his true colors at the earliest point in the hand where the limit has reached the maximum. In a single-limit structure, this person will normally play his hand strongly on the flop. With an outsize bet on the end structure, he may well try to conceal his strength until the river, when he can cause the maximum pain. In this section, we will only be talking about the standard two-tiered structure, such as $20 before and on the flop and $40 on the turn and river. Here, the turn will normally be the betting round revealing the truth.

In the standard structure, the betting round after the flop is "the phony betting round." People often use the cheap street to misdescribe their hand, trying to gain an advantage later on. This can be either acting tough when they don't have much or playing possum for a betting round with a strong holding. For example, a player with a modest-size drawing hand like an ordinary flush-draw might raise on the flop, figuring a free card can be taken on the turn if his ship does not come in. On the other hand, those with a strong holding often just call instead of raising, hoping that the bettor will fire again and they can extract the maximum by popping it at the higher limit. You have to attach a certain degree of importance to how a person has played on the flop, but you are dealing with people who often have the credibility of the proverbial used-car seller.

The turn betting round normally reveals the real situation. The barkers fail to bite, and the baggers spring to life. There is an old poker adage that says when a person takes action inconsistent with his previous betting, the action taken later in the hand is more likely to be the one reflecting that person's true colors. This adage applies particularly well to the turn betting round. Anybody who says to himself, "I think that if he really had a good hand, he would have been more aggressive on the flop, and not taken such a chance allowing a cheap card" is probably using incorrect reasoning. Often, it would have been superior poker for the person to play his hand strongly on the flop and not risk being beaten—this may well be the way you would have played a strong hand in that particular spot—but a lot of people habitually slowplay their good hands on the flop. If you pay one of these dudes off on the turn and river because he didn't show any strength on the flop, you are simply rewarding him for his bad playing. When you make an idiot look like a genius, that makes you the real idiot!

Proper play on the turn generally calls for aggressiveness. Follow-through is important in betting, and the turn betting round at holdem is the point where using follow-through is of most importance. Many players will fold when the limit doubles.

A number of players freeze up on the turn. A certain mindset comes over them once they get to the expensive street where prices double. It is almost like they are thinking, "Since my opponent has stayed with me this far and my mediocre hand could easily be beaten, I guess it is time to back off." But failure to follow through with a turn bet can be an expensive mistake when your opponent has done nothing but respond to your play. You can be giving a free card to an opponent who would have folded, but who now gets to see a river card that gives him the best hand. You can be put on the defensive by inducing a bet through showing weakness, then having to guess whether the opponent bet because you checked or because he has something that he thinks is good.

You might have to face a bet on the end instead of having the opponent check.

Here is the biggest reason why aggressive turn play is even more critical than in most other holdem situations. The fact that the limit is now twice that on the previous round means that many marginal flop callers are going to abandon ship. People will call on the flop, especially in a raised pot, on some really raggedy stuff. They are trying to get lucky at the cheap price, and often release their dish-rag when the limit doubles—if you bet again. So when you have been the bettor on the flop, it usually pays to fire another barrel. This applies when you have a solid hand like top pair or an overpair, and also if your bet was based on a draw or a speculative holding, if no one popped you on the flop.

You may be the preflop raiser with hands such as A-K or A-Q and fail to buy help on the flop. But because there are only one or two opponents, you attempt to purchase the pot with a flop bet. If someone calls and an innocent card comes on the turn, it is usually right to fire again and hope the double-size bet induces a fold. Of course, a bit depends on who called you. We are assuming you are up against the typical gambler, and not a rock or calling station.

Unfortunately, with most of your hands, there are a lot of possible board-cards on the turn that are not helpers for your hand, or blanks to hold the enemy at bay. You cannot take your foot off the gas pedal every time the turn-card could help someone. That would be wimpy poker that would often cause you to lose the initiative unnecessarily. So when an unpleasant turn-card arrives, you must ask yourself the question, "How bad is bad?"

Deciding whether to bet again on the turn requires the input of several factors. What is your position? How many opponents do you have? How many ways could that card help an opponent's hand? These and other questions need to be answered for you to make an intelligent estimate of the situation.

First, what is your position? Acting first means that a check reveals your weakness. A probable reaction to your blinking is a bet by the opponent. What usually happens when you have to act first is if you bet, he calls, and if you check, he bets. So if you call his bet, the fee for staying in may be the same amount as if you had bet yourself.

Of course, checking and calling deprives you of any chance to win the pot on that betting round. That is why good players tend to be aggressive optimists; a bet gives the chance for instant victory.

If you are last and check, at least you can stay for nothing. However, the fact that the enemy has checked reduces the chance that someone drew out on you. Also, a check in the passout seat is an almost sure sign of weakness (a check up front might be a trap). The opponents may be emboldened by your weak check, either betting on the end with a modest hand for value or running a bluff.

Many times, you bet on the turn to place yourself well on the last betting round, trying to get a free showdown. The free showdown on a marginal hand when you have position on an opponent is an important concept in understanding turn betting.

There will be many times when you have a little something, but it is not as good as the hand you are representing. (A bet on the turn can be thought of as representing top pair or an overpair, even though it is often made on a much lesser hand.) You would like to give the opponent a chance to fold. If he calls your turn bet, you are worried that he has you beat, and do not want to invest any more money. In such situations, your intention is that if he has shown some strength by a call on the expensive street, the pot is big enough already, and will turn your hand up if he checks the river. This is the "free showdown."

When acting last, betting on the turn can still be the same price to see the hand through, just like it usually was when you were acting first. Most of the time, if you bet the turn and get called, the opponent will check again at the river. Then you can turn your hand over and see if it is any good. The total investment for the last two betting rounds is one bet. The alternative, checking it back on fourth and calling your opponent's river bet, is the same amount of one bet. So the cost is one big bet either way, whether you bet or check, assuming you call at the river after having shown weakness that might have induced the aggression. The advantage of using that bet to get the opponent out, as opposed to just calling with it, is obvious.

Here is a common situation where you can use this technique of betting to get a free showdown. First, you have A-K, raise the pot preflop, get called, and bet the flop. Someone calls, and you do not know whether he has a draw, modest holding, solid hand, or monster. On the turn comes a blank and he checks again. Do not consider an A-K to be nothing, because it beats a busted draw, and you do not want to bluff on the end because you have a little something. So bet the turn, and when the opponent (you hope) checks the river, turn your hand over and see who wins. Do not bluff, because an opponent with a pair will call you, hoping you have exactly the hand you hold. You can have a pair that is less than top pair and use this same technique. Perhaps you have middle pair or second pair. Grit your teeth and bet the turn, if you have only one or two opponents.

What if you bet one of these marginal holdings and someone raises? This does not mean you should have checked. Since a check-raise on the turn shows a strong hand, you can usually fold with a clear conscience. You lose the same bet that you would have lost by checking on the turn and making a crying call at the river. (Surely, you would not check the turn and show weakness, then throw away your hand on the end after possibly inducing a bluff, would you?) Getting check-raised on this type of hand is not so big a disaster, because there are so few pots that you would have won by checking and drawing out with the free card. The impression that you have made a mistake by betting is an illusion.

Just as you use a bet on the turn to get a free showdown, you can also use a raise on the turn to get a free showdown! This is a valuable tool in varying your play. If you use the high standards that we recommend for starting hands, and play with the same group of people on a regular basis, it is inevitable that you will acquire a tight image. The raise on the turn to get a free showdown lets the opposition know that you do not always have a big hand when you make what looks like a power play. After seeing you throw in a raise on the turn with just top pair and a fairish kicker, they will not know what to expect the next time you pop them.

Betting the turn as a bluff comes into the picture when a scare-card shows up like an ace. The card can look just as horrifying to your opponent as to you, especially if you have been betting all the way. Perhaps you were the preflop raiser and little cards came on the flop. Now the hope that you were bulldozing the pot on two big cards like A-K or A-Q just evaporated. You will frequently pick up the pot by betting the ace whether or not you have improved with it.

When you bet the flop in late position and one or more players check to you, it is tempting to simply check yourself when holding a draw or tenuous holding. With a draw, you must evaluate the chance of winning the pot by betting again. Against only one opponent, it is usually a sound play to try and get him out. He may have something that cannot stand any heat. It also means that if you are both drawing, you get to bluff him at the river, rather than the other way around. The problem with not following through with a bet is that you set yourself up to get bet into at the river. By failing to bet, you tell your opponent you are weak and worried. This invites him to put you on a guess by betting the river.

Second, how many opponents do you have? When a bad card comes, the more opponents you have, the more likely someone helped. The degree of danger rises dramatically when you have two opponents instead of one, or three instead of two. Putting another opponent into a poker situation where you will either bet or check often changes your decision to the more passive action.

Against only one opponent, it is hard to find an excuse to check. All you have to do is get him out and you win. The key word is aggression. Your opponent does not rate to hold a good hand, and if you can get him to fold, you win the pot. Most of the time, you bet. Heads-up, the nature of your hand is not as critical to how you play. With a weak hand, you bet and try to steal the pot. With a mediocre hand, you bet to see if the opponent has anything. If you are lucky enough to pick up a good hand, you bet because you want to either make some money or induce surrender. Notice how checking fails to help you accomplish your goals.

The main reasons you check every once in a while in heads-up situations is to avoid being too predictable, or because the early betting has marked your opponent with a good hand. Once in a while, you check-raise, and once in a while you check and fold.

Against two opponents, you need to be more circumspect. You are not trying to win a place pool, so removing one player does not have the same reward as when you were heads-up.

Against three or more opponents, you usually check a marginal holding, since it is not likely that all of them will surrender, and the chance of running into a good hand has increased dramatically.

Third, just how bad is that ugly turn-card? Not all threats to your hand are equal. We have to look at the likelihood of an opponent having the right hand to capitalize on the situation, and how many different types of hands could have been helped.

Let us suppose you have two red queens, and receive a flop of J♣-9♣-3♥. You have an overpair, and of course a hand worth betting on the flop. Here are a few cards that could come; we want to analyze how severe the threat is to your hand.

The ace of diamonds is an overcard, obviously bad for you. But at least it can be used only to make a pair of aces. Worse is the ace of clubs, the suit of the two-flush. A flush-card is always annoying when you don't have any of that suit; you know a lot of hands get played simply because they are suited. The worst card in the deck is the club king, which is an overcard that can also make either the flush or complete an open-end straight-draw. Some poker players like to call a triple-threat card like that club king the "death card."

There are some other considerations involved in deciding whether to bet the turn. Especially with only one or two opponents, who they are and their style of play makes a difference. Does your opponent have some tricky moves, where a check might be a prelude to a check-raise? Is he aggressive enough to raise you on the turn when a scarecard comes? How well does he know your style of play? So in trying to analyze the situation, we will assume you are faced with rather ordinary players.

Let's take this situation of your having two red queens and the given flop of J♣-9♣-3♥ and ask this question for each of the cards that we talked about arriving on the turn. How many opponents would you need to have in order to prefer a check to a bet, if you were first to act? We think there would be a variance of opinion if you asked a group of top players to form a panel and provide answers, but here is our take on this.

The A♦: Against one player, it is ridiculous to let an overcard stop you from betting. We also prefer to fire into two opponents. But at some point, you have to say there is too large a field for you to bet. That point could be either three or four opponents.

The A♣: It can't be right to check with only one opponent. With two opponents you should be very nervous, and with three of them, definitely done with it.

The K♣: Even with the death-card, you still grit your teeth and bet into only one opponent. With the junk some people call you on, check and fold is too wimpy. There are a number of hands the person can have and not help, such as top, middle, or bottom pair (without a king for a kicker). However, we do not have enough guts to stomach a bet into multiple opponents.

It is not our purpose to present you with a table to be memorized. Rather, it is simply to show you how to go about analyzing the strength of a bad card against your hand. You must look at the number of opponents and the various ways they could have been helped by the turn-card. We also see that against one opponent, whenever the board changes status, you have to pretend to say, "That's me," and bet again. If the death-card for your hand didn't help your lone opponent, he will also be scared of it, and you'll probably win the pot.

All that about aggressive play being stated, there are times when you should just check on the turn. Sometimes, when a blank comes on the turn, you check in late position on a draw to get a free card, when you have multiple opponents. When the turn-card cripples your hand, the foot may need to come off the gas pedal. Against two or more people, we cannot blame a player who dogs it with top pair after an overcard that also makes a possible straight or flush comes, or a player on a straight-draw loses enthusiasm when the flush arrives. So do not take your action on auto-pilot; use your head.

If you are betting on the turn with a decent but not spectacular hand and someone raises, you are facing a tough situation. Most of the time, you have been served notice that one pair is not the best hand. It seems that when you call and try to draw out, you also wind up calling on the end, because it is only one more bet. You want to make sure the player really has you beat. Frankly, there is also a masochistic tendency to want to "See how they did it to me one more time." Chances are excellent that you will be viewing a hand that beats you, and one that had no business being played, to boot. This may not help you play your best poker afterwards.

It is hard to simply counsel you to fold whenever someone pops you on the turn. You are probably holding the hand you hoped to build—top pair or an overpair. So if you automatically give up every time you're raised, you will be folding too many winners, and asking to be used as a doormat. Whether you fold will depend on the precise situation and who the opponent is. But here are a few guidelines on whether to call or fold.

If you are heads-up, then against anyone other than a pure rock, you should likely pay the raiser off. There are a lot of power plays put on people in this situation because the opponent knows that if you fold, he wins. He might make a play hoping you have inadequate values, and you are actually holding a decent hand.

Things are different in a multihanded pot. There are fewer funky moves, because the player has to get through two or more people to make his play work. Particularly, if the others in the pot besides you are already in for one bet, the raiser is very likely to have exactly what he is representing, as at limit play a raise in this spot is not likely to clear out the entire field. This is a good place to give it up, especially if the player could have a straight or a flush against your one pair, putting him out of reach.

You not only pay a lot of attention to how many opponents are in the pot with you at decision time, but also how many were dealt in initially. For example, it is more likely that you are up against a top-quality hand like a set if there were ten people who got dealt in than if only seven people got dealt in, because the odds on someone having started with a pocket pair go up with the greater number of at-bats. Also, the tempo of the game is usually more aggressive with fewer people involved at the start. We will be visiting this concept again when we discuss shorthanded play in Chapter 38.

It is a lot more likely that an opponent who acts strong on the turn betting round has a big hand if you have been showing nothing but strength. When an unpleasant board-card comes, you always have to ask yourself just how odious it is. The number of opponents is often a critical factor, as a card that is bad for your hand increases in danger as the number of opponents goes up. When to continue betting and when to back off is an enormously complicated subject. But in general, tend toward betting, as if you show strength and get raised, you are probably beaten. If you check, it is less comfortable throwing in the towel, as the opponent might be betting simply because you showed weakness.

Holdem players sometimes sandbag with a strong hand by just calling on the flop, planning to raise when the limit goes up. But after you have bet the flop and been called, there isn't any way to be sure what's going on except to bet again. Chances are the enemy does not have anything of great value, because the odds favor having an ordinary or shaky holding, rather than a big hand. First, a big hand is harder to hit. Second, if a big hand is flopped, the person might decide to pull the trigger on the flop rather than the turn. So grit your teeth, bet again, and see what you are up against. If you do get popped, you will feel a lot more comfortable folding now than if you had shown weakness by checking and someone bet. A larcenous opponent finds it much easier betting when you have checked than raising when you have bet. There is a lot of bullying in poker, but bullies prefer to pick on the weak. Putting up a strong-looking front is essential to poker success.

When you are raised on the turn, chances are you are in trouble. Either the raiser was slowplaying on the flop with a strong hand, or improved on the turn-card. Either way, the raiser normally has a hand that can beat top pair or an overpair. If you were betting one of these kinds of hands, you may not have enough outs to continue, given the pot size and the cost of calling the raise. Of course, encountering a bluff is always possible. In deciding how much to trust that the raiser has a big hand, pay a lot of attention to the number of opponents. A solitary opponent is going to try a move on you a lot more than someone who is one of several flop callers. Your decision should take into account: (1) the number of opponents (2) your knowledge of the raiser (3) the texture of the board (4) the previous betting action.

When you are drawing, a draw like an open-ended straight draw or a flush-draw remains profitable because you have sufficient outs to merit continuing. Other drawing hands like gutshot straight draws, middle pair, or bottom pair should frequently be folded at this point. You normally do not have enough outs to continue, given the size of the pot and the fact that it is now costing you a double bet.

20 - INTRODUCTION TO TURN PLAY

If you bet or raise with a draw on the flop, and have position, the opponents may check to you on the turn. This gives you a choice between taking a free card or continuing the charade. Against only one opponent, the chance of winning the pot usually outweighs the opportunity for a freebie. With multiple opponents, taking the free card may be the prudent course of action.

Sometimes the betting heats up on the turn, and you have to face a bet and raise. If you are drawing, cold-calling a bet and raise even on a flush-draw or straight draw can often be a mistake. The pot odds may not be there to justify paying two big bets to see the river. Furthermore, the pot may get raised again, or between the bettor and the raiser the hand you are hoping to make may already be beat, which makes cold-calling a disastrous mistake. Particularly dangerous are situations where two different hands can have the nuts, as when a straight is the boss hand. The betting may well get capped before you get to see the river card.

Slow-playing and check-raising attempts on the turn can frequently backfire, resulting in you failing to collect some double-sized bets when you have the best hand and/or giving a free river card to an opponent who would have folded but ends up beating you. If you have something really good, leading with a bet may produce a desirable three-bet situation, since the modern player does not need the nuts to raise, and sometimes pops it after picking up an added drawing possibility.

The concept of not betting because a worse hand will fold and only a better hand will call applies at the river, not on the turn. Having the opponent fold at limit poker when there is another card to come is seldom a poor result. And a bet has value even if you get called. Do not be afraid to bet a hand, even one that will be a likely loser if someone calls. There is another card to come, and another betting round.

Summing up, the turn betting round acquires its character by the betting limit doubling. This doubling frequently reveals the truth about who has the best hand. It encourages betting. Bet to find out what is really going on, to get the weak hands out, to provide a chance to win the pot without a showdown, and to be placed well for the final betting round. All the top holdem players have a strong arm on the turn.

21 – TURN BETTING

This next group of hands illustrate some situations where you decide to bet or check on the turn. In many cases, the key is to follow through with a bet on the turn when you have a decent holding and your opponent or opponents have been just reacting to you. The texture of the board, the number of opponents, your position, and the previous betting actions are the main considerations that come into play.

(1) A $20-$40 game. You are on the button with the T♣-8♣. Two early players limp. You limp, and the small blind calls. There is $100 in the pot and five players. The flop comes: K♥-8♦-6♠, giving you middle pair. All four opponents check, and you bet. Both blinds fold and the two limpers call. There is $160 in the pot and three players. The turn is the 6♥. Both opponents check. What do you do?

Answer: Bet. Your hand is fragile and must be protected. If you get raised you can abandon ship, but you must bet and give your opponents a chance to fold, since any card that comes off on the river higher than an eight (other than a ten giving you two pair) may be bad news. You might even get someone who has an eight with a better kicker to fold, since you will have represented a top pair of kings at this point if you bet. You can also get a free showdown at the river by betting, and are less likely to be bluffed out at the river if another overcard to your eights shows up.

On the actual hand, the player checked. An ace came off at the river and was bet by the first limper. The second limper folded and the player made a crying call, only to lose to A♠-J♦. This is an example of the horrendous hands some people will call a flop bet with, especially if the bettor is the last person to act on the flop.

(2) A $30-$60 game. You are in the small blind with $20 posted in this structure, holding the J♣-9♣. An early player limps and a middle player raises. It is folded to you and you call the raise for another $40. The big blind and early limper call. There is $240 in the pot and four players. The flop comes: 5♣-3♣-2♠, giving you a flush-draw with two overcards. You bet. The big blind and the early limper fold. The preflop raiser raises. You call. There is $360 in the pot and two players. The turn is the A♠. What do you do?

Answer: Check with the intention of check-raising. If he checks it back, then you have been given a free card. This is a good scare-card if your opponent does not have an ace and was raising on a big overpair. You might get him to fold if you raise when he bets. Furthermore, since you were in the small blind, you possibly could have called the preflop raise with a four in your hand, now giving you a wheel. If he calls your check-raise semi-bluff, then you still have outs with your flush-draw.

On the actual hand, the small blind checked and the preflop raiser bet $60. The small blind now raised to $120. The preflop raiser thought for awhile and reluctantly folded.

(3) $10-$20 game. You open-raise from middle position with the 9♥-9♦. The button and both blinds call. There is $80 in the pot and four players. The flop is: Q♦-8♥-5♠, giving you second pair. Both blinds check. You bet and only the big blind calls. There is $100 in the pot and two players. The turn is the A♦. Your opponent checks. What do you do?

Answer: Bet. It is hard to tell where you stand, but there is a good chance your opponent fears the ace more than you do, since you raised preflop. A preflop raiser should normally bet into one opponent who checks after an ace comes. If he check-raises, then you can fold.

(4) A $10-$20 game. You are in the big blind holding the J♣-8♥. An early player, a middle player, and the small blind call. You get a free play in your big blind. There is $40 in the pot and four players. The flop is: J♠-8♠-3♦, giving you top two pair. The small blind checks. You bet. The early player and the middle player call. The small blind folds. There is now $70 in the pot and three players left. The turn is the J♦, making you the big full house. What do you do?

Answer: Bet. With the flush-draw on the table, you will get callers. You might even get raised by the case jack. Getting a free play in your big blind means you could have anything, including two pair without a jack. If both opponents call and a spade comes at the river, you could go for a check-raise. If only one opponent calls and a spade comes at the river, you should bet, because you can't be sure he was on a flush-draw.

(5) A $15-$30 game. You are in the small blind with the A♣-Q♣. Five players limp including the cutoff and the button. You raise and everyone calls. There is $210 in the pot and seven players. The flop is: A♥-K♦-9♠, giving you top pair. You bet and the cutoff and the button call. There is $255 in the pot and three players. The turn is the K♥. What do you do?

Answer: Bet. With all those players taking a flop, and now two callers, you may be up against trip kings, but you must bet in case you aren't. You need to protect your hand with a bet, having a large pot out there and a small number of opponents. If you check, you are inviting one of your two opponents to step in and bet on the expensive street, thereby putting you in a guessing mode as to whether or not you should call. If you check-call the turn and a blank comes at the river, you will probably be obliged to call a river bet as well. If someone raises on the turn and you don't think he's bluffing, you have a two-outer and can fold.

On the actual hand, the player checked. The cutoff checked and the button bet. The player thought awhile and reluctantly folded. The cutoff folded. The button took the pot while flashing the J♠-T♦. A short time later, I (JB) asked the button away from the table about his play. He stated that with both opponents checking, he could bet the expensive street representing a king and have a good chance of winning the pot outright. If he got called, he figured the pot would be large enough to play on for his gutshot. I asked the button if he would have raised had someone bet; he said no.

(6) A \$15-\$30 game. You are on the button with the T♥-T♦. An early player, a middle player, and the cutoff limp. You raise and everyone calls. There is \$180 in the pot and six players. The flop is: 9♣-5♠-5♥, giving you an overpair. Everyone checks and you bet. The blinds and the middle player call. There is \$240 in the pot and four players. The turn is the 9♠, pairing the top card on the board. Everyone checks to you. What do you do?

Answer: Check. It would be strange for three players to call your flop bet and none of them to have a nine or a five, given a rainbow uncoordinated board like that. You have too many opponents to bet, and the likelihood of getting check-raised on the expensive street after showing all this strength is very high. Check and take a free card to your two outer. The free card has extra utility here because you are the last to act.

On the actual hand, the player bet and got raised and reraised by both blinds. The player had to fold. The small blind called. The river was the T♠, which would have made the big full house. The small blind checked. The big blind bet; the small blind called. The big blind won, having the 9♦-8♦ for nines full on the turn.

(7) A \$10-\$20 problem. You are in the small blind with K♥-J♦. An early player, a middle player, the cutoff, and the button limp. You limp. There is \$60 in the pot and six players. The flop comes: K♣-8♦-5♥, giving you top pair, good kicker. You bet and everyone calls. There is \$120 in the pot and still six players. The turn is the 2♦. What do you do?

Answer: Bet. Although you still have a lot of opponents, you must bet what is probably the best hand and either get people out or make them pay to stay. With \$120 out there, you cannot afford to have it checked around, giving a table full of opponents a free card. There is a chance someone slowplayed a big hand, but a very reasonable chance your hand is good, so you must protect your money. What typically happens is that players bail out on the expensive street where prices double, and only the weaker kings or the diamond draws hang around.

(8) A $30-$60 game. You are in the big blind holding the Q♠-Q♥. Everyone folds to the cutoff, who only limps. The button limps, as well as the small blind. You raise and only the small blind folds. There is $210 in the pot and three players. The flop comes down: K♦-T♦-7♥, giving you second pair. You bet into two opponents despite the king-high flop. They call. There is $300 in the pot. The turn is the 3♥. What do you do?

Answer: Bet. Grit your teeth if need be, but bet. A flop containing a two-flush as well as a king and a ten means that opponents will frequently be calling on drawing hands, and not necessarily top pair type hands. Change the flop around to K♦-6♣-2♠ and you can reason that when your flop bet got called in two spots, someone probably has a king for a top pair of kings. But that is not the case here. If you check now, you may well get moved off the hand. If the next guy decides to bet as a semi-bluff, having a flush-draw for instance, and then the other guy calls, you will be on a tough guess as to whether or not to stay, since your hand could have only two outs.

On the actual deal, the player checked, and folded when it got bet and called back to him. The river was the 9♣ and it was checked down. The button won with J♦-T♠ for a pair of tens, while the cutoff had 9♠-8♠ for a pair of nines. The folded queens had been the boss throughout.

(9) A $15-$30 game. You are in early position holding the T♥-T♦ and raise an under-the-gun limper. The cutoff, the big blind, and the limper call. There is $130 in the pot and four players. The flop is: Q♥-2♠-2♣, giving you tens over deuces. The big blind and limper check. You bet and only the cutoff calls. There is $160 in the pot and two players. The turn is the A♦. What do you do?

Answer: Bet. The ace is a scare-card. It now puts two overcards on the table to your second pair, but you have to find a bet. The ace may frighten your opponent into folding even if he had top pair on the flop. You were the early position preflop raiser, and an ace would help hands you could have like ace-king or ace-jack suited. The other problem with checking is that you will encourage your opponent to bet and simply take the pot away from you. For all you know, he could have a small pair and have been hoping that you had A-K—until the ace came.

(10) A $15-$30 game. You are on the button holding the A♠-8♥. You open with a steal-raise and only the big blind calls. There is $70 in the pot and two players. The flop comes: J♠-T♠-9♣, giving you a one-card draw at an open-end straight, an ace overcard, and a backdoor nut flush-draw. The big blind bets. You call (raising would seem a better choice in this heads-up confrontation). There is $100 in the pot. The turn is the 3♠, now giving you a flush-draw and a straight-draw. Your opponent checks. What do you do?

Answer: Bet. Your opponent may well fold, and if you get raised, you can call with the nut flush-draw to fall back on. This would assume that your opponent is raising on a flush, making your straight outs worthless. If your opponent just calls, then you have 9 outs to the nut flush plus 6 more straight outs, for a total of 15 outs. An ace may be an out. This gives you as many as 18 outs, over a third of the deck, even when you are called.

(11) A $15-$30 game. You are on the button holding the A♥-K♥. The cutoff opens with a raise and you reraise. Only the cutoff calls. There is $115 in the pot and two players. The flop comes: J♠-8♦-7♣, leaving you with only overcards. Your opponent checks. You bet and he calls. There is $145 in the pot. The turn is the 2♣. He checks. What do you do?

Answer: Bet. It would be bad poker to check now. What you need is a cheap showdown if a blank comes on the river and all you have is the nut non-pair hand. When you check in these situations, here is what you are telling your opponent: "I don't have a thing. Feel free to step in on the next round with a bet and take the pot." Some might argue that you forsake getting a free card, but so what? If your opponent is strong enough to check-raise you on the turn, there is a good chance pairing an overcard would not be a winner. After all, he does not know whether you have A-K or a big pair on the betting to this point. Getting a free showdown is worth a lot, since you thus avoid an unpleasant guess on the end. And you may be able to win the pot outright.

(12) A $15-$30 game. You are in the big blind holding A♦-7♦. An early player limps and a middle player raises. Everyone folds to you. You call, as well as the early limper. There is $100 in the pot and three players. The flop comes: K♦-7♥-6♥, giving you middle pair and a backdoor nut flush-draw. You check, as does the early limper. The preflop raiser bets, you call, and the limper folds. There is $130 in the pot and two players. The turn is the 8♦, now giving you the nut flush-draw. What do you do?

Answer: Bet. You have just turned a big hand. You have the nut flush-draw (9 outs), a pair (2 outs), and an ace overcard (3 outs). This is 14 possible outs from 46 unseen cards. Against A-A you have 11 outs. Against top set you have only 8 outs (not nine, since the 6♦ pairs the board). Against A-K you have 11 outs. Against Q-Q, J-J, T-T, and A-Q, you have all 14 outs. Given your hand and the board, there are 3 ways for A-A, 3 ways for K-K, 8 ways for A-K, 12 ways for A-Q, and 18 ways for Q-Q, J-J, or T-T.

The point is that if you bet, your opponent will probably fold anything other than A-A, K-K, or A-K, which are only 14 hands from the 44 possible preflop raising hands he rates to have. Given the king and three parts to straight on the board, he will usually fold these other 30 hands on the expensive street for a bet. If he calls, you will draw out over a third of the time. If he has one of these other 14 hands, he will reraise only on K-K, and just call with top pair, top kicker or his overpair. Again, you still have a lot of outs when he does call, or even raise.

(13) A $30-$60 game. You are on the button with the J♠-J♣ when a middle player opens with a raise. You call (three-betting is a highly attractive alternative action) and the big blind calls. There is $200 in the pot and three players. The flop comes: K♥-T♠-7♠, giving you second pair and a backdoor flush-draw. Both players check and you bet. They both call. There is $290 in the pot. The turn is the 3♣. They both check. What do you do?

Answer: Bet. With the flop having both a two-flush and two cards in a playing zone, it is unlikely the preflop raiser is slowplaying a king or pocket aces. You should bet the turn (and fold if raised). If you get called, you will probably get a cheap showdown at the river if a blank comes. You could win right here on the expensive street. If you check, you may be giving your opponents free cards to beat you. The other problem is that if you check, you put yourself in a guessing mode at the river if someone bets.

On the actual hand, the player checked the turn. The river was the 9♦. The big blind bet and the preflop raiser called. The player thought awhile and reluctantly folded, figuring between the bettor and the overcaller, his jacks were beat. The preflop raiser won the pot with the A♦-T♦ for a pair of tens while the big blind mucked. Had the player bet the turn, the opponents would likely have checked the river, and he would have won the free showdown.

(14) A $10-$20 game. You are in the big blind holding the 8♦-6♦. An early player, a middle player, and the small blind all limp. You take a free play. There is $40 in the pot and four players. The flop is: K♣-4♦-2♦, giving you a flush-draw. The small blind checks. You bet, having only three opponents in this unraised pot. Only the early limper calls. There is $60 in the pot and two players. The turn is the K♠. What do you do?

Answer: Bet. If your opponent was calling your flop bet with top pair, then you will hear about it now on the expensive street when he raises. But if your opponent did not have top pair on the flop, he might fold, fearing that you have made trips. Checking would be bad against one opponent, because you are telling him that you are drawing, and he will know to stay with you. It is a lot harder to bluff the river successfully if you check the turn.

(15) A $15-$30 game. You raise from early position holding the A♥-K♦ after another early player limps. Only a middle player and the early limper call. There is $115 in the pot and three players. The flop is: 9♥-4♠-2♦, leaving you with only overcards. The early limper checks. You bet, and only the middle player calls.

165

There is $145 in the pot and two players. The turn is the T♥. What do you do?

Answer: Bet. If you check, then you must fold if your opponent bets. In these heads-up situations, the worst thing you can do is to check and call. If you get raised, you can fold. If you get called, you can check the river and have an ace-king to show down. In fact, you may get a cheap showdown, with your opponent not betting at all. By your betting now, the opponent may fold, since players often bail out on the expensive street if they have anything less than top pair or an overpair.

(16) A $20-$40 game. You are in the cutoff seat with the A♥-T♥. The game is shorthanded, with only seven players. An early player limps in and you raise. Only the big blind and the limper call your raise. There is $130 in the pot and three players. The flop comes: A♦-K♥-T♠, giving you top and bottom pair plus a backdoor nut flush-draw. Both opponents check. You bet and they both call. There is $190 in the pot. The turn is the Q♣, putting four parts to a straight on the board. Both opponents check. What do you do?

Answer: Check. Although it may be tempting to bet here, given the passive play on the part of your opponents, you have to believe that this board must have hit at least one of the two opponents who called your flop bet. You have the top and bottom two pair. But all anyone needs to have a straight is a jack. Check, and take a free card. If a blank comes at the river and you are bet into, then you can call. But you will not like betting the turn, getting check-raised, and having to make a tough decision about whether or not you should call. This would be followed by another annoying decision at the river when a blank comes and he bets again.

(17) A $30-$60 game. The under-the-gun player opens with a raise and you reraise, having the A♥-A♣. Only the raiser calls. There is $230 in the pot and two players. The flop is: K♥-Q♦-8♥, giving you a backdoor nut flush-draw as well as your overpair. He bets and you raise. He reraises and you call. There is $410 in the pot. The turn is the 7♦. He checks. What do you do?

Answer: Bet. The flop reraise by your opponent followed by his checking on the turn when a blank comes usually means he was just fooling around and your hand is still good. When a player takes an action on the flop indicating one hand strength and then his action on the turn is inconsistent with the previous action, the turn behavior is more likely to reflect the true hand. The limit has doubled, and the later the action, the less likely it is to be a lie.

(18) A $30-$60 game. You are in the small blind with the A♥-Q♣. The button opens with a raise. You reraise and only the button calls. There is $210 in the pot and two players. The flop comes: K♠-T♦-3♣, giving you a gutshot straight-draw and an overcard. You bet and the button calls. There is $270 in the pot. The turn is the 3♦, pairing the bottom card on the board. What do you do?

Answer: Bet. Preflop, you correctly three-bet a button steal-raiser, since your A-Q is a better hand than your opponent will usually have for this type of raise. On the flop, you led at your lone opponent, having a gutshot straight draw and an ace overcard, which was also aggressive and good poker. His flop call does not mean a lot at this point, since the pot is getting large and he is still on the cheap street. Now you have two choices. You can bet and hope he folds on the expensive street, but having outs if you get called, or you can check, and fold if he bets, since the pot odds are not there for continuing to play. Check-calling is a horrible idea, since you put yourself in a guessing mode throughout the rest of the hand. Reraised pots that are heads-up between a blind and a button steal-raiser have their own special rules. You are the aggressor, and should keep control of the betting.

(19) A $15-$30 game. You hold the K♠-K♣ and raise an early limper. The big blind and the limper call. There is $100 in the pot and three players. The flop is: A♦-J♠-T♥, giving you second pair and a gutshot straight draw. Both opponents check. You bet and they both call. There is $145 in the pot. The turn is the A♣. Both opponents check. What do you do?

Answer: Bet. You have only two opponents, who both keep checking. Find out the truth now. This is a classic "free showdown" situation. You are in position with a medium-quality hand. If someone has an ace, you don't have enough outs to care about a free card. However, you do want a free showdown with no one trying to bet you out of the hand at the river. If you get raised on your turn bet, you are against most players undoubtedly beaten, and can fold. By betting, you can frequently pick up the pot right away when no one has trip aces or better. Someone who is hanging around on a gutshot, middle pair, or bottom pair may decide to fold out of fear that he is drawing dead anyway. If he stays in, you make him pay to draw. The ace was not a bad card, since you could have drawn out with it (against bottom two pair) but the opponents did not draw out on you. It also reduced the chance that someone has an ace. If you are now behind, you were behind on the flop. Don't give worse hands than yours a free card.

(20) A $30-$60 game. You're on the button with the 8♦-8♣. An early player and a middle player limp. You limp. There is $140 in the pot and four players. The flop is: T♦-7♦-5♦, giving you second pair and a flush-draw. Everyone else checks. You bet and only the middle limper calls. There is $200 in the pot and two players. The turn is the K♦, giving you a flush with your 8♦. Your opponent checks. What do you do?

Answer: Check. You have a flush. If your opponent doesn't have a flush, he will fold if you bet. This does not help you if he doesn't have any outs. If your flush is good now, it will be just as good at the river. With two pair or a set, the opponent likely would have shown strength before now by either betting or raising on the flop or betting the turn. Check, and plan on calling if he bets at the river. Your check might even induce him to bluff on the end.

(21) A $15-$30 game. You are in the big blind holding Q♣-3♦. An early player, two middle players, the cutoff, and the small blind limp, so you get a free play. There is $90 in the pot and six players. The flop is: Q♠-8♠-3♥, giving you top and bottom pair. The small blind checks. You bet. Both middle players and the cutoff call. There is $150 in the pot and four players. The turn is the T♠, putting three spades on the board. What do you do?

Answer: Check. When called in three places on the flop, you should not bet the turn now that the third flush card has arrived. It is hard to believe that no one has a flush yet. The more likely scenario is that you are going to be raised if you bet.

(22) A $30-$60 game. You are in the small blind with the 7♠-6♠. An early player, a middle player, and the cutoff limp. You limp. There is $150 in the pot and five players. The flop is: K♦-7♣-3♥, giving you middle pair. Everyone checks. The turn is the J♣. What do you do?

Answer: Check. You probably have too many opponents to win the pot outright. The jack is likely to pair someone, since hands containing facecards are the kinds of hands players limp with. A bet will probably get called at least in one spot, if not more. This flop is also the type that some players with top pair like to check hands like king-queen or king-jack on the flop, planning to check-raise. When the flop doesn't get bet, they will bet or check-raise on the turn. If there had been only one or two other players, you could sometimes take a chance and bluff here. But four opponents is a whole crowd, too many to take on with your weak holding.

(23) A $30-$60 game. You are in the big blind holding the 6♥-2♥. An early player, two middle players, and the small blind limp. You get a free play. There is $150 in the pot and five players. The flop is: Q♦-T♠-5♥, giving you only a backdoor flush-draw. Everyone checks. The turn is the 9♥, giving you a flush-draw. The small blind checks. What do you do?

Answer: Check. While the heart gives you a flush-draw, the fact that it is a nine means that it probably has helped at least one of your four opponents, putting Q-T-9 now on the board. It is unlikely that betting will win the pot outright for you with this many opponents and that board. If someone else bets, fold. You are getting the right price for your flush-draw if it wins every time you hit—but it won't. Some of the time, an opponent will be betting on the turn because he has picked up a flush-draw, and his surely beats yours. When your flush doesn't win, you lose extras.

(24) A $30-$60 game. You open with a raise under-the-gun with the Q♥-Q♣. Only an early player and the big blind call. There is $200 in the pot and three players. The flop comes: A♥-8♥-5♦, giving you second pair and a backdoor flush-draw. The big blind checks. You bet and they both call. There is $290 in the pot. The turn is the 4♣. The big blind checks. What do you do?

Answer: Check. Heads-up, you should follow through with another bet on the expensive street in these situations, but here you face two callers. The texture of the board with nothing between a king and a nine makes it more likely that you were called with an ace. It is unlikely that both players are on heart flush-draws. You should check and hope the remaining player checks.

(25) A $30-$60 game. You are in the big blind holding T♣-9♦. The button open-raises and the small blind calls. You call. There is $180 in the pot and three players. The flop is: 9♥-7♦-4♣, giving you top pair. The small blind checks. You bet and both opponents call. There is $270 in the pot. The turn is the 5♥. The small blind checks. What do you do?

Answer: Bet. It is hard to know exactly where you stand, but you must follow through with a bet. You have top pair, which may be good. Your two opponents may fold on the expensive street, since it is unlikely that a board of nine-high helped them. Don't let a button raiser who could have been stealing on any ace or king get a free card to take the pot. If you get raised, you should strongly consider folding.

(26) A $30-$60 game. In the cutoff seat, you open on the A♥-2♣ with a raise. The button and small blind call. There is $210 in the pot and three players. The flop comes: A♦-K♦-3♦, giving you top pair, but with a three-flush on the board. The small blind checks.

You bet, and only the small blind calls. There is $270 in the pot and two players. The turn is the J♥. He checks. What do you do?

Answer: Bet. The board is scary and you only have top pair, no kicker, and lack any diamonds. But you are heads-up with an opponent who is just responding to your play. You simply have to grit your teeth and bet. If your opponent folds, you win the pot outright, and you deprive him of the opportunity of sucking out on you. Sometimes your opponent will fold a better ace, fearing the single-suited flop and/or the fact that you may have a bigger ace. If he has an ace, he may fold a hand like A♠-7♠, given your preflop raise, flop bet, and willingness to keep betting on the expensive street. He may figure he is playing two outs (7♣ or 7♥) at best or drawing dead at worst. By betting, you give him a chance to make a mistake. If he calls your turn bet, you can get a free showdown. You may induce a bluff bet on the river from a worse hand if he is on a diamond flush-draw that doesn't get there. The worst thing you can do heads-up is to dog it on the turn.

(27) A $20-$40 game. You are in the big blind with the 8♣-7♦. There is a call under-the-gun, and calls by a middle player, button, and small blind. The flop is 8♠-7♥-4♠, giving you top two pair. The little blind bets, you raise, and the under-the-gun three-bets. Everyone else folds, including the little blind, and you four-bet. The opponent calls. The turn is the 4♣, pairing the board. What do you do?

Answer: Bet. The opponent does not know your hand just got devalued. His three-bet on the flop looks like either an overpair or a big draw. Naturally, you are hoping for the latter, since an overpair now is in front. But if he was drawing, he may decide that the board pairing was too likely to have filled you for him to stick around. Of course, if he calls on a draw, you are still ahead.

(28) A $30-$60 game. You are in the big blind holding the 8♥-5♠ and get a free play when an early player, a middle player, and the small blind limp. There is $120 in the pot and four players. The flop is: T♥-5♥-2♥, giving you middle pair and a flush-draw. The small blind checks. You bet and the early player and the small blind call. There is $210 in the pot. The turn is the 2♦, pairing the bottom board-card. The small blind checks. What do you do?

Answer: Bet. No one raised your flop bet, so your hand might be good, and you may have the flush-draw to fall back on if it isn't. You might even pick this one up without fight. If you get raised with a board like this, you likely were drawing dead.

(29) A $10-$20 game. You are in the cutoff with the 9♠-9♥ and call a raise from a middle position player, with everyone else folding. There is $55 in the pot and two players. The flop comes: 7♣-2♣-2♦, giving you an overpair. Your opponent bets and you raise. He calls. There is $95 in the pot. The turn is the 9♣, putting a three-flush on board and making you a big full house. Your opponent checks. What do you do?

Answer: Bet. Your hand is nearly unbeatable, but you should bet anyway. There is nothing immoral about charging a price for drawing dead. If your opponent has something like A-K, A-Q, or A-J, or any two big overcards that contain a club, he will probably call, so make him pay to keep playing. He may even have a big pair (with a large club) or a flush, and be planning to check-raise.

(30) A $20-$40 game. You open with a raise from middle position having the A♦-K♠. Only a middle player and the big blind call. There is $130 in the pot and three players. The flop is: J♣-9♥-3♦, leaving you with only overcards. The big blind checks. You bet and both opponents call. There is $190 in the pot. The turn is the T♦, giving you a gutshot straight-draw along with your overcards. The big blind checks. What do you do?

Answer: Check. You have picked up four more outs with a queen, giving you 10 possible outs, but you should check. While the ten creates four new outs for your hand, it may actually hurt your other six outs. A king at the river gives anyone with a queen a straight. An ace at the river in a raised pot like this makes two pair more likely. The combination of having two opponents and a board of J-T-9 makes betting wrong here.

(31) A shorthanded $30-$60 game with only six players. The cutoff opens with a raise and you call on the button with Q♠-J♠. The big blind calls. There is $200 in the pot and three players. The flop is: A♦-T♣-9♣, giving you an open-end straight-draw. The big blind checks. The cutoff bets. You raise on your straight-draw and both opponents call. There is $380 in the pot. The turn is the 3♦, a blank. Both opponents check. What do you do?

Answer: Check. Checking is better than betting because you are the last to act, and taking a free card against two opponents who called your flop raise seems more prudent than trying to win the pot with another bet. It is unlikely betting will win the pot. If it were heads-up, you should bet, but an extra player often reverses your turn strategy.

(32) A $20-$40 game. You are in the cutoff seat with the K♣-T♠. An early player and two middle players limp. You limp, as well as the small blind. There is $120 in the pot and six players. The flop is: J♣-9♦-3♣, giving you a gutshot straight-draw, a backdoor flush-draw, and a king overcard. The small blind bets and only the early limper folds. You call. There is $220 in the pot and five players. The turn is the A♣, now giving you the nut flush-draw. It is checked to you. What do you do?

Answer: Check. While it is tempting to semi-bluff, having picked up the nut flush-draw, giving you a total of 12 outs with any club or queen, checking is better. You have four opponents, making it unlikely that you will win the pot outright by betting. One could argue that mathematically a bet would be sound because if all your opponents call your bet, this pulls into the pot another $80 for a $20 bet, and a 12-outer is only 34-to-12 against. But everyone may not call, and you could get raised, especially if someone was slow-playing a made flush.

22 - GETTING RAISED

How often do you bet a good flop like top pair, top kicker and follow it up with a bet on the turn, only to get raised or check-raised? Many players simply shrug their shoulders and pay off all the way to the river, only to find that they were playing with hardly any outs. While these players don't get bluffed out, it seems like an expensive way to play poker. On the other hand, if you are the type who runs for cover whenever your opponent throws some chips at you, the more astute ones will take notice, making you a target for any kind of strong betting on the expensive street.

There are many considerations that come into play when you are raised on the turn. The number of opponents, the texture of the board, the strength of your holding, and the betting action are the most significant. Your read on the raiser is also of prime importance, especially heads-up.

In general, when you get popped on the turn, the raiser can usually beat top pair or an overpair. This is especially likely if there is more than one opponent involved. You are also more in danger when the board is highly coordinated, containing flush or straight possibilities, or an open pair. The reason is the raiser is looking at the same board you are, and if he does not have a strong hand, he will be worried that you or one of his other opponents has one. While it is true that good players occasionally semi-bluff a raise or check-raise on the turn when they have a strong draw, this does not come up very often in middle limit holdem games. Another move that's rare in the middle limits is the positional raise on the turn followed by checking down a moderate hand at the river. You see these kinds of plays more often in high-limit games.

When you are facing a stronger hand on the turn (only one card to come), you normally do not have enough outs to justify playing on. Therefore, when you call, you are pinning your hopes on your opponent semi-bluffing, coupled with the possibility of your catching a miracle river card to win the hand. Calling a raise on the turn is usually a two-bet decision. If a blank comes on the river, you are more or less committed to call a bet. If part of your rationale for call on the turn was you felt the opponent might be semi-bluffing, a fold for one more bet at the river makes no sense.

174

The next set of hands cover many of these situations. Keep in mind that the problems assume the typical opponent. In many cases, we are advocating that you fold a pretty decent hand, one that only a very good player would know ought to be mucked. Because so few people would fold, not very many players would try to invest two bets to try and run them out. But some players are extremely aggressive, and a few astute enough to realize that you might well be dumping even a nice hand if you think it is beat. So against that type of player, you cannot afford to make the big laydowns that are good plays against the typical opponent.

(1) The game is $10-$20. A solid player limps in from early position. You are in late middle position and call with the J♦-9♦. The cutoff limps. There is $45 in the pot and four players. The flop is: K♠-7♥-3♣, missing you completely. Everyone checks. The turn is the 9♣, giving you a pair of nines. The big blind and the solid player check. You bet. The cutoff and the big blind fold. The solid player now raises you to $40. What do you do?

Answer: Fold. There is $105 in the pot and it costs you another $20 to call. You have five outs at best, which is an 8-to-1 shot. It is quite common for someone to slow-play on the flop with top pair in a small, unraised pot when facing an uncoordinated, rainbow board like this. A player with top pair of aces or kings is less afraid to give a free card than if his pair were lower in rank. On the actual hand, the player called both the turn raise and the river bet (when a blank came at the river). The solid player had K♥-Q♦ for a top pair of kings on the flop.

(2) A $20-$40 game. You are in middle position with the A♠-A♣. Two early players limp and you raise. Everyone calls except the small blind. There is $250 in the pot and six players. The flop is: T♠-6♠-6♦, giving you a backdoor nut flush-draw as well as having aces over sixes. The big blind bets. One of the early limpers calls. You raise. Everyone calls. There is $450 in the pot and five players. The turn is the 8♥. The big blind and the early limper check. You bet. The cutoff calls. The button raises and everyone calls. What do you do?

Answer: Call. Although you are quite likely up against trip sixes or better, with about $800 in the pot, the odds are almost sufficient to play your two-outer for $40. This pot could grow to $1000, and it is worth $40 to try and snag an ace at the river.

(3) A $15-$30 game. You are in middle position with the A♠-J♠. An early player opens with a raise, and you call. The big blind calls. There is $100 in the pot and three players. The flop comes: J♦-T♥-3♠, giving you top pair, top kicker as well as a backdoor nut flush-draw. The big blind checks. The early player bets. You raise and both opponents call. There is $190 in the pot. The turn is the 9♥. Both opponents check. You bet. The big blind now raises and the early player calls. What do you do?

Answer: Fold. There is $340 in the pot and it costs you $30 to see a card. There are three parts to a straight on the table (J-T-9) and you have been check-raised on the expensive street with the preflop raiser cold-calling. Against a straight or a set, you are drawing dead. Against jacks-up, you could have as few as three outs, which is a 15-to-1 shot, and the pot odds are not there. Against a lower two pair like tens over nines, you have eight outs with any ace, jack, or trey, with odds of about 5-to-1 against. Adding to your troubles is the presence of the preflop raiser, who could have cold-called with hands like A♥-K♥ or A♥-Q♥, and now is playing a flush-draw. This cripples your chances of improvement, plus the J♥ would give him a flush. Bottom line is that your hand is no longer any good, and you do not have enough outs to continue here when all scenarios are considered. On the actual hand, the player called. The river brought the T♣. The big blind checked and the preflop raiser bet. The player called and the big blind raised. The preflop raiser folded. The player called for another $30 with $490 now in the pot. The big blind won with the K♦-Q♣ for a king-high straight. The player was drawing dead.

(4) A $20-$40 game. You are in the cutoff seat holding A♠-Q♠. An early player limps and you raise. Only the early player calls. There is $110 in the pot and two players. The flop is: 9♥-8♦-5♦, leaving you with only overcards. Your opponent checks. You bet and he calls. There is $150 in the pot. The turn is the Q♥, giving you top pair, top kicker. Your opponent checks. You bet. Your opponent now raises. What do you do?

Answer: Call. You may well be beat by two pair and have only three to eight outs. But in a heads-up situation like this, you have to pay your opponent off. He could be raising on top pair, and you have the top kicker with your top pair. He could even be semi-bluffing a flush-draw.

(5) A $20-$40 game. You are in middle position with the K♣-J♣. An early player limps and a middle player limps. You limp. The button and small blind limp. There is $120 in the pot and six players. The flop is: 9♣-5♠-2♥, giving you two overcards and a backdoor flush-draw. It is checked to you and you check. The button bets. The small blind calls, as well as the middle limper. You call for another $20 with $180 in the pot because you have no concern about having it raised behind you, being last to act. There is $200 in the pot and four players. The turn is the K♥, giving you a top pair of kings. The small blind checks. The middle limper checks. You bet. The button raises. The small blind calls. The middle limper folds. What do you do?

Answer: Fold. With the button betting the flop and raising your bet on the expensive street, he will usually have kings-up, so you could be playing with as few as three outs, a 15-to-1 shot. If he flopped a set, you are playing with no outs. If he has two pair but not a king (it seems unlikely he would have limped in with nine-five, nine-deuce, or five-deuce), you have eight outs, a 5-to-1 shot. Besides, you have a third player in the hand who cold-called the bet and raise. If the small blind is on a draw, then the J♥ may not be an out for you, since it could give the small blind a heart flush.

On the actual hand, the player called. A heart came at the river and it was checked around. The button won, having 2♦-2♣ for a flopped set of deuces. The player was drawing dead.

(6) A $10-$20 game. You are in the big blind holding the A♥-7♥. An early player, a middle player, and the small blind limp. There is $40 in the pot and four players. The flop comes: 7♠-5♣-4♦, giving you top pair, top kicker. The small blind checks. You bet. The middle limper and the small blind call. There is $70 in the pot and three players. The turn is the 4♠, pairing the bottom flop-card. The small blind checks. You bet. The middle limper raises. The small blind folds. What do you do?

Answer: Fold. Unless you are up against a player who can read your mind or who knows exactly how you think, folding is best in a typical $10-$20 game against decent opponents. There is $130 in the pot and it costs you $20 to call. These are pot odds of around 6-to-1. What are your outs, assuming your opponent has a better hand? A seven for sure, but that is only two outs, a 23-to-1 shot. Is an ace an out? Only if he doesn't have trip fours or a straight. In the most optimistic case (other than a bluff), you have five outs with any ace or seven, which is an 8-to-1 shot, so the pot odds are still not there even in this rosy scenario. Bottom line is that there will be a high percentage of cases where you are playing two outs, making your call totally wrong. There will be a small percentage of cases where your call is only slightly wrong, because you happen to have five outs instead of two. To play on here is to basically put your opponent on a bluff or semi-bluff. Furthermore, at the time the middle limper raised, there are two players in the hand, you and the small blind. If he is bluffing or semi-bluffing, he is doing it in a multi-handed pot, which makes those types of plays more unlikely. The other problem with playing on, based on the shaky assumption that he is bluffing, is that you will end up calling a river bet as well, so it will cost $40 to see the hand through (not just $20).

(7) A $10-$20 game. You are on the button with the J♠-9♠. An early player, a middle player, and the cutoff limp. You limp, as well as the small blind. There is $60 in the pot and six players. The flop is: 6♠-3♥-2♠, giving you a flush-draw with two overcards. Both blinds check. The early limper bets, the next guy folds, and the cutoff calls. You decide to just call, since your flush-draw is only jack-high and your overcards are a bit shaky. The small blind folds. The big blind now check-raises and everyone calls. There is $140 in the pot and four players. The turn is the 6♦, pairing the top flop-card. The big blind checks. The early limper bets, the cutoff folds, and you call. The big blind raises and the limper calls. What do you do?

Answer: Fold. Actually, you should have folded when the board paired on the turn and a player bet, because there was strong betting on the flop, and your flush-draw is only jack-high. The big blind's check-raise on the flop usually means two pair and sometimes a set. With the board now pairing, his check-raise on the turn almost certainly means a full house. As an aside, the early limper may well be hanging around on a flush-draw which is bigger than yours. An interesting way of looking at this problem would be to examine what percentage of the time the big blind must not be full to make calling worthwhile (ignoring the presence of a third player for the time being). There is $240 in the pot and it costs you another $20. Assume you have nine outs, and that you will collect another $20 when you hit. These are implied odds of 13-to-1. The odds against you hitting are 37-to-9 against. If you go through the math, you will discover that the big blind has to not have a full house over 40 percent of the time to make calling correct. But in this betting sequence, you will nearly always be looking at a full house. Couple this with the times when some of your outs give the big blind a full house and the times that the third player is drawing to a bigger flush, and you will conclude that folding has to be right. On the actual hand the river was the 7♠, completing the flush. The big blind had sixes full and the early limper had A♠-T♠. The player was drawing dead—and hit.

(8) A $30-$60 game. You limp in under-the-gun with the Q♥-J♥. Two middle players and the small blind limp. There is $150 in the pot and five players. The flop is: T♥-9♠-3♣, giving you an open-end straight-draw, a backdoor flush-draw, and two overcards. Everyone checks (a bet by you looks right). The turn is the K♦, giving you the straight. Both blinds check. You bet. Everyone folds to the big blind, who raises. What do you do?

Answer: Reraise. You should reraise with the nuts now, and not slowplay your hand. You could get counterfeited at the river, which could kill your action. If a queen or a jack shows up, your opponent may not even call if you bet the river, but he will call your reraise here on the turn if he has two pair or a set. If a blank comes at the river, he will make a crying call on two pair or a set when you bet. On the actual hand, the player just called the raise and a jack showed up at the river. The big blind checked, and folded when the player bet, flashing the K♠-3♦ for kings-up as they hit the muck.

(9) A $10-$20 game. You are in the small blind with the Q♦-T♦. Everyone folds to the button, who opens with a raise to $20. You call. The big blind calls. There is $60 in the pot and three players. The flop is: Q♣-4♠-4♣, giving you queens over fours. You bet; both opponents call. There is $90 in the pot. The turn is the 6♥. You bet. The big blind raises; the button folds. What do you do?

Answer: Fold. A third party, the big blind, has now come out of the woodwork and shown strength by raising on the expensive street. There is an open pair on the table and the big blind could easily have a four in his hand. If so, you are dead to a queen. He could also possibly have a bigger queen and decided to wait until the betting limits doubled before raising. Bottom line is that unless he is bluffing, you are badly beaten, with nowhere near enough outs to continue. If he were semi-bluffing a club flush-draw, most players would have raised your bet on the flop rather than doing it on the turn. If you call now and a blank comes on the river, what will you do if the river gets bet? You will have to call, and likely lose another bet as well. In these cases where your outs don't justify a call on the turn, it is inconsistent to follow your call by a fold at the river if a blank comes. In for a penny, in for a pound.

(10) A $15-$30 game. An early player opens with a raise and you call with the A♠-Q♥. The early player is a decent-playing local who plays several times a week at this level. His opening standards can be a little loose at times, but once the flop comes, his play is good. The big blind calls. There is $100 in the pot and three players. The flop comes down: A♣-J♥-7♥, giving you top pair, good kicker. The big blind checks. The preflop raiser bets. Rather than raise, you decide to call. The big blind folds. There is $130 in the pot and two players. The turn is the 7♠, giving you aces over sevens with a queen kicker. Your opponent checks. You bet. He raises. What do you do?

Answer: Fold. The board is now paired, you have no flush or straight draws, and you have gotten check-raised by the preflop raiser. If you call now, you will most likely be calling at the river as well. You should fold, since you don't have enough outs when you are beat to continue. On the actual hand, the player called the raise. The river was a blank and the player called the river bet as well. The player was shown the K♣-7♣ by the preflop raiser for trip sevens. He was playing two outs. Afterwards, he argued that any guy crazy enough to open with a raise from early position with king-little suited has to be stayed with. But this is an expensive way to view these kinds of players. Many players have horrid preflop playing standards, including the tendency to play any two suited cards, sometimes even raising with them. But that does not mean that once the flop comes they continue to play poorly. On the turn, when these players raise or check-raise, they almost always can beat one pair.

(11) A $10-$20 game. You raise from middle position with the A♥-K♣ after an early player limps. Two middle players call as well as the early limper. There is $95 in the pot and four players. The flop is: 9♣-7♦-3♠, leaving you with two big overcards. The early limper checks. You bet and one of the middle players calls. There is $115 in the pot and two players. The turn is the A♠, giving you top pair, top kicker. You bet and get raised. What do you do?

Answer: Fold. Similar to many problems in this chapter, when you get raised on the turn, you are almost always beat when having one pair. (On occasion, you are up against a tricky player who likes to semi-bluff draws on the expensive street.) There is

$175 in the pot and it costs you $20 to call. These are pot odds of 9-to-1. If your opponent is raising on aces-up, then the number of outs you have depends upon his second pair. With him having aces over nines, you have three outs (any king). With aces over sevens, you have six outs (any king or nine). With aces over treys, you have nine outs (any king, nine, or seven). So one might conclude that on average you have about six outs, which is a 7-to-1 shot, and therefore you have a call. However, if your opponent does have two pair, you do not know which two they are, and thus may lose additional money on the river. Furthermore, your opponent may have a set, in which case you are drawing dead. Since he cold-called your preflop raise, he is more likely to have done this with 9-9, 7-7, 3-3, or A-9 than some other holding.

(12) A $15-$30 hand. You open limp from middle position with the Q♥-J♦. Only the cutoff and small blind limp. There is $60 in the pot and four players. The flop is: Q♣-8♠-7♠, giving you top pair, decent kicker. The small blind checks. The big blind bets. You raise and only the big blind calls. There is $120 in the pot and two players. The turn is the 8♥, giving you queens over eights with a jack kicker. The big blind checks. You bet and he raises. What do you do?

Answer: Fold. If your opponent has trip eights, then you are dead to a queen. There is $210 in the pot, so you are getting 7-to-1 pot odds to play. In these cases you have two outs to win, which is a 23-to-1 shot. If your opponent has a bigger queen, you have three outs with a jack, which is a 15-to-1 shot. There can be some cases where you have outs to tie, like when a third eight comes on the river, but none of this adds up to a call. The only way you have a legitimate play here is if your opponent is semi-bluffing with a spade flush-draw. If you have decided this is the case, then logic would dictate that if a blank comes at the river you will be calling there as well, so in many instances you are making a $60 decision here. Even in those rare cases where he happens to be making this play, you only win about 80% of the time, since 20% of the time he will make his spade flush anyway. The other consideration is that the big blind is less likely to be on a draw than any other hand.

(13) A $20-$40 game. You are in middle position with K♣-K♦ and raise an early limper. Only the small blind and the early limper call. There is $140 in the pot and three players. The flop is: Q♦-4♠-4♣, giving you kings over fours. The small blind bets. The early limper folds. Rather than raise, you decide to just smooth-call. You want your opponent to keep betting his queen so that you can raise him on one of the expensive streets. There is $180 in the pot and two players. The turn is the 7♥. The small blind bets. You now raise. He reraises. What do you do?

Answer: Fold. Unless you know your opponent to be extremely tricky or simply unpredictable, it is hard to believe that your hand is any good. His most likely holding is something with a four, giving him trip fours. There is $380 in the pot, and it costs you another $40 to call when you are dead to a king. The pot odds are not there to play two outs. Agreed that he called your preflop raise, but he was in the small blind. Many players will call raises out of either blind with any pair, any suited ace, any suited king, any suited connector, and so forth. For him to have a four in his hand is well within the realm of possibilities. If you call now and a blank comes, you must call at the river if he bets.

(14) A $20-$40 game. You raise with the A♦-Q♠ after an early player and a middle player limp. Both blinds and both limpers call. There is $200 in the pot and five players. The flop is: A♥-7♠-3♣, giving you top pair, excellent kicker. The small blind checks. The big blind bets. The early limper folds and the middle limper calls. You raise. The small blind folds and the other two players call. There is $320 in the pot and three players. The turn is the 5♣. Both opponents check. You bet. The big blind raises and the other player folds. What do you do?

Answer: Call. There is $440 in the pot and it costs you $40 to call. These are pot odds of 11-to-1. In these situations, against typical opponents, you will find yourself playing anywhere from nine outs to none. An A-3 in the opponent's hand gives you nine outs; he needs a set to kill your hand. A call for the pot odds is reasonable.

(15) A $30-$60 game. You are on the button holding the A♥-K♥ and open with a raise, which only the small blind calls. There is $150 in the pot and two players. The flop is: J♣-T♣-3♦, giving you a gutshot straight-draw and two overcards. The small blind checks. You bet and he calls. There is $210 in the pot. The turn is the 4♦. The small blind checks and you bet. He raises. What do you do?

Answer: Fold. There is $390 in the pot and it costs you $60 to try and get an ace, a king, or a queen. Ostensibly, with 10 outs, this seems like an easy call. The problem is that an ace or a king may not be an out. If your opponent has two pair or a set, you have only four outs with a gutshot queen, which figures to be an 11-to-1 shot. With just a top pair of jacks, your opponent might have bet the flop. But when you get check-raised on the turn, you may well up against two pair like jack-ten, or better. In rare cases, your opponent may be semi-bluffing some kind of draw like a flush-draw. He might have a pair and a flush-draw, giving him the best hand and a good draw. The A♣, K♣, Q♣, A♦, K♦, or the Q♦ may give your opponent a flush. Agreed that he cannot have all these holdings, but the point is that you will not win every time even when you hit one of your outs.

(16) A $20-$40 game. You are in the small blind with the K♣-Q♣. The under-the-gun player opens with a raise. The button, you, and the big blind call. The big blind is the tight, passive elderly lady discussed in previous problems. There is $160 in the pot and four players. The flop is: Q♥-8♥-7♦, giving you top pair, excellent kicker. You bet and everyone calls. There is $240 in the pot. The turn is the 4♣. You bet. The lady raises. The other players fold. What do you do?

Answer: Fold. When the lady pops you on the turn, you know you are badly beaten. This type of player doesn't make big semi-bluff moves on the expensive street. Some players might raise on a heart flush-draw here instead of doing it on the flop, but not this player. She has at least two pair, and she could have a set or a straight, in which case you are drawing dead. Against two pair, you have anywhere from three to eight outs. Overall, you are a long-term money loser to hang around here. On the actual hand, the player called. The river was the J♦. The player checked. The lady checked. The lady won the pot having the 6♠-5♠ for the second nuts. She correctly called the preflop raise from her big blind with six-five suited, flopped an open-end straight-draw, and made it on the turn. Despite her opponent's check, she didn't bet the river, because she saw her opponent could have made a bigger straight if he had a ten-nine. To her way of thinking, you cannot be too careful in a poker game.

(17) A $20-40 game. You are in the small blind with 9♠-9♦. The cutoff opens with a raise and the button folds. You three-bet, removing the big blind, and the cutoff calls. The flop comes down 8♣-7♦-3♣. You bet and your opponent calls. The turn is the 4♦. You bet again and the opponent raises. What do you do?

Answer: Call. What did the 4♦ do for your opponent? With this board, he needs a perfect holding of 6-5 to have a straight; there are no other possibilities. A straight seems unlikely, because he failed to raise you on the flop. If he had flopped a straight-draw, he might well have made an immediate play for the pot. (He does not know you have a pocket pair; you could easily have a big ace for your three-betting.) While it is true there are a number of hands that beat yours which he could be holding to raise, there are a lot of other hands he could have as well. A card that introduces a new two-flush provides an excuse for a holding that includes a couple of diamonds to make a play for the pot, tilting the scales in this type of situation a little more in favor of calling. He could have top pair and waited for the expensive street to pull the trigger. And of course, he could simply be putting a play on you with only a small pair, or something. You have too much hand to throw away in a heads-up situation. Call, and call at the river if he bets again. Besides everything else, it's possible that you will catch some help on the last card. The board pairing low would be nice, and another nine would be a beautiful sight.

23 - OTHER TURN PLAY

The remaining material covering play on the turn refers to situations where you are responding to the betting action of your opponents. Most of the decisions involve calling or folding, although there are a few problems where raising is the correct play. Typical situations involve hands where you are on some kind of draw and have to make a decision about whether or not to continue when the turn-card misses you. With hands containing eight or more outs (open-ended straight draws and flush-draws), the pot odds are usually there to play on if you do not have to cold-call raises on the expensive street. Gutshots, middle pairs, and bottom pairs frequently have to be mucked for a bet on the turn because the pot odds will seldom be there. Other situations involve multiple opponents in hands where you have either been showing strength all along with a decent hand, or you catch a turn-card that makes your hand look good, but start getting played with strongly. The next set of hands discuss some of these situations.

(1) The game is $10-$20. You are on the button with the Q♠-9♠. An early player and two middle players limp. You limp. The small blind limps. The big blind, a solid-playing local, does not raise. There is $60 in the pot and six players. The flop is: K♥-6♣-3♦, completely missing you. Everyone checks. The turn is the Q♥, giving you a pair of queens. The small blind checks. The local bets. The early limper folds. The first middle limper calls. The second middle limper folds. What do you do?

Answer: Fold. At this point there is only $100 in the pot and it costs $20 to call. This is a small pot and you have a weak kicker with your queen. Furthermore, the local, being a solid player who plays at this club all the time, probably would not bet into a large field like this without at least a queen. He might even have planned to check-raise the flop with a top pair of kings. Finally, you have another player to worry about who has called. He could also have a queen or be on some kind of a draw like a heart flush-draw, which kills one of your outs. On the actual hand, the player called. The river was the 9♥. The local bet. The middle limper raised. The player called (dubious), having two pair. The local folded, flashing the K♠-T♣ for a top pair of kings. The middle limper won the pot with the A♥-6♥, having made a heart flush. The player lost an extra $60 playing on with only four outs.

(2) The game is $30-$60. You open with a raise under-the-gun with the A♠-A♣. The player on your immediate left cold-calls. Everyone else folds. There is $170 in the pot and two players. The flop is: T♦-8♥-4♣, leaving you with your big overpair. You bet and your opponent calls. There is $230 in the pot. The turn is the K♥. You bet. Your opponent raises. What do you do?

Answer: Call. With your big overpair, the only choice is between reraising or calling. Folding would be wrong. You would be risking another raise by three-betting here, and your opponent could have a wide range of hands that beat a pair of aces at this point. While occasionally raises on the turn are semi-bluffs, these are rare among typical players. Instead, raises on the turn frequently denote two pair or better. He could have cold-called your preflop raise with pocket tens or eights and now have a set. He might have even called your preflop raise with king-ten suited and now have two pair. You will get four-bet if you are against a set, and will be drawing slim. By calling, you can check the river if a blank comes, and perhaps induce a bluff bet on the end if your opponent was semi-bluffing with something like a queen-jack suited. If your opponent has ace-king, you can call here, check on the end, and he will probably bet the river for you.

(3) The game is $15-$30. You are in the small blind with A♠-Q♦. The under-the-gun player raises. A middle player calls and you call. There is $105 in the pot and three players. The flop comes: A♦-K♥-9♦, giving you top pair, top kicker and a backdoor flush-draw. You bet. Both opponents call. There is $150 in the pot. The turn is the 7♠. You bet. The under-the-gun player calls. The middle player raises. What do you do?

Answer: Fold. Preflop, someone who raises under-the-gun will usually have A-A, K-K, Q-Q, J-J, A-K, or A-Q. A player who calls a raise cold will frequently have a similar hand. Your ace-queen is a vulnerable holding here. Furthermore, it would be difficult for you to improve, since your opponents often have cards that you need. However, because you are partially in, it is okay to call and see three cards. When the flop comes and it contains both an ace and a king, you can be in serious trouble, given the kind of holdings your opponents rate to have based on the preflop action. A flop containing both an ace and a king touches many hands these opponents could have. You can easily be up against the top two pair or even a set. When that is the case, you are practically drawing dead.

You bet the flop, and gave your opponents a chance to fold if they were raising or cold-calling with lower pairs like J-J or T-T or even 8-8. If one of them had ace-jack suited, he might fold. But when both opponents call, it looks like you may well be up against a powerhouse that is being slowplayed. A blank comes on the turn. You bet again, which is okay. But when you get called in one spot and raised in another on the expensive street, it is wrong to do anything but fold. There is $270 in the pot and it costs you $30 to play, but you are probably playing with no outs. At best you have three outs, which is a 15-to-1 shot.

(4) A $30-$60 game. A player opens with a raise in early position. You reraise sitting right next to him and having the A♠-A♣. Everyone folds and your opponent now four-bets. You decide to just smooth-call, because you are heads-up with position and want to disguise the strength of your hand. There is $290 in the pot and two players. The flop comes: K♣-9♦-7♣, giving you an overpair and a backdoor nut flush-draw. Your opponent bets and you raise. He calls. There is $410 in the pot. The turn is the 9♣, giving you the nut flush-draw. Your opponent bets. What do you do?

Answer: Call. When an early limper four-bets you out of position, his most likely holding is K-K, given that you have A-A. You should call the flop, call on fourth street, and call the river. Agreed that on the turn you have picked up the nut flush-draw, but this does not really change things that much, since with the board pairing your opponent has probably turned a full house. If he has K-K you minimize your loss. If he has A-K, he is playing with only two outs, and you should let him bet your hand for you.

(5) A $15-$30 game. You are in the big blind holding the J♠-4♥. An early player, a middle player, and the small blind limp. You get a free play. There is $60 in the pot and four players. The flop is: K♦-J♣-4♠, giving you bottom two pair. The small blind bets. You raise and only the small blind calls. There is $120 in the pot and two players. The turn is the 5♣. The small blind bets. What do you do?

Answer: Raise. Most people will go for a check-raise on the expensive street if they have two pair or better once the turn comes. Since you raised on the flop, your opponent will usually be confident that you will bet the turn when a blank comes, and check-raise with a better hand than yours. His bet most likely means a top pair with a flush-draw, or maybe he has five-four, which you can beat. His limping in from the small blind means he could have a wide range of holdings.

(6) A $10-$20 game. You are in the big blind holding the K♠-J♥. An early player limps and a middle player raises. The cutoff calls. You call from your big blind, since you are already halfway in. The early player calls. There is $85 in the pot and four players. The flop is: K♥-7♠-4♥, giving you top pair, decent kicker with a backdoor flush-draw. You bet. The early player folds. The middle player raises and the cutoff folds. You call. There is $125 in the pot and two players. The turn is the T♣. You check. Your opponent bets. What do you do?

Answer: Fold. In addition to being halfway in, part of the rationale for calling a legitimate raise preflop with a troublesome hand like king-jack offsuit is that you have the good sense to fold after you make top pair and catch heat. You aggressively bet with top pair into the preflop raiser and got raised. At this point it is okay to call and see the turn. Maybe you will help, and maybe he's not serious. But when a blank comes you must check, and fold when your opponent bets. He likely has A-A, K-K, A-K, K-Q, or some hand that beats yours. You are probably playing with no more than five outs (any king or jack versus A-A), maybe only three outs (only a jack versus A-K or K-Q), and you could even be drawing dead (no outs if he has K-K).

(7) A $30-$60 game. An early player opens with a raise and you call with the A♥-K♠. A middle player and the big blind call. There is $260 in the pot and four players. The flop is: A♠-J♥-3♣, giving you top pair, top kicker. The big blind comes out betting. The preflop raiser reluctantly calls. You raise. The next player folds. The big blind reraises and the preflop raiser now folds. You call. There is $470 in the pot and two players. The turn is the 2♦. The big blind bets. What do you do?

Answer: Fold. From the betting and the board, it is almost a certainty that your opponent has two pair or better for his flop reraise and lead here on the turn. Since he called a raise out of his big blind, he probably does not have jack-trey, but most likely an ace-jack or ace-trey suited. You are playing three outs at best, and could even be drawing dead. The pot odds aren't there to call and see another card.

(8) A $10-$20 game. You are on the button with the A♦-8♦. An early player, a middle player, and the cutoff limp. You limp, as well as the small blind. There is $60 in the pot and six players. The flop is: 4♣-4♦-3♦, giving you the nut flush-draw and two overcards. Both blinds and the early limper check. The middle limper bets and the cutoff calls. You call as well as the small blind. The big blind and the early limper fold. There is $100 in the pot and four players. The turn is the 7♣. The small blind checks. The middle limper bets. The cutoff now raises. What do you do?

Answer: Fold. It is an expensive mistake for players to play on and pursue their draw despite a paired board when it has been bet and raised to them on the turn. There is $160 in the pot and it costs you $40 to call, pot odds of 4-to-1. You have 9 flush outs from 46

190

unseen cards, odds of 37-to-9 against, or slightly over 4-to-1. Some might argue you rate to collect some extra bets after you hit your flush, so they reason they have a call here because of implied odds. But consider the following facts: (1) Someone may already have a full house, when you would be drawing dead. So you lose money by calling, and if you make your flush at the river, you will lose additional money. (2) An out for your hand like the 7♦ that double-pairs the board could easily give someone else a full house. So frequently you don't have nine outs, but a lesser number, thus reducing your chances of winning, despite improvement. (3) If someone has trip fours, a river card could come that gives you a flush but also pairs their sidecard, giving them a full house. This will cost you some additional money as well. (4) The pot could get raised again, which means that it might cost you $60 or more to pursue your draw, dropping your pot odds way down.

(9) A $10-$20 game. You are in the big blind holding the K♥-8♥. An early player limps, as well as the small blind, so you take a free play. There is $30 in the pot and three players. The flop comes: 7♣-6♥-5♣, giving you an open-end straight-draw with an overcard and a backdoor flush-draw. The small blind checks. You bet into two opponents in this unraised pot despite the two-flush on board. The early limper calls. The small blind now raises. You call, as well as the early limper. There is $90 in the pot. The turn is the 5♠. The small blind now bets. What do you do?

Answer: Fold. There is $110 in the pot and it costs you $20 right now to call, so these are pot odds of about 5-to-1. You have 8 outs to a straight from 46 unseen cards, so the odds are about 5-to-1 against. But you are in a situation beset with difficulties. The board has paired, which means there will be a certain percentage of the time when you are drawing dead. The small blind check-raising you on the flop means he is marked with a good hand like two pair, a set, or even a straight already made. He now leads right out on the expensive street. You have another player yet to act. There is a two-flush on board that could kill some of your outs. Also, you have a one-card draw, so the payoff is usually less when you hit, and there is a danger of splitting the pot. There are such a high number of cases where you're drawing dead or with hardly any outs that calling is unwise.

(10) A $20-$40 game. You raise from middle position with the A♥-Q♠ after an early player limps. Only the limper calls. There is $110 in the pot and two players. The flop comes: K♦-J♦-T♥, giving you the nut straight. Your opponent checks. You bet the nuts and he calls. There is $150 in the pot. The turn is the Q♥. Your opponent bets. What do you do?

Answer: Raise. For this to be right, the opponent has to be betting with two pair or a set and not fill. For this to be wrong, the opponent must have **both** a diamond draw **and** get there. If he had a straight and a flush-draw, he would likely not have just check-called the flop. The freeroll hands for him of A♦-Q♦ or A♦-T♦ are too remote to worry about at this stage, especially since he did not raise preflop. You are heads-up, reducing the chance that he holds a monster. He is far more likely to have two pair, a set, queen-nine, nine-eight, or just two diamonds.

(11) A $15-$30 game. You are in middle position and open with a raise on the A♦-K♣. Another middle player reraises and only the big blind and yourself call. There is $145 in the pot and three players. The flop is: Q♠-T♦-3♥, giving you a gutshot straight-draw with two overcards. The big blind checks. You check. The preflop reraiser bets and the big blind calls. You call. There is $190 in the pot. The turn is the 4♣. The big blind checks. You check. The preflop reraiser bets. The big blind folds. What do you do?

Answer: Fold. There is $220 in the pot and it costs you $30 to call, so your pot odds are about 7-to-1. You have 10 outs to improve, with any ace, king, or jack. A ten-outer is less than 4-to-1 against, so you appear to have a call here. But if an ace or a king comes, do you think you have the best hand? Will you bet the river if an ace or a king comes? It is doubtful. A preflop reraiser will typically have A-A, K-K, Q-Q, maybe J-J or A-K. Six of your outs are dubious and could actually cost you more money, not to mention the fact that the preflop reraiser may well hold cards you need to improve, so your outs may be fewer than you think.

(12) A $15-$30 game. You are in the big blind holding A♣-J♦. The under-the-gun player opens with a raise and only the small blind calls. You call. There is $90 in the pot and three players. The flop is: A♠-K♠-6♦, giving you top pair, good kicker. The small blind bets. You raise and both players call. There is $180 in the pot. The turn is the 6♣. The small blind bets. What do you do?

Answer: Fold. The board pairing just put your jack kicker out of play, so you have no wins, only ties. Even splitting the pot is unlikely, with a preflop under-the-gun raiser still in behind you and a small blind who keeps leading into you.

(13) A $15-$30 game. You open with a raise from early position with the A♣-Q♥. Only the big blind calls. There is $70 in the pot and two players. The flop is: A♠-T♠-2♥, giving you top pair, excellent kicker. The big blind bets. You just call. There is $100 in the pot. The turn is the 2♦. The big blind bets. What do you do?

Answer: Raise. You need to pull the trigger now while you still have the gun. He might fold a weak ace. If you just call, there are some river cards that hurt you, assuming your opponent is playing with a weaker ace. A king, an ace, or a deuce would then split the pot. If he hits his kicker, you lose. If he is semi-bluffing a draw, then he will call your raise. But if you just call and a blank comes, he might check and fold at the river, and you lost a chance to pick up an extra bet.

(14) A $30-$60 game. You are on the button holding the A♥-K♣. Everyone folds to the cutoff, who opens with a raise. You reraise and only the cutoff calls. There is $230 in the pot and two players. The flop is: 7♣-6♣-4♥, leaving you with two overcards and a backdoor flush-draw. Your opponent checks. You bet and he calls. There is $290 in the pot. The turn is the 5♠. He checks. What do you do?

Answer: Check. This is an exception to the rule about following through with a bet on the turn after showing all the strength before and on the flop. That low four-straight on the board is more dangerous for the preflop raiser than the caller (who is supposed to be tied in with the flop in some fashion). There are too many hands where your opponent has you drawing dead. By betting, you are also vulnerable to a check-raise bluff or semi-bluff.

(15) A $10-$20 game. After two early players limp, you raise with the A♥-K♠ in middle position. The button, big blind, and limpers call. There is $105 in the pot and five players. The flop comes: 8♥-7♦-4♠, leaving you with two overcards. Everyone checks. The turn is the K♦, giving you top pair, top kicker. The big blind checks. The first early limper checks. The next early limper bets. What do you do?

Answer: Call. You showed a premium hand like A-A, K-K, Q-Q, J-J, A-K, or A-Q when you raised preflop after other players limped in. When you checked the flop (which was correct), you told the table you had A-K or A-Q, since with an overpair you would have bet. Now a king comes off on the turn and an early player bets, knowing that this helps ace-king hands you could have. His bet frequently means two pair or he was slowplaying a strong hand on the flop. Raising is a bad idea, but you have to call.

(16) A $30-$60 game. You are in the cutoff seat with the 9♠-7♠. Two middle players limp. You limp as well as the button and the small blind. There is $180 in the pot and six players. The flop is: T♣-7♦-6♥, giving you middle pair and a gutshot straight-draw. Everyone checks to the button, who bets. Only a middle limper calls. You call. There is $270 in the pot and three players. The turn is the 3♣. Everyone checks to the button, who bets again. The middle limper folds. What do you do?

Answer: Fold. Taking a card off on the flop was okay, but doing it again on the expensive street where prices have doubled is not. There is $330 in the pot and it costs you $60 to continue. These are pot odds of about 5-to-1. A nine, an eight, and seven may all be outs for your hand. These are 9 outs from 46 unseen cards, so the odds are only 37-to-9 against. But a nine puts four parts to a straight on the table, meaning that if your opponent has an eight then he makes a straight, and it costs you another bet at the river when you make your crying call. An eight means that you could be splitting the pot with your opponent if he has a nine. Even a seven that gives you trips is not the nuts, since your opponent could have straight already made. Agreed that your opponent only has two cards and he cannot have everything, but the point is your outs have to be somewhat devalued, since they will not all win. Some tie or lose. Not only do you have fewer real outs than it appears, but an "out" that does not get you out burns up another big bet at the river.

(17) A $10-$20 game. You limp from middle position with the 7♠-6♠ behind two early players who limp. The small blind limps. There is $50 in the pot and five players. The flop is: 8♦-4♠-2♣, giving you a gutshot straight-draw and a backdoor flush-draw. The small blind bets. The big blind and one of the early limpers call. You call. There is $90 in the pot and four players. The turn is the pretty T♠, giving you a flush-draw and a double belly-buster straight-draw with any nine or five. The small blind bets. The big blind calls. The early limper folds. What do you do?

Answer: Call. You have 15 outs with any spade, five, or nine. The choice is between semi-bluff raising with your big draw or just calling. With two opponents, it seems unlikely that they will both fold if you raise. Heads-up, a raise on the expensive street might win the pot outright, depending upon the caliber of your opponent, but with two opponents, calling is likely better.

(18) A $20-$40 game. You are in the cutoff with the A♠-7♠. An early player and two middle players limp. You limp, along with the button and small blind. There is $140 in the pot and seven players. The flop is: K♠-Q♥-J♣, giving you a gutshot straight-draw and a backdoor nut flush-draw. Everyone checks. The turn is the J♠, giving you the nut flush-draw as well as a gutshot straight-

draw. Both blinds and the early limper check. The first middle limper bets and the next player folds. What do you do?

Answer: Fold. You have 9 outs to the nut flush and 3 more outs to a straight, so the odds are 34-to-12, or about 3-to-1 against. There is $180 in the pot and it costs you $40, which are pot odds of less than 5-to-1. On the surface, it would seem that you have a call here. But the implied odds are not in your favor. This board presents you with a whole host of difficulties that make playing on a mistake. Your straight outs, assuming a straight can even win, means that you will frequently be splitting the pot with anyone else who also happens to have an ace. Furthermore, the bettor likely has a jack, which kills one of your flush outs (the Q♠), and if one of your "outs" pairs his sidecard, that destroys another out. A coordinated board like this makes it very easy for you to be drawing dead. Hands like king-jack and queen-jack are the types of hands players limp in with. Finally, you could call only to find yourself getting raised by one of your other opponents. With five opponents, all kinds of horrible things become possible. You will lose a double bet here and at one or two more later if you make your flush and get beat by a full house.

(19) A $10-$20 game. You are in the cutoff seat holding A♦-K♠. Two players limp and you raise. They both call. There is $75 in the pot and three players. The flop comes: Q♣-9♥-5♠, leaving you with two overcards. Both opponents check. You bet and they both call. There is $105 in the pot. The turn is the T♦, giving you a gutshot straight-draw. The first opponent checks. The second opponent bets. What do you do?

Answer: Fold. Ostensibly, you have ten outs with any ace, king, or jack. There is $125 in the pot and it costs you $20 to call. A ten-outer is about a 4-to-1 shot, and your pot odds are over 6-to-1. But an ace or a king may give you a real problem. A king puts four parts to a straight on the table, so anyone with a jack has a straight. An ace could give one of your opponents aces-up, since hands containing an ace are the kinds of hands players limp in with. Both opponents called your flop bet, which would imply they may have a piece of the board other than an obvious jack-ten straight draw. Besides, one pair is a very beatable hand in holdem once all the boardcards are out and there are two or more opponents. You really only have four clean outs with any jack, which is an 11-to-1 shot. Your other "outs" are of dubious value, and cost additional money when they arrive and you lose anyway.

(20) A \$20-\$40 game. You are in the big blind holding A♦-T♣. An early player limps and a middle player raises. You call, as well as the early limper. There is \$130 in the pot and three players. The flop is: 9♣-8♣-7♣, giving you an open-end straight flush draw and an ace overcard. You bet and both players call. There is \$190 in the pot. The turn is the 8♦. You check. The early limper bets and the preflop raiser pops it. What do you do?

Answer: Fold. While it is exciting to be drawing to a one-card open-ended straight flush-draw, you quite likely have only two clean outs here (the J♣ or 6♣). All other outs that improve your hand are probably losers to a better hand held by either the bettor or the raiser. Furthermore, who knows when the raising will stop? You could be taken for a four or five bet ride here while playing only two outs.

(21) A \$10-\$20 game. You have the J♠-J♦ in middle position and raise an early limper. The big blind calls. The early limper now reraises. You call as well as the big blind. There is \$95 in the pot and three players. The flop comes: T♠-8♠-4♥, giving you an overpair and a backdoor flush-draw. The big blind checks. The early player bets. You raise to get out the big blind, who folds. The early player reraises and you call. There is \$155 in the pot and two players. The turn is the 9♠, so you have picked up an open-end straight-flush draw. Your opponent bets. What do you do?

Answer: Call. It would be a bad semi-bluff play to raise here given the power sequence both preflop and on the flop by your opponent. He likely has a bigger overpair than you, or possibly the A♠-K♠. Granted that you have 15 outs to a flush or a straight, and could even make a straight flush. But the problem is that your opponent will not fold when you raise, and he might even reraise. If he has a spade, it is surely bigger than yours, so your "flush outs" just cost you more money.

(22) A $10-$20 game. You limp in from early position with the 7♠-7♣ behind another early limper. A middle player raises and the small blind calls, as well as everyone afterwards. There is $100 in the pot and five players. The flop is: Q♠-6♠-3♣, giving you second pair and a backdoor flush-draw. Everyone checks. The turn is the Q♥. The small blind checks and the big blind bets. The early limper calls. What do you do?

Answer: Raise. Your hand has a reasonable chance of being good, and you should protect it with a raise. If anyone had a queen, they may well have bet the flop. Make it expensive for a player on a flush-draw or with overcards to your sevens to see the river. If the preflop raiser has a pocket pair smaller than queens, you of course want him out, as he will be able to beat your sevens. If you have the best hand, give yourself a decent chance to have it stand up. If you do not, you may be able to get a better hand out and beat a player who is drawing. It is worth the investment of an extra bet.

(23) A $10-$20 game. You are on the button with the A♥-7♥ and limp in behind three other players. There is $55 in the pot and five players. The flop is: 6♥-5♣-4♠, giving you an open-end one-card straight-draw, an ace overcard, and a backdoor nut flushdraw. Everyone checks. You decide to check, rather than betting your draw into a large field. The turn is the T♥. It is checked to the player on your right, who bets. What do you do?

Answer: Raise. Making a play for the pot is desirable when you have a lot of outs and the flop has been checked around. You have 9 outs to the flush, 6 outs to the straight, and 3 more outs to top pair. This is 18 outs against a player who has a ten in his hand. The player may be on a worse hand than that, such as a smaller pair, a heart draw underneath you, or even a cold bluff against all the checkers. You may win the pot right away, and have a lot of ways to catch a winner in case the bettor calls your raise.

24 – INTRODUCTION TO RIVER PLAY

The river card is the last card dealt during a poker hand, and the betting round following it is also called "the river." Play here is usually more straight-forward than on any other street. It is amusing to watch a player rapidly dump money into the pot on every round, then with the pot being huge, suddenly go into deep thought when the final river bet is made. With all those bets already in the pot, calling on the end in most situations is virtually automatic, especially in a heads-up situation. One prominent poster on the Internet has correctly observed that making tough folds at the river is not the way to make money in limit holdem. Of course, when there are multiple opponents involved, particularly if one or more of them have already overcalled, you may well have something to think about. The presence of one or more overcallers dramatically reduces your chances of winning when you hold a fair but vulnerable hand. Frequently, the pot is said to be "protected," meaning that the presence of multiple opponents will keep a player from attempting to buy the pot on the end.

Another phenomenon at the river is two players going to war by raising back and forth. When this happens, it usually means both players have the nuts and will be splitting the pot. But every once in a while, you will see a player raise and reraise his opponent until he raises himself out of money, only to have his opponent show him the nuts. In holdem, with the last card being shown, it is a simple matter to figure out what is the best possible hand, and to know whether you have it. To lose your entire stack in these situations is simply ridiculous. What usually happens is that a player puts the opponent on a hand, then stubbornly refuses to reassess the situation and double-check the board in the face of repeated raising.

One tactic at the river that can be effective, especially against an aggressive player or a maniac, is to check your hand hoping to entice your opponent into betting. You can do this in two situations. The first is when you know your hand is good and your opponent will probably fold if you bet, but he may try to steal the pot if you don't. The second situation occurs when you have a hand that is vulnerable, and there is great doubt in your mind that your hand is good. However, you also realize that your opponent may have a worse hand and may well bet it if you check.

There are two big mistakes that are often made on the river betting round. They are betting with a bluff-catcher and failing to bet a solid but not spectacular hand. Let's talk in some detail about each, as it pertains to a limit holdem game.

What is the most common raising hand in holdem? The answer is "big slick," A-K. This hand comes up with greater frequency than a pair of aces or kings combined, and most limit holdem players raise with A-K just about every time they get it. When you raise a pot, if the opponent knew for sure you had aces or kings, he wouldn't call. (At least, most people wouldn't call.) So when they do call, they are hoping that you have something like A-K instead of a big pair. It doesn't take any kind of miracle to beat big slick. And when they get a piece of the flop, most people will stick to the raiser like glue. True, they have only five outs to beat a big pair if they have paired on the flop themselves. But it is the very reasonable chance of finding you with A-K that makes them stay in. Consequently, at the end of the deal, even when they still have only the pair they flopped, if there is no ace or king on board, they drag out the last resort. They call at the river hoping you have been firing on A-K. Just about anyone is going to keep you honest in this spot, no matter how confidently you put the chips into the pot. They have already won hundreds of pots by showing down some scrawny pair and beating someone who had been charging hard all the way on a couple of high-cards (or a draw) and busted out. So they are going to call you the same way. Yes, it's a crying call, but sure as you're born the money is going in. If you can't beat their pair, they win the pot.

What does this mean for you, the person who raised on A-K (or maybe A-Q), fired all the way, and failed to ever help? It means that you cannot win the pot on the end against anyone who has you beat. No sir; no ma'am. If you are betting to frighten someone out of calling with a pair, you have erred, because you are getting called. So save your river bluffs for hands that are completely hopeless and cannot beat even a busted draw.

What about the other side of the coin, inducing a call by someone who you can beat? Pretty unlikely. You may get a play from A-Q, but that's rare. They must have that hand; then they need to call. So the simple question is, "Why are you betting your unimproved A-K at the river?" Since you cannot get someone who has you beat to fold and you hardly ever get called by someone you can beat, why are you betting? Many people bet because they say to themselves, "With all that money out there, I am not going to fold if my opponent bets, just in case he was on a draw, so I may as well bet myself." This is totally incorrect poker thinking. If you are acting first, and would call if he bet, you should check and then call. All you have is a bluff-catcher; inducing a bluff is the only chance to make any more money.

Checking with the intention of calling has two advantages over betting in this situation. First, you may win an extra bet if you actually have the best hand. Second, you cannot lose the pot if you have the best hand. (If you were to bet out and get raised, it would be tough to call, but conceivable that your hand was good.) As you can see, if no one with a pair is going to fold and no one without a pair will call, it is clearly right for A-K to check at the river. Yet there probably is not a poker game in the country where this error of betting A-K on the end is not made sometime during a session.

The other common mistake is failing to bet a solid but not spectacular hand. The reason for betting goes to the core of human nature. An opposing player does not want to fold a hand that can conceivably win. He also wants to see what beat him, rather than losing to an uncalled bet and having to wonder whether you pulled a fast one on him. In plain English, this means he is very likely to call a bet on the end, as mentioned before. He may well be making the right poker play also, as at limit poker he is getting such high odds for calling that he can't afford to be wrong by folding.

All this means that you should probably go into the firing line one more time on a decent hand. What qualifies for the term, "A decent hand"? If the board does not show a flush, or a straight that the opponent is likely to have, and there is one opponent left in the pot, then top pair with a good kicker is a decent hand. With this good a hand or better, you should bet whether the opponent has checked to you or is yet to speak. We are, of course, assuming that you are the one doing the betting and the opponent has not made an aggressive move on the previous betting round.

Here is a simple scenario. You have an A-J in middle position. Four of you see the flop, including the big blind. The spread comes A♠-10♠-3♣, giving you top pair with a jack kicker. The player that was in the blind bets and you make the automatic play of raising. The players behind you fold and the blind calls. On the turn comes the 7♣. The opponent checks, you bet, and he calls. At the river comes the Q♣ and your opponent checks again. There is now a potential flush on the board, but there was only one club on the flop. Furthermore, there is less than a twenty-five percent chance the blind was suited to start with. (We would guess that a player who voluntarily put money in before the flop is probably at least even money to be suited.) For a straight he would need a K-J, which is remote on both the betting and the logic of the situation.

There is only one holding that could be a threat to take seriously, and that is two pair. But if he had two pair on the turn, it seems that he would have either bet or check-raised, as there is a reasonable chance that you were drawing. If he made two pair with that last card, maybe he would have bet it. And which two pair does he hold? If he had A-Q, perhaps he would have raised the pot preflop. If he had Q-10, he probably would not have bet the flop. All in all, a little reflection should reassure you that your hand is still likely the best. Betting again at the river does not come with a money-back guarantee, because sure as you're born, some dude could show up with a hand that we have just explained is extremely unlikely. Still, poker is a percentage game, and the percentage play is to bet. One thing we can promise you. Since there was a flush-draw on the flop that did not get there, if your opponent has the hand he figures to hold—an ace with a worse kicker—you are going to get your river bet paid off.

In the sample hand used, it was pretty obvious to bet again. You do not need this clear a case to bet the river. There are more murky situations where it is still right to bet with top pair. Of course, there also are some other circumstances where top pair should be afraid and show the hand down, so betting is not an automatic process. But with a decent hand, you should be looking to max out instead of just being grateful if your hand is good. Greed can be a poker virtue.

A two-flush that goes the whole hand without turning into a three-flush has a substantial effect on betting after all the cards are out. Was the bettor throughout the hand pushing a flush-draw that busted out? Was the caller throughout the hand hoping to make a flush, and now betting on the end with nothing? Value-betting at the river does well because people will call with very light hands, hoping the person who bet on the end is on a cold bluff.

We have seen some fine poker plays made in this type of situation where someone's sniffer detected a busted draw. Here's one that Ciaffone was on the wrong end of. This happened a long time ago in a $20-$40 game in Nevada. He had an 8♥-7♥ that caught a great flop; the 10♥-9♥ and some little card were on the board, giving him an open-end straight-flush draw. He bet the flop and bet the turn, getting called in two places. At the river he wound up with—you guessed it—an eight-high nothing. Being unwilling to give up, he bet $40 on the end. The man on his left, a long-time Vegas professional player who we will call "Mr. Diddley," made it $80. The third man in the pot folded quickly. Ciaffone showed the raiser the 8♥-7♥, said something like, "You caught me speeding," and threw his hand away. His opponent smiled and replied, "You could have gotten half the pot," and showed him the 8♣-7♣. It takes a hell of a player to win a pot when the opponent has bet all the way with the identical hand plus a total freeroll!

As you go through the problems in the following chapters, remember that the odds received for calling the last bet are often in the 8-to-1 to 20-to-1 range. This means throwing your hand away for one last bet has to be right nearly all the time to be the right play. The opponents know this also, meaning your bet is liable to get called if they have anything at all. Be aggressive; squeeze every bit of milk out of the cow that you can. Make that value bet.

25 - BETTING ON THE END

Players are frequently in a quandary at the river when they think they might have the best hand, but are unsure whether to bet. Maxims are many. For example, we have been told by some that whenever we bet on the end and get raised, we have put at risk two bets to win one bet, since we will usually be obliged to call the raise. Therefore, it is argued that we need to have a better than even chance of having our hand be good to merit betting. Our preference is to cross bridges when we come to them. If you check whenever afraid of getting raised, you are playing too passively. At holdem, it is not easy to have a smooth trip with no scare-cards.

Another reason given for betting is when we cannot survive a showdown and we think our opponent might fold for a bet. This last scenario often occurs when we have been betting with a strong draw all along (for example, an open-ended straight flush draw), we bust out at the river, and can't even beat ace-high.

A common situation often misplayed is playing too aggressively when the river card nullified much of the strength of your hand. The following example represents a mistake that was made by a poker author. The hand involved a late-position player who limped with A♠-7♠ behind two other players. The flop was: A♦-J♣-4♠. One player bet, the other player called, and the late position player called. The turn was the T♥. It was checked around (a mistake, in our opinion, but not the point of the example). The river was the T♦. The flop bettor now bet and the next player folded. The author recommends raising because he wrongly believes that the late position player's hand improved from having a seven kicker to having a jack kicker. But it would be very bad poker to raise. The running pair of tens put your seven out of play, so all the bettor needs is an ace to have as good a hand as you. He may well be betting a superior hand. He may have been checking a big hand on the turn hoping to check-raise. He may have a ten in his hand. Regardless, the running pair of tens did not improve your hand at all. It was damaged, and you will be lucky to split the pot. Raising here is a clear-cut poker error.

The next few hands cover many of these situations, and should give the reader a better understanding of when to bet the river.

204

25 - BETTING ON THE END

(1) The game is $10-$20. You are in early position with K♥-K♦. An early player opens with a raise. You reraise. A middle player, both blinds, and the early player call. There is $150 in the pot and five players in the hand. The flop comes: 9♦-7♥-6♦, giving you an overpair and a backdoor flush-draw. Both blinds and the early player check. You bet. The middle player and the small blind fold. The big blind calls. The early player raises. You call; the big blind calls. There is $210 in the pot and three players. The turn is the 2♥. The big blind checks. The early player bets; you call. The big blind folds. There is $250 in the pot and two players. The river is the 7♠, pairing the board. The opponent checks. What do you do?

Answer: Bet. From the betting so far, your opponent either has nines full, pocket aces, or a worse hand than yours. Since he checked, he almost certainly has a worse hand. You beat Q-Q, J-J, T-T, A♦-Q♦, and A♦-J♦. You lose to A-A and 9-9, but neither hand is likely. He might not open-raise in early position with 9-9, or check when filling up; he would likely reraise preflop with aces. He could conceivably have A♦-Q♦ or A♦-J♦ and been on a draw which busted out at the river, so he hopes to get a cheap showdown with a good ace. He actually had pocket jacks.

(2) The game is $20-$40. You are in the big blind with A♣-J♦. A middle player opens with a raise, the cutoff calls, and you call. There is $130 in the pot and three players. The flop is: T♦-8♦-7♣, giving you a gutshot straight-draw, a backdoor flush-draw, and two overcards. Everyone checks. The turn is the 6♥. You now bet, representing a nine for a made straight and hoping to win the pot outright against only two opponents, neither of whom bet the flop. You have some outs if you are called. Only the cutoff calls. There is $210 in the pot and two players. The river is the J♠, which finally gives you a pair. What do you do?

Answer: Check. It is unlikely that a worse hand will call, since you have represented a straight by your bet on the turn. A better play is to check. You now have enough to show down. You might induce a worse hand to bet, which you will call. On the actual

205

hand, it made no difference, since the player bet and was called by his opponent, who held the Q♣-9♣ for a straight on the turn. The guy had the nuts and didn't raise the river bet. Amazing!

(3) A $30-$60 game. You are in early position holding the Q♠-J♠. A player limps in ahead of you. You limp. A middle player, the button, and the small blind limp. There is $180 in the pot and six players. The flop is: Q♥-T♥-7♦, giving you top pair, decent kicker. Both blinds and the early limper check. You bet. The button and the big blind call. There is $270 in the pot and three players. The turn is the 2♠. The big blind now bets. You just call. The button calls. There is $450 in the pot. The river is the 8♠. The big blind now checks. What do you do?

Answer: Check. The board is cluttered and you have the button behind you. The river card being an eight puts four cards close together in rank (the Q-T-8-7), making a straight or two pair more likely than otherwise. The big blind could be checking a better hand because he is worried about a straight. If the last card were a total blank like a trey and you were checked to, then betting would be okay.

(4) The game is $20-$40. You are in the big blind with K♣-Q♥. An early player limps and another early player raises. Everyone folds to the small blind, who calls. You call. The early limper calls. There is $160 in the pot and four players. The flop comes: A♦-K♥-Q♦, giving you bottom two pair. The small blind checks. You bet. Everyone calls. There is $240 in the pot. The turn is the 4♣. The small blind checks. You bet and everyone calls. The pot is now $400. The river is the 2♠. The small blind checks. What do you do?

Answer: Bet. When you have two pair, bet the turn, and no one raises, your hand is probably good when a blank comes at the river. Some of your opponents were hanging around on draws that didn't get there. With $400 in the pot, you might as well bet and pick up some crying $40 river calls from guys with one pair. If someone had a better hand, they probably would have shown some strength on the turn. Finally, you are unlikely to get raised by a better two pair, since they may fear you have jack-ten for the nuts.

(5) A $10-$20 game. You are in early position holding Q♣-Q♠. The first two players limp in and you raise. Two middle players and the two early players call. There is $115 in the pot and five players. The flop is: Q♥-9♠-5♥, giving you a top set of queens. Both early limpers check. You bet and only the two middle players call. There is $145 in the pot and three players. The turn is the 7♥. You bet despite the flush possibility. No one may have a flush, and you have 10 outs to beat a flush. The next player raises and the third player folds. You call. There is $225 in pot and two players. The river is the Q♦, giving you quads. What do you do?

Answer: Check with the intention of check-raising. At this point you have represented an overpair like A-A or K-K or maybe A-Q. Your opponent probably has a flush, and will most likely bet if you check. But if you bet, he may get cold feet with the board pairing and just call.

(6) A $10-$20 game. This hand was posted on an Internet forum and it generated a big thread and lengthy debate. You are in middle position with the Q♥-T♥. Two early players limp in. You limp in. The player behind you limps and the next player raises. Everyone folds to the first limper, who calls, as well as everyone afterwards. There is $115 in the pot and five players. The flop is: 9♥-7♦-3♣, leaving you with overcards and a backdoor flush-draw. Everyone checks. The turn is the 2♠. Everyone checks. The river is the T♠, giving you a pair of tens. Both early limpers check. What do you do?

Answer: Check. This situation comes up often and is highly instructive. This is a classic case of a worse hand not calling, but better hand always calling. After the turn, it seems nobody had anything, not even top or medium pair. But you do have four opponents taking the flop and getting free boardcards. If a ten helped anyone else, it probably helped them more than you. It could easily give someone a straight, two pair, or even a pair with a better kicker than yours. If it did not help anyone, no one rates to call if you bet. Adding to your woes is the possibility of getting raised by one of the two opponents yet to act. On the Internet, some posters argued that you will get calls from ace-high type hands. But if you are one of the players yet to act, would you call a bet with no pair and players behind you? Probably not. Furthermore, your check might induce a bluff bet from one of the two players behind you, which you can call. Checking is the superior play even though you may have the best hand.

(7) A $10-$20 game. You are in the small blind with the A♥-Q♠. Everyone folds to the button, who raises. Since you have a good hand and the button might be on a steal, you reraise. The big blind folds and the button calls. There is $70 in the pot and two players. The flop is: A♣-T♣-3♥, giving you top pair, excellent kicker. You bet and he calls. There is $90 in the pot. The turn is the K♦, adding a gutshot straight-draw. You bet and he calls. There is $130 in the pot. The river is the 7♠. What do you do?

Answer: Bet. If your opponent had anything good, you would have been raised on the turn. He will call with any ace and lose to your kicker. He may well call with a lower pair, hoping you were betting a come hand, since there was a two-flush on the flop.

(8) A $15-$30 game. You are in middle position with the A♦-K♠. Two early players limp in and you raise. The cutoff, the blinds, and the limpers call. There is $180 in the pot and six players. The flop is: A♥-T♥-7♦, giving you top pair, top kicker. Both blinds and both limpers check. You bet. The cutoff and the first early limper call. There is $225 in the pot and three players. The turn is the 9♦. The early limper checks. You bet, the cutoff folds, and the early limper calls. There is $285 in the pot and two players. The river is the 3♦, putting a backdoor three-flush on the board. Your opponent checks. What do you do?

Answer: Bet. Since your opponent did not raise you on the turn, you can probably rule out him having two pair, a straight, or any hand that beats yours, except for a flush. The 3♦ does makes a flush, but it is backdoor. Your opponent cannot be sure you will bet here if he does have a diamond flush, so the odds are that he does not have a flush, given that he has now checked. You probably have the best hand. Will a worse hand call? Any weaker ace will certainly call. With all this dough in the pot, he might even call you down on less, hoping you were on a busted draw.

(9) A $15-$30 game. You are in the small blind with the A♥-K♥. An early player limps and the button raises. You reraise and only the button calls. There is $120 in the pot and two players. The flop is: 5♥-4♥-2♠, giving you the nut flush-draw, a gutshot straight-draw, and two big overcards. You bet. Your opponent calls. The turn is the 7♣. You bet and your opponent calls. The river is the 5♦. What do you do?

Answer: Check. You should check because you have a big ace to show down. With any pair, he will almost always call, hoping you were three-betting preflop on ace-king and not an overpair. The other advantage to checking is that you might induce him to bluff. If he bets the river, you will call, hoping he has a busted draw.

(10) A $20-$40 game. You are in the cutoff with the J♥-J♦. An early player and a middle player limp. You raise. The big blind and both limpers call. There is $170 in the pot and four players. The flop is: 8♠-2♠-2♥, giving you jacks over deuces. The big blind checks. The early limper bets, the middle limper folds, and you raise. Only the bettor calls. There is $250 in the pot and two players. The turn is the 5♦. Your opponent checks. You bet and he calls. There is $330 in the pot. The river is the 3♥. He checks. What do you do?

Answer: Bet. You have a solid hand for your betting. Your opponent has done nothing but respond to your play, and there is little likelihood that the river card helped him, especially given his river check. There are many worse hands that he will call with, like top pair, or lower overpairs like pocket tens or nines.

(11) A $10-$20 game. You are in the big blind holding A♣-8♥. Two early players and two middle players limp, with everyone else folding, so you take a free play. There is $55 in the pot and five players. The flop is: A♠-Q♥-8♦, giving you top and bottom pair. You check your two pair, figuring one of your four opponents will bet, allowing you to check-raise. Both early players and the first middle player check. The second middle player bets. You raise. An early player calls and the other players fold, including the original bettor. There is $105 in the pot and two players. The turn is the 9♠. You bet and your opponent calls. There is $145 in the pot. The river is the 9♦. What do you do?

Answer: Check. The running pair of nines has just counterfeited your second pair of eights. If your opponent has an ace, the best you can do is tie. You can also lose to trip nines or a straight. You should check, and call if he bets.

(12) A $20-$40 game. You are in the big blind holding A♦-K♦. An early player and a middle player limp. The second middle player raises and the third middle player calls. The cutoff calls. The button and small blind fold. You call, as well as the other players. There is $250 in the pot and six players. The flop comes: 7♥-4♦-4♣, leaving you with two big overcards and a backdoor nut flush-draw. It is checked to the preflop raiser, who bets. The other two players fold. For $20, you call, with $270 in the pot. The other two players fold. There is $290 in the pot and two players. The turn is the 8♦. You check your flush-draw. Your opponent checks. The river is the 4♠, making open trips. What do you do?

Answer: Check. He will call if he has you beat or tied and fold if he doesn't. The only hand he might pay you off with is ace-queen. Of course, you will call if your opponent bets. Actually, the place to make a play for the pot was on the turn, because you picked up a flush-draw and could have represented a straight with the 8. Your being in the big blind would make this believable.

(13) A $10-$20 game. You limp from middle position with the A♠-J♣ behind an early limper. Everyone else folds. There is $35 in the pot and three players. The flop comes: T♠-8♠-2♥, leaving you with overcards. The big blind checks. The early limper bets, you call (dubious), and the big blind folds. There is $55 in the pot and two players. The turn is the Q♦, giving you a double belly-buster straight-draw with any king or nine. Your opponent bets and you call. There is $95 in the pot. The river is the 3♠. Your opponent checks. What do you do?

Answer: Bet. You should bet because your opponent may fold, fearing that you have just made a spade flush or that you have a bigger pair than his, assuming he was betting top pair on the flop. If he has a lower pair than tens, then from his standpoint, you were either playing with a better hand or you were on a draw. If you were on a draw, it looks to him like you got there.

(14) A $10-$20 game. You are in the big blind holding the 4♣-3♣. An early player limps, along with the small blind. You get a free play. There is $30 in the pot and three players. The flop comes: K♠-7♣-5♥, giving you a gutshot straight-draw and a backdoor flush-draw. The small blind checks. With only two opponents (one who has checked), you bet, representing kings, and having some outs if you are called. Only the limper calls. There is $50 in the pot and two players. The turn is the 2♦. You now have an open-ended straight-draw, and only one opponent, who has shown no strength. You bet and he calls. There is $90 in the pot. The river is the 5♣. You have nothing; what do you do?

Answer: Bet. Since you have no hand to show down, you cannot win by checking. You should bet and hope your opponent folds. If he happens to be on some kind of a draw, then this river card probably didn't help him, and he might fold if you bet. Since your opponent did not raise your flop bet, he is unlikely to have a top pair of kings himself, and he might fold a lower pair, convincing himself that you must have a top pair of kings for your betting. He only has to fold one time in four for you to show a profit.

(15) A $15-$30 game. You open with a raise from middle position with the A♦-Q♣. Two other middle players call. There is $115 in the pot and three players. The flop comes: 9♦-7♦-5♥, giving you a backdoor nut flush-draw and two overcards. You bet into two opponents. Only one opponent calls. There is $145 in the pot and two players. The turn is the 9♠. You bet again because the top card has paired, your opponent did not raise your flop bet, and you might win the pot outright. He calls. There is $205 in the pot. The river is the 3♦. What do you do?

Answer: Check. The reason this problem is included is because the player bet the river, and later argued that if his opponent did not have a flush, he was worried that the person would have a pair, and that he could not survive a showdown. Checking and calling is much better, since you gain $30 when he is bluffing. Betting here would be bad because he will call with any pair and raise with a made hand like a flush. He might fold an ace-king, but with this hand, he might not even be in the pot at this point.

(16) A $15-$30 game. You limp in behind three other players with the K♦-Q♥. The cutoff and small blind limp. There is $105 in the pot and seven players. The flop comes: K♥-7♥-5♥, a three-flush, giving you top pair, excellent kicker and the second nut flush-draw. The small blind bets and four of your six opponents fold. You raise. The cutoff and the small blind call. There is $195 in the pot and three players. The turn is the 6♣. The small blind checks. You bet and both opponents call. There is $285 in the pot. The river is the 2♠. The small blind checks. What do you do?

Answer: Check. Normally you should bet what you think might be the best hand, and collect something on the end. However, this is an exception. There are all kinds of better hands which will call if you bet, but which are concerned about a possible heart flush with the board flopping all of one suit. One of your opponents could easily have two pair or a set or even a straight, and have been just calling because of the heart flush possibility. You raised the flop bet and have been leading all along. You should hope it gets checked around and be grateful if your hand holds up.

(17) A $10-$20 game. You are in the big blind holding A♥-A♦. An early player, two middle players, the cutoff, and small blind limp. You raise and everyone calls. There is $120 in the pot and six players. The flop is: 8♥-7♥-5♣, giving you an overpair and a backdoor nut flush-draw. The small blind checks. You bet. Only a middle limper folds. There is $170 in the pot and five players. The turn is the 5♦, pairing the bottom card on the board. The small blind checks. You bet and everyone calls. There is $270 in the pot. The river is the 3♣. The small blind checks. What do you do?

Answer: Bet. You were worried on the turn with the board pairing and having so many opponents, but when no one raised, you have to assume you are still in the lead. The 3♣ only beats you if someone were hanging around with pocket treys, which is highly unlikely. You should bet and collect some chips from river calls.

(18) A $20-$40 game. You are in the small blind with the J♠-J♥. A middle player opens with a raise and only you and the big blind call. There is $120 in the pot and three players. The flop comes: 5♠-5♥-4♠, giving you jacks over fives and a backdoor flush-draw. You bet, the big blind folds, and the middle player calls. There is $160 in the pot and two players. The turn is the Q♦. You bet and your opponent calls. There is $240 in the pot. The river is the Q♣. What do you do?

Answer: Bet. You were a bit worried when the first queen hit, but he didn't raise your turn bet, so your hand still looks like it is good. If he had A-A, K-K, or A-Q, you would have been popped on the turn. The river card obviously did not let your opponent go from loser to winner, so is actually a good card. You will get called by a lower pocket pair like tens or nines. Be aggressive in value-betting on the end when there was a flush-draw on the flop; the opponents don't want to get bluffed by a busted draw.

(19) A $15-$30 game. You are in the big blind holding the 5♣-3♣. Two early players and the small blind limp. There is $60 in the pot and four players. The flop is: 6♣-4♦-3♥, giving you bottom pair, an open-end straight-draw, and a backdoor flush-draw. The small blind checks, you bet, and only the two limpers call. The turn is the 9♣, now giving you a flush-draw. You bet and the middle limper calls. There is $165 in the pot and two players. The river is the Q♠. What do you do?

Answer: Check. You have a pair to show down and can beat any ace-high hand. Your opponent may have had a five and missed his straight-draw. He won't be folding a pair on the end anyway in this sequence with that board, so you should check. Plan on calling if he bets, and you will be surprised how often you pick up an extra $30. The other nice thing about checking here is that you are not subject to a bluff-raise on the end, an unusual play, but within the arsenal of certain players, especially at higher limits.

(20) A $10-$20 game. You are in the big blind holding A♥-2♦. An early player, two middle players, and the small blind limp. You get a free play. There is $50 in the pot and five players. The flop is: A♣-7♦-2♠, giving you top and bottom pair. The small blind bets and you raise. Only a middle player folds. There is $130 in the pot and four players. The turn is the 3♥. The small blind checks. You bet and only the early player calls. There is $170 in the pot and two players. The river is the 3♠, putting a running pair on the board. What do you do?

Answer: Check. Your second pair of deuces just got counterfeited by the running pair of treys. If your opponent has an ace, which is likely, since he cold-called your raise on the flop and stayed with you on the turn, you are reduced to playing the board for your kicker. If his ace has any kicker except a 4, 5, or 6, you lose.

(21) A $30-$60 game. You are on the button holding the A♥-T♥ and open with a raise. Only the big blind calls. There is $140 in the pot and two players. The flop comes: 9♣-8♥-3♥, giving you the nut flush-draw and two overcards. The big blind bets. You raise and he calls. There is $260 in the pot. The turn is the 4♠. He checks. You bet and he calls. There is $380 in the pot. The river is the 3♦, pairing the board. He checks. What do you do?

214

Answer: Check. A bet may get ace-queen or ace-jack to fold, but he is unlikely to have such a hand. Nearly any other hand that beats yours will call. On rare occasions, you will be exposing yourself to a check-raise bluff by a tricky player who has a busted draw. A ten is a big enough kicker for you to show down an ace.

(22) A $30-$60 game. You open with a raise from middle position with the K♣-Q♦ and only the big blind calls. There is $140 in the pot and two players. The flop is: J♣-8♣-3♥, giving you two overcards and a backdoor flush-draw. The big blind checks. You bet and the big blind calls. There is $200 in the pot. The turn is the A♥, giving you a gutshot straight-draw. The big blind checks. You bet and your opponent calls. The river is the A♦. Your opponent checks. What do you do?

Answer: Check. You have the no-pair nuts. If your opponent has a pair, he will probably not be folding, after having called all the way. Hope he was on a busted flush-draw.

(23) A $30-$60 game. You are in the cutoff seat with the Q♣-Q♠ and open with a raise. The button and big blind call. There is $200 in the pot and three players. The flop comes: A♣-J♠-9♥, giving you second pair. The big blind checks. You bet and only the big blind calls. There is $260 and two players. The turn is the T♦, giving you a straight-draw with your second pair. The big blind checks. You bet and your opponent calls. There is $380 in the pot. The river is the 2♦. The big blind checks. What do you do?

Answer: Check. Hope your queens hold up. Your opponent will not be folding even a weak ace once he calls your turn bet. The reason you followed through with a bet on the turn was to get a cheap showdown. You got it, so use it.

(24) A $20-$40 game. You are in the cutoff seat with the A♣-9♣. Two early players and a middle player limp. You limp, the button raises, and both blinds fold. Everyone else calls. There is $230 in the pot and five players. The flop is: A♦-J♦-3♥, giving you top

215

pair. Everyone in front of you checks. You bet, the button raises, and everyone folds. You call. There is $310 in the pot and two players. The turn is the 2♣. You check. The button checks. The river is the 7♠. What do you do?

Answer: Bet. His check on fourth coupled with a blank at the river tells you that he is weak. However, he quite likely has something to show down, since he raised preflop. You will get a call from pocket kings or queens. Even a common button raising hand like king-jack suited or queen-jack suited will probably call.

(25) A $20-$40 game. You are in the cutoff with the A♣-8♦ and open with a raise, which only the big blind calls. There is $90 in the pot and two players. The flop is: A♥-7♣-3♠, giving you top pair. Your opponent checks. You bet and he calls. There is $130 in the pot. The turn is the 6♠. Your opponent checks, you bet, and he calls. There is $210 in the pot. The river is the K♠. Your opponent checks. What do you do?

Answer: Bet. Unless your opponent hit a backdoor spade flush, there is no reason to think your ace with a playable kicker is not still good. Your opponent will call with a weaker ace or a decent pair like nines, eights, or even middle pair. With a bigger ace like ace-king, ace-queen, or ace-jack, he likely would have shown more strength before the river.

(26) A $20-$40 game. You are on the button with Q♠-Q♥. Two middle players limp and the cutoff raises. You reraise and the blinds fold. The two limpers and the raiser call. There is $270 in the pot and four players. The flop is: 8♠-5♦-3♥, giving you an overpair. Everyone checks to you and you bet. They all call. There is $350 in the pot. The turn is the 2♠. Everyone checks to you and you bet. Only the cutoff calls. There is $430 in the pot. The river is the 6♣. Your opponent checks. What do you do?

Answer: Bet. Your overpair looks like it's still good, and you will get called if he can beat A-K. If the cutoff had a four (for a straight), he probably would not have raised preflop. If he had two

216

pair, he would have raised your turn bet. The reason he might not bet top pair or an overpair on the flop is because you were the preflop raiser marked with a good hand, and he was "checking to the raiser" like he sees everyone else do.

(27) A $10-$20 game. You are in the big blind and hold K♠-K♥. A middle player opens with a raise and everyone else folds. You reraise and he calls. There is $65 in the pot and two players. The flop is: 5♠-2♦-2♣, giving you an overpair. You bet and he calls. There is $85 in the pot. The turn is the A♣. You bet and he calls. There is $125 in the pot. The river is the A♦. What do you do?

Answer: Bet. You can beat queens, jacks, tens, nines, eights, and other hands he might perhaps call with. With two aces on the table, it is less likely that he has an ace. One thing is for sure; the river card did not beat you.

(28) A $10-$20 game. You have the A♣-K♦ in the small blind. An early player opens with a raise and two middle players call. You call and the big blind folds. There is $90 in the pot and four players. The flop is: K♠-T♠-9♦, giving you top pair, top kicker. You bet. The preflop raiser pops it and the other two players fold. You just call, since your opponent raised preflop and there are three cards in the playing zone. There is $130 in the pot and two players. The turn is the 8♣. You check and he bets. You call. There is $170 in the pot. The river is the K♣. What do you do?

Answer: Check. If your opponent had a better hand than you on the flop like a straight, a set, or kings-up, he is still in the lead. If he had something you can beat like the bottom two pair (tens over nines), he probably won't call. In all likelihood, he would not have raised preflop from early position with ten-nine anyway. He might have king-queen or king-jack, but this would mean he has the case king **and** he was open-raising from early position with one of these hands, which seem unlikely. If he was pushing a busted draw of some kind like a flush-draw, he might bluff-bet you on the end if you check, but he will of course fold if you bet.

26 - OTHER RIVER PLAY

Other play at the river primarily deals with situations where you have to decide whether to call or fold when your opponent bets. In responding to your opponent's play at the river, you must realize that when calling is wrong, it is usually only wrong by a fraction of a bet. You occasionally win the pot by calling because you have picked off a bluff. Even when you lose, you send a message that you cannot be easily moved off a hand at the river. This will discourage future attempts to steal from you.

On the other hand, you do not want to be always calling at the river when it is obvious you are beat. When you have multiple opponents, especially when some of them have overcalled, this has a double effect on your decision to call. First, it makes it less likely that the bettor is stealing. A guy may try to move one player off a hand, but as the number of opponents increases, he instinctively realizes that the likelihood of a bluff attempt working goes down dramatically. Second, the chance of someone having a good hand goes up with an increasing number of opponents.

This set of problems outlines some important considerations in deciding how to play in these river situations.

(1) A $10-$20 game. You are in the small blind holding T♦-8♦. An early player, a middle player, and the cutoff limp. You limp. There is $50 in the pot and five players in the hand. The flop is: J♠-5♦-3♦, giving you a flush-draw. Everyone checks to the cutoff, who bets. You call, as well as the big blind. There is $80 in the pot and three players. The turn is the 2♠. You check. The big blind checks. The cutoff bets. You call, as well as the big blind. There is $140 in the pot. The river pairs you with the T♥. You check. The big blind checks and the cutoff bets. What do you do?

Answer: Call. With $160 now in the pot, you have a clear call for another $20. You are probably beat by a top pair of jacks, but if the cutoff was betting a draw or second-rate holding, you can easily have the best hand. The cutoff could have been betting a flush-draw or straight-draw and decided to bet the river because it was his best chance of winning the hand. On the flop, the cutoff

218

was last and everyone had checked. He could have bet initially with nothing, then kept firing. An alternative to calling is raising, to knock out the big blind, but this looks unnecessary.

On the actual hand, the player folded and the big blind called. The cutoff won a $180 pot with the 7♣-3♣ while the big blind had the 6♥-3♥ for a worse kicker.

(2) A $30-$60 game with a $20 small blind. You are in the big blind with the Q♦-T♥. A middle player limps and everyone folds to the small blind, who raises. You call. The middle player calls. There's $180 in the pot and three players. The flop is: Q♥-7♥-3♥, giving you top pair with a flush-draw. The small blind bets. You raise. It would help to get out a hand with the J♥ or K♥. The middle player folds. The small blind reraises. You call. There is $360 in the pot and two players. The turn is the 2♣. The small blind bets; you call. There is $480 in the pot. The river is the T♣, giving you top two pair. The small blind bets. What do you do?

Answer: Raise. It is highly unlikely that your opponent was raising out of his small blind and three-betting the flop with a made flush unless he held specifically A♥-K♥, A♥-J♥, or maybe K♥-J♥. A far more likely holding is pocket aces, pocket kings, or maybe even ace-queen. There are 20 ways for him to have a hand you can beat and only 3 ways for him to have the flush. There is a remote chance he holds the other two queens, so maybe there are 4 ways you are beat. Nevertheless, you almost certainly have the best hand with the top two pair, and you will get crying calls from an overpair or top pair, top kicker type hands. On the actual hand, the player called, and won as the small blind showed the K♠-K♣.

(3) The game is $20-$40 in Las Vegas (a bet and four raises allowed). A player opens under-the-gun with a raise. You are sitting on his left holding the Q♠-Q♣, and reraise. A middle player makes it four bets and the cutoff caps the betting. The button and small blind fold; everyone else calls. There is $510 in the pot and five players. The flop is: J♠-7♦-3♥, giving you an overpair. The big blind checks. The under-the-gun player bets.

You raise. The middle player calls. The cutoff reraises. The big blind folds and everyone else calls. There is $750 in the pot and four players. The turn is the 2♣. Everyone checks to the cutoff, who bets. The big blind and the under-the-gun player fold. You call. The middle player folds. The river is the T♦. You check. The cutoff bets. What do you do?

Answer: Call. While you are almost certainly beat here by pocket aces, pocket kings, or maybe even a set of jacks, with $870 in the pot you have to call for the last $40. The cutoff could be betting ace-king and you only have to be right about one time in twenty to show a profit here.

On the actual hand, the player mucked and the cutoff flashed the A♠-K♠, winning an almost $900 pot.

(4) A $10-$20 game. An early player limps and a loose middle player raises. You call with the A♥-Q♥. Both blinds and the limper call. There is $100 in the pot and five players. The flop is: A♠-8♠-7♥, giving you top pair, excellent kicker and a backdoor nut flush-draw. It is checked to the raiser, who bets. You raise and only the bettor calls. The turn is the 8♥, giving you the nut flush-draw. Your opponent checks and you bet. He raises and you call. The river is the K♠. Your opponent bets. What do you do?

Answer: Fold. Although there is $240 in the pot and it costs you $20 to call, you should fold. Your queen kicker is useless, so any ace ties you. There is now a spade flush possibility out there. Your opponent's check-raise on the turn means he probably has big slick or trip eights.

(5) A Las Vegas $20-$40 game. You are on the button with the 9♦-8♦. An early player, a middle player, and the cutoff limp. You limp. The small blind limps. The big blind raises and everyone calls. There is $240 in the pot and six players. The flop comes: A♦-T♥-7♠, giving you an open-end straight-draw. The small blind checks. The big blind bets. The early player folds. The middle player raises. The cutoff folds. You call. The small blind folds. The big blind reraises and the middle player makes it four bets. You call. The big blind caps the betting. The middle player and yourself call. There is $540 in the pot and three players. The turn is the J♣, giving you a straight. The big blind bets. The middle player calls. You raise. Both opponents call. There is $780 in the pot. The river is the Q♠, putting four parts to a Broadway straight on the board. The big blind bets. The middle player calls. What do you do?

Answer: Call. No one has king-queen, since your turn bet was not raised. The big blind raised after several players limped in preflop. This could mean A-K. But would he have three bet and capped the betting on the flop with just top pair, top kicker, or would he be more likely to have done this with two pair or a set? What about the middle player? He cannot have A-K, since he did not raise preflop. We have already ruled out K-Q. There is no other hand containing a king that would have caused the middle player to raise and then four-bet on the flop. Since there is a slight chance that the big blind may not have A-K, but rather have been playing two pair or a set, you have to call for another $40 with $860 in the pot. The big blind was holding the A♠-T♠. The middle player had the A♥-J♠. You win.

(6) A $10-$20 game. An early player who has a lot of tricky moves opens with a raise. Four players fold to you. You reraise with the A♠-A♥. Everyone folds to the early player, who makes it four bets. Rather than give away the strength of your hand, you decide to just smooth-call in this heads-up situation with you having position over your lone opponent. There is $95 in the pot and two players. The flop is: Q♦-6♥-2♠, giving you an overpair. Your opponent checks. You bet and he calls. There is $115 in the pot. The turn is the J♣. Your opponent checks. You bet and he calls. There is $155 in the pot. The river is the 7♦. Your opponent checks. You bet and get raised. What do you do?

Answer: Call. With $215 in the pot, you must call the $20 raise with your big overpair. It is obvious that your opponent probably has pocket queens or pocket jacks and has you beat with a set. But for a fold to be correct, you would have to be right over 90% of the time. Your opponent might have pocket kings, which you can beat. He might be fooling around and putting in a last-minute raise in a desperate attempt to win the pot. Regardless, there is too much money in the pot for you to fold on the end. When folding hands like this on the end against one opponent, do not ever show anyone your hand. If you do, your more observant opponents will start taking pots away from you.

(7) A $15-$30 game. You are in the big blind and are holding the Q♥-J♠. An early player and the small blind limp. You take a free play. There is $45 in the pot and three players. The flop comes: A♠-K♠-Q♠, giving you bottom pair and a royal flush-draw. The small blind checks. You bet. Only the small blind calls. There is $75 in the pot and two players. The turn is the K♥, pairing the board. Your opponent checks. You check. The river is the 7♦. Your opponent bets $30. What do you do?

Answer: Fold. Having decided to check it back on the turn, you should fold. This is a small pot with $105 and it costs you $30 to call. It is too easy for your opponent to have an ace, a king, a flush, or a straight. He could be bluffing a busted flush or straight draw, but this is unlikely (you have the J♠). There is not enough money in the pot to pay and find out. Had you decided to bet the turn and he just called, then his leading here on the river when a blank comes would be more suspect. Furthermore, the pot would be bigger, and the pot odds would be much better for calling.

(8) A $30-$60 game. You open-raise under-the-gun with A♦-K♦. Only the small blind calls. The small blind is an eccentric lady who plays very loose preflop but decently once the flop comes. She is stuck about three grand in this game. There is $150 in the pot and two players. The flop is: J♥-T♦-5♣, giving you a gutshot straight-draw and two overcards as well as a backdoor nut flush-draw. She bets and you call. There is $210 in the pot. The turn is the 9♦, giving you the nut flush-draw. She bets. You just call, because she is not the type to fold on the turn when raised in a heads-up situation. There is $330 in the pot. The river is the 2♠. She bets. What do you do?

Answer: Fold. Calling is bad because the nine on the turn helped many non-pair type hands she might have like K-Q, 9-8, or 8-7. The only hand you can beat would be specifically A-Q.

(9) A $20-$40 game. You are in the big blind holding the 9♦-7♣. An early player, two middle players, and the small blind limp. You get a free play. There is $100 in the pot and five players. The flop is: 9♣-7♥-7♦, giving you a full house. The small blind checks. You check. The early player bets and one of the middle players calls. The small blind folds and you raise. Both opponents call. There is $220 in the pot and three players. The turn is the A♦. You bet and both opponents call. There is $340 in the pot. The river is the J♣. You bet. The early limper folds. The middle player raises. What do you do?

Answer: Reraise. With a full house, you should make it three bets. With pocket aces or jacks, he would have raised preflop. With pocket nines or a seven in his hand, he may well have raised on the turn. The only likely holding he can have is 10-8 (suited for his preflop call), and he now has made a straight, which he thinks is good. You know it isn't, so punish him by three-betting.

(10) A $20-$40 game. You open with a raise from middle position with the 9♥-9♣. Only the big blind calls. There is $90 in the pot and two players. The flop is: 7♣-5♠-4♦, giving you an overpair. The big blind checks. You bet and he calls. There is $130 in the pot. The turn is the 2♠. The big blind checks, you bet, and he raises. He may have a straight with 8-6, 6-3, or A-3, which means you are drawing dead. It seems unlikely that he would call a raise even out of his big blind in a heads-up situation with the first two of these holdings. You have eight outs against two pair, which is a 38-to-8 shot, and you are getting better than 6-to-1 pot odds. You decide to call. There is $290 in the pot. The river is the J♥. Your opponent bets. What do you do?

Answer: Call. In a heads-up situation with $330 in the pot, you should put in another $40; your opponent may be bluffing or

223

betting a worse hand. It is unlikely that the J♥ helped him. You only need to catch a bluff about 15% of the time to show a profit. The player folded at the river. The big blind had held 8♠-8♦. The big blind knew that his opponent would open-raise from middle position with any two big cards, as well as a medium or big pocket pair. He would follow this up with a bet on the flop, and probably bet the turn as well, since he is aggressive. The big blind figured that by waiting until the turn to raise, he might get his opponent to fold at that point. If his opponent called, he would figure he was beat, but that he had outs to a set or straight. When his opponent called his raise on the turn and a blank came at the river, he figured his only chance to win was to keep betting and hope for a fold, which is what happened.

(11) A $15-$30 game. You are in the small blind with the K♥-5♠. An early player and a middle player limp. You decide to toss in another $5 and limp. There is $60 in the pot and four players. The flop is: J♠-J♣-3♣, missing you completely. Everyone checks. The turn is the K♣, giving you top pair. You bet and only the early limper calls. There is $120 in the pot and two players. The river is the A♠. You check. Your opponent bets. What do you do?

Answer: Call. With trip jacks, your opponent might have raised on the turn. It looks like he has a king (but not ace-king, since he did not raise preflop). Call and expect to split the pot.

(12) A $15-$30 game. You are in the cutoff seat holding J♠-J♦. Two middle players limp and you raise. The big blind and the limpers call. There is $130 in the pot and four players. The flop is: 8♣-7♣-6♥, giving you an overpair. The big blind bets, one limper calls, and the other folds. You raise and both opponents call. There is $220 in the pot and three players. The turn is the K♠. Both opponents check. You bet and they both call. There is $310 in the pot. The river is the 8♦. The big blind now bets. The other opponent folds. What do you do?

Answer: Call. While you are probably beat, most likely by trip eights, you have to call, since you are getting better than 11-to-1 odds. There is a decent enough chance that the big blind is betting a busted flush-draw or straight-draw.

(13) A $15-$30 game. You limp in under-the-gun with K♣-Q♦. Two middle players limp. There is $70 in the pot and four players. The flop is: Q♠-J♦-8♥, giving you top pair, excellent kicker. The big blind checks. You bet and everyone calls. There is $130 in the pot. The turn is the 8♣. The big blind checks. You bet and only the limpers call. There is $220 in the pot and three players. The river is the A♠. You check. The first limper checks. The second limper bets. What do you do?

Answer: Call. You correctly checked the river when the ace arrived, but you invited a bet by the last player when you did so. There was a straight-draw on the flop which may not have gotten there (a pair plus a gutshot like Q-10, Q-9, J-10, or J-9). With $250 in the pot, you have to pay off for another $30.

(14) A $30-$60 hand. You are in the small blind with the K♦-4♦. An early player, a middle player, and the button limp. You limp. There is $150 in the pot and five players. The flop is: K♥-Q♥-8♦, giving you top pair and a backdoor flush-draw. You bet. The big blind folds. The early player raises and the other two players fold. You call. There is $270 in the pot and two players. The turn is the J♣. You both check. The river is the 9♠. You check. Your opponent bets. What do you do?

Answer: Call. It is too easy for your opponent to be betting a busted heart flush-draw, especially after his check on the turn. You are probably beat by a ten or a bigger king, but with $330 in the pot, you should call for another $60.

(15) A $20-$40 game. You limp from middle position with the K♠-T♥ after an early player limps. The small blind limps. There is $80 in the pot and four players. The flop is: K♥-J♦-T♦, giving you top and bottom pair. The small blind bets. The big blind folds. The early limper calls. You raise and both opponents call. There is $200 in the pot and three players. The turn is the 4♠. Both

225

opponents check. You bet and only the limper calls. The river is the A♥. Your opponent bets. What do you do?

Answer: Call. Your opponent could have been on a flush-draw that missed. There is $320 in the pot and it costs you $40, so you only have to be right about 13 percent of the time to make the call correct in this situation.

(16) A $20-$40 game. You are in the big blind holding K♣-Q♠. An early player limps and another early player raises. You call, as well as the limper. There is $130 in the pot and three players. The flop is: A♦-Q♥-7♣, giving you middle pair. It is checked to the raiser, who bets. You call (a shaky decision) as well as the limper. The turn is the T♣, giving you a gutshot straight-draw. Everyone checks. The river is the 3♥. You bet, the limper raises and the other player folds. What do you do?

Answer: Fold. Everyone checking the turn made it look like your middle pair of queens might be good, so you bet the river. But the early limper's actions are suspect. The 3♥ appears to be a blank, so what is the early limper suddenly so excited about that he wants to raise? He probably checked the turn thinking that the preflop raiser would bet. He rates to have at least a pair of aces, and maybe something more like two pair or a straight, that he was planning to check-raise on the turn.

(17) A $30-$60 game. You are on the button holding the A♥-K♣. The cutoff opens with a raise and you reraise. Only the cutoff calls. There is $230 in the pot and two players. The flop comes: 7♣-6♣-4♥, leaving you with overcards and a backdoor flush-draw. Your opponent checks and you bet. He calls. There is $290 in the pot. The turn is the 5♠. Your opponent checks. You check. The river is the 7♠. Your opponent bets. What do you do?

Answer: Fold. This hand runs counter to the principle that when you show weakness on the turn by checking, you must pay off at the river. There are players who don't bluff, no matter how juicy the opportunity. Your opponent didn't act aggressively on the flop, like he might have with a flush-draw. He had a golden opportunity to bluff the turn when the four-straight came, but he checked. The bet on the end looks like he was trying to get you to bet his hand all along, rather than someone finally waking up to bluff the river.

(18) A $15-$30 game. You open with a raise from middle position with 9♥-9♣. It is folded to the small blind, who reraises. You call. There's $105 in the pot and two players. The flop is: J♣-5♣-3♦, giving you second pair and a backdoor flush-draw. The small blind bets and you call. There is $135 in the pot. The turn is the 6♣, giving you a flush-draw. The small blind bets and you call. There's now $195 in the pot. The river is the 2♥. The small blind bets. What do you do?

Answer: Call. There is no ace, king, or queen out there and you have a pair. You were heads-up with position the entire time. You beat A-K, A-Q, and K-Q suited, which your opponent might have been betting, especially if one of his cards was a club.

(19) A $15-$30 game. You are in early position holding T♠-T♥ and raise an early limper. Only the limper calls. There is $85 in the pot and two players. The flop comes: 9♥-4♠-3♠, giving you an overpair and backdoor flush-draw. Your opponent checks. You bet and he raises. You reraise, since you can beat top-pair hands he might raise with. He calls. There is $175 in the pot. The turn is the 2♥. He checks. You bet and he calls. There is $235 in the pot. The river is the A♥. Your opponent now bets. What do you do?

Answer: Call. You were heads-up from the start. Your opponent could have a heart flush, an ace, or even a five for a wheel. But hearts weren't the flush suit on the flop. The ace is a scare-card for him to represent. Even though you are probably beat, with $265 in the pot, there is too much money to fold for $30. You must catch him with something like a busted spade flush-draw or just a worse hand only about 12 percent of the time to show a profit by calling.

27 – INTRODUCTION TO SPECIAL TOPICS

Having completed study of the game sectioned by the betting round, it is now appropriate to discuss some specialized topics. Much has been written by various poker writers about strategic concepts, and some players attempt to learn post-flop play through a discussion of these concepts. The problem with this approach, as opposed to a concrete study of examples, is that many of these concepts may or may not apply in a given situation. The texture of the board, the number of opponents, your position, the previous betting action, and, of course, your hand all influence whether or not it is right to utilize a certain poker concept. Consistent with the rest of our book, we believe the best approach for learning when to employ a concept is by viewing specific problems. As you work your way through the problems in this section, compare your thinking with ours. If you find yourself coming up with an answer that is different, it may be the result of one of the following things.

First, you may be tailoring your answer to a type of opponent you play with regularly. For example, it may be that in the games you play in, your opponent bets virtually every time when it is checked to him. Some players do this regardless of how many opponents they have or the texture of the board. In such a case, our answer may not be the right one for your specific situation. We are addressing the scenario when your opponent is a stranger or a typical middle limit player.

Second, maybe we are considering more factors in arriving at our answer than you are. For example, from our postings on the Internet, we have learned that when some players analyze a problem, they don't always consider the full texture of the board. Things like two-flushes, number of cards in the playing zone, and the closeness in rank of board-cards all play a major role for us in deciding what action to take. From our experience in teaching others about the game, we find that many players overly focus on one element in a decision and overlook another. Leave out a pertinent element and you may well come to a different answer— an incorrect one.

28 – BLUFFING

Bluffing is an interesting and enjoyable aspect of poker. To win because one was willing to make a bet on a bad hand makes you feel that the money was earned. At limit holdem, bluffing is an important part of the game. Its basic nature of getting only a two-card starting hand, but three cards at once on the next round, is that a hand able to stay in contention after the flop has been fortunate. A holdem player gets a pocket pair on 3 hands out of 51, which is 1 out of 17. If he does not start with a pair, he will hit a pair or something else playable on the flop on only one out of three pots. So in shorthanded pots, especially those where no one was strong enough to raise preflop, there is a realistic possibility that no one has a hand worthy of the name. However, the dealer is going to have to push the pot to someone, decent hand or not. This means if you are willing to make a bet or raise on a weak holding, the winner is more likely to be you than a player who always sits back to wait for something respectable before risking any money.

One of the great myths surrounding poker is that you have to bluff a lot in order to be a winning player. "It is important to advertise so that you get paid off when you have a good hand," according to many players. We do not believe the purpose of a bluff is to advertise in order to get your good hands paid off. Rather, we believe the advertising is a natural byproduct of good play when the situation is right for running a bluff. The purpose of a bluff is to give yourself the opportunity to win a pot when your hand quality is insufficient to accomplish the job. We bluff when we think it is the right play and has a chance to work. We do not bluff every time we have nothing to show down.

Many of the ideas that some players have concerning bluffing emanate from the world of big-bet poker (pot-limit or no-limit). Someone makes off with a big pot with a nervy bet on nothing. Bluffing is a critical skill in big-bet poker. In big-bet poker, a bluffer can make a large enough bet to move his opponent off a better hand often enough so a lot of pots are won this way.

Bluffing is also an important skill in limit poker—but not to the extent that many people seem to think. In a full-table limit holdem game, pots with either lots of players or lots of money are normally won by the best hand. In these pots, a potential caller is frequently getting 10-to-1 or even better pot odds to call. A potential bluffer simply cannot bet enough money in a limit game relative to what is already in the pot to move an opponent off a hand that has even an outside chance of winning a big pot.

The pots presenting a successful bluffing opportunity are mostly those where there are few players and no one has shown strength preflop. It is important to your bankroll that you pick up a lot of these small pots where no one has much. If you aspire to winning a big bet an hour, or even a small bet an hour, you can make a day's wages or close to it just by picking up a few of these pots in a session. Even though the stolen pots are seldom large, some successful steals will often prove to be the margin that turns a losing session into a winning one.

To show a plus from your bluffs, you do not have to be successful bluffing more times than not. The pot is laying you odds, so do not pull in your horns because a bluff does not work. The math in limit games is you only risk a fraction of what you can win, so winning one time out of perhaps every four or five bluffs means you have shown a long-run profit.

There are many times in limit poker when a bluffing opportunity will present itself. It is important that you recognize it and capitalize on the situation. We have already mentioned that most bluffs aim at a small pot and few opponents. Here's some other things you should look for in a bluffing opportunity.

Prospects are brighter when no one has shown any strength. One obvious place for this to happen is when you are on the button and everyone has checked. Someone has to be responsible for preventing pots from dragging out to the end, or the money might rot out there. If you are on the button, be willing to perform the task of ending these pots where no one has much. It's a dirty job, but someone has to do it. Button bets by both you and your opponents are suspect because of this. Making off with this type of pot is sometimes done by check-raising the button bettor on little or nothing, in the hopes that player was on a steal. It helps to be observant of how often a player bets on the button when checked to, because the thieves are easier to hijack than the honest folks.

28 - BLUFFING

The blinds are often in good position to steal a pot. When the button relinquishes a chance to bluff and the flop is checked by all, the pot is for sale. It is first come, first served. The little or big blind will have the first chance to put in a purchase order. Be especially eager to do so when the boardcards are mostly or all lower than the playing zone of the "free-will" players. That means they are in the blind's "stealing zone." When a blank comes, opportunity is knocking. If the card that comes is not a blank, consider a bluff anyway if there are not very many opponents. For example, suppose the flop comes all small cards, like 8-6-3 rainbow. Now a facecard comes. With only one or two opponents, there is a good chance that it missed everyone. Go ahead and bet. If no one made a pair with it, you are likely a winner. When the pot is very small, you might not get called even by a player who picked up a flush-draw, as he is not getting the right pot odds to draw at his hand. The card that comes does not have to be a potential top pair. When the flop is checked, no one is supposed to have top pair or better. (If someone has checked top pair, it is often one of the blinds, hoping to find out that the coast is clear for a top pair, weak kicker hand.) For a flop of K-6-3, a card in the playing zone like a jack ten, or nine also presents a possible bluff against a small field.

Look for a board where there may be few hands connecting. You have a better chance of success when the cards on the board are not coordinated with each other. Also helpful is having cards mostly lower than the playing zone of ace through nine.

Persuade the opponents that you are out of reach. You have brighter prospects when you can persuade people that you not only have them beaten, but are so far ahead that you are hard or impossible to catch. Having one big card on the board (that you supposedly have a pair of) and the rest small cards is helpful in this regard. It is actually easier to steal with this type of flop than if it comes all little cards. A couple of other examples where you might be out of reach are when you represent a flush when they are likely to have only one pair, or when you have shown strength on the flop and the top board-card pairs on the turn.

Put a tight image to work. If you play poker like we advocate, waiting for good starting hands and not trying any fancy stuff against a big crowd, you will acquire a tight image. Opponents may wrongly equate your tight play with reluctance to bluff. Don't bemoan your image or try to give action to undo it. Instead, use it. You have a better chance of a successful bluff in potential steal situations than most of the others, so take advantage of your image when opportunity knocks.

Don't appear to be a clepto. You are not the only player in the game that recognizes these easy steal situations. (The vigilance of others will increase as the stakes are higher, so there is a lot of action in a $40-$80 game that is lacking in a $10-$20 game.) If you try to pig everything in sight, your appetite will be apparent. Some of the other players are going to start playing back at you rather than folding. A good way to conceal your interest in thievery is to every so often, when on the button with a raggedy flop that's checked to you, let one go by and check yourself. Another way that gives up little is to occasionally just limp in when you are the button or cutoff and no one has opened yet. A wolf should occasionally masquerade as a sheep.

Look for situations where your hand might help and win. Be more eager to bluff when holding a hand that could still get lucky when the bluff fails to work. We have already discussed many times the widespread use of betting on the come (semi-bluffing).

Sometimes you ought to bluff with no outs. Yes, outs are desirable. But certain flops do not present any drawing chances to a straight or flush. For example, if a flop comes down 9-9-2 rainbow, there is no draw anyone can be betting (except overcards). Yet with this character flop, someone still has to get the money when no one has anything. Only in deals with weak and passive players involved does such a pot get checked out all the way and the biggest no-pair hand win.

The next group of hands illustrate some of these situations where a bluff may come into consideration.

(1) The game is $20-$40. You are in the big blind with A♥-K♠. A middle player limps and another middle player raises, with everyone else folding to you. You call as well as the middle limper. There is $130 in the pot and three players. The flop comes: J♥-7♦-3♣, leaving you with two big overcards. It is checked to the preflop raiser, who bets. You call and the other player folds. There is $170 in the pot and two players. The turn is the J♠. What do you do?

Answer: Bet. This is normally a decent time to bluff. As a preflop caller (rather than a raiser) you have certain advantages. Your hand is more likely to be tied in with the flop than a preflop raiser, so you should be quick to represent something that appears on the board at the turn or river. Here you can represent trip jacks, since you called out of your blind and your opponent does not rate to have a jack. He will sometimes fold, fearing that he is playing with only two outs if he has a pocket pair, or no outs if he has two overcards. (The confrontation of A-K vs. A-K is fairly common in holdem, and a lot of these are not split pots.)

(2) A $20-$40 game. You are in the big blind holding the J♠-7♠. An early player, a middle player, and the button limp. You take a free play. There is $90 in the pot and four players. The flop is: T♦-3♠-2♠, giving you a flush-draw with an overcard. You bet. Only the middle player calls until it gets to the button, who raises. You call, as well as the middle player. There is $210 in the pot and three players. The 6♥ comes on the turn. Now everyone checks. The river is the T♣. What do you do?

Answer: Bet. You bet the flop, representing a top pair of tens, into three opponents. You just called when raised, and this is what a player with top pair, weak kicker might do. You checked to the raiser on the turn when a blank hit, and got a free card. This tells the table that the button raiser was drawing, hoping to see the river for free. The river card now pairs the top flop-card, making it look like you could now have trip tens. You cannot win by checking, and have a decent chance to win by bluffing.

(3) A $30-$60 game. You open-raise from middle position with the A♣-T♠. Only the big blind calls. There is $140 in the pot and two players. The flop is: K♣-6♥-3♦, leaving you with an overcard. Your opponent checks. You bet on a cold bluff and he calls. There is $200 in the pot. The turn is the 6♠. Your opponent checks. What do you do?

Answer: Check. A bluff is unlikely to work here. When your opponent called your flop bet after you raised preflop and a board of K-x-x rainbow, he probably has a top pair of kings, or at least some kind of made hand he will play. This is a type of flop that is often checked and slowplayed by a player with top pair up front, because it is relatively safe to give out free cards here.

(4) A $10-$20 game. You are in the big blind holding the 4♣-3♦. Only the under-the-gun player and the small blind limp in. You get a free play. There is $30 in the pot and three players. The flop is: K♠-7♣-5♥, giving you a gutshot with any six. The small blind checks. What do you do?

Answer: Bet. This is a perfect situation for a bluff. You have only two opponents. No one has shown any strength, since the pot is unraised. One of your two opponents has checked. A rainbow flop came one big card and two little cards, so a draw is unlikely.

(5) A $15-$30 game. You are on the button with the T♣-8♣. An early player limps. You limp, as well as the small blind. There is $60 in the pot and four players. The flop comes: A♥-Q♦-4♥, giving you nothing. It is checked to you. What do you do?

Answer: Check. This is not a good time to bluff. A two-flush coupled with an ace-queen combo means that there will be all kinds of draws out there. Besides a flush-draw, there are numerous gutshots with the common playing hands of K-J, K-T, and J-T. You are unlikely to win the pot outright by betting into three opponents. Furthermore, if the flop were more ragged (like rainbow ace-nine-deuce), then you know that when you are called you are up against some kind of made hand, not a draw. But with this flop, you really don't where you are at when you get called, so the decision whether to bet the turn is more muddled. Also, an ace-high flop gets sandbagged a lot. Lastly, button bets are suspect, and someone will often call or even check-raise such a bet.

(6) A $20-$40 game. You are in the big blind holding the J♣-6♦. An early player, a middle player, and the small blind limp, so you get a free play. There is $80 in the pot and four players. The flop is: A♥-Q♣-3♠, missing you completely. Everyone checks. The turn is the Q♦. The small blind checks. What do you do?

Answer: Bet. This is an excellent spot to bluff. No one bet the flop, so no one may have an ace. It would be logical for you to have a queen and not bet the flop when an ace shows. You have only three opponents, and one of them has now checked twice. This is a good example of a hand with no outs where a bluff is quite reasonable. Outs are desirable, but not a necessity.

(7) A $10-$20 game. You raise from middle position with A♥-K♣ behind two early players. The button and the early players call. There is $95 in the pot and four players. The flop is: J♦-8♦-5♦, giving you two overcards. It is checked to you. What do you do?

Answer: Bet. Despite the single-suited board, you should take a stab at the pot with only three opponents. The bluff will fail more often than work, but you are getting over 7-to-1 on the money. The board is scary, so maybe no one will try to run you down on a marginal pair. If you get called, then you are done with it.

(8) A $10-$20 game. You are on the button with the A♣-T♣. Two early players and two middle players limp. You decide to vary your play and raise. Everyone calls. There is $140 in the pot and seven players. The flop is: K♥-9♣-8♣, giving you the nut flush-draw and an ace overcard. Everyone checks and you bet. Only an early player and a middle player call. There is $170 in the pot and three players. The turn is the 2♦. It is checked to you and you bet. Both opponents call. There is $230 in the pot. The river is the 8♥. Both players check. What do you do?

Answer: Bet. With two opponents, your decent ace will most likely not be strong enough to survive a showdown. It is worth another bet to try and get middle pair or bottom pair to fold.

(9) A $10-$20 game. You are in early position with A♠-J♠. You raise after two other players limp in. The cutoff and the two limpers call. There is $95 in the pot and four players. The flop is: K♦-8♠-3♦, leaving you with an overcard and a backdoor flush-draw. It is checked to you. What do you do?

Answer: Bet. You should bet a flop of K-8-3 despite the two-flush, having only three opponents with two of them checking. You are the preflop raiser, marked with a good hand. Your opponents will frequently put you on ace-king, and may well fold a pair lower than kings.

(10) A $20-$40 game. You are in the big blind holding A♣-Q♣. An early player and a middle player limp. You raise and they both call. There is $130 in the pot and three players. The flop comes: 7♥-6♦-2♠, so all you have is two overcards. You bet and only the middle player calls. There is $170 in the pot and two players. The turn is the 3♣. You bet and your opponent calls. There is $250 in the pot. The river is the 9♠; no help. What do you do?

Answer: Check. Your opponent has been hanging around all along, hoping you have only overcards. Having decided to call your bet on the turn, he will not be folding for a bet on the river when a blank comes. Your only hope is that maybe he has some kind of busted draw, giving him a non-pair hand you can beat. If he bets, a call should be strongly considered.

(11) You are in the big blind with the A♠-9♠. A player limps in under-the-gun and the little blind calls. You take a free play. The flop comes J♠-6♦-3♣. The little blind checks, and you bet, trying to steal (though you may actually hold the best hand with ace-high). Both opponents call. On the turn comes the J♥, pairing the top card on the board. The little blind checks; what do you do?

Answer: Bet. You should bet again when you have a go at it on the flop, no one raises, and the board pairs with the top card. You represented top pair with your flop bet, and their failure to raise here makes it unlikely they have a jack. (If the player who limped in under-the-gun has a jack, he figures to have a good kicker, and may well have raised you on the flop.) If the first player had a jack, he probably would have bet it on the flop. The pair on board leaves them with few or no outs if you now have three jacks.

(12) You are in the cutoff seat, returning to the game, and have to post a blind. You pick up the 4♠-2♠. Everyone folds to you. What do you do?

Answer: Raise, unless the opponents yet to act are known calling stations. If you play the kind of poker we advocate, you will not be playing a lot of starting hands, and are liable to get a tight image because of this. Here is a chance to exploit it. You are only investing a small bet, and may win the pot outright. If not, you have the initiative in a shorthanded pot. If instead you rap the table, another player may seize on your weakness and raise, so you will have to pay another small bet to stay in anyway. Your raise here is far different than raising on trash with nothing invested.

(13) You pick up the Q♠-J♠ and call in middle position. Two players call behind you, and the little blind calls. The big blind, an experienced and decent player, raises. Everyone calls, so five of you see the flop, which comes A♠-9♦-8♠, giving you a flush-draw and a gutshot straight-draw with any ten. The little blind checks, the big blind bets, and you call. The others fold. The turn is the 2♦. The opponent bets again and you call. On the end comes the 5♥. Your opponent checks; what do you do?

Answer: Check. It is an error to bet on the end anytime you cannot win a showdown. This opponent is not going to check on the end after betting throughout, if he was on a draw. He has something. If you bet, he will beat you into the pot to call. He sees the flush-draw that came on the flop and never got there. He isn't going to put you on a 7-6 for a straight when you have opened the pot in middle position. So be a meek mouse, check, and cut your losses. There's no reason to throw good money after bad.

(14) You have 6♣–6♠ in middle position and open with a raise. A player in late position calls and everyone else folds, so just the two of you are in. The flop is K♣-7♣-7♦, making a two-flush on the board. You bet, and he calls. The turn is the 8♥. You bet, and he calls again. The last card is the K♠, counterfeiting any semblance of a hand that you may have had. Do you check or bet?

Answer: Bet. Pray that the opponent has a busted flush-draw. You cannot let some clown win with nine-high.

(15) You hold K♥-J♥ in the big blind. A solid player opens with a raise, the button calls, and you call, so there are three players. The flop is: A♣-A♦-6♠. You check, the raiser bets, and the button folds. What do you do?

Answer: Call. Of course, there is nothing wrong with throwing your hand away, since you have nothing. But this is not a bad spot for a little larceny, particularly if the opponent is one of those mutterers who regards you as a tight player. The idea is whatever comes, you will then bet. A phony call on the flop can be used as preparation for a bluff on the turn. This ploy of faking a call before bluffing often works better than an immediate raise.

(16) You are in the big blind with the 7♦-3♦. An early player and two middle players call, so four of you are in for the flop, which comes K♠-9♦-5♣. Everyone checks. The 2♥ comes on the turn, giving you zero. What do you do?

Answer: Bet. Don't let the fact that you have no outs stop you from running a bluff when everything else is just about perfect. Three opponents is a bearable number to bluff against. Since the top two flop cards hook up, it is doubtful that anyone slowplayed a king. Nobody picked up a flush-draw on the turn; the board is still rainbow. It would be surprising if someone made a pair with the turn-card, or got any help other than maybe a gutshot at a wheel.

(17) You have the K♣-J♣ in middle position and call. The cutoff and small blind call, so four of you see the flop of Q♥-7♣-4♥.

238

You have a king-high backdoor flush-draw and an overcard. The two blinds check and its up to you. Do you check or bet?

Answer: Bet. The flush-draw would be a deterrent to betting if you were first, because there are more card combinations that would be playing hands. But now that two people have checked, the flush-draw is more help than harm to a bluff. A player will seldom check a good hand like top pair or better when there is a flush-draw on the board, because even if no one draws out, he may lose his market for betting. True, there is still one player behind you, but he is not a favorite to call.

(18) A \$15-\$30 game in Las Vegas. You have the A♣-Q♣ in the big blind. A solid fellow opens with a raise in early position and everyone else folds. You call. The flop is a good one; J♣-7♣-2♦, giving you the nut flush-draw with two overcards. You bet (a check-raise is also to be considered). He raises, and you call. There is \$130 in the pot. The turn is the 4♥. You check, he bets, and you call. There is \$190 in the pot. The river is the disappointing J♥, so you have zero. Do you give up or bluff a bet?

Answer: Bet. The top board-card pairing on the turn or river presents a bluffing opportunity to someone who is not the preflop raiser and has shown some strength on the flop. His hand is apt to be tied in with the board-cards. Despite your opponent's preflop and flop raises, he may not have an overpair. He could easily have only A-K or an intermediate pair. Maybe he should call with either of these hands, because there was a flush-draw on the flop, but if he thinks you are a real tight player, he may fold. (Frankly, this type of bluff works better if there was a rainbow flop and you have busted out on a straight-draw.)

On the actual hand, the opponent thought for quite a while, but finally mucked his hand. Penny wise, pound foolish. This is an example of a type of bluff that will not work against certain players, so it helps to know your opponents. It also shows that having a tight image has an upside; bluffs work more often.

(19) A $10-$20 game. You are on the button and are holding the T♠-8♠. Only an early player, a middle player, and the cutoff fold. You limp in, as well as the small blind. There is $70 in the pot and seven players. The flop is: Q♥-9♠-6♠, giving you a flush-draw plus a double belly-buster straight-draw (a jack or seven). It is checked to the player on your right, who bets. You raise. Only a middle player and the bettor call. There is $130 in the pot and three players. The turn is the 5♣. Both opponents check. You bet and only the middle player calls. There is a $170 pot and two players. The river is the 8♣, pairing you. The opponent checks. What do you do?

Answer: Check. You intended to bluff if a blank had come. But now you have something to show down that beats a busted draw, so a bet is unneeded—and unwise. Your opponent will call if he has you beat (since he called your turn bet) and fold if he doesn't.

(20) A $20-$40 game. You are in the cutoff seat with the J♠-T♠. A middle player limps, you call, and the button calls. The small blind folds and the big blind raps, so four of you are in for a $90 pot. The flop comes Q♣-7♣-4♥, a clean miss. You have no pair, no draw, and not even any overcards. The big blind and middle player check. What do you do?

Answer: Bet. Of course, we could hardly consider it a terrible poker play to check, since you don't have a darn thing, but be aware of the dynamics of this situation. The flop is queen-high and has a flush-draw. The two players who checked are unlikely to have anything decent, because if they did, they would want to protect it by a bet. Their giving a free card would have some danger because there are a couple of potential overcards and a draw to contend with. This means you are probably home free with the pot if you get through the button. A bet in the cutoff seat look less like a possible bluff than a bet on the button, so there is a good chance you will not get called (or raised) on suspicion. If you have a tight image, so much the better. On balance, this is such a good spot for a bluff that we recommend you give it a try despite having no outs. You don't need any outs if you don't get called!

29 – CHECKING AND CALLING

A good friend of ours who is a strong player has told us on more than one occasion that he hates checking and calling. If he is in the pot, he wants to be the bettor or the raiser. He feels the key to success at poker is to be aggressive and deceptive, making him unreadable to his opponents. "You cannot be a winning player when you are checking and calling," he proclaims. "Good players get the money by winning with the worst hand and getting paid off on their good hands, so you must keep your betting arm in motion once you decide to play." We have heard this philosophy from quite a few other people as well. Of course, there is an element of truth here. The general approach to poker success is to play good hands, those worth backing by a bet or raise. You can't win a pot before the deal is over by only checking and calling.

However, it is our view that success at poker involves making good decisions by selecting the best action from a variety of options. Betting, checking, calling, raising, and folding are simply options. Like a master craftsman, the good player selects the right tool from his tool kit, depending upon the particulars of a given job. To rule out checking and calling is to limit your options and make it harder to get the job done optimally.

In a limit holdem game with a pot that involves multiple players, checking and calling can easily be the proper course of action. It is what you do when the pot odds justify playing, but aggressive action is unwarranted because your hand is weak, and the number of opponents, board texture, and prior betting tell you that there is little chance of winning the pot by a bet or raise.

The following hands illustrate some of the factors that come into consideration when passive play by just calling is an option. Since aggressive play has been deeply covered in the other chapters, this set of "problems" consists only of those hands where you ought to tread gently, but the explanations should be helpful.

(1) The game is $10-$20. You are in the big blind with the 9♠-7♣ and get a free play after two early players and the button limp in. There is $45 in the pot and four players. The flop is: 7♦-4♥-2♣, giving you top pair. You bet; only the button folds. There's $75 in the pot and three players. The turn is the 6♥. What do you do?

Answer: Check. Having your flop bet get called in two spots given the rainbow board means that someone either has a bigger seven or was on a draw, in which case the six has helped him.

(2) A $10-$20 game. You are in the big blind holding the Q♣-8♥ and get a free play after an early player, two middle players, and the small blind limp in. There is $50 in the pot and five players. The flop is: Q♦-J♦-8♣, giving you top and bottom pair. The small blind checks. You bet. Everyone calls back to the small blind, who raises. You reraise and everyone calls. There is $200 in the pot. The turn is the 3♠. The small blind checks. You bet and only a middle player folds. There is $280 in the pot and four players. The river is the A♠. The small blind checks. What do you do?

Answer: Check. The ace is a bad card, making a straight possible, as well as a higher two pair. You also have two players yet to act.

(3) A $10-$20 game. You raise from middle position with Q♠-Q♣ after an early player limps in. The next player as well as the cutoff and the big blind call. There is $105 in the pot and five players. The flop is: T♦-8♦-7♣, giving you an overpair. It is checked to you. You bet, the other two players call, and the big blind raises. The early limper folds. What do you do?

Answer: Call. Do not reraise on the flop with an overpair when there is a possible straight on the board and you have this many opponents. There is also a two-flush on the table. The pot could get raised again or capped, your hand may not be best, and there are a number of cards that can come off on the turn that kill your hand (for example, a diamond, a nine, or a ten).

(4) A $10-$20 game. You limp in under-the-gun with 9♠-9♣. An early player, a middle player, the cutoff, the button, and the small blind call. There is $70 in the pot and seven players. The flop is: 8♣-6♥-5♦, giving you an overpair and a gutshot straight-draw.

29 - CHECKING AND CALLING

Both blinds check; you bet. The early player, middle player, cutoff, and small blind call. The pot has $120 and five players. The turn is the 8♥. The small blind checks. What do you do?

Answer: Check. On the flop, we were nervous betting our one middle-sized pair into six opponents with a possible straight on the board. With the top flop-card now pairing and us still having four opponents, the likelihood of someone having trip eights or a slowplayed straight is too high to be leading off here.

(5) A $10-$20 game. You are in the small blind with the Q♦-2♦. An early player and two middle players limp. You limp for another $5. There is $50 in the pot and five players. The flop is: Q♥-T♠-9♣, giving you top pair. What do you do?

Answer: Check. With four opponents and three cards in the playing zone, it is right to check here. You are unlikely to win the pot outright by betting, and your top pair, no kicker hand is too weak to be leading into this large a field.

(6) A $10-$20 game. You limp in under-the-gun with the 9♠–9♣. Everyone calls except the other two early players and the small blind. There is $75 in the pot and seven players. The flop comes: Q♣-T♥-6♠, putting two overcards to your pocket pair of nines on the table. Everyone checks. The turn is the 5♥ and everyone checks. The river is the 9♦, giving you a set of nines. The big blind checks. What do you do?

Answer: Check. The nine makes some possible straights, and there are five other players still to act. Anyone helped by the nine probably made a straight, since you have two nines, and there was no betting on either of the two previous betting rounds. You are unlikely to get called by a worse hand, and could easily run into a better one. To bet for value on the end in poker, we need a reasonable chance of getting paid off by a losing hand.

(7) A $10-$20 game. You are on the button holding the A♥-A♣. Two early players, a middle player, and the cutoff limp. You raise

243

and everyone calls except for the big blind, who folds. There is $130 in the pot and six players. The flop is: Q♦-8♦-3♣, giving you an overpair. It is checked to you and you bet. The small blind and the two early players call. There is $170 in the pot and four players. The turn is the 6♦, making a possible flush. It is checked to you. What do you do?

Answer: Check. With this many opponents taking a flop, four players wanting to see the turn, and that board, betting again would not be a good idea despite your big overpair. You may get check-raised. Against a flush, you have no outs; against two pair, you might have as many as eight outs. You hate to give out a free card to four opponents, but it is too dangerous to bet.

(8) A $10-$20 game. You are on the button holding the Q♠-Q♣. Everyone limps except a middle player, who folds. You raise. Everyone calls. There is $180 in the pot and nine players. The flop is: J♣-9♥-3♥, giving you an overpair. Both blinds check. An early player bets. Everyone calls except for another early player and the cutoff, who fold. You raise and only the small blind folds. There is $300 in the pot and six players. The turn is the Q♥, giving you top set. The big blind checks. Both early players check. The first middle player bets and the next one calls. What do you do?

Answer: Call. You are surely beat, but have 10 outs to a full house or quads. These are odds of 3.6-to-1 against. Some would argue you should raise, because for every $1 you wager, if you are getting more than $3.60 pulled into the pot from the other players, you will show a profit. But a raise looks wrong here. Often, even when your draw is getting overlay odds, it's a mistake to make a piggy raise and possibly alter the favorable situation. Some players may fold, and your raise would reopen the betting for a reraise.

(9) A $20-$40 game. You are in middle position, an early player limps, and you raise with the J♦-J♣. The button, both blinds, and the early limper call. There is $200 in the pot and five players. The flop is: K♣-T♠-9♥, giving you second pair and a gutshot straight-draw. Both blinds and the limper check. What do you do?

Answer: Check. A flop of K-T-9 will connect with many hands that players limp in with preflop. You have a second pair and a gutshot straight-draw with four opponents. If you bet, it is very unlikely you will win the pot outright. With this board and so many opponents, you will frequently get raised. You are getting 10-to-1 pot odds, which are slightly less than the odds for hitting a gutshot, and the problem is that your draw is a one card straight-draw. This means that you will be occasionally splitting the pot even when a queen arrives. Your jacks may or may not be good. A king-high flop touches many hands players limp in with, and many players simply check to a preflop raiser, rather than bet, even with top pair. If you catch a jack, this puts four parts to a straight on the table, so anyone with a queen has you beat. There is also a player behind you who probably has a decent hand, since he cold-called your preflop raise.

(10) A $10-$20 game. You are in the big blind holding the 7♣-4♣. An early player, a middle player, and the button limp, so you take a free play. There is $45 in the pot and four players. The flop is: A♦-7♦-4♥, giving you the bottom two pair. You bet and only the button folds. There is $75 in the pot and three players. The turn is the A♠. What do you do?

Answer: Check. If you had but one opponent, it could be argued that betting again might be right because he may be on a flush-draw. But with two opponents, it is unlikely that they are both flushing. It is too easy for one of them to have an ace. Furthermore, if one of them has a pocket pair higher than sevens, your second pair just got counterfeited by the aces.

(11) A $15-$30 game. You are in the big blind holding K♥-J♥. An early player and the small blind limp. You raise and they both call. There is $90 in the pot and three players. The flop comes: Q♦-Q♣-J♣, giving you queens over jacks. The small blind checks. You bet and only the small blind calls. There is $120 in the pot and two players. The turn is the J♠, giving you jacks full of queens. Your opponent checks. What do you do?

Answer: Check. You save money if your opponent has a queen, which is a distinct possibility based on his flop call. You may induce a bluff or a call on the end from a worse hand. He will not draw out on your boat with the free card if you are ahead, and may pay you off on the end or bluff if you show weakness now.

(12) A $10-$20 game. You raise from early position with A♦-J♦. A middle player, the cutoff, the button, and both blinds call. There is $120 in the pot and six players. The flop is: 7♠-4♦-3♥, giving you two overcards and a backdoor nut flush-draw. Everyone checks. The turn is the J♠, giving you top pair, top kicker. The small blind checks. The big blind bets. What do you do?

Answer: Call, don't raise. Despite having top pair, top kicker, you cannot be sure you are not up against a straight, which would mean you have no outs. If the big blind is betting two pair, than you may have sufficient outs to play on. If the big blind is betting a worse jack, than be happy to let him bet your hand for you.

(13) A $10-$20 game. You are in middle position with the K♠-J♥. An early player and a middle player limp. You limp as well as the cutoff and the small blind. There is $60 in the pot and six players. The flop is: J♦-8♥-7♥, giving you top pair and a backdoor flush-draw. The small blind bets, the big blind folds, and the two limpers ahead of you both call. What do you do?

Answer: Just call. Despite having top pair, good kicker, raising is bad, because you cannot get any more players out at this point except for the cutoff, who may fold anyway. You want to see the turn-card before committing any real money to this hand. Six players took this flop and all three cards are in a playing zone, putting a possible straight on the board. There is also a two-flush on the table, so a heart likely beats you.

(14) A $15-$30 game. You are in early position with the Q♠-Q♦. Another early player opens with a raise and you reraise. Only the small blind and the early player call. There is $150 in the pot and three players. The flop is: T♠-7♠-3♠, giving you a flush-draw as well as an overpair. Both opponents check. You bet and only the small blind calls. There is $180 in the pot and two players. The turn is the 2♠, Making your flush. Your opponent checks. What do you do?

Answer: Check. Induce a river bet by a worse hand. And if he is sandbagging with a bigger flush, you will save money.

(15) A $20-$40 game. You open with a raise from early position with the A♦-A♣. Two middle position players and the big blind call. There is $170 in the pot and four players. The flop comes: K♣-T♣-7♣, giving you the nut flush-draw in addition to your overpair. The big blind checks. You bet. The first middle player calls and the second middle player raises. The big blind folds. What do you do?

Answer: Call. Reraising is a bad idea when out of position. When the board flops all of one suit and there is a bet and a raise to you, then at least one of your two opponents has either a made flush or the nut flush-draw. Since you have the A♣, it is apparent that someone has a flush, and they will not be laying it down. Save yourself some money by checking and calling.

(16) A $10-$20 game. You raise with the A♥-Q♥ from middle position after two early players limp. The next player calls and the cutoff reraises. Both the button and small blind fold, but everyone else calls. There is $185 in the pot and six players. The flop is: A♣-Q♣-5♣, giving you the top two pair. The players in front of you check. You bet and the next player calls. The preflop reraiser pops it. The big blind calls. It is folded to you. What do you do?

Answer: Call. With the board flopping all of one suit and three opponents willing to call bets and raises, the likelihood of you being up against a flush or just a better hand is too high to reraise. Six players took this flop and four of them are paying premium prices to see the turn. You may well have very much the worst of it. On the actual hand, the player reraised. The preflop reraiser had a set of aces, and capped the flop betting. The big blind had a small flush. The turn was a blank and the river was the Q♠, filling him. While the player would have had a lot of difficulty getting away from his hand, he lost more money than he should have, even with queens full versus aces full.

(17) A $10-$20 game. A shorthanded game with only seven players. You raise from middle position with the 9♠-9♣ behind two early limpers. Only the limpers call your raise. There is $75 in the pot and three players. The flop comes: A♥-5♦-3♣, giving you second pair. They both check and you bet. Only one limper calls. There is $95 in the pot and two players. The turn is the Q♠. Your opponent checks. What do you do?

Answer: Check. You should not bet on the turn when you get called on an ace-high flop, after raising preflop, unless the opponent could be drawing at a flush or straight. The caller is marked with an ace, given that board. Also, having another overcard show up on the turn is a detriment.

(18) A $15-$30 game. You are in early position with the K♦-Q♣ and limp in behind another early limper. A middle player raises and both blinds call. The early limper calls and you call. There is $150 in the pot and five players. The flop is: T♣-9♣-3♥, giving you a gutshot straight-draw. Everyone checks. The turn is the Q♦, giving you top pair. The small blind checks. The big blind bets and the early limper folds. What do you do?

Answer: Call. The board is now Q-T-9, and even if your opponent is betting a queen, his kicker could easily be paired with the board, or he might have you outkicked. Either you are beat, tied, or he has specifically queen-jack. You also have a preflop raiser still in the hand, who may have decided to not bet this flop with A-Q and four opponents. Once in a while, the preflop raiser will have flopped a set (or have A-A or K-K), and decided to slowplay. While this is not likely, it is part of the spectrum of possibilities.

(19) A $10-$20 game. You limp in from middle position with the A♦-2♦ behind an early limper. The cutoff, the button, and the

248

small blind limp. There is $60 in the pot and six players. The flop is: A♣-7♥-3♦, giving you top pair and a backdoor nut flush-draw. The blinds and the early limper check. You bet and only the cutoff folds. There is $110 in the pot and five players. The turn is the K♣. It is checked to you. What do you do?

Answer: Check. With top pair, no kicker, you should not bet the turn after five players call your flop bet. There is no flush-draw or logical straight-draw on the flop, so at least one of your numerous opponents must have a better ace than you.

(20) A $10-$20 game. You are in early position having the J♥-J♣ and raise an early limper. A middle player, the big blind, and the limper call. There is $85 in the pot and four players. The flop is: 8♦-7♦-3♦, giving you an overpair. The big blind checks and the early limper bets. What do you do?

Answer: Call. With the board flopping all of one suit, it would be out of line for you to raise. If another diamond appears, your hand is instantly dead, unless it is specifically the J♦. Call and await developments. If a blank comes on the turn and you are checked to, then you can bet. Otherwise, you may be glad you just called.

(21) A $30-$60 game. You open with a raise under-the-gun having the Q♥-Q♦ and only the cutoff calls. There is $170 in the pot and two players. The flop is: A♣-7♥-3♦, giving you second pair. You bet and he calls. There is $230 in the pot. The turn is the 2♠. What do you do?

Answer: Check. What is out there for your opponent to be calling a flop bet if he does not have an ace? If your opponent is an aggressive type who will bluff or semi-bluff a lot, then you can simply check, and call when he bets. But there is no point in you betting here. If he has an ace, he will not fold. If he is chasing, he probably does not have very many outs to beat you.

(22) A $10-$20 game. You are in middle position with A♣-4♣ and limp behind an early limper. There is $35 in the pot and three players. The flop is: K♣-7♣-3♦, giving you the nut flush-draw and an ace overcard. The big blind bets and the early player calls. You raise. The big blind reraises and the early player folds. You call. There is $105 in the pot and two players. The turn is the A♥, giving you top pair as well as the nut flush-draw. The big blind bets. What do you do?

Answer: Call. While it is tempting to raise on the expensive street with top pair and the nut flush-draw, the strong flop betting by the big blind makes two pair or better quite likely, especially since he got a free flop.

(23) A $10-$20 game. You are on the button with the 9♦-8♦. An early player and two middle players limp. You limp. The small blind limps. There is $60 in the pot and six players. The flop is: T♦-7♦-4♦, giving you a flush and an open-ended straight flush-draw. They all check. You bet and only the early limper calls. There is $80 in the pot and two players. The turn is the 2♦, putting a four-flush on the board. Your opponent checks. What do you do?

Answer: Check. Betting here is overly exposing yourself to a raise and is unlikely to get a call from someone you can beat. Your opponent is not likely to be drawing at a full house; if he had a set or two pair, he probably would have bet or check-raised you on the flop. The probable situation is that if you have the best hand, he has no outs. If he stays with you, he almost certainly has a bigger diamond, and you might even get check-raised. You have a chance to get a free card to your straight flush-draw, so take it.

(24) A $10-$20 game. You are in the small blind with the K♣-K♦. An early player limps and a middle player raises. Another middle player calls, as well as the cutoff. You reraise and everyone calls. There is $180 in the pot and six players. The flop is: Q♥-T♦-4♣, giving you an overpair. You bet. The big blind and the early player fold. The preflop raiser pops it. The other two players call. You reraise and everyone calls. There is $300 in the pot and four players in the hand. The turn is the A♣. What do you do?

Answer: Check. Betting when an ace turns up into three other players who paid three bets to take cards off is too risky. Someone likely has an ace, and you are playing six outs at best, with any king or jack. A king may not be an out, since a jack in someone's hand gives that person a straight. After checking, you are getting the right pot odds to play on.

(25) A $30-$60 game. You are on the button holding the A♥-K♣. Everyone folds to the cutoff, who opens with a raise. You reraise and only the cutoff calls. There is $230 in the pot and two players. The flop is: 7♣-6♣-4♥, leaving you with two big overcards and a backdoor flush-draw. Your opponent checks. You bet and he calls. There is $290 in the pot. The turn is the 5♠. Your opponent checks. What do you do?

Answer: Check. This is an exception to the rule about following through with a bet on the turn after showing all the strength before and on the flop. With an open-ended straight on the table, there are many hands where your opponent has you drawing dead. By betting, you are also exposed to a check-raise bluff or semi-bluff.

(26) A $20-$40 game. An early player who is a rich maniac opens with a raise. A middle player reraises. You are on the button with the K♠-K♣ and make it four bets. They both call. There is $270 in the pot and three players. The flop is: 5♣-4♥-4♦, giving you kings over fours. It is checked to you. You bet and they both call. There is $330 in the pot. The turn is the 2♠. The maniac bets and the next player folds. What do you do?

Answer: Call. Your hand may not be good, so you should minimize your loss by just calling. If your hand is good, then let the maniac bet it for you. The key here is that you have position, so you can make sure that every betting round gets bet.

30 - CHECK-RAISING

A poker player with a good hand faces this decision; should he lead out and bet with the hand or try for a check-raise? If he always bets, the opponents will know when he checks that he does not have a top-quality hand. But when he checks, he risks that all the opponents will check behind him. They are getting a "free card." By not betting, the player with a good hand in this spot has reduced the amount he can win. Worse yet, it is possible that an opponent who would have folded for a bet will actually take the pot away from him. This could happen when the free card on the flop allows a longshot to hit on the turn, when an opponent uses the free card to pick up a draw and completes the hand on the end, or when the turn-card scares him into checking and allowing a longshot to hit at the river. It can also cause him to lose the pot on a bluff when a scare-card hits and someone bets. Whether to check and allow the possibility of a free card is a weighty decision that can seriously affect your result for the session.

Few poker plays are more fun than the check-raise. You act like you are weak, the opponent tries to take advantage of the "weakness" by betting, and you put him in his place by now raising, which lets him know where the power lies. There is a joyful feeling in entering a phone booth, stripping off your rather ordinary outer garments, and coming out as the Man of Steel.

There a chess story involving Emmanuel Lasker, a World Champion during the early part of the 20th century. Lasker was on a trans-Atlantic voyage, and one of the passengers asked him to play a game of chess, having no idea who he was. When Lasker was hesitant, the man misjudged the reason why, and offered to spot Lasker a queen (a monster spot, as the queen is the most powerful piece). Lasker played the man a game getting queen odds and deliberately lost. Lasker then said, "I think it helped you to be without a queen. Let's play another game, and I will give you a queen." The man protested, and probably thought his opponent a bit crazy, but Lasker insisted, so they played another game with Lasker giving the queen spot. Lasker trounced the man. Then the World Champion said, "I told you having a queen was a disadvantage." Later on, the man found out who Lasker was, and felt quite embarrassed.

The check-raise is for many players an overly-used poker play, mostly because it is such a psychologically satisfying play to use. If you are playing poker mainly for fun, we will not try to take away part of your entertainment. But if you are trying to win money, perhaps you are going for too many check-raises. If so, you should give up that fondness for that pleasure of check-raising, that coming out of the bushes to show who's really boss, and instead get your poker kicks from counting your winnings.

After gaining some playing experience, a number of holdem players become quite enamored with check-raising. They like to check-raise because it gets more money in the pot when they have the best hand. They also use it as a tool for eliminating players by forcing them to call two bets cold, thereby protecting their hand. Many of them see it as a nifty tactical weapon to be used in varying your play and confusing your opponents.

However, check-raising has some difficulties. It requires someone else to bet your hand for you. When this does not happen, you can lose some bets. You may also inadvertently give out a free card to an opponent who would have folded had you bet. This can cost you the pot, as in the following example.

This hand was played many years ago, in a $10-$20 game at the Stardust cardroom in the late seventies. I (BC) was still pretty much a rookie at holdem. I held a 9-7 of hearts in middle position. Everyone in front of me called the blind, so I called. (I would not make such a call today.) Then the raising started. By the time the flop came, there were nine players in for a capped pot—and the cap was a bet and five raises. There was over half a grand in before the flop, which came A-3-5 rainbow, and was checked by everyone. The turn-card was a heart (I forget which one), giving me a four-flush. The under-the-gun player bet, and I called. The third heart on board came at the river to make my flush, and when the player bet again I raised. He called, I showed my flush, and he flashed me a 4-2 before mucking his hand. He had flopped a straight, checked it, and no one had bet his hand for him. I would not have called a bet on the flop to draw at a nine-high backdoor flush, so his check on the flop had cost him a gigantic pot. This hand illustrates an important poker principle; when the pot is big, you try to protect your hand rather than win extra bets.

There are a lot of good holdem players who would have also checked that flop with his hand. In fact, we are not even saying the player actually made a poker error, even though on this particular hand trying for a check-raise turned out to be an extremely expensive decision. But what we will say is any player who checks in this type of situation should be doing so in order to confront the field with a double bet and thus eliminate players, not with the idea of simply gaining some extra bets.

From this example, we see that there is an additional danger of losing the pot by checking besides having the player receive a free card that he would not have stayed in and paid for. There is also the danger a player will pick up a draw, then be receiving sufficient pot odds to call a bet and draw out on you.

The pot size is an important factor affecting the decision of whether to risk going for a check-raise. When the pot is very large, protecting your hand comes first. If we are going for a check-raise just to vary our game, it would be wise to do so in unraised pots, where not as much money is at stake. In raised pots, when we try for a check-raise, the main reason is we are hoping a certain specific person will bet. Then we can confront the field with a double bet, which is more likely to move people out of the pot. So when we check, it is usually because we expect the preflop raiser to bet. In fact, it is not so unusual for a check-raise to be the only way we could have won the pot, because it eliminated a player who was going to call a single bet. For the double-bet strategy to work, the preflop raiser needs to be on or near our right. With the preflop raiser on our left, we can usually better protect our hand by betting, as the raiser may well pop it, hoping he has us beaten. Of course, we also relish the three-bet opportunity.

The number of opponents is very important when contemplating a check-raise strategy. It is axiomatic that the fewer opponents you have, the less dangerous it is to give a free card. In most cases where you can go for a check-raise, the pot is either heads-up or threeway. The risks of a drawout go up sharply as the number of opponents grows. With more than two opponents, you need to be persuaded that one of the opponents is extremely likely to bet. Perhaps if a very aggressive player is the preflop raiser, or something like that. Against a large field, do not check a hand intending to raise unless you have the game plan of using a double bet to move players out of the pot.

Giving a possible free card when trying for a check-raise is a gamble. You are gambling someone is going to bet. When taking such a gamble, the big question is how likely a free card is to beat you. If the card was only going to get the opponent in trouble if he hit, than we do not need any kind of assurance that someone will bet. For example, suppose we limp in with a pair of kings up front—an action that is itself the kind of gamble we have been discussing. The pot goes unraised, we get some callers, and see a flop of K-7-2 of three different suits where we have top set. At holdem, when we check and the field checks behind us, this is no disaster. We hope someone will make a pair, two pair, or a set on the next card, and be either stone dead or close to it. Even if someone were to pick up a flush-draw, the pot odds would not be such that we had made a serious error. The player will be about a 4.5-to-1 dog, and the pot odds normally will be in that neighborhood.

Unfortunately, if the only hands we check-raised with were whoppers such as top set with no straight or flush draw, our play would be way too predictable, because such situations are so rare. So we need to vary our play, and do some check-raising with only one pair. Naturally, checking this weak a hand is risky business, but the risk can be cut down to an acceptable level if you go about it the right way.

The most important factor that affects whether you can check one pair trying for a check-raise is the rank of your pair. If you have aces—either pocket aces or an ace that matches a card on the board—then overcards do not exist. If the next card beats you, the opponent will have to make two pair or better with it. As we all know, it is a lot harder at holdem to make two pair than one pair.

With any lower pair, there exists the possibility of an overcard coming. This is always bad. Even if it doesn't beat you, it may scare you into checking, or hinder your chance of getting called.

The following is a good rule of thumb. If more than one overcard beats you, do not check top pair or an overpair. Here are some examples. With K-Q and a king or queen being the top card on the board, you can sometimes gamble a check, because only an ace beats you. But if there is more than a one rank of card that beats you, go ahead and bet the hand. Even though this is being a bit predictable, betting is absolutely necessary. Frankly, anybody who checks a hand like A-10 after turning top pair with the ten is making a grave error.

Note that the same principle applies when there is an overcard to your pair. If you have pocket kings or pocket queens, an ace comes on the flop, and the texture of the flop is raggedy, there is less need to bet. If you are not beaten already, the next card is not likely to turn the enemy's loser into a winner. But with something like pocket tens or nines, you should bet when an overcard flops, if there is a reasonable chance that the hand is good, because the next card might beat you.

There is another drawback to using a check-raise besides allowing players to draw out when no one bets your hand for you. Even when someone gratuitously bets, using a check-raise can cost you money instead of gaining. The reason is you have both announced a strong hand and created a place where a player is informed of this early on. If you try for a check-raise on the flop and are successful because someone bet, the player may dump his hand, either when you check-raise or when you bet the turn. If instead you bet the flop, bet the turn, and bet the river, your opponent does not really know that you have something very good. He may well go all the way with you on a modest holding.

Should you stop using the check-raise as one of your poker plays? No; just use it in moderation. Don't overwork the play. Some people automatically check whenever they hit a big hand. This is bad poker. An astute opponent who picks up on this leak is going to know that you do not have a super-strong hand when you bet. When you do, he will go out of his way to put heat on you.

Some forms of poker, notably Omaha, allow drawing hands that are so big it is normally too dangerous to allow a free card. For holdem, the degree of danger varies widely, depending on the number of opponents, board texture, and type of hand you have. That is why concrete situations must be examined.

A good poker player knows the risk of giving a free card, and how this varies with each situation. Checking a hand hoping for a check-raise is not something you do depending on your mood. It is a calculated risk that varies greatly from one situation to another in the danger attached. You must know these factors and use them in your calculations to be successful at the poker table.

The following hands bring out some of the important considerations that come into play before deciding whether to try for a check-raise. Keep in mind that the plays we suggest apply when you are up against a stranger, or a typical player. An important factor in the decision to check-raise is the likelihood that the opponent will bet. If you are up against someone whose play you know well, and that person is a very aggressive player, you can take more liberties in going for a check-raise, so there the answer to some of these problems may be different.

(1) A $10-$20 game. You are in the small blind and have 8♥-7♥. Two early players, a middle player, and the button limp. You call. There is $60 in the pot and six players. The flop is: 8♦-3♦-2♣, giving you top pair. You bet, two other players fold, and an early player raises with the other players folding. You call. There is $100 in the pot and two players. The turn is the 7♠. You now have the top two pair. What do you do?

Answer: Bet. Before attempting a check-raise, you need to picture what your opponent may have. First, a very likely holding is a diamond flush-draw. If you check, he may well take a free card, which you do not want. Second, he might have a very powerful holding like a set. This means it will cost you three bets to take a card off, rather than two. Third, he may have been fooling around with second pair such as pocket sixes, fives, or fours. Fourth, he could have wheel cards like ace-five, ace-four, or five-four, and be planning to take a free card if you check. Fifth, he may have raised on a good hand like top pair or an overpair. Only in this last case would check-raising be right.

(2) A $10-$20 game. You are in the big blind having the A♣-K♦. An early player opens with a raise and the cutoff calls. You call.

There is $65 in the pot and three players. The flop is: A♠-8♥-3♦, giving you top pair. What do you do?

Answer: You should go for a check-raise in this situation. You have a preflop raiser who figures to bet, having only two opponents. His bet will put the third player in the middle, so you can trap him for an extra bet before announcing your power. You have top pair, top kicker on a raggedy, rainbow board. In the rare case where it gets checked around, there are no overcards to your hand. Should you bet the turn after a flop check by all, the opponents will have no idea you have this big a hand.

(3) A $10-$20 game. You limp in from middle position with the A♣-9♣ behind an early limper. The next player raises. The big blind and the early limper call; you call. There is $85 in the pot and four players. The flop comes: A♦-K♣-8♣, giving you top pair with the nut flush-draw. It is checked to you. What do you do?

Answer: Bet. Betting is superior to attempting a check-raise. With the ace-king combo on the table there are a lot of gutshot draws out there, so you need to charge them a price. The preflop raiser may not bet this board if he was raising on pocket queens, jacks, or tens (18 hands).

(4) A $15-$30 game. You limp in under-the-gun with the K♠-Q♠. Everyone folds to the button, who raises, and it is folded to you. You call. There is $85 in the pot and two players. The flop comes: Q♣-T♦-9♠, giving you top pair, a gutshot straight-draw, and a backdoor flush-draw. What do you do?

Answer: Bet. Your hand is not strong enough to check-raise, but you have a good betting hand with top pair, excellent kicker. Don't check and run the risk of giving your opponent a free card when there are three parts to a straight on the table. His "button raise" could have been made on a wide variety of hands, and may not be legitimate in the sense that he does not have to have a big pocket pair or two big cards headed by an ace. On the actual hand the player checked, hoping to check-raise. The button checked.

258

The turn was the 4♥. He bet and got raised. He called. The river was the K♣. He checked and the button checked. The button won having pocket fours for a set of fours on the turn, beating his two pair. Had he just bet his hand on the flop, the button would almost certainly have folded rather than play going for two outs.

(5) A $20-$40 game. You are in the big blind having the Q♦-2♦. An early player and the small blind limp so you take a free play. There is $60 in the pot and three players. The flop is: Q♥-7♣-3♦, giving you top pair and a backdoor flush-draw. The small blind checks and you bet. The early player raises and the small blind folds. You call. There is $140 in the pot and two players. The turn is the 2♥, giving you two pair. What do you do?

Answer: Check with the intention of check-raising. With no flush-draw or straight-draw on the flop, your opponent does not figure to be drawing. This turn-card appears to be totally innocent to him, so he will probably bet. You are a big favorite to have him beat and he rates to pay you off.

(6) A $20-$40 game. You are in the cutoff seat having the K♣-Q♠ and open with a raise. The button reraises and you call. There is $150 in the pot and two players. The flop is: A♣-8♣-3♣, giving you the nut flush-draw. What do you do?

Answer: Bet. In these heads-up reraised pots you need to make a play, and a bet is better than a check-raise. His button reraise preflop could be done on a lot of hands, since he was responding to your steal-raise. He might well fold a hand like 7♥-7♦ rather than play what to him might look like a two-outer or a one-outer. If he calls or raises, you have the nut flush-draw to fall back on.

(7) A $10-$20 game. You are in the big blind holding the 10♠-8♠. An early player limps and a middle player raises. It is folded to you and you call. The early player calls. There is $65 in the pot and three players. The flop is: 5♠-4♠-2♦, giving you a flush-draw with two overcards. You bet. The early player folds but the middle player raises. You call. There is $105 in the pot and two players. The turn is the A♥. What do you do?

Answer: Bet. This is a good scare-card if your opponent does not have an ace and was raising on a big overpair. You might get him to fold. Furthermore, since you were in the big blind, you could easily have called the preflop raise with a trey in your hand, now giving you a wheel. If he calls, then you still have a lot of outs with your flush-draw. If we were up against an aggressive player, than we might even plan to check-raise instead of betting right out. But the typical player might well check the ace, and we want to make a play for the pot on the turn, when we threaten him with a loss of two big bets.

(8) A $20-$40 game. You are in the big blind holding the K♦-J♥. An early player and a middle player limp. The cutoff raises. You call as well as the limpers. There is $170 in the pot and four players. The flop is: A♣-Q♠-T♦, giving you the nut straight. What do you do?

Answer: Bet. Forget about attempting a check-raise move here. This is a raised pot with all three flop cards in the playing zone. With that flop you will get played with and your bet will probably get raised by someone, especially the preflop raiser. This will allow you to reraise. Your goal in these situations is to protect your interest in the pot. This has priority over trying to finagle an extra bet or two downstream in raised pots with lots of players. Besides, there is no reason to think going for a check-raise will build a bigger pot, since the chance of being able to three-bet is quite bright.

(9) A $10-$20 game. This game is temporarily shorthanded with only five players. You are in the small blind with the K♥-2♥. A middle player opens with a raise and the button calls. You call, as well as the big blind. There is $80 in the pot and four players. The flop is: 9♥-8♥-4♣, giving you a flush-draw. You bet and only the big blind folds. There is $110 in the pot and three players. The turn is the 3♥, giving you a flush. What do you do?

Answer: Bet. The problem with attempting a check-raise is that when you do it after a flush card comes off, it is very obvious to your opponents what is going on and they can get away from their hands quite easily. By betting, you might get calls from a lower heart, who assumes you were betting top pair or an overpair. You may even get calls from top pair hands or overpairs who are suspicious that you are semi-bluffing a heart flush. This allows you to then bet the river and frequently get a "curiosity call."

(10) A $20-$40 game. You are in early position holding J♦-J♥. Two players limp in ahead of you and you raise. Two middle players and the two limpers call. There is $230 in the pot and five players. The flop is: J♣-9♣-2♦, giving you top set. Both early limpers check. You bet your top set with a two-flush on the table, and only the middle players call. There is $290 in the pot and three players. The turn is the 3♣, completing a possible flush. You bet anyway; no one may have a flush, and you have ten outs if someone does. The next player raises and the third player folds. You call. There is $450 in the pot and two players. The river is the J♠, giving you quads. What do you do?

Answer: You should check, planning to check-raise. You have been representing an overpair like aces, kings, or queens or perhaps top pair, top kicker with ace-jack. After the flush card comes on the turn and you get raised, your opponent most likely has a flush. This means he will bet if you check, allowing you to raise. But if you lead at him, he probably will get nervous with the board pairing and just call.

(11) A $20-$40 game. You are in the big blind holding K♥-3♠. An early player, two middle players, and the button limp. The small blind folds and you take a free play. There is $110 in the pot and five players. The flop is: K♠-Q♠-3♥, giving you top and bottom pair with a backdoor flush-draw. What do you do?

Answer: Bet. Prefer a bet over a check-raise attempt because there is both a flush-draw and a straight-draw on the flop. Don't run the risk of handing out free cards to four opponents. Instead, hope that someone raises so that you can reraise. Lots of players love to raise pots on come hands. Be a sport; give them a chance to do so.

(12) A $15-$30 game. You limp in from middle position with the 6♦-6♣ behind two early players. The cutoff calls and the button raises. Both blinds fold but everyone else calls. There is $175 in the pot and five players. The flop is: 4♥-2♥-2♠, giving you sixes over deuces. It is checked to you. What do you do?

Answer: Bet. Having four opponents, the preflop raiser may just check it down with a hand like ace-king rather than bet so a check-raise attempt could easily backfire. You cannot afford to give out a free card with your tiny overpair to this large a field. Any card higher than a six that comes off could kill your hand.

(13) A $10-$20 game. You are in the small blind with the Q♠-J♠. Two early players, two middle players, and the button limp. You limp. There is $70 in the pot and seven players. The flop comes: Q♦-Q♥-T♣, giving you trip queens. What do you do?

Answer: Bet. Trying to check-raise or slow play is a mistake with this board and so many opponents. It is quite likely that someone has an open-end straight draw or a gutshot draw and will be happy to take a free card trying to run you down. It is almost a certainty that among six other players, someone has A-J, K-J, or some other holding that fits that flop. If the ten were a seven, taking away any possibility of a straight coming on the next card, then checking with the intention of check-raising would be a reasonable play.

31 – RERAISING

When is it right to three-bet? Should it always be done when you think you have the best hand? Should it ever be done on a draw? As with many poker decisions, the texture of the board, the number of opponents, the previous betting action, your position, and other factors come into play when deciding what to do. You should be more inclined to three-bet when you do not have position. First, having back position means you were check-raised, which is much more likely to mean you have run into a strong hand. Second, when you have position, the opponent cannot get a free card on the next betting round unless you decide to allow it.

Be wary of reraising if a substantial number of turn-cards that could come will make you ill. If you have an overpair, your hand is dead if they make a straight or a flush, but their straight-draw or flush-draw is still alive even if you buy one of the few helping cards that could come on the turn.

Here are a set of problems involving whether to reraise.

(1) The game is $20-$40. An early player opens with a raise and you reraise from the cutoff seat with the K♦-K♣. Only the early player calls. There is $150 in the pot and two players. The flop is: 6♦-2♠-2♥, giving you kings over deuces. Your opponent checks. You bet and he raises. What do you do?

Answer: Reraise. An early preflop raiser would not have been helped by this board. He is check-raising an overpair and your overpair is probably bigger than his. There are 18 ways he can have pocket queens, jacks, or tens and only 6 ways he can have pocket aces. If he had been dealt aces, he probably would have reraised with them preflop. If he is the type who would open raise from early position with a medium pair like pocket nines or eights, then you are a huge favorite to have the best hand. Just smooth-calling because you want to wait until the expensive street to pop him is dangerous, because a scare-card could come off on the turn that might keep him from betting. For example, suppose his overpair is jacks and you just call. If a queen, a king, or an ace comes off on the turn, he may check.

263

(2) A $40-$80 game. The under-the-gun player puts up a live straddle. You raise from early position with the A♠-A♣. A middle player, both blinds, and the straddler call. There is $600 in the pot and five players. The flop is: Q♦-J♥-8♦, giving you an overpair. Both blinds and the straddler check. You bet and the middle player raises. The small blind calls, the big blind folds, and the straddler calls. What do you do?

Answer: You should just call, not reraise. The raise on your left with a board of Q-J-8 is very ominous. You could easily be facing two pair or a set. Furthermore, the raiser may make it four bets, costing you that much more to continue when it looks like you are chasing. It is possible he could be raising on a flush-draw, but it seems unlikely, given your early preflop raise and his call of $120 cold, although A♦-K♦ is possible.

(3) A $30-$60 game. You open with a raise under-the-gun having the A♠-A♣. The player on your immediate left cold-calls your raise and everyone else folds. There is $170 in the pot and two players. The flop is: T♦-8♥-4♣, giving you an overpair. You bet and your opponent calls. There is $230 in the pot. The turn is the K♥. You bet and your opponent raises. What do you do?

Answer: Call. You are risking another raise if you three-bet here, and your opponent could have a wide range of hands that beat a pair of aces at this point. While occasionally raises on the turn are semi-bluffs, these are rare among typical players. Instead, raises on the turn frequently denote two pair or better. He could easily have cold-called your preflop raise with K-K, T-T, or even 8-8, and now have a set. You will get four-bet if you are against a set, and you only have two outs. You have eight outs against the top two pair, and again you could easily get four-bet. By calling, you can check the river if a blank comes, and perhaps induce a bluff bet on the end if your opponent was semi-bluffing with something like queen-jack suited. If your opponent has ace-king, you can call here, check on the end, and he will probably bet the river for you.

(4) A $10-$20 game. You are in the small blind holding T♥-T♦. Two early players limp and you raise. The big blind and the limpers call. There is $80 in the pot and four players. The flop is: 7♠-3♠-2♥, giving you an overpair. You bet and the big blind calls. The first early limper raises and the next player folds. What do you do?

Answer: Reraise. You can beat top pair, top kicker type hands, and even some overpairs that the early player could be raising with. He may even be raising on a draw hoping for a free card. By reraising, you confront the player on your left with a double bet, greatly increasing the likelihood of inducing a fold.

(5) A $10-$20 game. You raise under-the-gun with A♠-K♠. A middle player and the button call. There is $75 in the pot and three players. The flop is: K♥-Q♥-9♦, giving you top pair, top kicker. You bet. The middle player calls and the button raises. What do you do?

Answer: Just call. You could reraise, but it is better to call and then possibly lead on the turn if a blank hits. The problem with reraising is that there are a lot of cards that can come off on the turn which kill your hand, given the highly coordinated nature of this board. Any heart, any jack, or any ten could all be bad news. Reraising does put added pressure on the third player to fold, but this does not offset the risk of getting four-bet by a better hand or having a bad card show up on the turn that kills your chances.

(6) A $10-$20 game. You call in middle position with the K♦-J♦ behind two early limpers. The cutoff calls, leaving $55 in the pot and five players. The flop is: K♣-Q♥-J♣, giving you top and bottom pair. The big blind checks. An early player bets and the other early player raises. What do you do?

Answer: Call. Normally, top and bottom pair is a strong holding that should be played aggressively. But this board is highly coordinated, with three cards in sequence, and all in the playing zone. Making it even worse is the two-flush. With this many opponents, it is too easy for someone to have a straight or the top two pair. Even if your hand is good, you will get drawn out on a high percentage of the time. When you are behind, you are practically buried, and when you are ahead, you may well get drawn out with this many opponents. Any club, ace, ten, or nine that shows up on the turn or the river is likely lethal. These are 20 cards you have to dodge on both the turn and the river.

(7) A $10-$20 game. You limp in from middle position with the J♠-T♠ behind an early limper. The button and small blind limp. There is $50 in the pot and five players. The flop is: K♠-Q♦-3♠, giving you a flush-draw and an open-end straight-draw. It is checked to you. You bet and the button raises. Everyone folds. What do you do?

Answer: Reraise. With 15 outs and two cards to come, you are a mathematical favorite to make a flush or a straight by the river, and you will be going all the way there with this hand. The button may be raising on a come hand himself, hoping for a free card. Not only should you reraise, you should plan on betting the turn unless your opponent four-bets you here on the flop and a blank comes on the turn.

On the actual hand the player just called. The turn was the 7♣. He checked and the button bet. He called. The river was the 2♣. It was checked down. The button won a $130 pot with the Q♥-T♥ for a middle pair of queens. Had the player reraised on the flop and followed through with a bet on the turn, the button would have been hard-pressed to find a call. One of the virtues of the big draw is the ability to put down so much heat that you do not always have to hit in order to win.

(8) A $20-$40 game. You are in the small blind with the Q♠-Q♥. An early player limps, a middle player raises, and the cutoff calls. You reraise and everyone calls. There is $300 in the pot and five players. The flop is: T♠-T♣-9♣, giving you queens over tens. You bet and the big blind folds. The early limper raises and your two other opponents call. What do you do?

Answer: Just call. A flop with an open pair and touching cards in the playing zone coupled with a two-flush means that you could be in trouble here. Furthermore, you would be reraising players who called $40 cold. A player who flops a full house often sandbags on the flop betting round.

(9) A $30-$60 game. You are in middle position with the A♣-3♣. An early player limps and you limp. The cutoff limps as well as the small blind. There is $150 in the pot and five players. The flop is: K♦-5♣-4♣, giving you a gutshot straight-flush draw. The small blind bets and the big blind raises. The early player folds. What do you do?

Answer: Reraise. With the nut flush-draw, a gutshot straight-draw, and an ace overcard, you have a huge draw. This could be as many as 15 outs with two cards to come. The reraise gets extra money out there if you hit, and may buy you a free card if you miss. We should mention that if you get a chance for a free card, you should take it in this kind of betting sequence, because the strong betting to here indicates that you will not get everyone to fold with a turn-card bet.

(10) A $30-$60 game. You are in the small blind with the A♠-J♣. An early player limps, a middle player limps, and another middle player raises. The cutoff and the button both call. You call as well as everyone else. There is $420 in the pot and seven players. The flop is: J♦-8♦-3♥, giving you top pair, top kicker. You bet. The big blind raises and only the preflop raiser calls, with everyone else folding. What do you do?

Answer: Call. See what comes off on the turn. At this point you are not confronting anyone with a double bet, so your reraise will get called. The preflop raiser could be cold-calling on an overpair and waiting until the turn to pull the trigger. If the big blind is raising on a flush-draw, then one of your outs is killed. The only scenario where three-betting would be right is when the big blind is raising on a weaker jack and the preflop raiser just has overcards like ace-king or ace-queen. But it is unlikely that the preflop raiser would cold-call on just overcards unless they were both diamonds.

(11) A $10-$20 game. You open raise from middle position with the A♥-T♥. Only the cutoff calls. There is $55 in the pot and two players. The flop is: K♥-T♣-9♥, giving you middle pair and the nut flush-draw. You bet; your opponent raises. What do you do?

Answer: Reraise. This is a heads-up situation. You have the nut flush-draw (9 outs), a middle pair of tens (2 more outs), and an ace overcard (3 more outs). This is 14 outs with two cards to come. You are about even money to make a flush, trips, or two pair by the river, and you will be going all the way with this hand. It is possible that your opponent may decide to fold a weak king, fearing that you have pocket aces, a set of kings, or big slick. Most of the time he will call. If he continues to bet, you have a ton of outs. You have a big enough hand that you should keep your foot on the gas pedal.

(12) A $30-$60 game. You raise from middle position with the T♠-T♥ after two early players limp in. The cutoff and the big blind call as well as the limpers. There is $320 in the pot and five players. The flop is: 6♥-5♦-2♦, giving you an overpair. It is checked to you and you bet. The cutoff raises. The big blind folds but the early limpers call. What do you do?

Answer: Call. You should avoid reraising because you are not confronting the other players with a double bet. Your reraise will not drive out anyone, and all turn-cards are hazardous except for a ten. Any card ace through jack makes a bigger pair possible. Any diamond makes a flush possible. A trey, four, seven, eight, or nine makes a straight possible. With this many players, nearly every card in the deck is bad.

(13) A $15-$30 game. You are in the small blind with the J♠-T♣. An early player, a middle player, the cutoff, and the button limp. You limp and the big blind raises. Everyone calls. There is $180 in the pot and six players. The flop is: J♥-T♦-9♣, giving you the top two pair. You bet, and the big blind raises. The early player, the cutoff, and the button all call. What do you do?

Answer: Call. Having the top two pair is a powerful holding and should normally be played strongly. But this particular board is highly coordinated. You could easily be up against a straight or a set, with all this action and so many opponents. There are a lot of cards that can come off on the turn like a king, a queen, an eight, or a seven that will make you glad you have not reraised.

(14) A $10-$20 game. You are in the big blind holding A♣-K♦. An early player raises and a middle player calls. You call. There is $65 in the pot and three players. The flop is: A♦-Q♦-J♥, giving you top pair and a gutshot. You bet. The preflop raiser pops it and the other player calls. What do you do?

Answer: Call. While it is tempting to three-bet with top pair, top kicker, calling is better. With this board, you can easily be up against two pair or a set. The other problem is that some of your outs are of a dubious value. For example, a king gives you two pair, but anyone with a ten now has a straight. A ten gives you a straight, but anyone with a king has the same straight, so you win only half the pot. If you reraise, it could get raised again.

(15) A $20-$40 game. You are in the big blind holding T♥-9♦. An early player, two middle players, the button, and the small blind all limp, so you get a free play. There is $120 in the pot and six players. The flop is delightful; Q♣-J♠-8♥, giving you the nuts. The small blind checks. You bet. The early player and the first middle player fold. The second middle player calls. The button raises and the small blind folds. What do you do?

Answer: Reraise. Don't slowplay. You have the nuts right now, but with three cards in the playing zone, you must pound the pot and make opponents pay the maximum to try and draw out. Your hand can be counterfeited if a nine or a ten shows up on the turn. If an ace or king comes, a bigger straight is possible. Of course, the board pairing would be ominous.

(16) A $10-$20 game. You open on K♥-K♦ with a raise from early position. A middle player, the cutoff, and the big blind call. There is $85 in the pot and four players. The flop is: 9♦-8♥-6♦, giving you an overpair and a backdoor flush-draw. The big blind checks. You bet. The middle player calls and the cutoff raises. The big blind folds. What do you do?

Answer: Call. With this board, there are a number of bad cards that can come off on the turn which hurt your hand. A ten, a nine, a seven, and a five are all bad, unless they include a diamond. Even with a diamond, you may be chasing instead of leading. If a blank comes on the turn you can bet. Just calling now does not obligate you to check on the turn.

(17) A $20-$40 game. You open with a raise from early position with Q♥-Q♦. Only the big blind calls. There is $90 in the pot and two players. The flop is: K♠-Q♠-5♥, so you have middle set. The big blind checks. You bet and he calls. There is $130 in the pot. The turn is the K♦. The big blind checks. You bet and he raises. What do you do?

Answer: Call. Plan on raising him at the river. You cannot get him out and protect your hand, so guard against a bluff and max out on the hand. When you are full and have position, it is usually better to smooth-call when you get check-raised on the turn.

(18) A $10-$20 game. You open with a raise in early position on A♦-A♣. An early player, the button, and the big blind call. There is $85 in the pot and four players. The flop is: 8♣-5♣-3♣, giving you the nut flush-draw to go with your aces. The big blind checks. You bet and everyone calls. There is $125 in the pot. The turn is the A♠, giving you trip aces. The big blind checks. You bet and both other players fold. The big blind raises. What do you do?

Answer: Reraise. You may have the best hand. If not, then you have 17 outs (9 full house cards, 1 card to quads, and 7 clubs to the nut flush) to beat a flush. Furthermore, your opponent cannot have the nut flush because you have the "Ace of Trump" (A♣), so he is unlikely to four-bet. Finally, by reraising, you discourage your opponent from betting the river when a blank comes, giving you a free showdown. So if you lose, the financial damage caused by the reraise is no greater than calling at the turn and river.

(19) A $15-$30 hand. You raise from middle position with the A♠-A♣ after an early player limps. The big blind and the early player call. There is $100 in the pot and three players. The flop is: J♥-T♣-7♥, giving you an overpair. It is checked to you and you bet. The big blind calls. The early player raises. What do you do?

Answer: Call. There are three parts to a straight on the table, as well as a jack-ten and a two-flush. Just call the raise now and see what the turn brings. If it is a heart, a queen, a nine, or an eight, you will be glad you didn't reraise. If it is a blank, see how the action develops. Bet the turn if checked to after a blank comes.

(20) A $15-$30 game. You are in the small blind with the 6♣-6♠. An early player limps and you limp. There is $45 in the pot and three players. The flop is: 8♣-6♦-4♠, giving you middle set. You check. The big blind checks. The early player bets and you raise. The big blind calls. The early player folds. There is $120 in the pot and two players. The turn is the A♦. You bet and your opponent raises. What do you do?

Answer: Reraise. You should three-bet now and plan on betting the river. Your set is a powerful hand given this betting and that board. Your opponent's raise is likely being done on just a good ace or two pair, which you can beat.

(21) A $20-$40 game. You are in middle position and raise with the Q♦-Q♣ after an early player and two middle players limp. The cutoff and the limpers call. There is $230 in the pot and five players. The flop is: 7♥-5♥-4♣, giving you an overpair. Three opponents check and you bet. The cutoff folds. The early player raises. The first middle player folds and the second middle player calls. What do you do?

Answer: Call. You have a coordinated board with a two-flush. You have a large field taking this flop and you are now getting check-raised. Just call the raise and see what happens on the turn. If a heart, a six, an eight, or a trey turns up, you will be happy you did not three-bet on the flop. If a blank comes, you can resume betting if the opponents both check.

(22) A $40-$80 game. You hold J♥-J♣ in middle position and open for a raise. The cutoff calls and everyone else folds. You are heads-up. The flop comes 8♦-5♦-3♠, giving you an overpair. You of course bet, and your opponent raises. Do you call or reraise?

Answer: Reraise. You should three-bet because you do not want to give up the initiative. When you are heads-up on the flop, particularly in the bigger games, expect to get tested. It is almost automatic for an opponent who intends to play anyway to throw in a raise when the pot is heads-up. While you do not have a powerhouse, two jacks with this flop is a solid hand. Frankly, against an aggressive player, we would be inclined to bet the turn no matter what comes, assuming the opponent just calls our reraise on the flop. Cross each bridge as you come to it.

(23) You hold the A♦-Q♦ in the cutoff seat. A player opens under-the-gun with a raise, and you call. The field folds. The flop is to your liking: J♦-10♦-8♣. You have a gutshot royal flush and a nine makes you a straight. The opponent bets, you raise, and he reraises. You are playing in a cardroom with unlimited raises heads-up. Do you raise again or just call?

Answer: Reraise. You don't intend to keep raising down to the cloth, since you are an underdog to a set. But against K-K, you have 18 outs, so another raise is in order. If the opponent does not have a set, he will just call, because you could easily have a set yourself here. Putting in an extra raise with a big draw varies your play, and could get you a "free" card on the next betting round.

32 – SLOWPLAYING

By slowplaying, we are referring to situations where you have a very powerful holding and you are deliberately checking or just calling in order to get additional bets on later betting rounds by concealing the high quality of your hand. There are a few things to consider when contemplating a slowplay. First, can you really afford to give out a free card or a cheap card? In other words, is your hand really as invulnerable as you think, or can it be overtaken on the next card? We prefer a situation where an opponent who improves after getting a free card is going to lose his money, not win ours. Second, what is the likelihood that a future round will get bet? Frequently, with lots of players and large pots, players will bet on the cheap street, but then check it down on the later, more expensive streets. Third, is simply betting your hand really going to cost you any money? By betting the flop, you frequently pick up several small bets because of the size of the field and the texture of the board. If it gets checked around, when you bet the turn, you may get few callers, if any. The bet is twice as much. Furthermore, players will raise on the flop much more often than on a later betting round where prices double. When they raise, you can reraise and get additional money right away, which may more than offset collecting an extra big bet downstream.

As with check-raising, many players become quite enamored with slowplaying, and will do it routinely with any powerful holding. This can be an expensive mistake. Consult the chapter on check-raising to see the downside of underplaying your hand.

We remind you that our advice is for what we think will work best against a casual player or stranger. In most cases, we prefer to simply bet or raise, instead of slowplaying. However, we do not want to get you into the habit of always betting your strong hands, any more than always checking them. One area of poker where you need to vary your game is how you play your good hands. Please refer to our chapter on deception for a discussion of how often you need to do something contrary to your normal approach.

The next set of hands discuss some situations where you have a strong holding and slowplaying may or may not be best.

(1) The game is $20-$40. You are on the button holding T♦-T♣. An early player, a middle player, and the cutoff limp. You raise, the small blind folds, and everyone else calls. There is $210 in the pot and five players. The flop comes: K♣-T♠-3♥, so you have middle set. The big blind checks. The early limper bets and the other two opponents call. What do you do?

Answer: Raise. This is not a good time to slowplay your middle set. This is a raised pot with a lot of players, and you have two cards in the playing zone (a king and a ten). You don't want to give a cheap card to a bunch of gutshot draws or to someone with a queen-jack. Focus on protecting your hand and not trying to finagle an extra bet later on. Maybe the original bettor will reraise to try and confront the field with a double bet. If so, this is great for you, whether the field plays or folds.

(2) A $10-$20 game. You are in the small blind with the K♠-Q♠. An early player and a middle player limp in. You call. There is $40 in the pot and four players. The flop is nice: K♣-K♦-4♥, giving you three kings. What do you do?

Answer: Check. You can slowplay here. There is no two-flush or straight-draw on the table for anyone to be hanging around with, so you are not giving up much if it gets checked around. If someone bets, you can call, and plan on check-raising the turn. Given the absence of a preflop raise, your queen kicker is strong.

(3) A $10-$20 game. You are in the small blind holding 8♠-8♣. An early player and a middle player limp. You call. The big blind now raises and everyone calls. There is $80 in the pot and four players. The flop is: Q♥-9♥-8♦, giving you bottom set. What do you do?

Answer: Bet. Hope you get raised so you can reraise. With three cards in a playing zone plus a two-flush, you need to make sure the flop gets bet and no free cards are handed out. You may well get raised by a player with top pair or a come hand.

274

(4) A $20-$40 game. You are in the cutoff seat holding T♠-T♥. An early player opens with a raise, everyone folds to you, and you call. The button calls and both blinds fold. There is $150 in the pot and three players. The flop comes: T♦-7♠-3♣, giving you top set. The preflop raiser checks. You bet because you know that you will almost always get called by a preflop raiser even when he just has overcards. Only the preflop raiser calls. There is $190 in the pot and two players. The turn is the A♥. Your opponent now bets. What do you do?

Answer: Call. Slowplaying is clearly right here. The ace coming on the turn is a good money-making card for you, since it touches all the A-K, A-Q, A-J, and similar type hands your opponent may have. Your opponent has virtually no outs and figures to bet the river, in which case you will raise. If he is bluffing and does not have an ace, it would obviously be a bad idea to pull the trigger now; urge him to bet the river by slowplaying.

(5) A $15-$30 game. You limp in from middle position with the A♥-2♥ behind an early limper. The small blind limps. There is $60 in the pot and four players. The flop comes: Q♥-T♥-3♥, giving you the nuts. The other players all check. You bet because there are two big cards on the table, which make the likelihood of someone calling quite high, plus anyone with a heart might call as well. Players don't expect an opponent to bet the nuts on the flop. Only the early limper calls. There is $90 in the pot and two players. The turn is the J♦. Your opponent bets. What do you do?

Answer: Raise. Don't slowplay. If a heart comes at the river, you may well lose your market. If he is betting a set, a straight, or a flush, he will likely call your raise, and may well make a crying call at the river even if he doesn't improve.

(6) A $20-$40 game. You are in the cutoff seat holding Q♦-Q♣. An early player and two middle players limp. You raise and the button plus both blinds fold. Everyone else calls. There is $190 in the pot and four players. The flop is: Q♠-7♠-5♥, giving you top set. Everyone checks and you bet. The early player raises and your other two opponents fold. What do you do?

Answer: Call. This one you can slowplay. You have only one opponent. You have position. A reraise doesn't protect your hand any better versus a flush-draw; he will call.

(7) A $10-$20 game. You limp in with the K♦-Q♣ behind another middle limper. The cutoff limps. There is $45 in the pot and four players. The flop is: Q♠-Q♦-7♦, giving you three queens. The big blind and the middle limper check. What do you do?

Answer: Bet. With a two-flush and three opponents, you should not try to slowplay. A flush-draw might even try a semi-bluff raise or check-raise, allowing you to reraise if you choose. Some bad things can happen when you allow it to be checked around here. A guy with a pocket pair gets a free card on the flop and then hits his two-outer on the turn to take the pot away from you. This is rare, but both annoying and expensive when it happens. Or another diamond shows up, and some guy with the A♦ now has a legitimate play for the pot. You should bet a strong hand when there is a two-flush on board and multiple opponents.

(8) A $20-$40 game. You are in the cutoff seat holding A♠-J♠. An early player and two middle players limp. You raise and everyone calls. There is $280 in the pot and seven players. The flop is: J♦-J♣-5♣, giving you three jacks. Both blinds check. The early player bets and the two middle players fold. You raise and everyone folds to the early player, who reraises. What do you do?

Answer: Call. Just smooth-call and don't make it four bets. Your lone opponent most likely has the case jack with a worse kicker than yours. Now that it's heads-up with you having position, let him lead on an expensive street before lowering the boom.

(9) A $20-$40 game. An early player limps in. You limp from middle position with the A♦-T♠. Everyone else folds. There is

$70 in the pot and three players. The flop comes: A♥-T♦-9♣, giving you the top two pair. It is checked to you. What do you do?

Answer: Bet. Don't slowplay your top two pair even on a rainbow board with only two opponents when you have all three flop-cards in the playing zone like this. There are many gutshot straight-draws as well as normal open-end straight-draws out there. A lot of opponents will not be playing as solidly as you do when up front, so if someone hits, it will be even more damaging if they connect with some kind of strange hand you wouldn't normally expect to be lurking.

(10) A $20-$40 game. You are on the button holding the A♣-A♥. The under-the-gun player opens with a raise and everyone folds to you. You notice that the blinds look like they are about to fold. What do you do?

Answer: Call. This is a perfect spot to slowplay preflop. You have the best possible hand and the best possible position, with what looks to be only one opponent. Let your opponent take a flop having no idea what is in store for him.

(11) A $20-$40 game. You are in middle position with the K♣-T♣ and limp behind an early limper. The cutoff limps. There is $90 in the pot and four players. The flop comes perfectly: Q♠-J♦-9♥, giving you the nut straight. The big blind checks. The early player bets. What do you do?

Answer: Raise. Don't slowplay when you flop the nut straight with big cards on the table. You rate to get played with, and someone might even reraise. Your situation may be more precarious than you think, since a ten or a king showing up on the turn can easily counterfeit your hand. Strike while the iron is hot.

(12) A $15-$30 game. You open with a raise from middle position with the A♦-9♦ and only the big blind calls. There is $70 in the pot and two players. The flop is: J♥-8♦-3♦, giving you the nut flush-draw. The big blind checks. You bet and he raises. You

277

reraise and he calls. There is $160 in the pot and two players. The turn is the Q♦, giving you the nut flush. Your opponent checks. What do you do?

Answer: Bet. The opponent will almost surely call, because when you reraised on the flop, it looks to him like you have a big overpair. He will not put you on a flush. He will call if he is drawing to a flush or a straight. He might even have two pair or a set and be planning to check-raise.

(13) A $10-$20 game. You are on the button holding the 5♠-5♣. One early player, two middle players, and the cutoff limp. You limp as well as the small blind. There is $70 in the pot and seven players. The flop is: 7♠-5♦-3♣, giving you middle set. It is checked to a middle player, who bets, and the cutoff calls. What do you do?

Answer: Raise. You should not slowplay or sandbag on the flop in a big multi-handed pot like this with six other players. It is better to raise immediately, since any six or four coming off on the turn would be bad news, especially with this many players.

(14) A $10-$20 game. You are in the big blind holding A♣-9♣. An early player, a middle player, the cutoff, the button, and the small blind limp. You take a free play. There is $60 in the pot and six players. The flop is: K♣-6♣-2♣, giving you the nut flush. The small blind checks. What do you do?

Answer: Check. When you flop the nut flush and the board is otherwise ragged, it is okay to slowplay even with a large field. There are no straight draws or open pairs out there for anyone to play with. The likelihood of someone catching something on the turn good enough to possibly run you down at the river is very remote, so if it gets checked around you are still in good shape. Who knows, someone may bet top pair or a pair and a flush-draw thinking that they have a hand. You will probably just call when this happens, and wait until an expensive street to pounce.

33 – FREE CARDS

When someone bets, if you have position, you can use it to throw in a raise on a drawing hand or some other holding that does not figure to be the best hand at that point. The idea is that if you have a drawing hand, then you raise on the flop, hoping the opposition will just call your raise, then check to you on the turn. If a blank comes, you can simply check and get to see the river for free. When this scenario unfolds, you save a half-bet, since the limit on the turn was double that on the flop. If you hit, there is extra money already in the pot.

This tactic, the free card raise, is a standard tool for many players. However, we see it applied too mechanically and too often. When it is right to raise in order to try and get a free card on a later betting round?

There is a problem with raising on a come hand in order to get a free card later. When you get checked to on the turn and simply check back, you are telling your opponent that you were drawing, which allows him to play more accurately from that point. Specifically, he knows he has the best hand, or can likely pick up the pot by representing the best hand with a bet at the river if the draw misses. If you are both drawing, the likely result is he wins by bluffing the river, instead of you continuing the charade by following up with a turn bet, then successfully bluffing him at the river.

It is possible that this drawback of losing the initiative will persuade you to use your raise to try and steal the pot by betting the turn if checked to, rather than taking the free card. When you make a raise in position and have the opportunity to get a free card, you are not required to take it. Perhaps a bet on the expensive round will knock the opponent out of the pot. Maybe you have something like middle pair to go with your draw, and thus would prefer to get your free card on the end. When you have enough to show down that will beat an opponent who is also drawing, or perhaps are pushing a very modest holding like middle pair with a worse kicker, you have a strong interest in being in for the showdown. How you play a hand from the flop onward affects how much this will cost. So a raise in position when drawing can be followed up in different ways. Sometimes you take a free card if it is offered, and other times you keep betting.

Raising on the come has another drawback. In a multi-handed pot, a raise may have the effect of eliminating players, which is seldom desirable when you have a drawing hand. There are several ways that others can be driven out. Players who haven't acted yet may fold because your raise confronts them with a double bet. Players who have called the original bet may be confronted by a double bet if the bettor reraises. Lastly, someone else may stick his nose in and reraise. Of course, when there is a reraise, you have lost a bet, not saved one, if a blank comes on the turn and your opponent continues betting.

With a standard draw (an open-end straight draw or a flush-draw with no other outs) you do not want players to fold. If you are drawing, you want these people in to provide better pot odds. Of course, if someone with a higher-ranking draw than yours goes out, this helps you, but such a person is not the one likely to be forced out by your raise (nor are you so likely to pop it without a nut draw).

When you are drawing to a hand that is superior to the hands that others in the pot aspire to, it's nice to have company. For example, if you are drawing to the nut flush and hit it, you want to win a bigger pot as a result of others having contributed by paying to draw. You also want those players who are trying to hit a smaller flush, straight, set, or two pair to remain in the pot so they can hit their second-best hand and pay you off.

Since a hand such as the nut flush-draw can be helped in more than one way (making the flush or pairing the ace), your proper strategy is not always perfectly clear. If hitting the ace would beat the original bettor, you don't want anyone in position to make a bigger ace or aces up; you want to remove someone who has an ace with a paired or bigger kicker. But you cannot have things both ways, driving ace-holders out but keeping all other players in, or know the full layout of cards around the table. Having your raise win a pot after pairing the ace that would have been lost if you had not raised is a remote possibility, requiring an improbable parlay of events. So it is almost always better for the nut flush-draw to play to retain the other contestants in the pot when it is multi-handed. Only if the pot were already gigantic from being jammed preflop would you want to concentrate on driving people out with this type of hand.

Some players reason that it is good to raise on a flush-draw, which is only about a 2-to-1 dog, as long as you have more than two callers. They feel they have an overlay on the pot odds, so raising is right. But they are paying insufficient attention to the possibility of their raise worsening the good odds they are getting at the point the raise is made. The original bettor may be itching to reraise and protect his hand to the maximum.

We are not saying that you should avoid employing this tactic of raising on the flop when drawing and in position. However, we believe it is overused by many players. They seem to raise automatically on the flop, regardless of their type of draw, and then always give the show away by checking the turn. You must learn when to make the positional raise with a draw, and vary how you follow it up.

This set of problems will help illustrate when raising in position on a draw is a good idea, and how to play thereafter.

(1) The game is $20-$40. You are on the button holding T♦-9♦. An early player, a middle player, and the cutoff limp. You limp. The small blind folds. There is $110 in the pot and five players. The flop is: A♦-K♣-2♦, giving you a flush-draw. The big blind checks. The early player bets and your other two opponents call. What do you do?

Answer: Raise. This is a good situation for a free card raise. The bettor figures to have an ace, given his lead into four opponents. However, with a big ace like ace-king or ace-queen, he probably would have raised preflop from early position, and it is unlikely that he would limp in from early position with ace-deuce. Therefore, your raise is unlikely to get reraised by the initial bettor. You have two opponents already tied in for one bet, so your raise will not drive them out. Furthermore, you know you will have to make your flush to win, so if a blank comes on the turn and you are checked to, you can check and take a free card. Notice that you do not figure to be giving up anything by checking on the turn when a blank comes, because with this many opponents, you were highly unlikely to win the pot by betting.

(2) A $10-$20 game. You are in the cutoff seat holding 9♠-8♠. An early player and a middle player limp in. You call. The button and the small blind call. There is $60 in the pot and six players. The flop is: K♠-5♠-2♦, giving you a flush-draw. It is checked to the middle player, who bets. What do you do?

Answer: Call. Don't raise trying for a free card. When you raise in this situation, you are now confronting your other four opponents with a double bet. With this board, the most likely scenario is that they will all fold except for the bettor, who probably has a king. When you are drawing like this, you want bottom pairs and middle pairs to call, not fold. It is unlikely that in a heads-up situation you will be successful in getting the bettor to fold a top pair of kings on any street, so you must make your flush to win.

(3) A $20-$40 game. You are on the button with the A♣-J♦ and open with a raise. Both blinds call. There is $120 in the pot and three players. The flop is: Q♥-T♠-3♥, giving you a gutshot with an overcard. Both blinds check. You bet and only the small blind calls. There's $160 in the pot. The turn is the 8♣, giving you four more outs to a straight. Your opponent checks. What do you do?

Answer: Bet. The player in question checked because he thought he wanted a free card. But when you are heads-up with position over your opponent, and the turn-card is unlikely to have helped him, you should bet again. You may win the pot outright if your opponent was hanging around on middle pair or bottom pair. Furthermore, with eight outs to a straight plus three more overcard outs, you will catch something good at the river about a fourth of the time anyway. Finally, if he is on a flush-draw, then you are giving a free card, not taking one, and a check would invite him to rob you at the river. It is seldom right to take a free card on the turn (and thereby reveal you are on some kind of draw) when you have one opponent and something to show down.

(4) A $10-$20 game. You are in middle position with the A♦-K♥ and raise after an early player limps. The big blind and early limper call. There is $65 in the pot and three players. The flop is: J♦-8♥-3♠, so all you have is two overcards. Both players check. You bet; only the limper calls. There is $85 in the pot and two players. The turn is the T♣. He checks; what do you do?

Answer: Check. Taking a free card looks right here. The ten probably helped your opponent more than you if he was drawing. If not, then he was calling your flop bet with a better hand than yours. This means he will be calling your turn bet as well. There is no flush-draw on the flop, and the only open-end straight-draw just hit to make a pair. Your opponent is very likely to have a made hand, one he will not turn loose if you bet, so save your money. You don't need a free showdown when you are almost certain you're beat.

(5) A $20-$40 game. You are in middle position with the A♣-6♣ and call behind two early limpers and another middle player. The small blind limps. There is $120 in the pot and six players. The flop is: 5♠-4♦-3♥, giving you a one-card open-end draw to a straight, plus an overcard. It is checked to you. What do you do?

Answer: Check. Take a free card. You have five opponents and a highly coordinated board. Your straight draw is not nearly as good as it looks, because it is a "one-card straight draw," meaning that you are using only one of your two cards. With only one card working, your hand can be easily counterfeited, possibly resulting in your splitting the pot or losing it altogether. Your ace overcard is of dubious value, since an ace turning up would put four parts to a wheel on the table, and with this many opponents, someone could easily have a deuce and make a straight when you pair the ace. Also, your kicker is weak. You may well get raised, costing you two bets to take off a card. Betting now does not mean that your opponents will check to you on the turn, given that board.

(6) A $10-$20 game. You limp in from middle position with the A♦-7♦ with only the small blind calling. There is $30 in the pot and three players. The flop is: K♥-K♦-3♠, so all you have is a weak-looking backdoor flush-draw. The two blinds check. You bet, trying to steal the pot, and only the big blind calls. There is $50 in the pot and two players. The turn is the 2♦, so you have picked up a flush-draw. Your opponent checks. What do you do?

Answer: Check. Taking a free card to your flush-draw and ace overcard may well depend upon the kind of opponent you are up against. Most players would have led at the board in a three-way, unraised pot on the flop unless they had trip kings. With trip kings, they will frequently check, intending to bet the turn, or try to check-raise the turn if the flop gets bet. Against this type of player, it is too easy to find yourself getting check-raised. Since you have outs against trip kings, checking is better than betting.

(7) A $20-$40 game. You open with a raise from middle position having the A♠-9♠. Only the small blind calls. There is $100 in the pot and two players. The flop is exciting: J♦-8♠-2♠, giving you the nut flush-draw as well as an ace overcard. Your opponent checks. You bet and he raises. What do you do?

Answer: Reraise. This may well be a "free card reraise." Yes, there are times when we still try for a free card even after the opponent has shown strength. If the opponent bets the flop, you raise, and he reraises, it can be right to pop him again. The also applies if you get check-raised on the flop. In making this type of decision, it is helpful to know the rules on caps in heads-up play for the cardroom you are in. The better rule is to allow unlimited raises when heads-up at the point when a raise would normally be a cap. But some cardrooms say if there was anyone else in the pot at the start of the betting round, the cap applies. Naturally, it is more attractive to throw in another raise if it is a cap. You have a lot of hand here with the nut flush-draw and an ace overcard, facing only one opponent over whom you have position. He may well be check-raising on a big jack, but even if he is doing this on something more, you have a lot of outs with two cards to come. If he calls, a blank comes on the turn, and he checks, you can decide how you want to proceed, but certainly taking a free card would be an attractive option. We are more inclined to take a free card on the turn when the opponent has shown power in the flop betting.

(8) A $10-$20 game. You are in the cutoff seat holding A♦-K♠. An early player and a middle player limp in. You raise. The big blind and the two limpers call. There is $85 in the pot and four players. The flop is: Q♦-Q♣-J♠, so you have "two overcards" and a gutshot. It is checked to you. What do you do?

Answer: Check. A board like this can easily have hit one of your three opponents. Don't be fooled by all the checking. They may well be merely "checking to the raiser." You have no clean outs, and any pair could be bad news for you, since both your overcards complement the board. Even the gutshot might not win.

(9) A $20-$40 game. You are on the button and are holding the T♦-8♦. An early player, a middle player, and the cutoff limp. You limp, as well as the small blind. There is $60 in the pot and six players. The flop is: Q♦-8♣-4♠, giving you middle pair. It is checked to you. What do you do?

Answer: Check. Middle pair with no kicker is too weak a holding to bet into five players despite all the checking. You are beat by a second pair, a better eight, or someone with a weak queen who decided not to lead into a large field. Take a free card and hope all five of your outs are working. The free card has great utility, since you are the last to act. In the middle limit games, you find a lot of flop bets by the button when all have checked, so many players try to counter this by check-raising if the button bets. This could be done by a sandbagged strong hand, a moderate hand like top pair no kicker, or simply as a bluff.

34 – AVOIDING TROUBLE

One of the many differences between a good player and a mediocre player is that when the good player sees dark clouds on the horizon, he seldom waits until the storm hits before paddling to safety. The ability to duck out of a bad situation and escape at minimal cost, despite having a promising hand, is one of the reasons good players show a nice profit over the course of a year.

For many of these hands, trouble announces itself when two or more players get into a raising war on the flop. While this can be players with made hands, each of the opinion that his is the best, it is often the case that one of the wave-makers is pumping a big draw. At holdem, big draws nearly always include a flush-draw, and the player who is willing to keep raising has the nut flush-draw as part of his holding. If you have a flush-draw, getting pinned between the nut flush-draw and a good made hand is a disaster. Big pot odds are useless if you are drawing dead.

The following set of hands illustrate some of these hazardous situations. Although the answer to nearly every problem is to fold, we believe there is a lot of benefit in reviewing the rationale.

(1) The game is $20-$40. You are in the big blind with the 7♥-4♥. Two early players, two middle players, the button, and the small blind limp. You get a free play. There is $140 in the pot and seven players. The flop is: K♠-Q♥-3♥, giving you a tiny flush-draw. The small blind checks. You check. An early position player bets, a middle player calls, and the button raises. The small blind calls both bets cold. What do you do?

Answer: Fold. You should not cold-call a bet and a raise on the flop with a small flush-draw in a large field like this. It may seem strange to fold a flush-draw on the flop, since this is normally a promising holding that we will usually take to the river. But given all these players who are willing to call bets and raises to see the turn when a two-flush flops, the likelihood of someone else being on a flush-draw quite high. When this happens, not only is it important that you be drawing to the bigger flush, but the odds of making it are reduced even if you are drawing live. Here, an opponent drawing to a flush almost certainly has a bigger draw than yours. The threat of drawing dead is very strong. On the actual hand, the player stayed all the way to the river and made his flush, only to be shown the nut flush by the small blind. There is nothing like drawing dead and getting there to ruin your day.

(2) A $30-$60 game. You are in the small blind holding 9♥-9♦. An early player limps, a middle player raises, and the remaining players fold. You call, as well as the big blind. There is $240 in the pot and four players. The flop comes: Q♠-J♦-8♦, so you have a pair with a one-card straight-draw. It is checked to the raiser, who bets. What do you do?

Answer: Fold. There is $270 in the pot and it costs you $30 right now to call. On the surface, you might believe that you have a lot of outs, with any ten making a straight, any nine giving you a set, a diamond giving you a flush-draw, and so forth. But your "outs" are a mirage. A ten means that anyone with ace-king or king-nine has you beat. Even someone with another nine has you tied. Therefore, your one-card gutshot straight-draw is actually weak. A nine puts four parts to a straight on the table, giving anyone with a ten in his hand a straight. Your backdoor flush-draw is nowhere near the nuts. Anyone who happens to have a big diamond in their hand has you beat. In fact, you have no nut draws.

On the actual hand the player called, as well as the big blind. The early player folded. The turn was the T♥. The player bet his straight and got called by the big blind and then raised by the preflop raiser. He called, as well as the big blind. The river was a blank. It was checked to the preflop raiser, who bet. The player made a crying call, as did the big blind. The preflop raiser won, having the A♦-K♦ for the nuts on the turn. The big blind had the J♠-9♠. The player lost an extra $210 playing a one-out draw.

(3) A $10-$20 game. You raise from early position with T♠-T♣ after another early player limps in. A middle player calls and another middle player reraises. The cutoff and button fold, but everyone else calls. There is $180 in the pot and six players. The flop is: 5♣-4♠-2♣, so you have an overpair. Both blinds check. The early player now bets. What do you do?

Answer: Fold. Despite having an overpair, you have some serious problems here. The board is highly coordinated with a two-flush. You are being bet into with a preflop reraiser yet to act, plus four other players. If the preflop reraiser has an overpair, it is probably bigger than yours, and he will definitely raise. If he has an A-K that includes a club, he may well raise. You don't expect to see another card for just $10. Raising will not drive out anyone you can beat, nor will it drive out any legitimate draws. On the actual hand, the player raised with his overpair and got reraised. It got capped back to him and he found the good sense to fold. It ended up being a huge pot with bets and raises on every street. The early player won the hand when he made a club flush at the river, having the A♣-9♣. The preflop reraiser was holding the K♠-K♣.

(4) A $20-$40 game. You are in early position holding A♥-A♣ and raise an early player. Two middle players call, as well as the early limper. There is $190 in the pot and four players. The flop is: T♠-7♠-6♣, giving you an overpair. The early player checks. You bet. The first middle player raises and the next middle player reraises. The early player folds. What do you do?

Answer: Unclear. This is a difficult problem, and a lot of your decision is based on who reraised. A straight-forward player has you beat, but this is a spot for possible tactics to get you out. Against a person who has what he represents, you are either badly hurting or buried. You have no outs against a straight, ignoring perfect-perfect. You have two outs against a set, five outs against two pair. If one of your opponents is on a flush-draw, then one of your outs is killed; if not, redraws get created. If you are in the lead, you will still lose about a third of the time against a flush-draw or against someone with a pair and a gutshot. Finally, it could get raised again after you call. On the other hand, a player could have something like an overpair and simply be trying to use the leverage of a double bet to muscle you out of the pot.

(5) A $15-$30 game. You limp in from middle position with the T♦-9♦ behind three other players. The cutoff raises and the button and small blind both fold. Everyone else calls. There is $190 in the pot and six players. The flop comes: K♣-8♦-3♦, giving you a ten-high flush-draw. The big blind bets. Everyone calls to the button, who raises. The big blind reraises and everyone calls to you. What do you do?

Answer: Fold. One thing is for sure. When six players are willing to pay three bets each to see the turn when a two-flush flops, there has got to be more than one person on a flush-draw. A bigger flush-draw is almost certainly out there, which means you are drawing dead. On the actual hand, the player stayed with his draw, only to catch a diamond at the river and lose to a king-high flush. He thought he took a bad beat. But this was a "bad beat" he did not have to take. Very often, when the flop is bet and raised, one of the pumpers is on a draw.

(6) A $30-$60 game. You are in the big blind holding the 6♠-6♥. An early player, a middle player, and the button limp. The small blind folds so you get a free play. There is $140 in the pot and four players. The flop is: 9♦-7♥-5♥, giving you a pair and a one-card gutshot. Everyone checks. The turn is the 6♣, giving you three sixes. What do you do?

Answer: Check. This seems wimpy, but with four parts to a straight now on the table and three opponents, it is too easy for someone to have an eight for a straight. Occasionally, two players will have a straight, and when this happens, you can get taken for a four or five bet ride here on the turn, costing you $300 to see the river. You have 10 outs, so your drawing odds are 3.6-to-1 against. The problem is that the pot is a small one because no one bet the flop. With only $140 in the pot, you should check, and call if someone bets.

On the actual hand, the player checked. It was bet and raised back to him with his third opponent folding. He called. It got reraised and four-bet; he called that as well. When it was capped, he had paid $300 to see the river. The river was a blank, and he folded when it was bet and raised to him. His two opponents split the pot, each having ten-eight. He spent $300 on the turn to win $740, plus whatever bets he would collect at the river if he hit. He needed 3.6-to-1 odds to play, but was getting well under 3-to-1.

(7) A $20-$40 game. You limp in under-the-gun with the K♥-Q♥. An early player calls and a middle player raises. The big blind calls, as well as you and the early player. There is $170 in the pot and four players. The flop comes: J♥-6♥-6♠, giving you a king-high flush-draw, but with an open pair on the board. It is checked to the preflop raiser, who bets. The big blind calls and you call. The early player now raises. The preflop raiser then reraises. The big blind calls. What do you do?

Answer: Fold. With an open pair on the table and three players excited about their hands, it is best to fold here. Your situation is doubly bad, because your draw is not to the nut flush and you have serious problems if someone has trip sixes, since some of your outs get killed. When there is an open pair on the table, you should usually dump even a big flush-draw when the betting sequence is raise, reraise, cold-call.

(8) A $15-$30 game. You are in the cutoff seat holding T♠-T♥. An early player limps and a middle player raises. You call, as well as the big blind and the early limper. There is $130 in the pot and four players. The flop is: 7♠-5♥-3♦, so you have an overpair. The big blind bets. The early limper raises and the middle player calls. What do you do?

Answer: Fold. This is a rainbow board with just small cards, so it is unlikely all these players are pounding the pot on a come hand. Among your three opponents, which include a bettor, a raiser, and a cold-caller, someone surely has a better hand than yours, and you are probably playing two outs. If by some miracle you are in the lead, you will get overtaken about a third of the time against one opponent who has a pair and a gutshot. Against multiple opponents whose hands all fit that flop, you will get overtaken by one of them the majority of the time.

35 – NON-STANDARD GAMES

In this section, we will be dealing with some non-standard game conditions. Most holdem games are played with a two-tiered betting structure. The bet on the first and second betting rounds is a small bet; the bet on the third and fourth betting rounds is a big bet of twice the small bet. However, in some parts of the country, particularly near the Gulf Coast in Louisiana and Texas, a holdem structure which allows a double big bet on the last betting round is quite popular. The most common one is a limit of $10-$20-$40, where the bet on the last round can be either $20 or $40. The big river bet creates a profound impact on strategy, not just on the last betting round, but throughout the whole deal. For instance, there is a lot of sandbagging on the turn, as a player holding a behemoth usually waits one more round for the maximum limit before revealing his strength. Of course, there is more leverage created for a bluff on the end. We are not fond of this structure, because it provides such a large reward for someone lucky enough to draw out on the person who was in front. But the action is often too good to pass up, so if this structure is played in your locale, it is worth it to learn how to beat the game.

The blind structure in most holdem games is half a small bet for the small blind and one small bet for the big blind. But games like $15-$30 holdem and $30-$60 holdem have the small blind at 2/3 of a small bet. This impacts your play from the small blind, as well as your propensity to try and steal the blinds. For example, in a $30-$60 game, if you are in the small blind, it costs you only $10 to call in an unraised pot, because you had to put up a $20 small blind. Suppose three players limp in. When you call, there is $140 in the pot, so you are getting 14-to-1 pot odds to take a flop. If the small blind had been $15, one half of a small bet, then it would cost you another $15 to take a flop, and your pot odds would bet $135-to-$15, which is only 9-to-1. This has a significant impact on hand selection for calling when in the small blind. Suppose you are in late position and are considering opening with a steal-raise. With $50 in blind money already in the pot, a $60 steal-raise looks more attractive than if there were only $45 in the pot.

We have a chapter on playing in games that are less than a full game of eight to ten players. As the game becomes shorthanded, you will be putting up more blind money over the course of an hour. In a ten-handed game you might have the small blind three times and the big blind three times, resulting in your putting up $150 an hour in blind money in a $30-$60 game. If the game becomes five-handed, you are now putting up $300 per hour in blinds. This means you play more aggressively against the blind money in a shorthanded game than you would in a full game. Furthermore, hand values change when shorthanded.

Frequently, a new player will arrive in the game and want to get into action by posting right away rather than waiting for the big blind. You may want to do this yourself when you first sit down in a game. Such a post is normally made in the cutoff seat, to obtain the maximum number of free hands before having to take the regular blinds. The same type of post is often made by a player who has missed the blinds, except there is the extra amount of the little blind that is taken into the center of the pot by the dealer, creating even more of a feeding frenzy.

The posting of an additional blind builds a bigger pot and gets more people involved, making a major impact on the hands you play and how they are played. The tendency when holding any hand good enough to open is to raise, so there isn't anyone getting a free ride to see the flop.

Occasionally, a gambler will want to straddle. A straddle is a blind raise made by the player under-the-gun before the cards are dealt. With so much money in the pot already, and a double bet to play, a lot of extra action is induced. This is why the straddler put up the money. Often, he is stuck and trying to get even, and this is his method of choice to increase the monetary fluctuation. Of course, he is more likely to be inducing an outflow than an inflow for his stack, so anyone who objects to the straddle is not trying to win money in the game. Do not raise a straddle bet thinking you are going to get a walk; the straddler hardly ever folds. He may reraise, souping up the action even more.

All these departures from the usual betting and blind structure impact the game, and the all-around player needs to know how to adjust to the new environment.

36 – THE BIG RIVER BET

Some games are structured to allow a double-size big bet on the end after all the cards are out. An example of this is a limit holdem structure of $10-$20-$40, called "Ten and twenty, forty on the end." This is a $10-$20 game with an optional $40 river bet available. At the river you can bet or raise either $20 or $40 (instead of just $20). For example, if someone bets $20 at the river, you can raise to either $40 or $60. Of course, when someone makes a bet or raise of $40, only a $40 raise is allowed thereafter. This follows the standard poker law requiring any raise be at least the amount of the last bet or raise (except when going all-in).

What are the advantages and disadvantages of allowing a $40 bet at the river? There is more deception on the turn, as players try to derive the maximum benefit (or the minimum pain) from the increased limit on the end. The element of bluffing is intensified by the extra leverage. More drawing hands are playable after the flop because of the bigger payoff when hitting. Obviously, this structure aids the drawing hand, as opposed to the made hand carrying the betting on the early rounds. The draw has extra leverage, whether it is getting paid off after hitting or running a bluff after missing.

Frankly, a good player is more likely to be the person in front as the deal proceeds, rather than the person trying to improve. A good player's advantage in the game is diminished by allowing a larger bet on the end than can be made to protect his hand in the earlier stages.

Those players who want to play a lot of hands and seek lively action like the big bet on the end. If playing strictly for entertainment, we would be in favor of this structure. For the purpose of trying to win as much money as possible, it is inferior to a standard structure. However, allowing a big river bet does attract the kind of people you should like to gamble with, so do not boycott such a game. It is beatable despite its drawbacks.

When you find yourself in a structure like this using the big river bet, there is a large influence on the play, especially on the last betting round. You need to fully adjust to the special requirements of this structure to optimize your results. If you make no adjustments, you might not even beat the game.

In a regular betting structure, the truth usually comes out on the turn betting round. This is where the big hand normally chooses to make its move. The reason is the limit is not going to get any higher, so the incentive in sandbagging for another round has been reduced. But in a structure where the limit will double on the last card, it is tempting for a big hand to slowplay until the limit has reached the maximum. You cannot assume in a big river bet structure that your hand is still good if you were just called on the turn and a blank comes at the river. When the opponent makes a bet or raise on the end, you will in many cases not know whether he has just drawn out or has simply been laying low until he could milk you for the maximum. Of course, he may be bluffing.

Because of the frequent sandbagging, the big river bet reduces the amount of value betting you can do on the end. In a normal structure you should be aggressive, because people play and pay off with cheesy hands. But you definitely need to tone this down a notch with the big river bet in use. This particularly applies in the passout seat. Your opponent who checked to you all the way is unlikely to have enough hand to call $40 (though he might be looking to raise you). And betting only $20 when last reopens the gates to a $40 raise, so it is a type of bet to be avoided.

Here is an example of how value betting is affected by the big river bet. You hold K♠-Q♠ and call the blind in middle position. The button and small blind also call, so four of you see the flop, which comes K♦-J♦-3♠. The blinds check and you bet. The button and little blind fold, and the big blind calls, making it heads-up. On fourth street comes the 6♦, creating a three-flush on board. Your opponent checks and you bet. A bet in this spot is clear, as the blind is less likely than a voluntary player to have been playing a suited hand. Naturally, you would be unhappy to get check-raised, but to play correct poker you must cross those bridges when you come to them. At any rate, the opponent only calls. The last card is a blank, the 8♥. Your opponent checks; what do you do?

In a regular structure you should bet again, because your hand is probably good. The opponent may well have something like top pair with a bad kicker and pay you off. But with a $40 bet on the end, the chance of getting paid off is less, and getting check-raised would be really unpleasant. There is also a greater chance of the opponent having a flush than in a regular structure, because the big river bet encourages slowplaying, so his check-call on the turn is less meaningful. Here you should simply turn up your hand, expecting to win the money, but avoiding unpleasantness.

You too can be one of the sandbaggers. You pick up J♠-J♣ and open in early position with a raise. You get several callers and the flop comes 8♦-8♠-3♦. The blinds check and you bet your overpair. Two players behind you call. Lo and behold, your dream-card the J♦ jumps off the deck, giving you the big full house and creating a possible flush. You bet out, praying to get raised. The first player folds, but the second one produces that hoped-for raise. With that $40 river bet coming up, it may be better to just call and hope to get in a check-raise on the end. That double-size bet is simply too hard to resist.

Bluffing on the end should become more attractive because you can bet $40, putting heavier pressure on your opponent to fold. However, it has been our experience that against typical players, the use of the $40 river bet is normally done on their good hands, even though some of the better players will occasionally make use of the big river bet to bluff.

The $40 bet produces some good bluffing opportunities. Some situations that at a standard structure are a bit unclear should be taken advantage of here with the extra leverage available. Here's an example. You pick up Q♥-J♥ in middle position. There is an early limper and you also call. Two players call behind you, so there are a total of five seeing the flop, which comes K♣-10♣-4♠, giving you an open-end straight-draw. The blind bets, the early limper folds, you call, and someone in late position also calls. On fourth street comes the 7♦, a blank. The blind bets again, you call, and the player behind you folds. The last card is the 2♣, making a three-flush on board. The blind checks. Do you give up or bluff? A major factor in the decision to represent the flush is how much weight your bet will carry. At pot-limit you should almost surely make a big bet. At limit poker, a player with top pair in a regularly structured game is likely to call on the end. But with a big river bet available, the opponent has something serious to think about, and you should strongly consider running a bluff.

There are some significant adjustments you should make in this structure to your preflop and flop play as well. Drawing hands like straight-draws and flush-draws have increased implied odds, because when you make your hand at the river you are collecting four small bets instead of just two. Sometimes you may even collect eight small bets (when you raise and get called). So suited connectors, suited aces, and even other suited cards go up in value in this type of structure, especially against the right lineup of players. Therefore, it may well be correct to limp in early with hands like jack-ten suited, ten-nine suited, and ace-little suited when playing in this kind of game if there is not much preflop raising. Drawing hands are more attractive if the game is loose and passive and you know you will probably get paid off when you hit your hand.

Any change in the betting structure produces some change in strategy. You must adjust to the new circumstances; poker is not supposed to be a game that you play by rote. A big river bet means you cannot play your regular game; these are a few of the ideas you can put to work for you. One of the hallmarks of the top player is the ability to modify his regular game when operating in a new environment.

The next group of hands highlight some of the significant differences between this structure and the traditional two-tiered betting structure.

(1) You are in the big blind with the A♦-A♣. An early player, a middle player, the cutoff, and the small blind all limp. You raise and everyone calls. There is $100 in the pot and five players. The flop is: T♠-T♥-3♣, giving you aces over tens. The small blind checks. You bet and the early player as well as the cutoff call. There is $130 in the pot and three players. The turn is the 5♦. You bet and only the early player calls. There is $170 in the pot and two players. The river is the Q♥. What do you do?

Answer: Check. In a normal $10-$20 game, you should bet again. But in this structure, with the big $40 river bet available, you should check. Players love to slowplay until the river in this structure. In a normal game, if your opponent had trip tens, he would raise your turn bet. But in this game, he will usually wait until the river to reveal himself by popping you. When you bet into a board of T-T-3 rainbow and get called in two spots, you cannot be overly optimistic.

(2) You are in the big blind with the Q♣-9♥. An early player, the cutoff, and the small blind limp, so you get a free play. There is $40 in the pot and four players. The flop is: Q♦-5♣-3♥, giving you top pair. The small blind checks. You bet and only the early player calls. There is $60 in the pot and two players. The turn is the A♦. You bet and your opponent calls. There is $100 in the pot. The river is the 4♦, completing a possible backdoor flush. You check. Your opponent makes the $40 river bet. What do you do?

Answer: Fold, unless you think the opponent is bluffing. The big $40 river bet makes a large difference, when compared to a normal $10-$20 game. In a normal game, your opponent could only bet $20, so you would be getting 6-to-1 pot odds to call and try to pick off a bluff. But in this game, having to call $40 reduces your pot odds to 3.5-to-1, almost cutting them in half from a normal game. Top pair with a shaky kicker is not a hand where you can bet or call with on the river, so a bluff is all you can beat.

(3) You are in middle position with the K♣-Q♠ and call behind three other players. The cutoff raises and only the limpers call. You call. There is $115 in the pot and five players. The flop is: Q♣-9♦-6♦, giving you top pair. It is checked to you and you bet. The cutoff raises, an early player calls, and you call. There is $175 in the pot and three players. The turn is the 8♦. Everyone checks. The river is the 4♣. The early player checks. What do you do?

Answer: Check. In a traditional betting structure, you can assume that the absence of any betting on the turn means that your top pair, excellent kicker is probably good. If someone made a flush, they would have bet the turn. If the cutoff, who raised preflop, had an overpair or top pair, top kicker, he would have bet the turn after being checked to. So normally you should bet the river. But in this structure, the big $40 river bet distorts everything. A player with a flush or with a better hand than yours will wait until the river to reveal himself, since there is such a large payoff for doing so. The threat of getting raised $40 is quite real, and you do not want to invest $60 or $80 to avoid getting faked out, with a pot having less than $200 in it. Of course, you will call if the cutoff bets (assuming the early player does not raise).

(4) You are on the button with the A♥-Q♣. An early player limps in and you raise. He calls. There is $55 in the pot and two players. The flop is: A♦-Q♠-T♣, giving you the top two pair. Your opponent checks. You bet and he calls. There is $75 in the pot. The turn is the 8♣. Your opponent checks. You bet and he calls. There is $115 in the pot. The river is the 4♥. Your opponent now makes the $40 river bet. What do you do?

Answer: Call. Don't raise to $80. In this structure, there is so much slowplaying that you do not know if the 4♥ helped him or if he had something all along. In a regular $10-$20 game, you could raise a $20 bet to $40 nearly every time with the top two pair when a blank comes at the river, but not in this structure.

(5) You are in the big blind with the K♣-8♣. An early player, a middle player, the cutoff, the button, and the small blind all limp. You take a free play. There is $60 in the pot and six players. The flop is: T♣-6♣-4♥, giving you a flush-draw with a king overcard. It is checked to the cutoff who bets. It is folded to you and you call. The middle player calls. There is $90 in the pot and three players. The turn is the 3♠. Everyone checks. The river is the K♥. You bet $20 with your top pair. The next player folds. The cutoff raises $40 more (making the total bet $60). What do you do?

Answer: Fold. A $40 river raise is a big move in this game. Against most players, your top pair of kings with an eight kicker is almost certainly no good. You should fold unless you think your opponent is the type of player who would make a big bluff river bet on a busted draw.

(6) You are in the cutoff seat with the J♦-9♦. An early player and two middle players limp. You limp. There is $55 in the pot and five players. The flop is: J♥-5♦-2♦, giving you top pair as well as a flush-draw. It is checked to the player on your right, who bets. You raise and only the middle limpers call. There is $115 in the pot and three players. The turn is the Q♣. The first player now bets and the next player folds. You call. There is $155 in the pot and two players. The river is the A♦. Your opponent bets $20. What do you do?

Answer: Raise. Make the big $40 river raise for a total of $60. With a king-high or queen-high flush your opponent would make the big $40 river bet instead of just betting $20. He probably has a smaller flush than you, or some other hand you can beat.

(7) You limp in from early position with the A♦-J♥ behind another early limper. Two middle players call and everyone else folds. There is $55 in the pot and five players. The flop comes: J♦-9♥-7♣, giving you top pair. The big blind and the early limper check. You bet and only one of the middle players behind you fold. There is $95 in the pot and four players. The turn is the 9♠. It is checked to you. You bet and all three opponents call. There is $175 in the pot. The river is the 3♥. The big blind and the early limper check. What do you do?

Answer: Check. In a normal structure, if one of your three opponents had flopped a middle pair of nines and then made trip nines on the turn, they would have raised your turn bet. But in this structure, players love to sandbag, hoping to pick up a big $40 crying call at the river. Therefore, the lack of raising on the turn does not mean anything. You should check and be happy to get a free showdown, while hoping your hand is good.

(8) You are in the cutoff seat with the T♣-9♦ and limp in behind an early limper and a middle limper. The small blind calls and the big blind raises. Everyone calls. There is $100 in the pot and five players. The flop is: Q♣-J♥-8♠, giving you a straight, which is the nuts right now. It is checked to you and you bet. Only the early limper and the middle limper call. There is $130 in the pot and three players. The turn is the T♥. It is checked to you and you bet. Only the early limper calls. There is $170 in the pot and two players. The river is the 3♥, so a backdoor flush has arrived. Your opponent checks. What do you do?

Answer: Check. Any nine ties you and there is a runner-runner heart flush threat. It is unlikely that a hand worse than yours will call with four parts to a straight on the table plus a three-flush. It would be prudent to check it down here, especially in this structure where you run the risk of facing a big $40 river raise. Resist the temptation to bet $20 trying to milk your opponent. When you are acting last, avoid making a small bet that subjects you to a big raise. A play of betting $20 when checked to at the river should never be used.

(9) You raise from early position with the Q♠-Q♦ after another early player limps in. A middle player, the cutoff, and the early player call. There is $95 in the pot and four players. The flop is: T♥-7♥-3♣, giving you an overpair. The early player checks. You bet and the middle player calls. The cutoff raises and the early player folds. You reraise and the middle player now folds. The cutoff calls. There is $165 in the pot and two players. The turn is the J♥, putting a three-flush on the board. You bet and your opponent calls. There is $205 in the pot. The river is the 3♠. What do you do?

Answer: Check. Again, in a normal structure if you were beat, you would likely hear about on the turn. But in this structure, you can be getting slowplayed very easily.

(10) You are in the big blind with the K♣-3♠. An early player and the small blind limp, so you get a free play. There is $30 in the pot and three players. The flop is: T♣-7♣-3♣, giving you bottom pair and a flush-draw. The small blind checks. You bet. The early player calls and the small blind folds. There is $50 in the pot and two players. The turn is the 5♦. You bet and your opponent calls.

300

36 - THE BIG RIVER BET

There is $90 in the pot. The river is the 3♦. You make the big $40 river bet, having made trip treys. Your opponent now raises to $80. What do you do?

Answer: Fold. While making good folds at the river is not the way to make money in limit holdem, this is one time where folding is right. Your opponent has been calling all along. He either had a hand or was on a draw. At the river, a club did not arrive and the board paired small. You made the big $40 river bet expecting to get calls from two pair-type hands and expecting a busted flush-draw to fold. Obviously, your opponent was not drawing, since a blank came and your $40 river bet is being raised, which is a big move in this game. His raise means he has a hand that can beat trip treys. The most obvious hand for him to have is a flopped flush that he was slowplaying all along. A call might be warranted against a tricky player, a maniac, or some player who was capable of bluff-raising on the end. But against typical opponents, folding is right. On the actual hand, the raiser holding the A♣-9♣ had flopped the nut flush.

(11) You open with a raise under-the-gun with the Q♠-Q♣. Another early player reraises. The big blind calls and you call. There is $95 in the pot and three players. The flop is: J♥-7♥-6♦, giving you an overpair. The big blind checks. You bet. The preflop reraiser pops it. The big blind calls. You call. There is $155 in the pot. The turn is the 4♣. The big blind checks and you bet. The preflop reraiser calls. The big blind folds. There is $195 in the pot and two players. The river is the 2♦. What do you do?

Answer: Check. At this point your opponent either has no pair, like ace-king, or he has you beat. Betting is pointless. It is unlikely a guy with ace-king will call, and if he has a pair, it is probably better than yours based on his preflop action and play on the flop and turn. Since a better hand won't fold and a worse hand likely will not call, you should check, then decide what to do if he bets. On the actual hand, the player bet $20. His opponent raised $40 more and the player called. The opponent won with A♠-A♣.

301

37 – SMALL BLIND 2/3 BIG

In most holdem games, the small blind is half a bet. But in $15-$30, the small blind is $10, which is 2/3 the size of the $15 big blind. In $30-$60, if the game is played with all ten-dollar chips, the small blind is $20, which is 2/3 the size of the big blind.

When playing in a game with this type of irregular structure, what changes should you make in your play? Areas where you might consider making strategy changes would be in limping from the small blind, stealing the blinds, defending against steal-raises out of your small blind, and calling legitimate raises from the small blind.

The area where we feel there are significant strategy adjustments is limping in from the small blind. The pot odds are usually very favorable, especially when several players limp in. Suppose you are playing in a $10-$20 game where the small blind is $5. Further, suppose three players limp in before the action gets to you. At this point there is $45 in the pot and it costs you $5 to call, assuming the big blind does not raise. These are pot odds of 9-to-1. Now compare this to a $15-$30 game with a $10 small blind. With three players limping, it costs you the same $5 to call. But with $70 in the pot, your pot odds are 14-to-1. Typically, there is a big enough difference in pot odds to allow you to limp in with a much larger array of hands.

Recalling our earlier guidelines on calling from the small blind, we stated that any pair was playable, as well as suited connectors down to six-five suited and offsuit hands as bad as nine-eight. With the small blind being 2/3 of a bet and several players in, the pot odds are there to play any two suited cards and any two connecting cards. This is because you are frequently getting better than 10-to-1 pot odds to call and see three cards. When you have two suited cards, your odds on flopping a flush-draw are only 7-to-1 against. It is about the same with regard to flopping a straight-draw when you start with two connecting cards. Furthermore, the odds of flopping two pair or better are 28-to-1 against. Bottom line is that when you have suited cards and connecting cards, the likelihood of you catching a flop you like is usually well under 10-to-1 against. Since your current pot odds in

302

this structure are frequently greater than that, these hands become playable.

We still don't play unsuited trash like 9-4, 8-3, or 7-2. These hands have no flush or straight potential, so we hope to flop two pair or better, which is about a 28-to-1 shot. A fold is indicated.

On occasion, you may wish to depart from this general advice and play even a total trash hand. This would be when there is only one limper, a passive player, and the big blind is also a passive player. The intent is to use your presence in the pot to rob your opponents; making a hand would be frosting on the cake.

Regarding a raise by us to steal the blinds, we do not feel that the extra blind money already in the pot here (a sixth of a bet) is large enough to make any strategy difference. The slight increase in money is counter-balanced by the greater likeliness of being called, because the small blind has a larger amount already in the pot. Similarly, with regard to defending the small blind against late position steal-type raises, we don't believe there is enough difference to alter our strategy here by a significant amount.

What about the "Ciaffone Rule" regarding calling legitimate raises from your small blind? If you recall, in our section on preflop play, we stated that if you would not cold-call a raise from the button with a given hand, you should not call from the small blind either with the same hand. This is because position in a raised pot should be worth about half a small bet. Again, the additional sixth of a bet is not enough for us to change this.

In order for you to take advantage of the extra money you have posted by playing more hands than in a standard structure, you have to play carefully and well when out-of-position. If you flop a small flush-draw and the pot gets bombarded on the flop, get out. If you flop top pair with a weak kicker, don't try to run down an opponent who says he has you beat.

Not all your stellar play lies in folding. Know when to go for a steal by betting the turn when the flop is checked by all. On occasion, use your position to check-raise a suspicious button bet, confronting the other players with a double bet and isolating on a possible bluffer. Calling on weak hands out-of-position because of favorable pot odds must be backed up by proper play, or you have no overlay, and should get out of harm's way by folding.

Here are some hands which discuss play in situations with the small blind two-thirds of the big blind.

(1) A $15-$30 game. You are in the small blind holding 6♦-5♣. An early player, a middle player, the cutoff, and the button limp in. What do you do?

Answer: Call. There is $85 in the pot and it costs you $5 to call. Your pot odds to take a flop are 17-to-1. The probability of flopping a straight draw is only 9-to-1 against. Add to this the probability of flopping two pair or better. You can also flop a pair and a draw plus other things. You still have to make your hand after flopping your draw; that's why you need an overlay. Here you have a playable hand, provided you are a good player who seldom gets nailed for big bucks chasing out-of-position.

(2) A $15-$30 game. You are in the small blind with the A♠-2♣. A middle player and the button limp in. What do you do?

Answer: Call. There is $55 in the pot and it costs you $5 to see the flop. These are pot odds of 11-to-1. The odds are only 4-to-1 against flopping a top pair of aces. It is possible you could lose additional money if one of your three opponents has a bigger ace when you flop aces. But the fact that no one raised diminishes the chance of hands like ace-king, ace-queen, and ace-jack suited. Again, you are getting such a large overlay that calling is right. You can also flop two pair or better along with some other things. However, to play this kind of hand, you have to be prepared to fold it if an opponent's betting indicates your weak ace is beaten.

(3) A $30-$60 game. You are in the small blind with the A♥-4♣. An early player and the cutoff limp. You limp. The big blind raises. Everyone calls. What do you do?

Answer: Fold. Initially calling was correct because you were getting 11-to-1 pot odds to call against players who showed no strength. But now there is $210 in the pot and it costs you a full $30 to play. Your pot odds have been reduced by a substantial amount, to 7-to-1. Furthermore, the presence of a big blind who is willing to raise after three other players have entered the pot means he has a premium hand like A-A, K-K, Q-Q, A-K, or A-Q. The threat of being dominated by a larger ace is too strong to get involved any further. It is common in this structure to have a small blind limp in, then fold when the big blind raises.

(4) A $30-$60 game. You are in the small blind holding T♥-6♥. An early player, a middle player, and the button limp in. What do you do?

Answer: Call. There is $140 in the pot and it costs you $10, so your pot odds are 14-to-1. The odds against flopping a flush or a flush-draw are about 7-to-1 against. Couple this with the chances of flopping two pair or better or a flush-draw with a pair, and you have a big enough overlay to call.

(5) A $15-$30 game. You're in the small blind with J♠-8♥. A middle player and the button limp in; you call for $5. Four of you see a flop of K♥-J♣-5♠, giving you middle pair with an eight kicker. Everyone checks to the button, who bets. What do you do?

Answer: Raise. A fold is also fine, of course, and indicated if against a solid-passive type button player. The one thing you must not do is call. Being first to act on the flop gives you the most credibility for having checked a good hand. We generally bet our good hands rather than check-raise, but we do vary our play enough to be able to raise here with credibility. You are positioned well for putting a play on the button (possibly with the best hand). He may be stealing; he may have a light hand that he thought was good; he may fold top pair with a weak kicker on the turn (you intend to keep betting). Calling, which lets the button charge us to play and lets the field in cheap to draw at who-knows-what, is abhorrent poker. We could construct lots of problems with this theme of coming to life after the field has shown weakness on the flop, but only one is needed to understand our philosophy when up front. Being first to act has upsides as well as downsides.

38 – SHORTHANDED PLAY

By playing shorthanded, we are referring to situations where there are less than eight players dealt in. We will try to divide the material into two categories. Initially, we will discuss four-handed and five-handed games. Later on in this chapter, we will discuss six-handed and seven-handed play. (Maybe we should call such a game "semi-short.") Of course, the two categories have quite a bit in common.

Many players prefer to avoid shorthanded games. When a game becomes shorthanded, they will stop playing altogether, or get up and go for a walk. The cardroom will usually lower the rake to keep the remaining players from leaving the table.

An all-around poker player needs to know how to adjust his play so he can do all right in a shorthanded game. Most cardrooms have "must move games" in order to make sure that the first game spreading a given limit such as $20-$40 will always be full, rather than having multiple $20-$40 games that have less than a full complement of players. To keep your place as a player waiting for the main game, you may be asked to play in the must-move game.

If you are a tournament poker player, knowing how to play shorthanded is an absolute must. The crucial part of play for the big-money places takes place at the end of a tournament event, where you have to know how to play even in a heads-up game. The difference in payoff for a higher place finish can be huge.

Here is the truth about whether you have more or less advantage at shorthanded games than in a full game. If the other players are weak, your advantage is greater. You will be able to win a great many pots without the burden of having to make the best hand. But if the other players are the loose and aggressive type, your edge in shorthanded play is less. Pumping pots on weak hands is a more effective tactic shorthanded then in a full game.

An important area where a good player has an advantage over a bad player is preflop play. The good player does not play very many starting hands, especially in early position. The bad player does. Consider a hand like K-10 offsuit. In a full game, the good player rarely plays this hand. Unless he can limp in from late position, steal-raise from late position, or he is playing out of his blinds, he will usually muck this piece of cheese. But the bad player thinks king-ten offsuit is a real hand and will play it from any position, maybe even cold-call raises with it. The good player makes money from the bad player because of this loose play. When the bad player comes in with king-ten offsuit and a good player is involved, the good player will frequently have a dominating hand of A-K, K-Q, or K-J. But since the good player normally doesn't play K-10 offsuit, the reverse rarely happens when the bad player happens to have a bigger king.

But suppose the game is reduced from a ten-handed game to a five-handed game. A king-ten offsuit becomes a much more playable hand. So the good player adjusts his play and starts coming in with this hand. He has to, or the blinds will eat up his money mercilessly. But the bad player is already playing this hand. In other words, the bad player who plays too many hands before the flop is actually playing correctly in many cases because the game is shorthanded. So for many deals, both the good player and the bad player are playing the same hands. Therefore, the edge the good player had over the bad player by being more selective before the flop becomes dissipated in a shorthanded game. This means that the good player has only three betting rounds instead of four to make up for the edge he had in a full game.

Here is why you are forced to play a lot of hands in shorthanded play. Suppose you have a ten-handed $30-$60 game. Let us assume they deal 35 hands per hour. Every ten hands you are putting up a $20 small blind and a $30 big blind, so you are putting up $50 in blinds each round. This averages roughly $175 per hour you are putting up in blind money. Now reduce the game from being ten-handed to being five-handed. It then costs you about $350 per hour in blind money. If you play as tightly five-handed as you did ten-handed, you will hardly ever win enough pots to keep from blinding off your money. This means you have to start playing weaker cards than is your norm.

When you have to play more marginal holdings, two things happen, both of which are bad. First, as stated previously, your preflop play starts to look like everyone else's. Second, once the flop comes, you will find yourself thrown into more marginal situations. You may find yourself having to play middle pair or bottom pair with or without a good kicker because of the pot size and the fact that you cannot be as sure that you don't have the best hand. It may be harder to tell where you are at and whether you are leading or chasing. There is a big difference between dealing in ten players to start with and having three of them take a flop versus dealing in only five players and having three of them play. Three who took a flop from a starting field of ten will have a better average starting hand then three from a base of only five players.

Furthermore, what happens in a shorthanded game is that many players will start raising with hands they only limp with in a full game. Ace-ten offsuit is usually a limping hand. It becomes a raising hand in a shorthanded game. This means that more pots are getting raised. So, with a shorthanded game, you have the double-barreled impact of having to play more hands in raised pots. Having to put up more blind money, having to play weaker cards, and having to pay multiple bets to take a flop, all mean that you are gambling more and incurring higher fluctuations. This is why many players at middle and lower limits avoid shorthanded play.

In a shorthanded game, a pair or even ace-high will frequently win the pot. The reason is because many pots become heads-up almost immediately. In general, you want high card strength and medium pairs. Small and medium suited connectors go down in value. You do not need to make a straight or a flush to win, and you will seldom get the multi-handed action needed to make these hands profitable.

Many hands which were playable in a full game become raising hands in a shorthanded game. Hands like ace-jack, ace-ten, ace-nine, king-queen, king-jack, and even king-ten are raising hands if no one has entered the pot. Any medium pocket pair down to sixes becomes a raising hand. In a shorthanded game, you should be much more inclined to enter the pot with a raise if you want to play. Preflop, there are more "raise or fold" situations in shorthanded play. You can sometimes call with suited connectors behind others who have limped, but is not a good idea to raise with them, since these hands do much better in volume pots.

In games with experienced shorthanded players, one hardly ever sees someone open by just limping. However, there are many games that are shorthanded because the players are hoping and expecting the game will soon fill up. Their attitude may be one of, "I don't want to get stuck too bad before the real game starts." In such a game, it is okay to put on sheep's clothing and limp in on occasion to show that you are "one of the boys," and encourage others to be passive. Just make sure you do not overdo this Mr. Nice Guy act.

More money changes hands in a shorthanded game, so expect some big fluctuations. A lot of hands get played. The blinds will play much more loosely, because they expect any player who enters their pot to be a potential thief, regardless of his position. Many pots are hard-fought, because a player feels he is within striking distance, as big hands are rare.

From the blinds, you need to reraise with all your decent hands, not just your premium ones. Reraise with pocket tens, ace-ten suited, and ace-jack offsuit, especially against a cutoff or button raiser. Chances are you are the one on top. Also, you send a message that you are willing to play back at your opponent on a wide-range of holdings.

Your flop strategy will change quite a bit in a shorthanded game. You should frequently be raising or check-raising with hands that seem like they are only worth calling. Even top pair with a weak kicker becomes a strong hand. This is because players will semi-bluff a lot, hoping you will fold, but having outs if you call. You need to make these kinds of aggressive players pay. In addition, you should be semi-bluffing more and trying to win the pot without always having the best hand. Against certain people, you can win a lot of money just by betting.

Our style of play changes in a shorthanded game. You can see that in a regular game, we generally play rather straight-forwardly much of the time. In shorthanded play, we don't. It is less detrimental to give a free card (many pots are heads-up), so checking good hands happens much more often. Use of the check-raise, both as a move and a value-getter, is more frequent.

Let us discuss six-handed and seven-handed play, the semi-shorthanded game. Poker writers seem to only talk about two types of games, full tables or short-handed tables. For holdem, a full game generally is taken to mean eight to ten players; short-handed generally refers to three to five players. Hardly anybody has talked about the intermediate-size game, which should be the way we refer to six-handed or seven-handed play. The assumption has been that if you know how to play in a full game and know how to play short-handed, you can logically figure out what you should do anywhere in between. Well, it won't hurt to talk specifics instead of generalities, so lets discuss strategy for seven-handed holdem.

One strategy you can use is to go for a walk anytime the game deteriorates to seven-handed or less. This option has both social and monetary repercussions. The other players, who themselves are likely going a little out of their way to hold the game together, will not appreciate your action. If you are paying a time charge, as is typical at mid-level play in places like California, then you are paying out of your pocket for your walk. Surely it is better to stay put and learn how to play properly when a few players are absent or a game is just starting. This skill assumes greater topicality these days as casinos increasingly adopt a no-smoking policy, and the nicotine addicts have to go for a short walk to get their fix, leaving the poker table short two or three players for a while.

Now that you have decided to stay and play in the seven-handed game, the first question arises. Which hands do I play? The scale of hand values is a sliding one, and you can come down a notch or two in your caliber of starting hands as the number of players at the table decreases. In a full game, for pairs, 8-8 or 7-7 is your suggested minimum if a lot of pots are being raised (as in the typical California or Nevada middle-limit games). In a seven-handed game, it is reasonable to play 6-6 up front. For big unsuited cards in a full game, a player up front holding an ace likely needs at least a jack with it to enter the pot. For seven-handed, the A-10 is fine. If you are suited, then hands composed of two cards ten or larger are normally playable.

It is also important to ask the question, "How should these hands be played?" More often than not, if you come in at all, it should be with your guns blazing. Prefer to raise rather than just call when holding A-10, 7-7, and 6-6. Naturally, you also raise on the good hands that are worth a raise in a full game. With suited facecards, you should vary your game, sometimes raising and sometimes just calling. Whether and how to play these hands depends on a number of factors. Are the opponents calling your raises cold? Are they playing back at you? How well do they play poker? Test them and see how they react to your aggression.

Since you are being a bit more aggressive than usual, it is extremely important to notice which opponents are also loosening the throttle, and which ones are behaving the same as they did when the game was full. The ones that are more aggressive can be reraised on lighter values at seven-handed than you would need for a full game. If an opponent opens with a raise in early position when the game is full, the normal standard for making it three bets is a pair of queens or better. For seven-handed, you should surely pop the raiser on J-J, and maybe even 10-10, depending on who the raiser was. With A-K, suited or unsuited, we seldom would make it three bets if the game was full, but prefer to reraise at seven-handed. Depending on who is the raiser, you may well do this even holding A-Q, though this is a bit riskier.

A big adjustment in play is not necessary in late position or on the button when the game is seven-handed from what you would do in a full game, even though the deck is probably not quite as rich in high-card strength. Naturally, a hand such as A-9 has a slightly better chance of being the best hand when you are in an unopened pot on the right of the button in a seven-handed game than its chance would be a full game, because the fact that more hands have been folded in a full game makes it somewhat more likely one of the remaining players has you beaten. The deck is supposed to be slightly richer in high-card content. But you do not need to make a big adjustment because you are seven-handed.

Because more pots are being raised, and there are fewer players at the table to start with, most pots in a seven-handed game are heads-up or threeway pots. We have stressed that the number of opponents frequently determines your strategy. With four opponents, do not get out of line; with three, take some liberties now and then. With only one or two obstacles blocking the cheese, the mouse suddenly acquires a set of teeth; just about always bet an open-ended straight-draw or any kind of flush-draw, because there is a good chance of capturing the pot without a fight. It is not unusual to make a cold bluff, with no hand and no draw, if the opponents have shown weakness by checking, or the texture of the flop gives hope that nobody was able to get help. You have got to play aggressive poker in three-handed and heads-up situations.

In seven-handed poker, there is usually more emphasis put on stealing the blind money. Here again, it is critical to be aware of who has adjusted to the situation, and who is so busy watching the ball game or the cocktail waitress that they are still playing their solid nine-handed or ten-handed game. Against the people who have altered their play and are now being more aggressive, you must fight fire with fire. If you are in the little or big blind with a decent-looking hand like A-J or pocket sevens, and someone in middle position opens with a raise, by all means play back at him if he is an action player. Of course, if he is a real solid player who always has a good hand when he raises, you will not fare well with this tactic, so know your customers. And it should go without saying that if you are heads-up and have made it three bets before the flop, you are going to bet on the flop whether you help or not.

Now that we have distinguished the seven-handed game from the full table, we should also distinguish it from the short-handed game. At seven-handed, you should still fold the tiny pairs. Some people think two treys is some kind of decent hand. They are always raising with this type of hand trying to eliminate players, knowing that if they can get heads-up it would improve their chance with a small pair. Hey, you cannot make a silk purse out of a sows ear. Many times, when you try to isolate on one player, someone else will unexpectedly stick his nose into your business. Three-betting is more common in a smaller field. Since a small pair is no big bargain even against only one player, and in trouble against two or more players, it is better to simply muck the hand and wait for a better one.

Small connectors like 9-7 suited or 7-6 suited are bad hands even in a full game, and very bad in a game where you seldom get a volume pot and a lot of pots are being raised. The fact that you are on the button does not mean that you should take one of these miscast hands and try to steal the antes; they are bad ante-stealers. Muck those connectors fast in a seven-handed game.

Being suited is not as great an asset in a seven-handed game, because you are seldom against a field so large that you need a flush to win. At seven-handed, an A-10 offsuit is a clearly better hand than an A-2 suited. A suited hand looks pretty, but do not fall for its good looks and over-value it.

When you try to steal the antes, you are hoping to make a pair if you get called. Save your steals for hands with decent high-card content, and try to build a reasonably big pair.

The hands that are in this chapter clarify many of these ideas.

(1) A five-handed $20-$40 game. A good player opens with a raise under-the-gun. You are in the small blind with the K♣-Q♥ and everyone folds to you. What do you do?

Answer: Call. In a full game, when a good player opens with a raise in early position, you should fold king-queen offsuit unless you are in the big blind. The reason is because the good player rates to have A-A, K-K, Q-Q, J-J, A-K, or A-Q, and many of these hands dominate yours. But in a five-handed game, a good player will raise on a much wider range of hands like pocket eights, sevens, and sixes, as well as ace-jack, ace-ten, ace-nine suited, king-jack, queen-jack suited, and so forth. Your hand is worth a play, especially since you are already partially in. We would also cold-call a raise on the button having to put in the full amount.

(2) A five-handed $10-$20 game. You are on the button with the A♥-J♥. The under-the-gun player opens with a raise and the next player folds. What do you do?

Answer: Reraise. In a full game, against an early position raiser, ace-jack suited is a calling hand, not a three-bet hand. But in a shorthanded game, two big cards headed by an ace that are suited become a much stronger hand. The raiser will usually not have a premium hand like he would in a full game. Your hand could easily dominate his. Furthermore, being suited will allow you to get out of a trap easier if you run into an A-K or A-Q. If you are up against one of those hands, you are a bit more than a 2-to-1 underdog, compared to a nearly 3-to-1 underdog if you are offsuit.

(3) A five-handed $20-$40 game. You open the pot with a raise under-the-gun having the K♠-J♦. An early player and a middle player call. There is $150 in the pot and three players. The flop comes: K♥-8♠-7♥, giving you top pair. You bet. The next player raises and the other player calls. You call. There is $270 in the pot. The turn is the 7♦, pairing the bottom board-card. You check. The flop raiser bets. Your other opponent calls. What do you do?

Answer: Call. Just as you adjust your hand values preflop in a shorthanded game, you must adjust your hand values after the flop as well. You still have top pair with a playable kicker, so your hand may be good. The flop raise could have been done on any king, and the third player could easily be on a flush-draw or a straight-draw. In fact, both players could be drawing. In a full game, you expect anyone with a king who cold-called an early position raiser to have a bigger king than yours. But this is not true in a shorthanded game. A lot of players in a five-handed game will cold-call a raise with any suited king and some unsuited kings like king-ten offsuit. Players will also semi-bluff more with drawing hands in a shorthanded game, so someone on a flush-draw or even a straight-draw will frequently raise a flop bet.

(4) A four-handed $20-$40 game. You are in the big blind with the Q♥-5♥. The first player in opens with a raise and the other two players fold. You call for another $20 with $70 in the pot. You are calling because of the pot odds you are getting, the fact that about a third of the time you will flop a pair, which can easily end up as the best hand in a shorthanded game like this with only opponent, and the fact that you will flop a flush-draw about a seventh of the time, allowing you to play on. Furthermore, the raiser in a four-handed game might well have just about any pocket pair, any two connected cards that are suited, and so forth. There is $90 in the pot and two players. The flop is: 8♥-3♣-2♥, giving you a flush-draw with an overcard. What do you do?

Answer: Bet. You have a strong hand in this four-handed game against one opponent, and you must play it as such. It is imperative that you be aggressive in these shorthanded games and give yourself a chance to win without having to always make a hand. Much of your earn in these shorthanded situations comes from being aggressive and simply betting your opponent out of the pot. If he stays and has you beat right now, you have nine flush outs and three overcard outs with two cards to come, making you almost even money to end up with a winner.

On the actual hand, the player merely checked, then called the flop bet and the turn bet. The river was a blank and his opponent won with a bare ace, a ridiculous outcome. Had he check-raised the flop and bet the turn, his opponent would have probably folded, having no pair, no draw, and no hand. Instead, he put himself in a check-calling mode, allowing an unimproved ace to take the money. People who play this way should avoid shorthanded games—or read our book.

(5) A $20-$40 game. You are in the cutoff seat with the 8♣-8♦. The game has six players. You open with a raise. The button reraises and you are the only caller. There is $150 in the pot and two players. The flop comes: T♣-T♦-6♠, giving you tens over eights. You bet and the button calls. There is $190 in the pot. The turn is the 8♥, giving you a full house. What do you do?

Answer: Bet. Your opponent in all likelihood either has overcards or an overpair. An overpair will sometimes raise your turn bet, allowing you to three-bet with your full house. If your opponent has overcards, he may decide not to bet, which costs you the money he would have paid to draw. One of the more detrimental poker traits is to habitually check or slowplay every hand that looks as if it is unbeatable. Most of the time, the opponent has no idea he is up against a colossus, and would be willing to pay to improve. On this hand, you are a favorite to be holding a hand that will lose to kings up or aces up, so he may be trying to run you down with only two overcards. Why should you be so generous as to let him get cards for free just because he is drawing dead? There is pleasure in watching someone wrestle with the decision whether to stay in drawing to what you know is a certain loser, a chance to pay back the catch-artists for the times they beat you on the end.

(6) A five-handed $20-$40 game. You open with a raise under-the-gun having the A♦-K♥. Both blinds call. There is $120 in the pot and three players. The flop is: K♣-9♥-2♣, giving you top pair. The small blind bets; the big blind folds. What do you do?

Answer: Call, for now. In a full game, we have been advocating raising with top pair, top kicker especially in raised pots when there are two-flushes and cards in the playing zone like king-nine. But in a shorthanded game, the likelihood of your lone opponent having a drawing hand is less than normal. For example, with this flop, it is less likely that your opponent has two clubs and is on a draw when he was one of only five players dealt in than if he was one of ten players dealt in. Your top pair, top kicker is a powerful holding in a shorthanded setting like this. Furthermore, this is now a heads-up situation, so there are no other opponents to eliminate by raising. Plan on pulling the trigger after he bets the turn.

(7) A six-handed $20-$40 game. You have the K♦-Q♥ and open with a raise under-the-gun. Two players behind you plus the big blind call. There is $160 in the pot and four players. The flop is: 10♣-8♥-2♣, giving you two overcards. The big blind bets. What do you do?

Answer: Fold. Even though the scale of hand-values is reduced at shorthanded play, some things don't change. The bet is coming through you with two people behind you who have not acted. You have no hand, so hit the door.

(8) A seven-handed $20-$40 game. You are under-the-gun having the K♦-T♥. What do you do?

Answer: Fold. This is the same answer as you would get asking the question in a nine-handed game, "Two players have folded and it is up to you." The hand would be an obvious fold in that situation. For up-front hands, comparing with a full game in this manner is a good way to gauge whether you belong in the pot. Just pretend that enough people have folded to bring the field down to your size, and you will be oriented properly.

39 – EXTRA MONEY IN THE POT

By extra money in the pot, we are referring to situations where one or more players other than the regular blinds have posted before the cards are dealt, or the under-the-gun player puts up a blind raise (referred to as a "straddle bet"), so that there is additional money in the pot. If a game is being played with a kill, the extra money is treated much as you would a straddle bet. The purpose of this chapter is to discuss how you should adjust your play for the extra money.

An additional blind results when a player does not want to wait for the big blind to play. The two most common situations are when a new player enters the game, or when an established player who missed taking the blind returns to his seat. A new player posts the amount of the big blind. An established player puts up both blinds, with the little blind taken to the middle of the table as dead money. Normally, a player chooses to post an extra blind on the deal when in the cutoff seat. That way, he gets the maximum number of hands for the amount spent.

When a player has posted some extra blind money, what effect does this have on the strategy used by the other players? Quite a bit. There is a simple poker principle that pertains to this situation. The more money there is in the pot, the harder you fight for it. Let's see how that principle is applied to a limit holdem deal with a third blind posted.

When someone posts a late-position blind, if you are going to play, assuming you are the first to enter the pot, you should strain to find a raise with those hands where you normally limp. If your hand is worth playing, raise with it. If you are reluctant to raise, muck it. Consider yourself in a raise-or-fold situation.

In a normal deal, you may well raise more often than call when the first person to enter the pot. Still, there are some hands and occasions when you prefer to limp, especially in early position. But if there is extra blind money posted, it would be hard to find a situation where you would not prefer to bring it in for a raise. It is bad enough to let one or two people in the pot who have not even looked at their cards, let alone three people. A mere call is now inappropriate.

Here is a deal that occurred in a $15-$30 money game at Binion's Horseshoe during the 1998 World Series Of Poker. Ciaffone was on the immediate left of the big blind and picked up K♥-Q♦. There are some people who do not play a K-Q offsuit in first position, but their numbers are few, and he is not one of them. However, he does not like to raise with this hand. A raise involves a commitment. If you raise on big cards and miss, you are obliged to make a play for the pot anyway, provided the board is not too threatening and there are only one or two callers. When you bet the flop and buy a blank on the turn, you should bet again. So far, so good, but what happens on the end? If you have raised on A-K or A-Q, the prudent play is to check, trying to show it down. A bet has little point, since your opponent figures to call if he has you beaten and fold if he does not. However, if you have raised on a K-Q, you do not have enough hand to check, since an opponent beats you with an ace, which is a fairly common holding. The right play in most situations is to fire another barrel. We prefer to avoid this "commitment" to keep betting with nothing by not raising in the first place.

However, on this particular deal, there was a new player who had posted a blind in the cutoff seat. Therefore, Ciaffone altered his usual play with the K-Q and brought it in with a raise. The new player called, but both the little and big blind folded. He had the feeling of accomplishment even before the dealer put out the flop, because getting heads-up against a "blind man" already justified the raise by making him a favorite to win the pot. As it happened, the flop was friendly, Q-8-4 rainbow. He bet and the player folded.

Here is another hand from the same game. This time the cutoff seat had posted both the big blind and a dead little blind, as he was already in the game. A player in early position opened with a raise. Ciaffone was in middle position looking at a pair of jacks. Under ordinary circumstances, this hand is not really considered strong enough to automatically make it three bets by reraising when someone raises in early position. (You prefer queens against a decent player to pop it again.) However, with all that extra money in the pot, it is criminal not to make it three bets here.

First, the original raiser may be straining a little bit for his raise, instead of having a solid hand. Many other players follow the raise-or-fold policy that we encourage you to adopt.

Second, it is far harder for the other players to continue contesting the pot after your reraise. So this hand illustrates an important poker principle. There are many situations where you should raise or reraise where you do not have the faintest idea whether you have the best hand. If you try to argue that two jacks are a pretty nice hand and a favorite to be good here, let us tell you that a pair of nines would have been played the same way. It is simply a situation that demands a reraise.

Here is a deal taken from Ciaffone's book, "Improve Your Poker," where he played a hand in an abnormal manner because of a made-up blind. He was on the button holding A♦-Q♦ on a deal where the cutoff seat was a new player who has posted a blind. A lady who is an aggressive player brought it in with a raise and the cutoff called. It is normally not his habit to reraise an early-position raiser when holding A-Q, whether suited or not. However, reraising is called for here against many opponents. The original raiser may be straining a bit for her raise, and the player posting the blind is not going to be happy about putting three bets into the pot. Moreover, you would like to get the blinds out, as they may otherwise be drawn in by the extra money. The reraising ploy worked, and three players saw the flop, which came K♠-8♣-3♦. They check, he bet despite missing the flop, and they both called. On the turn the K♥ came, pairing the board. They checked, he had another go at it, and they both folded.

Suppose you are the one posting the late position blind just behind the button and everyone folds to you? Most of the time, you should look at your cards and then raise regardless of what they are. The reason you look at your cards, even though you intend to raise, is because you do not want your opponents to know what you are doing. Make them think you have some kind of hand for your raise. Strangely enough, a lot of opposing players think you are likely to have a good hand in this spot because "you were already in."

Raising automatically may seem like strange advice, but the likelihood of you winning the pot outright with only three opponents holding random cards is high enough to make this ploy correct. You also have position over two of your three opponents if they choose to play. This situation is a lot different than if you didn't have anything invested toward playing, because here it costs only half as much to give yourself a chance to win the money.

Let's discuss when you should post a blind. There seems to be a difference of opinion as to the better strategy to use when entering a game; to take the big blind or wait for the button to go by. Some players sit down on their big blind and ask to be dealt out, and other players sit down in the immediate position behind the button and wait for the big blind before playing. Here is our opinion on the matter.

An important question in this decision is whether the blind structure is the standard one where the little blind is half the size of the big one, or something else. By taking the big blind, the player gets three extra hands for the additional price of the little blind. (He gets to play the big blind, the little blind, and the button.) In a nine-handed game, this means a third of the total number of hands dealt in a round. If the little blind is less than half the big blind, as in a $3-$6 game using a $1 and $3 blind, it must be right to take the big blind, as you get three extra hands for only one dollar. (This type of structure is not used in middle-limit games, but sometimes occurs in tournament play.) If the little blind is more than half the big blind, as in a $15-$30 game using a $10 and $15 blind, the player is getting overcharged for those three hands, and is advised to wait for the button to go by.

The only situation where it is not obvious what to do is in the standard structure of the little blind being half the amount of the big blind. If you come in behind the button, the money is put up in position, which of course is desirable. If you take the big blind, you get to play the button, which also is desirable. If you were to put the situation under a microscope, getting your money posted in position is the slightly more important factor. However, for a good player, prefer to take the big blind rather than being dealt out for three additional hands, if that is the earliest you can get into action at the point you sat down. Time equals money. Also, waiting for the button to go by conveys some information to the opponents as to what type of player you are. Do you want to look like a shrewd penny-pinching bargain hunter?

Let us now discuss the straddle bet. You should strain to find a raise on many hands that you would normally just limp in with. The reason is because you want to drive out the other players and isolate the straddler, who has a random hand. The additional money in the pot makes this correct. For example, in a $10-$20 game without a straddle bet, when you raise, you are putting in $20, with $15 already in the pot for the blind money. But when someone straddles and you raise, you are putting up $30, with $35 already in the pot. This is a much more favorable risk versus reward ratio. Furthermore, you want to put pressure on the remaining players to fold, because isolating the straddler (who always will call) is your prime goal. You probably have the best hand and you have position. So if you are going to play and you are the first player to act after the straddler, just calling the straddle bet is normally not good poker. You might just as well post a sign saying, "I don't have much; I couldn't even raise a player who hasn't looked at his hand." Calling a straddle bet might make some sense if anyone had called in front of you, but otherwise you should raise.

If you notice that another player is raising the straddler on a light hand, you should reraise him with many hands that are normally worth only a single raise. This is because a good player who raises a straddler will frequently not have a premium hand, but just a limping hand under ordinary conditions. Again, when you have good hand, you want to force everyone else to pay through the nose to take a flop with you. Typically, you will drive out everyone but the raiser, and perhaps the straddler.

You can see the ideas at work when there is a straddle or a made-up blind. Play is more aggressive with added blind money in the pot. Not only is there more money to be won, but the other players are extending themselves a bit to win that money also (or at least they should be). An opponent who raises might not have full values, and a player who fails to raise shows a weak hand, ignorance of the game, or both. You must raise and reraise lighter than usual to properly take advantage of the situation and maximize your opportunity to win the extra money.

39 - EXTRA MONEY IN THE POT

The following hands discuss some of these situations where there is extra money in the pot.

(1) A $20-$40 game. You are in early position holding the 8♦-8♣. The player under-the-gun puts up a straddle bet. The action is on you. What do you do?

Answer: Raise. Pocket eights is usually a limping hand in early position, but with $70 in blind money now in the pot, it is worth paying $60 to drive out the other players and get it heads-up with the straddler. Your opponents don't know that you have less than a premium hand, and frequently a player with a hand like ace-queen or pocket nines will fold rather than call three bets cold. Your medium pocket pair is a good hand against a straddler, who holds random cards, plus you have position. Limping in with this hand is not good, because you are just encouraging other players to limp in behind you, reducing your chance of winning.

(2) A $10-$20 game. You are in middle position with the A♥-K♣. The under-the-gun player puts up a $20 straddle bet. A good player, sitting right next to him, makes it $30. It is folded to you. What do you do?

Answer: Reraise. Ace-king offsuit is a reraising hand in any position with extra money in the pot. The good player does not need a premium hand to raise a straddler. He may simply have a decent hand and be trying to isolate the straddler. And as long as he doesn't have aces or kings, it's right to reraise. You want to put maximum pressure on everyone else at the table to fold, thereby giving you position over the straddler and the raiser. It may seem like you could be overplaying your hand, but this is no different than any other situation like facing a late-position open-raise, where the raiser may well have a hand of less quality than usual. Most of the money put into the pot was by players holding random cards. A good player will capitalize on this by raising with medium pairs, and even two big cards like ace-jack, king-queen, or other hands containing high cards that you dominate.

322

(3) A $15-$30 game. You are in early position holding the 9♥-8♥. The under-the-gun player puts up a live straddle. You are next to act. What do you do?

Answer: Fold. This is not a good hand to try and isolate two blinds and a straddler. Furthermore, with six players yet to act, anyone who calls you probably has a better hand, with position over you. You still do not want to be playing in raised pots with small and medium suited connectors, especially out-of-position. You want some kind of hand to fall back on when you get played with. This usually means a medium pocket pair, or two big cards, preferably headed by an ace.

(4) A $30-$60 game. You are in middle position with the Q♣-J♣. The under-the-gun player puts up a $60 straddle bet. The next player raises to $90. A player folds and the action is on you. What do you do?

Answer: Fold. Queen-jack suited is not a good enough hand to call three bets cold with only a straddler and one other player in the hand. You have hand that wants lots of opponents and a cheap entry fee to take a flop. Playing in this situation is bad because you are unlikely to get the multi-handed action you need to make this hand profitable, and you are paying a high entry price, which damages your implied odds.

(5) A $10-$20 game. You are on the button with the J♦-T♦. The under-the-gun player puts up a $20 straddle bet. Three other players call with no one raising. What do you do?

Answer: Call. Normally, jack-ten suited is not worth calling two bets cold to take a flop. But here, since no one raised, you do not have to worry about being up against a premium hand like a higher-ranking pocket pair. With four players already committed (the straddler plus the three callers), you are getting the multi-handed action needed to make this hand profitable. The likelihood of the one or both blinds playing is quite high in these situations, so you will normally be taking this flop five-handed and sometimes six-handed. Also, you're on the button.

(6) A $15-$30 game. You are in the small blind with the A♣-T♠. The under-the-gun player puts up a $30 straddle bet. Everyone folds to you. What do you do?

Answer: Raise. You must drive out the big blind and get it heads-up with the straddler even if you are out of position. You have an excellent playing hand under the circumstances, and your two opponents have random cards. Don't just call and make it easy for the big blind to play. In these situations, unless you are reraised, you will betting the flop regardless of what comes.

(7) A $20-$40 game. You are on the button with the K♦-J♥. The player has just come into the game and posts a late position $20 blind. It is folded to him and he checks. What do you do?

Answer: Raise. Having two big cards is a good hand under the circumstances, when all three of your opponents have random hands. This is especially true when you have position. The player on your right figures to have nothing, since he did not raise after everyone folded to him. With $50 of blind money in the pot, it is worth raising to $40 to get players out. You may win the pot outright, and you will flop a decent-sized pair about a third of the time anyway, which can easily hold up against a small field.

(8) A $30-$60 game. You are in the big blind holding the A♥-Q♦. The new player in the cutoff seat posted a $30 blind. It is folded to him; he raises. The button and small blind fold. What do you do?

Answer: Reraise. The poster is most likely raising with a worse hand than yours under the circumstances. Had someone else limped in, then his raise would have been more meaningful. As it is, you have an excellent playing hand, and should three-bet despite your poor position. You would normally three-bet the cutoff when that player opens with a raise, and here you have even more reason to do so.

(9) A $20-$40 game. You are a new player to the game and post a $20 blind in the cutoff seat. You look at your hand and see 6♠-5♠. It is folded to you. What do you do?

Answer: Raise. There is $50 in the pot and it only costs you another $20 to raise. Your raise may force the button out. You may even win the pot outright. These two factors alone make raising worthwhile regardless of your hand. In this case, your little suited connector represents some semblance of a hand. There are many flops you can catch which allow you to play aggressively with position over a small field, giving you a chance to bet your opponents out of the hand.

(10) You have pocket nines on the right of a player who has made up a blind in the cutoff seat. The player on your right opens with a raise. What do you do?

Answer: Reraise. Maybe you are beat, but if you have the best hand, you have a much better chance of victory by confronting the remaining players with a double bet. With a pocket pair, you must reraise or fold here, and 9-9 looks big enough to take the aggressive play. A pair prefers heads-up play if ahead preflop.

(11) You are playing in a $20-$40 game where the rule is anyone who wins two pots in a row must kill the third one. You win the required two pots and have a $40 kill posted under-the-gun. The player on your left raises and the button reraises. You hold the Q♥-9♥. What do you do?

Answer: Where are you playing? This is a close decision. Our inclination would be to call if the last raise were a cap, as in most cardrooms. But some places use a bet and **four** raises as the cap. We are not inclined to put our money into a pot on a marginal hand like this one if we can get charged any more for admission after committing ourselves by a call. This is a good illustration of why you find out the rules before getting into action. Here, you do not want to be asking about the cap while deciding whether to call.

40 – LOW LIMIT POKER

Our book *Middle Limit Holdem Poker* has produced a frequently asked question: "Can the material in this book be used for low limit play?" This is of course a very logical query, considering those words "middle limit" in the title of the book. We added this chapter because we know some low-limit players will be buying this book, and a middle limit player may decide to take a seat in a smaller game on occasion. The short answer is MLHP can be quite helpful, but should be applied to low-limit play only after making some adjustments.

In our book, we arbitrarily define "middle limit" as $10-$20 through $40-$80, so low-limit means games smaller than $10-$20. Low-limit games do not all fit the same mold; far from it. There are $3-$6 games that look like a party of drunks, and $3-$6 games that are filled with loose, passive players (yum!). There are also some $3-$6 games that strongly resemble middle-limit games; having relatively few people involved in the pot, but fighting aggressively for the money. But no matter what type of game it is, you can use the ideas in our book, decide how it applies to the game you are in, and apply those ideas accordingly. So with care and intelligence, you can use the ideas in MLHP to your advantage at low-stakes poker. Now let's go into more detail on this subject.

Keep in mind the way most low-limit players differ from their higher-stakes counterparts. They call too often and do not bet aggressively enough. These traits are reflected in their play as follows:

First and foremost, they play far more starting hands. Some do this because they do not know any better, but many realize they are erring. However, since the amount of money involved in their poker games is relatively small, they prefer to have fun rather than do their best to make money. So in lowstakes poker you find yourself facing more opponents in each pot, on the average. You see throughout this book how much importance we place on the number of opponents in planning your strategy.

Secondly, they chase by calling on the flop and turn on low-quality hands. Playing is more fun than folding. Technical

326

deficiencies include ignorance of percentages and unawareness of how a hoped-for card may help the opponents.

The other main way they differ is by failing to bet or raise when they should. In particular, a raise is used only on a premium holding, instead of the many tactical uses for a raise employed by the middle limit player. They also stick to a preconceived scale of values on what constitutes a betting hand, instead of simply trying to determine if their hand is better than yours. Your check against a calling type player shows weakness, but much of the time you will not suffer because you blinked, because that person elected to also check, instead of realizing how weak you must be to not bet. Part of their passive play is a result of knowing from past experience in low-limit play that their bets are going to get called most of the time even if their opponent has initially checked.

Before we talk about how to play in a low-limit game, lets talk about finding the right one to plunder. Your first task at any limit is to find a good poker game. It is easy for a low-limit player to fall into the trap of thinking that a hold'em game where many pots are reraised and capped before the flop is a juicy place to light. Although such games are beatable, the truth is they are far from a piece of cake. Here is why. By putting a huge amount of money (relative to the betting limit) into a pot preflop, you minimize the abilities needed to handle postflop situations. All that loose play you see at low limits like chasing non-nut gutshots and backdoor non-nut flushes is either right on these jammed pots, or only marginally wrong. And the best hand always wins; forget about bluffing or reading your opponent. Furthermore, most of your hands are no longer playable. You should not be putting three and four bets into the pot preflop on 7-7, A-7 suited, and so forth. To beat a low-limit game, you want to be able to hit flops cheaply and get your good hits paid off. Lastly, with everyone held hostage to continue by the large amount of money preflop, your good hands are going to get cracked more often. So even though the ones that hold up make a mint, there is a lot of fluctuation in your results.

Now that you have found a good game, you will find our advice on using tactical tools more applicable to pots where there are only one to three other players. In this setting, poker skills can be brought into play, and the best hand doesn't always win. You can bluff, raise to get a free card, make a play for the pot on a light hand, and so forth. Low-limit games have a lot more callers preflop on most deals, but there still are pots where most of the players fold.

We often base our strategy on the number of people in the pot. At low-limit play, you will have plenty of company in contesting most pots. Our strategy for this type of situation is simple: skip the tricky stuff. This is even more applicable to low-limit games than middle-limit games. Your chances of buying a pot by betting a draw into a large field is nearly zero. If you have what looks like the best hand, bet it; you'll have plenty of callers.

Following all the middle-limit strategy concepts in our book to the letter would lead to some errors at low-limit. Here are a few tips for the cheaper games that differ from our regular strategy.

In low-limit games, there are more players in for the flop on each deal. In a passive game with little preflop raising, the larger fields mean more hands are playable. So you can loosen up somewhat, and play hands like 4-4 and A-x suited in early position. But beware of hands that play poorly with a large field. We are talking about unsuited cards like K-J offsuit and A-T offsuit. You will be running into hands such as A-K, A-Q, and A-J in unraised pots, plus top pair does not stand up as well in a large field. So keep to the strict standards we suggest for unsuited moderately large cards.

There are some adjustments you need to make concerning your post-flop play at the lower limits. These adjustments are driven by the fact that many low limit players will call flop bets with the most horrid of holdings. This is especially true in the large pots that were built because so many players stayed for the flop, sometimes cold-calling raises to do it. Things like the number of opponents, texture of the board, odds against improving, and improving without winning don't enter their thought process.

Here are a couple of examples in our book where course of action we recommend at the middle limits might well be different at lowstakes poker.

Hand #1 on Pages 241-242, repeated for convenience below, has you checking top pair, weak kicker on the turn when you get called in two spots after betting the flop. Here was that hand.

(1) The game is \$10-\$20. You are in the big blind with the 9♠-7♣ and get a free play after two early players and the button limp in. There is \$45 in the pot and four players. The flop is: 7♦-4♥-2♣, giving you top pair. You bet; only the button folds. There's \$75 in the pot and three players. The turn is the 6♥. What do you do?

We said to check. In a middle limit game, this is correct for the reasons we discussed. But in a low limit game, your two opponents could have easily been calling on bottom pair, a small pocket pair, or just overcards. It would be a mistake to not bet again on the turn.

Hand #4 on Pages 242-243, given below, is another example where you likely should bet again on the turn with your overpair despite the top flop-card pairing.

(4) A \$10-\$20 game. You limp in under-the-gun with 9♠-9♣. An early player, a middle player, the cutoff, the button, and the small blind call. There is \$70 in the pot and seven players. The flop is: 8♣-6♥-5♦, giving you an overpair and a gutshot straight-draw. Both blinds check; you bet. The early player, middle player, cutoff, and small blind call. The pot has \$120 and five players. The turn is the 8♥. The small blind checks. What do you do?

We said to check. But at low-limit people call on a wider range of hands, and a large field does not indicate so strongly that someone has top pair. There could be several hands composed of only overcards, which will often be folded if you bet after the board has paired with the card you've been representing.

Don't be too aggressive against people who seldom bet and usually call. We do not like to check a hand at middle limit that we intend to play, because our opponent is encouraged to bet by our show of weakness. We don't want to surrender the initiative. At low-limit, your opponent is much more likely to check it back after you check, being grateful for a chance to see another card without having to spend anything. Yet if you bet, he is going to stick like glue. So the wise low-limit player does not need to be so pushy with a moderate hand.

Here are a couple of problems that were constructed specifically to show how you might wish to play differently facing weaker players.

(A) $2-$4 limit. You hold A♣-Q♣ and open in early position with a raise. A middle position player, the button, and the big blind call you. The flop comes K♠-9♣-5♦. The big blind checks; what do you do?

Answer: Check. At middle limit, it is worth a bet in most games to see if all the opponents have missed the flop and are willing to fold, fearing a hand like A-K. At low-limit, you are more likely to be wasting a bet—and if you decide to follow through by betting the turn, wasting some more money. Three players is the dividing line between betting and checking at middle limit play. For most low-limit games, do not fire into three opponents on a hand like this even if one of them has checked.

(B) $3-6 limit. You hold 9♣-9♠ in middle position. The first two players limp and it is your turn. What do you do?

Answer: Just call. At middle limits it would be tempting to raise the pot, hoping to narrow the field to only two opponents and confronting the blinds with a double bet. But against frequent callers, chances of a threeway pot are significantly worse. With an intermediate pair, we do not want to have a large pot with several opponents, because they will too often stay in and outdraw us even if the flop is a nice one, like an overpair.

You will find that many ideas in *Middle Limit Holdem Poker* can be applied to low-limit games. But as you see, a few do not, so you must apply good judgment when using it as a guide in a low-limit poker game.

CONCLUSION

We hope and trust that our book has been both educational and enjoyable for you. By writing it, we wanted to make people realize that a poker book needs to have many practical examples, to see how theory is actually applied for a particular hand and situation, to be of greatest efficacy. We have great faith that our teaching method can turn the typical holdem player into a strong one.

Now that you have read our book, you are ready to put your skills to work. We wish you all the best, and feel confident that we have equipped you with the knowledge of holdem you need to be a big winner. But keep in mind that a successful player of any poker form needs good gambling skills to go with superior knowledge. Since our book is about holdem, we have not discussed poker in general. There are two very important ingredients for poker success, besides a mastery of the form that you play.

First, you need a good game to play in. Your advantage is determined by how well you play relative to the opposition, not by your skill level as measured by an objective scale. Since there is a charge for playing in most poker games (the rake), you need a good-sized advantage to be a big winner. So try to find a game where most of the opposition has not read our book!

Second, there is an old chess quote of Grandmaster Siegbert Tarrasch that could easily be applied to poker. "You need more than just to be a good player; you must also play well." To win demands your best effort. This means being well rested and in a good frame of mind. Particularly important is the ability to keep your head together when things go badly. Short-term poker results vary widely because of the luck element. You cannot let the psychological weight of bad luck, getting loser in the game, throw your play out of whack in an effort to get even at all costs. The 1995 World Champion Dan Harrington says, "I have a much bigger edge over someone else in the game when we are both losing than when we are both winning." In other words, he is able to keep his head together under adversity; the opponent may not. Play your best at all times, not just when things go your way!

INTERNET POKER
by Bob Ciaffone

The 21st century has seen an enormous expansion in the popularity of poker. The two largest driving forces behind this are televised programs on tournament poker and poker websites on the internet that provide an alternative place to play the game. Let's discuss internet poker.

Live poker games provide a social setting and the opportunity to view your opponents. But internet poker, despite drawbacks, has many advantages over live play. Here are ten of them.

(1) You can enter or quit a game whenever you want.

(2) There is a far wider menu of games and tournaments to play in.

(3) The opponents are much less skillful, on the average, than those encountered in live play.

(4) Because the extra overhead for spreading each additional table is negligible, games for microscopic stakes are available, as well as games just for fun. This makes the internet a terrific training ground for new players.

(4) You can play in more than one game at the same time. This enables a good player to make more money, and also reduces the boredom of waiting for a decent hand.

(5) You can take notes on your opponents, and refer to these notes on a player any time that person is in your game.

(6) You can get a "hand history" printed of any pot of interest to you, which records everything that happened on that deal. It will be it instantly emailed to you, and you can preserve it in a file for future reference.

(7) You can have your statistics tracked for such things as how often you enter a pot and how often you win one.

(8) You can either play in a totally smoke-free environment or light up whenever you want.

(9) If you wish, you can play without anyone knowing who you are, your sex, age, citizenship, or anything else about you.

(10) Internet poker is less expensive to play. The rake is usually lower, travel expenses are nil, refreshments are cheaper, and you do not have to tip.

INTERNET POKER

Some people shy away from internet poker because they are overly concerned about being cheated. Here is the truth. Unlike sites where you gamble against the house, at poker sites, you gamble only against other players. This means the house has less interest in producing an altered outcome. Running an internet poker site is big business, one that would destruct rapidly of tainted by a scandal, so the house has a powerful incentive to not cheat in any way. There is far more money to be gained in being totally honest with this business than in cheating customers by favoring one player over another.

At internet poker there is no dealer to collude with a player, so that is one less form of cheating you will encounter on the internet. Yes, there is a chance of being cheated by players colluding with each other. This can happen in a regular cardroom game and this can happen in an internet cardroom game. But I believe the internet to be a safer environment in certain respects. First, there is a wide choice of games. Cheaters usually go to the place where they can make the most money. I do not think there is much hanky-panky in the lowstakes games. Second, the website has a complete record of every hand played by anyone on their site. This makes it much easier to detect collusion than in a regular cardroom. There is software that can search for suspicious behavior and flag it, and anything that gets flagged can be examined more closely by a human being to detect if there is collaboration between players.

Where should you play? There are a number of good sites. I am an affiliate of PartyPoker, presently the most popular poker website. There you will find the widest choice of games. PartyPoker does a fine job of attracting new players to its site. Translation: the tables there have a lot of novices, often abysmally weak players, so the games are very attractive.

If you would like to play poker on the PartyPoker website, simply go to their website, www.partypoker.com, download their software, and sign up to play. You can help us both out by giving a referral to this book when you sign up. You will receive some bonus chips when you make a deposit of funds to play on, and I will get a bonus for referring you. Simply use the signup code CoachMLHP when registering. (My nickname is "The Coach," and MLHP will show you were sent to PartyPoker because you read my book, Middle Limit Holdem Poker.) This code is repeated for convenience on the inside of the back cover. You have nothing to lose by using this code, and something to gain.

The sister site for Party Poker is Empire Poker, which is run by a different company but uses the same platform. My bonus code for signing up to play at Empire Poker is CPLNL.

I am now closely associated with a new site coming online in the fall of 2004 called "ChecknRaise Poker." I have visited the parent corporation's headquarters in Canada several times (the company and server site is based in Curacao). They have an impressive leadership, and staff who are dedicated to their work. The company philosophy is aimed heavily at retaining their player base as well as initially attracting it, so they will have many benefits for their players. I have contributed to their website content, and worked closely with their programmers in designing the graphical display for their interface. I expect the ChecknRaise Poker site to be the best poker website on the internet for screen design. Give it a try.

FLOP ODDS AGAINST
IMPROVING ON NEXT CARD
(There are 47 unknown cards out of 52)

Type Of Hand	Outs	Flop Odds	Rounded Off To
Set over set	1	46-to-1	46-to-1
Pocket pair vs. pocket pair	2	45-to-2	23-to-1
Same pair with worse kicker	3	44-to-3	15-to-1
Gutshot	4	43-to-4	11-to-1
Middle pair vs. top pair	5	42-to-5	8-to-1
Two overcards	6	41-to-6	7-to-1
Gutshot plus an overcard	7	40-to-7	6-to-1
Straight-draw	8	39-to-8	5-to-1
Flush-draw	9	38-to-9	4-to-1
Gutshot with two overcards	10	37-to-10	7-to-2
Straight-draw plus overcard	11	36-to-11	3-to-1
Flush-draw plus a gutshot	12	35-to-12	3-to-1
Straight-draw with a pair	13	34-to-13	5-to-2
Flush-draw with a pair	14	33-to-14	7-to-3
Straight-flush draw	15	32-to-15	2-to-1

The odds on improving a different hand than one listed above would of course be identical if the number of outs is the same.

Drawing hands that are stronger than those given in the table are also possible. For example, a flush-draw combined with a gutshot straight-draw and two overcards is 18 outs, about a 3-to-2 underdog to help on the next card. A flush-draw combined with a straight-draw and two overcards is 21 outs, about a 5-to-4 dog. An example of this would be the K♠-Q♠ with a flop of J♠-10♣-3♠.

The turn odds on making a hand are not significantly different than the flop odds given above, since the only difference is there are 46 unknown cards instead of 47, so the chance of improvement is a tiny bit better. For example, with pocket pair over pocket pair, the odds on improving go from 2 out of 47 to 2 out of 46, which is from a 22.5-to-1 underdog to a 22-to-1 underdog.

HELPING WITH EITHER OF TWO CARDS

Calculating the odds on being helped by either the turn or river cards is much more involved than calculating the odds on only the next card. It is better to see how two hands actually match up against each other than simply present a table, because improvement can be insufficient to win the pot. The opponent may lock you out by improving enough to have you drawing dead, or redraw on the last card to win. Cutting the odds in half is workable for approximating longshots, but off the mark for other hands. The reason is because for hitting on both cards (rare for longshots but common for strong hands) you do not get paid double.

The way to calculate the odds on each hand winning in a heads-up confrontation is to examine the chance that each card in the deck provides to the contestants, and then total the results. Here is an example of how we do this. You hold A♥-A♣. The flop is K♥-8♣-3♠. The opponent has K♦-Q♦ for top pair. Looking at both of the hands plus the flop, there are 7 cards known out of 52, leaving 45 unknown on the flop, and 44 on the turn. The total possibilities are 45 x 44, or 1980. Here is how this is calculated:

Card	# in deck	Wins on end for draw	Outs
A	2	0	0
K	2	42	84
Q	3	36	108
8,3	6	2	12
Other	32	5	160

Total wins for draw out of 1980 possible combinations = 364

Here is how to read the table. An ace locks out the draw. A king makes the aces needing an ace on the end, so the draw wins on 42 last cards. A queen allows the aces to win with an ace for trips, or an 8 or 3 for two pair, so the draw wins on 36 last cards. An 8 or 3 means the draw has to hit a king, winning on only two last cards. For the remaining 32 cards (out of 45), the draw has 5 wins (a K or Q). We multiply the number of cards times the outs on the end to see how many wins each card gives the draw, then add them.

ODDS TABLES

Below are some tables for frequently seen match-ups. All the odds in this table were calculated by hand. In the odds column, odds listed are against the draw, unless marked otherwise. The odds will vary somewhat, depending on the exact hands. The examples used here do not have any backdoor draws, so the odds against the draw in this table are slightly longer than would often be the case in practice. The odds on a straight-draw vs. top pair or a flush-draw vs. top pair are worth memorizing. Please note the odds on a straight-draw with two overcards vs. top pair, because it is exactly even money, making it a demarcation line for draws; a 14-out draw is the dividing line between a draw being an underdog and a favorite, assuming the made hand has only one pair.

Note the big change in odds if the made hand is two pair or a set, especially the latter. Here, there is a serious danger of making the draw and still not winning the pot. With a big draw, when considering a raising war on the flop, give a lot of thought to the probable nature of your opponent's hand, as well as your own.

Hand Types	Draw	Hand	Flop	Odds
Top pair vs. overpair	K♦-Q♦	A♥-A♣	K♥-8♣-3♠	4.44-to-1
Middle pair vs. top pair	A♥-7♥	Q♠-J♦	J♣-7♦-2♠	3.70-to-1
Two overcards vs. top pr	A♥-J♥	9♥-8♥	9♣-4♦-2♠	3.52-to-1
Straight-draw vs. pair	T♥-9♥	A♣-5♠	A♣-8♦-7♣	1.92-to-1
Straight-draw vs. two pr	T♥-9♥	Q♣-J♠	Q♦-J♣-2♠	2.32-to-1
Straight-draw vs. set	T♥-9♥	8♣-8♠	8♦-7♣-2♠	2.87-to-1
Flush-draw vs. top pair	J♥-9♥	A♣-T♠	A♦-6♥-2♥	1.70-to-1
Flush-draw vs. two pair	J♥-9♥	A♣-6♣	A♦-6♥-2♥	2.36-to-1
Flush-draw vs. set	J♥-9♥	6♣-6♠	A♦-6♥-2♥	3.06-to-1
St-dr + ovcd vs. top pair	Q♣-T♣	A♣-J♣	J♥-9♦-2♠	1.42-to-1
Fl-dr + ovcd vs. top pair	A♥-7♥	T♣-9♣	9♥-4♦-2♥	1.28-to-1
Fl-dr + gutshot vs. top pr	9♣-8♣	A♥-J♦	A♣-6♦-5♣	1.10-to-1
St-dr + 2 ovcd vs. top pr	J♣-T♣	A♣-9♣	9♥-8♠-2♥	Even
Fl-dr + pair vs. top pr	9♣-8♣	A♥-J♦	A♣-8♥-2♣	1.03 fav.
Fl-dr + 2 ovcd vs. top pr	Q♥-J♥	A♣-7♣	7♥-4♦-2♥	1.12 fav.
St-dr + fl-dr vs. top pair	9♣-8♣	A♦-J♦	J♣-T♠-2♣	1.31 fav.
St-dr + fl-dr vs. overpair	9♣-8♣	A♦-A♥	J♣-T♠-2♣	1.29 fav.
St-dr + fl-dr vs. set	9♣-8♣	J♦-J♥	J♣-T♠-2♣	1.49 dog

ODDS TABLES

PREFLOP ODDS

What follows is a table of the preflop odds of one hand against another. These odds were determined by use of the Poker Probe, a computer program designed by Mike Caro. We ran a simulation of a million deals for each match-up. Here are some of the things you should notice by studying the table.

First, the basic nature of holdem is clearly seen, where the best hand has a good chance to prevail. The only close match-up is a pocket pair against two overcards, where the pair has only a small advantage.

Second, the basis for domination is shown. A hand is dominated in the case of pair against pair, same-rank cards where someone has a bigger kicker, or a pair against two cards where one of those cards is the same rank as the pair. This latter is particularly toxic if the odd card is lower-ranking than the pair.

Third, if you do get into a trap where you have a dominated hand, your chance to win is definitely improved by being suited.

This simulation does not resemble the actual practical chances in a limit holdem game where there is betting (it is as if both players were all-in before the flop). Some of these hands are in worse shape than it looks. If the flop is not hit, the stronger hand may well stay in, but the weaker hand may have to fold. Thus, the overlay of the boss hand in practice is often even stronger than this table implies.

For each match-up, the number after the hand is the percentage of the time it wins against the opposing hand next to it.

Preflop Match-ups For Various Hands

A♠-A♣ 81, K♥-K♦ 19   9♠-9♣ 56, A♥-K♦ 44
A♠-A♣ 77, T♦-9♦ 23   9♠-9♣ 52, A♦-K♦ 48
A♠-A♣ 93, A♥-K♦ 7   A♠-K♣ 74, A♥-Q♦ 26
A♠-A♣ 88, A♦-K♦ 12   A♠-K♣ 70, A♦-Q♦ 30
K♣-K♠ 72, A♦-Q♣ 28   A♥-K♣ 59, T♦-9♦ 41
K♣-K♠ 68, A♦-Q♦ 32   A♣-K♣ 61, T♦-9♦ 39
K♣-K♠ 70, A♥-K♦ 30   J♣-J♥ 68, A♦-T♦ 32
K♣-K♠ 66, A♦-K♦ 34   J♠-J♥ 71, A♦-T♣ 29

GLOSSARY OF HOLDEM TERMS

Backdoor: Improvement from helping on both the turn and river cards. Same as runner-runner.

Big slick: Nickname of the holdem hand A-K, sometimes shortened to just "slick."

Blind: A bet posted by a player before the cards are dealt.

Bottom pair: A pair formed with the lowest-ranking board-card.

Button: The person last to get cards and who acts last during a deal (with the exception of the blinds on the first betting round).

Cap: To prohibit further raises on a round because the maximum allowable number has been reached.

Clean out: A card improving your hand that does not figure to improve someone else's hand.

Counterfeit: To have a board-card cripple the value of a hand by matching either a card in that hand or a card already on the board.

Cutoff: The seat to the immediate right of the button.

Dominated hand: A hand in trouble because another starting hand is stronger and has a card in the weaker one tied up.

Double Belly-buster: A drawing hand capable if making either of two gutshots, thus having the same number of outs (8) as an open-end straight-draw.

Drawing dead: Trying to hit a hand that cannot win the pot, either because a player has a better hand than the one being drawn at, or an opponent is drawing at the same hand with bigger cards.

Flop: The three board-cards dealt simultaneously after the preflop betting round is over.

Four-bet: To put in a third raise, making the total number of bets four on the round. This term implies a bet and four raises are allowed in that cardroom, or the term "cap" would be used. A bet and four raises is a common rule in higher-stakes Nevada cardrooms, and in tournament play.

Freeroll: being presently tied with another hand, but having the chance of improving to win the whole pot. An example would be when two hands have the same straight, one of them having the freeroll of a flush-draw to break the tie.

Holdem: Usually spelled "hold'em," an abbreviation of "hold them." Same as Texas hold'em. The poker form using two personal cards and five board-cards. This layout means that a full house is not possible unless the board is paired, and a flush or straight is not possible unless there are three parts to it on the board. The board-cards are dealt 3-1-1. The first three are called "the flop," fourth card "the turn," and fifth (final) card "the river."

Limp: To just call the blind.

Gutshot: A straight makable with one rank of card. An inside-straight draw, sometimes called "belly-buster" or "middle-buster."

Lockout: A card that prevents an opponent who is drawing from winning the pot even if hitting his hand.

Middle pair: A pair formed with the second-highest flop card.

Overpair: A pocket pair bigger than any card on the board.

Out: A board-card that (hopefully) improves the hand to a winner.

Playing Zone: The rank of board-cards from ace to nine inclusive, which is the rank of cards most frequently played.

Position: The order in which a hand is required to act (the later, the better). Also, location with respect to the preflop raiser, who frequently is the person doing the betting after the flop.

Preflop: The initial betting round, before board-cards are dealt.

River: The last card, and associated betting round.

Redraw: To help a hand that was beaten by a draw on the turn.

Runner-runner: Requiring two running cards to be successful. Same as backdoor.

Running pair: A pair formed by the last two board-cards matching each other in rank.

Second pair: A pair higher than all of the board-cards except one.

Set: Trips formed by a board-card matching a player's pocket pair.

Steal position: Position of a player who acts late on the preflop betting round when no one has yet opened. Arbitrarily defined in this book as the cutoff, button, or little blind positions.

Straddle: Voluntarily posting a blind double the big blind. This is only allowed to the first player clockwise from the big blind.

Tainted: Said of a draw that may well help opponents more if hit.

Three-bet: The second raise, making a total of three bets.

Top pair: A pair formed with the highest-ranking board-card.

Turn: The fourth board-card and associated betting round.

Under-the-gun (UTG): The player on the immediate left of the big blind, who is required to act first on the preflop betting round.